The **Newspapers**
H A N D B O O K

The Newspapers Handbook is the first comprehensive guide to the job of the newspaper reporter. It offers advice on a range of different types of newspaper writing, looks at how newspapers cover events and shows how reporting styles can differ in mainstream and non-mainstream newspapers.

The Newspapers Handbook encourages a critical and reflective approach to newspaper practice. In this new edition, Richard Keeble explores the theoretical, moral and political dimensions of a journalist's job and examines changing newspaper ownership structures and recent ethical controversies. New and up-to-date chapters from Henry Clother and John Turner explore the specialisms of court and local government reporting.

The Newspapers Handbook is essential reading for journalism and media studies students, freelances and anyone hoping to work in today's newspaper industry.

Richard Keeble is Senior Lecturer in journalism at City University, London. He was editor of *The Teacher* and has also worked on local newspapers in Nottingham and Cambridge. He is the author of *Secret State, Silent Press: New Militarism, the Gulf and the Modern Image of Warfare* (1998).

D0265576

Media Practice

edited by James Curran, Goldsmiths College, University of London

....

The *Media Practice* handbooks are comprehensive resource books for students of media and journalism, and for anyone planning a career as a media professional. Each handbook combines a clear introduction to understanding how the media work with practical information about the structure, processes and skills involved in working in today's media industries, providing not only a guide on "how to do it" but also a critical reflection on contemporary media practice.

....

Also in this series:

The Radio
H A N D B O O K

....

Peter Wilby and Andy Conroy

The Television
H A N D B O O K

....

Patricia Holland

The Advertising
H A N D B O O K

....

Sean Brierley

The **Newspapers**
H A N D B O O K

....

Second Edition

....

Richard **Keeble**

London *and* New York

·LEEDS METROPOLITAN
UNIVERSITY
LEARNING CENTRE

1702986163
BT-BV 24-8-00
1239731

070.4 KEE

First published 1994
by Routledge
11 New Fetter Lane, London EC4P 4EE

Simultaneously published in the USA and Canada
by Routledge
29 West 35th Street, New York, NY 10001
Reprinted 1995, 1997

Second edition 1998
Reprinted 1999

© 1998 Richard Keeble

Typeset in Times by The Florence Group, Stoodleigh, Devon
Printed and bound in Great Britain by Biddles Ltd, Guildford and King's Lynn

All rights reserved. No part of this book may be reprinted or reproduced or utilised in any
form or by any electronic, mechanical, or other means, now known or hereafter invented,
including photocopying and recording, or in any information storage or retrieval system,
without permission in writing from the publishers.

British Library Cataloguing in Publication Data
A catalogue record for this book is available from the British Library.

Library of Congress Cataloguing in Publication Data
  Keeble, Richard
    The newspapers handbook/Richard Keeble.–2nd ed.
      p.   cm. – (Media practice)
    Includes bibliographical references and index.
      1. Newspaper publishing–Handbooks, manuals, etc.
      2. Journalism–Handbooks, manuals, etc.   I. Title.   II. Series.
    PN4783.K44   1998
    070.4–dc21   97–34625

    ISBN 0–415–18409–6 (hbk)   0–415–15827–3 (pbk)

Dedicated to the memories of my former students Sophie O'Neill, David Irwin, William Nyadru-Mia and Zodwa Mshibe

The struggle to learn, to describe, to understand, to educate is a central and necessary part of our humanity. The struggle is not begun at secondhand after reality has occurred. It is itself a major way in which reality is continually formed and changed.

Raymond Williams, *Communications*

Contents

Notes on contributors

Henry Clother was a lecturer in journalism at City University from 1977 until 1996. His career in journalism has included working as news editor on *The Teacher*, and as first industrial reporter and then education correspondent at the IPC (pre-Murdoch) *Sun*. From 1970 to 1977 he was Head of Public Relations for the National Union of Teachers.

John Turner is a principal lecturer in politics in the Department of Politics of Oxford Brookes University, where he lectures in British politics, media policy and electoral studies. He has been a member of the Midlands Regional Consultative Committee of the Independent Television Commission and is currently a political consultant with ICM Research who carry out opinion surveys for the *Guardian* and *Observer*. During the 1997 general election he carried out focus group studies for the *Guardian*.

Preface

··

This is a textbook on newspaper reporting skills with a difference. It attempts, for the first time, to draw together two traditions so often in conflict. There is the dominant newspaper culture which stresses learning of skills "on the job". Then there is a tradition, embedded in many mass communication and journalism courses in colleges, which encourages a more reflective, critical approach to the press. As a result of this split, journalists and media theorists speak different languages; they seem to inhabit different worlds.

So this book is rooted in an examination of the ever-changing, everyday skills of newspaper reporting – as highlighted in the updated profiles and interviews throughout this second edition. And an important new section examines the role the Internet is having on reporters' sourcing techniques. But at the same time the handbook draws on some of the theoretical writings to throw helpful insights into reporters' routines, news values and myths.

My underlying message is simple. Since all practice is based, consciously or unconsciously, on theory, journalists' standards would improve if they reflected more on the crucial political and ethical dimensions of their work.

I have sought to represent the rich diversity of the press by focusing, not just on mainstream national and local newspapers, but also on the ethnic, leftist and other alternative media. In all cases the good, the bad and the unacceptable are identified. Too much of English newspaper journalism is narrowly localised, Anglocentric or, at worst, xenophobic so a large number of the examples are deliberately focused on foreign news. Journalism is by its nature ephemeral, always produced at speed: this is acknowledged. Indeed my comments on the cuttings should be seen as the basis for future discussion rather than definitive.

Can a journalist be compassionate and succeed? This question lies at the heart of this book. Certainly the best journalism can draw on the whole personality: it can, for instance, give evidence of sensitivity, courage, political intelligence, wit and a command of complex research, language and social skills. It can inspire you to political action; it can move you to tears. Indeed, while conventional journalism stresses "objectivity", this book promotes the notion of "subjectivity". It highlights the difficulties behind the surface simplicities of newspaper writing but always seeks to inspire students to be creative and daring in their journalism: to challenge dominant news values, lies, myths and stereotypes.

The new ethics/efficks chapter, symbolically placed near the start of the book, examines the press coverage of the spate of corruption/sleaze scandals that enveloped the Conservative Party in the final years of the Major administration. But it looks behind the screaming headlines, arguing, controversially, that one of the major factors was the collapse of the Soviet Union.

During the Cold War, the constraints imposed by the national security state meant that the elite had to stand relatively united in the face of the common enemy (the Russian Bear), the danger it posed being always exaggerated. With the crumbling of the Berlin Wall everything changed. The common enemy disappeared and elite members were left bickering among themselves. Newspapers (pursuing a reactionary moral/political agenda) helped provide the theatre in which these elite squabbles could be played out.

This new edition examines the changing ownership structures of the national and provincial mainstream press and draws on some recent surveys of journalists' stress levels, the roles of women in newspapers and journalists' salary structures. Pay levels of journalists in the provinces remain scandalously low, and managements might consider that one of their basic responsibilities is to provide decent wages to their increasingly over-stressed staff.

The chapter on training highlights the recent explosion of opportunities with journalism and media studies courses springing up all over the country. Vocational/academic courses provide the ideal place where best practice (from both home and abroad) can be identified and where dominant news values can be examined and challenged. Yet Fleet Street has panicked in the face of this training explosion, possibly because it sees an emerging culture of reflection and critique as a threat.

Kiss – keep it short and simple – is a much-used journalistic maxim. The selection here of newspaper assignments aims to keep it short and simple too. Examples are given to help the reporter, perhaps facing National Council for Training of Journalists (NCTJ), National Vocational Qualifications (NVQ), diploma or degree assignments, and the freelance, alone and wondering how to make the break into the somewhat intimidating world of reporting. In addition, the general reader and mass communications student should find here a different perspective on the origins and application of reporters' news values.

Jargon words such as "freebie", "embargo", "mug shot", "podding" and "quote" are used throughout and those new to journalism might have to consult the glossary (brought up to date in this edition to incorporate some of the cyberspace jargon) at the end of the book from time to time.

Many people have helped with the writing. At City University, Professor Hugh Stephenson, Bob Jones, Bruce Hanlin, Michael Bromley, Milverton Wallace, Isabelle Marcoul and Colin Bickler have been particularly helpful. Humphrey Evans had some good words of advice on the freelancing chapter. Robert Satchwell and Helen Montgomery (*Cambridge Evening News*); Sarah Knight and Jeff Humphreys (*Derby Trader*); Daniel Nelson, Kanina Holmes, Glyn Roberts, Dupe Owodunni and Paul Slater (Gemini News Service); Richard Garner (the *Mirror*); Angella Johnson (*Weekly Mail and Guardian*, Johannesburg); David Shaw (London *Evening Standard*); Gertrud Erbach (News International); and Tim Gopsill (the National Union of Journalists) all also helped through interviews.

Thanks also to Waltraud Boxall (Liverpool University) and my editors at Routledge, Rebecca Barden, James Curran, Christopher Cudmore and Caroline Cautley. Special thanks to Maryline Gagnère and Gabi Keeble-Gagnère for all their support over the years.

If you have any comments on this book please send them to me at City University, Department of Journalism, Northampton Square, London EC1V OHB or R.L.Keeble@city.ac.uk

Great Abington, Cambridgeshire
August 1997

Acknowledgements

The author and publishers gratefully acknowledge permission to reproduce copyright material from the following:

Cambridge Evening News, Daily Express, Daily Mail/Solo, *Derby Evening Telegraph, Evening Standard*/Solo, *Guardian, Herts and Essex Observer, Liverpool Daily Post, Liverpool Echo, Mail on Sunday*/Solo, *Matlock Mercury, Morning Star, News of the World*, Newspaper Publishing plc, *Nottingham Evening Post, Nottingham Weekly Post and Recorder, Observer, Peterborough Evening Telegraph, Ripley and Heanor News, socialist, Sun, Sunday Express, Sunday Mirror, Telegraph, The Times*/Times Newspapers Ltd, *Wakefield Express*, William Hall.

Every attempt has been made to obtain permission to reproduce copyright material. If any proper acknowledgement has not been made, we would invite copyright holders to inform us of the oversight.

1

Behind the Hollywood myths
The journalist's job

···

ONE of the most striking features of the British press is its diversity. There are many "journalisms".

The poorly paid journalist on a local freesheet is living almost in a different world from a top columnist on a national. The reporter on a trade union monthly, similarly, has little in common with a freelance travel writer. Their salaries, sources and working routines will all be different. So might their ethical values and notions of what they expect to achieve through their jobs.

The London-based, national mainstream press comprises ten Sundays (the *Sunday Business* being the most recently launched – in April 1996) and 12 dailies (*Today* being the most recent casualty, closed by Rupert Murdoch in November 1995). The regional mainstream press can be divided into paid-fors and frees. The first category incorporates some 90 morning and evening dailies, ten Sundays and around 430 weeklies; the second takes in about 950 freesheets, mainly weeklies though some appear less frequently.

Behind the diversity: *domination*

YET behind the façade of extraordinary diversity lies an industry dominated by monopolies and conformism. There is an "alternative" press including leftist, religious, municipal, trade union and ethnic minority publications. But their circulations are relatively small and their impact on the national debate only marginal.

Power, influence and financial resources lie with the mainstream local and national press. Here competition has not promoted variety. By 1974 only London, Edinburgh and Belfast had directly competing local morning or evening papers. Since then, the concentration of media ownership has intensified, reducing many newspapers to tiny outposts in vast multinational empires (*Britain's Media: How They Are Related: Media Ownership and Democracy*; Granville Williams; Campaign for Press and Broadcasting Freedom; London; 1994).

The "free revolution"

DURING the 1960s and 1970s a consumer and advertising boom helped inspire a "free revolution" in the provinces. Lionel Pickering, founder of the Derby Trader Group, and Eddie Shah, creator of a series of weeklies in the Manchester area and later of *Today* newspaper, were typical of the local entrepreneurs who pioneered the revolution (*Eddie Shah and the Newspaper Revolution*; David Goodhart and Patrick Wintour; Coronet; Sevenoaks; 1986).

As a result, the number of paid-for weeklies was halved between 1981 and 1991. But by the early 1990s, the frees had come to be dominated by the older established companies and the Association of Free Newspapers, which had aimed to promote their interests, had been wound up.

Bob Franklin and David Murphy showed in their study of the local press in the early 1990s that 70 per cent of freesheet distribution was controlled by the 22 top publishers (*What News? The Market, Politics and the Local Press*; Routledge, London; 1991). And Jeremy Tunstall records (in *News Power: The New National Press in Britain*; Clarendon Press; Oxford; 1996) how the Big Five regional newspaper publishers – Thomson, Reed, Northcliffe, United and Westminster Press – were by 1994 also the biggest freesheet publishers.

Monopolies rule: *at the local level*

THE mid-1990s witnessed a major shake-up in the ownership structure of the regional press. In November 1995, the Chester-based Trinity International Holdings, which grew out of the *Liverpool Post* group in the 1980s, purchased Thomson Regional Newspapers (for £327.5m) making it the largest group in the country with well over 130 titles; while Newsquest bought out Reed Regional Newspapers, the UK's largest free newspaper publisher (for £205m) ("For sale: a snip at £200m", the *Independent*; Mathew Horsman; 4 June 1996). Also in this month, Southnews bought Portsmouth and Sunderland Newspapers for £12.95m.

Then in July 1996, Johnston Press paid £211.1m for Emap Regional Newspapers while in the following month Pearson sold its regional newspaper business, Westminster Press, to Newsquest for £305m. As the National Union of Journalists commented: "The decision of the Department of Trade and Industry to allow the takeover of Emap by Johnston without a Monopolies Commission inquiry shows how the government was prepared to bend the rules to accommodate the need for Emap to get the cash into the hands of its bankers." Indeed, despite these significant changes the overall monopoly structure of the regional press remained intact. By 1997, Northcliffe, a subsidiary of *Daily Mail* and General Trust and Newsquest accounted for more than 36 per cent of all UK regional newspapers.

Monopolies rule: *at the national level*

AT the national level, monopoly ownership has similarly intensified. In 1947, the three leading corporations accounted for 62 per cent of the national daily circulation and 60 per cent of national Sunday circulation. By 1988 these figures had increased to 73 and 81 per cent (*Power without Responsibility: The Press and Broadcasting in Britain*; James Curran and Jean Seaton; Routledge; London; fourth edition 1991).

In February 1996, United News and Media (owners of the *Express*) merged with MAI to form a £3 billion conglomerate.

Such trends have been a feature not only of the European media but also of the global industry. For instance, Rupert Murdoch's four British nationals (*The Times, Sunday Times, Sun, News of the World*) constitute a small subsidiary of a vast empire ("The global visage"; the *Guardian*; London; 24 July 1995). This includes:

- a principal share of BSkyB satellite TV company, which distributes programmes throughout Europe (with exclusive screening rights to many top sporting events), and the News Datcom technology subsidiary;

- a 13 per cent stake in PA, Britain's leading press agency;

- newspapers in Hungary, Fiji, Papua New Guinea and Hong Kong;

- an American film company and a US television network; *TV Guide*; *New York Post*; *Standard Magazine*; Delphic On-Line; his purchase of New World Communications television stations in June 1996 (for $2,500m) gave him access to more than 40 per cent of homes in America;

- book publishing houses in the US, UK and Australia;

- Asia's dominant satellite company, Star TV (by satellite to 54 countries); Indian Zee TV; AsiaSat2 satellite system; Star Radio; half of Pacific Magazines;

- a near-monopoly of the Australian mass-selling press, owning the *Australian*, the *Herald-Sun* and more than 100 other titles in individual states;

- a growing interest in Internet technology: in June 1995 Murdoch's company, News Corporation, announced the launch of a joint deal with the *People's Daily*, the powerful newspaper of the Chinese Communist Party, to explore a range of possibilities in the information technology sector including electronic publishing, on-line information databases, data transmission networks and digital mapping;

- and LineOne service launched together with BT in 1997 to compete directly with AOL and CompuServe, its content featuring the *Sun*, *News of the World*, Press Association's news, games and entertainment.

In October 1995, *Vanity Fair* magazine voted Murdoch No. 1 in a list of 50 members of the New Establishment, ahead even of Microsoft chief Bill Gates. The magazine commented: "Rupert Murdoch is arguably the most powerful private citizen in the world."

According to Andrew Marr, editor of the *Independent*: "It is abundantly clear that Murdoch is trying to create a de facto national newspaper monopoly in Britain. The price war is intended to destroy the *Independent* and the Hollinger group which own the *Telegraph* and then they'll go after the rest."

Accompanying this growing monopoly ownership has been a serious decline in sales; since their peak in the mid-1950s nationals' sales have slumped 21 per cent ("The British keep reading despite the box"; Brian MacArthur; *British Journalism Review*; Vol. 3, No. 4; 1992). Circulation of regional mornings and evenings has fallen 20 per cent since 1978; weeklies have lost a massive 40 per cent. Moreover, the continuing drop in the number of newsagents and proposed EU legislation banning under-16s from delivering papers posed new threats to newspaper circulations in the late 1990s.

The jobs revolution

JOURNALISM remains a job carrying enormous personal rewards. It is difficult, challenging (politically, ethically, physically) and fun. It requires a formidable range of knowledge and skills. Reporters must be both literate and numerate. They need to master the law as it affects newspapers and the social skills to develop contacts and interview many different kinds of people. Many will want to speak at least one foreign language. All will need to possess computer and Internet skills. According to Jan Boucek, of Dow Jones News Service: "Things can go wrong when technical support isn't immediately available and it's of great help if the journalist can at least assess what the problem is rather than just groan that the computer doesn't work. Computer-literate staff can also make a big contribution to maximising the efficiency of news production."

Reporters should be curious, persistent, imaginative and daring: prepared to challenge stereotypes, expose myths and lies. Or in the words of the late Nicholas Tomalin, journalists should cultivate "ratlike cunning, a plausible manner and a little literary ability". In addition, he said, they should be able to display "an ability to believe passionately in second-rate projects", and should possess "well-placed relatives" and "an implacable hatred of spokesmen, administrators and public relations men". There is a glamorous side to the job which Hollywood has helped to promote. No wonder the queues for entering the profession are so long.

Since the arrival of new technology and with the decline in advertising revenue, the job has been through many changes, not all of them positive. Staffing levels have been reduced. At the national level, the *Express* titles, the *Financial Times*, the *Sun* and *Mirror* have been particularly affected. The *FT* managed to axe its entire picture desk in one fell swoop. One major factor behind the series of swingeing redundancies was the price war launched by Rupert Murdoch in the summer of 1994 ("Serious newspapers cost money"; Alan Rusbridger; *Press Gazette*; 22 March 1996).

In the regions, newspapers lost hundreds of jobs as owners "downsized" reducing staffing levels in advance of selling off titles to the emerging conglomerates ("A war of pros and cons"; Roy Greenslade; the *Guardian*; 30 December 1996). Particularly under threat were journalists aged over 50.

At the same time, working hours have been extended. Early Saturday morning "sunrise" editions are adding further demands. As Andy Read comments: "It's predicted that within the next two or three years many papers will be, in effect, providing 24-hours-a-day coverage for six or even seven days a week" ("The morning after"; the *Journalist*; February/March 1996).

Local branches (chapels) of the National Union of Journalists (NUJ) have been left fighting for recognition and personal contracts have been increasingly forced on staffers. It is impossible to establish the level of unemployment among journalists since most journos will try to scrape a living as a freelance. But between 1989 and 1990 the total cost of the basic benefit of £20 a week for six months, paid by the NUJ to unemployed members, rose from £10,000 to £100,000.

Accompanying these trends has been growing casualisation. Many staff members have been turned into "permanent part-timers". Managements have found it cheaper, while job insecurity always favours conformism. With the decline in unions' power, opportunities for exploitation by management have increased.

Multi-skilling or de-skilling?

One consequence has been "de-professionalisation" with reporters forced to perform promotional, distribution and other non-journalistic jobs. "Multi-skilling" schemes are being introduced on some papers with reporters, photographers and sub-editors learning from each other – and sparking fears of further job cuts and a decline in standards. At Trinity International titles, for instance, teams of writers, subs and designers work as integrated teams. Many local papers are training reporters in sub-editing skills so that they can fill in during absences.

At the *Eastern Daily Press*, reporters and photographers are encouraged to think about the best ways of displaying their stories. As Pete Waters, *EDP* special projects editor and author of the *Guide to the Tabloid: Best Practices for a Better EDP*, argues: "If the best form [of presenting a story] is a graphic and the reporter is asked to research details rather than write a story, then that is what we must do."

"Flexibility" is the buzzword.

And as some local newspaper chains move into cable television, how soon will it be before multi-skilling will incorporate filming and video editing?

Young reporters have had to fund their own training; some work without any contractual protection. Many entrants, desperate to get their foot in the door, are being cynically exploited by managements, having to work long periods on unpaid attachments.

"Commercial features" geared to promoting business and infotainment specials (reflecting the growing power of market researchers on editorial content) have mushroomed; serious investigative journalism has been marginalised ("Retreat of the investigators"; Alan Doig; *British Journalism Review*; Vol. 3, No. 4; 1992).

Tabloid values have crept into the serious and regional press. As Harold Evans, president of Random House and former *Times* and *Sunday Times* editor, told the Guild of Editors in November 1996: "Sexual allegations make the front pages and the decision to do that is defended on the grounds the story is about 'character'. This is no more than prurience on stilts." And he continued: "If only one tenth of the energy spent on snooping on private lives can be spent on monitoring real power, on analysis, on improving the writing and the accuracy, we will be a helluva lot better off."

Many press commentators have argued that profits are the prime concern of managements rather than editorial quality. As Roy Greenslade, former editor of the *Mirror*, argues: "The pressure is constantly on managing directors and directors. They must cut costs, they must make savings. This means redundancies and greater productivity from those who stay." He continues: "The most important person on a newspaper is no longer the editor. It is the managing directors. They rule the roost."

Significantly, the move towards more human interest, infotainment-style news has been accompanied by job cuts. This is how Phil Walker, editor of the *Daily Star*, announced plans to cut 45 jobs in June 1997: "The emphasis has moved from hard news to showbiz, glamour and features. Much of our material is bought in because it cannot be home-grown. We do not need and cannot afford as many staff as we have now" ("*Daily Star* journalists fear for the future"; Jean Morgan; *Press Gazette*; London; 6 July 1997). And many cash-strapped national newspapers have cut their foreign staffs to the bone.

Money matters: the scandal of low pay

Salaries for many in the newspaper industry remain scandalously low; for trainees they can be appalling. Significantly in 1996, the NUJ launched a campaign against widespread "pitiful" rates of pay. Union vice-president Jeremy Dear said he knew local papers where trainees started on £6,900 a year. "This union supports the minimum wage of £4.26 an hour. Well, 15 to 20 per cent of provincial journalists would actually benefit from that." According to a 1995 survey commissioned by the Guild of Editors, four out of five trainees were earning less than £10,000. Many had fallen deep into debt or were leaning heavily on their families for financial support (*Survey of Editorial Training Needs: Summary of Findings*; Guild of Editors; London; March 1995). A 1996 survey by the NUJ found that 11.1 per cent in provincial newspapers earned less than £10,000 and 22 per cent between £10,000 and £15,000. Across all media sections one-fifth of the sample earned between £15,000 and £20,000.

The survey also identified significant gender differences: whereas one-third of the male members earned £30,000 and above, only 19 per cent of the women did so.

At the same time top executives on national newspapers can earn more than £50,000 and some star columnists £100,000 plus. Rupert Murdoch's wealth has been estimated at £250m; *Daily Mail* owner Viscount Rothermere's at £850m, *European* owner Frederick Barclay's at £215m.

In contrast, for many freelances salaries have either stood still over recent years or dropped. A 1996 NUJ survey found that nearly a fifth of freelances (19.1 per cent) earned below £10,000. The highest wages in the media industry were found to be in national television where 51 per cent earned more than £30,000 a year. In comparison, the figure for local newspapers was just 6.4 per cent.

The news machine

REPORTERS work in close liaison with their news desk. The number of titled executives on the desk will differ according to the size of the operation. A weekly freesheet might have just one news editor doubling up as deputy editor and feature writer. An evening may have a city desk headed by a news editor alongside a district desk organising (through computer link-up) the operations of the district offices.

In contrast, a national might have as many as five journalists assigned to the home news desk. They will be drawing up the diary and news lists, liaising by phone with reporters out on stories and feeding in follow-up and news ideas into the operation. In addition, they will be monitoring the wires, the other media and the flow of copy from staff reporters, attending news conferences to review past issues and plan future ones.

The amount of initiative allowed individual reporters differs from paper to paper. General reporters on local weeklies and dailies will be "fed" a considerable number of their stories by their news editor. They will arrive in the office at 8 am, say, often with no idea what they are to cover until they are briefed by their news editor.

Specialists, who are generally more experienced reporters, will tend to originate far more of their own material. An evening might have them assigned to the crime, education, industrial, local government, farming (where relevant) and environment beats. A national broadsheet's specialists, on the other hand, might include education, the environment, crime, arts, local government, the media, consumer affairs, defence, labour, Westminster, health, religion, politics, transport, the law.

At the core – the conference

At the centre of the news operation of all but small weeklies will be the conference. A national broadsheet may have as many as six in one day; a regional evening two or three; a weekly just one at the start of an operation. Attendance differs from paper to paper. At a small newspaper all staff will attend. At a national, one meeting may be open to all staffers while at other times only heads of departments such as features, sports, finance, news, foreign, arts, together with top executives (often called the backbench team) will be present.

Discussions tend to focus around the news list extracted from the diary with reporters, and where relevant photographers, artists and cartoonists, being assigned tasks.

In or out of the office?

One of the consequences of new technology and the staffing cuts has been the increased amount of newsroom-based work by reporters. Many local reporters say as much as 90 per cent of their work is done by phone; national reporters can spend 70 per cent of their time and more in the office. Journalism is an increasingly desk-bound job. When a story is completed journalists no longer carry the copy to a file on the news editor's desk. It is routed through the computer system. They often don't get up and talk to each other. Instead, they send (both serious and un-serious) messages through the computer.

The role of the subs

ONCE the story has passed the news editor it will go through the computer system to the sub-editors. They check the piece for accuracy, with the reporter contacted if there are any queries, and for any legal problems such as libel and contempt. (In addition, some nationals have teams of lawyers to offer advice.) They may re-jig the story if a clearer structure is required, or reduce its length if necessary. They will ensure style is followed throughout and compose any accompanying headlines, captions, standfirsts and panels. And they design the pages, increasingly directly on the screen.

The amount of subbing of copy differs from paper to paper and from section to section. But all reporters have to accept that their copy might be hacked about. News copy on a national tabloid might be almost entirely rewritten to fit the small space available though features on the same paper may be only slightly touched by the subs. National broadsheets are "reporters' papers" and their copy is generally only lightly subbed. Given the number of words, there is not the time to do regular re-jigs.

Journalists new to local papers will tend to have their copy subbed a lot as they get used to the house style. Once settled their copy will tend to be heavily subbed only rarely. Indeed, reporters come to sub their own copy (checking style, clarity, conciseness and accuracy) before passing it on.

To illustrate the work of reporters, five journalists from differing sectors of the industry talk about the challenges, routines, the stresses, the necessary skills and the rewards of their jobs. A local evening, a local free weekly, a national tabloid and broadsheet (*Guardian* journalist Angella Johnson having moved to South Africa) and an "alternative" news agency are all represented.

Profile

Promoting the positive:
profile of
● ● ● ● ● ● *Cambridge Evening News*

EDITOR Robert Satchwell says his award-winning *Cambridge Evening News* is committed to promoting the positive in the local community.

"When so many people are knocking the health service, business and schools, people in them must get demoralised. And an awful number of them are doing superb things. We are not making any political point – simply saying that they are doing things which should be feted."

Part of the Yattendon group, which also incorporates the *Burton Mail*, Herts and Essex Newspapers and the *Staffordshire Newsletter*, the *News* has district offices in St Ives, St Neots, Royston, Saffron Walden, Haverhill, Newmarket and Ely. With a circulation of around 42,000 on weekdays and 35,000 on Saturdays, it has six editions Mondays to Fridays and two on Saturdays. The first goes at 10.30 am; the last at 2.30 pm.

Campaigns form an important ingredient in the newspaper's activities. For instance, in September 1996 it launched the "Community Challenge" campaign with financial backing from the city's universities, business and councils and with messages of support from Prince Charles, TV personality Anneka Rice, Prime Minister John Major and Terry Waite, the former Beirut hostage. The centrepiece of the campaign is an awards programme split into seven categories: youth support, age support, the environment, crime prevention, security, children's support and institutional support.

Satchwell explains: "Community for us is strategy. If you look at the decline of local newspaper sales it has accompanied the decline in community spirit. It is more and more difficult for people to relate to their communities, they are more mobile and less likely to buy city papers. This is why newspapers must help stimulate communities. We are already closely involved and it is working for us." Indeed, the *News* has won the Newspaper Society award for the best sales increases in 1993, 1994 and 1996; in 1993 it was *UK Press Gazette* Evening Newspaper of the Year and in 1996 it was voted Community Newspaper of the Year in the Newspaper Society's sales awards.

To help tackle the city's drugs problem, the newspaper launched a "Shop a pusher" campaign and Crimestoppers immediately recorded an increase in telephone calls providing them with useful leads.

In addition, the *News* operates a "Have your say now" line. As Satchwell explains: "This encourages readers to complain, praise or simply give us information and we guarantee to ring them back within 48 hours."

To help promote local industry, the *News* has been running Business Excellence Awards for the last four years. And because of the importance of science in the city's universities and high-tech industries, it is one of the very few local newspapers to boast a science specialist.

A third of the editorial staff are women though numbers have varied over recent years. The paper went full colour in April 1992 and moved to full-page design (using QuarkXpress) the following year. News conferences are held at 7.15 am for the department heads and at 2.45 pm for planning the next day. In addition, every Thursday afternoon representatives from the circulation and promotions departments attend and canvass returns are examined, with the newspaper determined to ensure all areas and social groups are being catered for.

Satchwell, Journalist of the Year in the British Press Awards 1977 and a former assistant editor at the *News of the World*, has strong views about the journalist of the future. "All the new breed of journalists will have to have a readiness to take on marketing concepts and techniques because they will have an increasing responsibility for the sales of their paper. They will be asked to look closely at the sales penetration in their particular patches and seek out potential for sales increases."

He also believes local newspapers must exploit all the possibilities of the Internet. The *News* launched its own site on the Web in May 1996 (www.cambridge-news.co.uk) incorporating a brief digest of the whole paper and links to other local information sources. "We are still in the early days of development but newspapers have got to become the major sources of news, information and advertising both on paper and electronically." Moreover, the journalist of the future will have to be multi-skilled, able to work in print, broadcasting and on the Internet, he says.

The *News* currently has five trainees (all graduates from pre-entry courses) on its staff, while Satchwell receives many applications to join his newspaper every week. So what does he look for when considering trainee applicants?

"A good general education. Good A levels – I have no set preference for graduates though they do have the advantage of an extra three years of maturity. I have to say I dislike media studies as a discipline. Not all the programmes are, of course, bad. But I am looking for graduates with a more general background. They must show an interest in life around them and be involved in something more than simply the academic. They might play a sport, be involved in a political organisation or even be a Girl Guide. I like to look for local people because they come with a whole range of contacts – friends and relatives. But people move around the country far more these days making local recruitment more difficult."

| Profile | Still learning, following in her father's footsteps: |

● ● ● ● ● ●   profile of

Helen Montgomery, reporter

HELEN Montgomery grew up in a family where all the national newspapers were present every day. Her father has been a Fleet Street sports reporter most of his working life and so it is perhaps not surprising that Helen has followed in his journalistic footsteps. But she is quick to stress: "I don't think you are a born journalist. Newspapers have certainly always been a big part of my life. I've seen that being called up all the time is not particularly glamorous but I've also seen how exciting it can be; the buzzes it gives. The crucial skills are being able to talk and get on with people – and these you have to learn."

Montgomery, 25, trained on the Westminster Press scheme in Hastings in 1995 and worked on the *St Alban's Herald* and *Welwyn and Hatfield Times* before moving to *Cambridge Evening News* in December 1996 as a senior reporter.

She much prefers working on the daily. "You can do a story and it will be correct at the time of going to press. On a weekly you are constantly having to update stories. If there is something big in your area the nationals can easily pick it up before you have the chance to publish. And then you might have some controversial complaint about the health service which could all be sorted out by the time you go to press. That sort of thing used to annoy me."

Her work routine is different each day. "Some days are busy when everything you touch seems to produce a story. Then there are days when you can't file any copy; people aren't in when you phone them or don't ring back. And I never like going home without thinking I've done a lot of productive work."

She has had to do a number of "death knocks", interviewing relatives and friends after deaths. "This is certainly the hardest thing to do. But at the same time it gives you the biggest buzz when they actually talk." And she advises: "As long as you are not pushy with them, people usually want to talk. They want you to print good things about their family member in the paper."

The job, she finds, can be very stressful. "You have to learn you can't do everything. When I started here I was working ridiculously long hours, finding my feet. Now I've learnt to prioritise."

A lot of her work is done on the phone where she finds her 100 wpm shorthand invaluable, but she tries to leave the office on a story at least once every day.

A week in the life of Helen Montgomery

Monday

Drives to meeting of South Cambridgeshire District Council in Cambridge which starts at 2 pm. On the previous Saturday the News has run a big story (picked up from the meeting's agenda) that villagers in Hauxton were hoping to win council support to launch a volunteer community shop following the shopkeeper's recent death. "I was quite surprised that they wouldn't give any money so that was a big follow-up for us." In addition, the council agreed to donate £100,000 to Ely Cathedral, and security at its offices was to be improved, while a new enforcement officer was to be employed to cover local travellers' sites. "This was a good meeting for me. Sometimes I can come back and there isn't anything."

Back in the large, open-plan office on the outskirts of Cambridge, the news desk asks her to follow up some important stories: a dangerous patient has gone missing from a local hospital so she has to ring the hospital's director for an update quote; a woman has been arrested on suspicion of killing her husband so the police are contacted.

At 6 pm, she begins a series of routine telephone calls: to the duty inspector at Cambridge police station, and to the taped phone messages of the police in Essex, Cambridgeshire, Suffolk, Hertfordshire, Bedfordshire and Northamptonshire. In addition, all the fire service tapes in the same counties (with the exception of Northamptonshire) are rung. All this takes around 20 minutes. Television news is also closely monitored. "We see these as our direct competitors. If they have any stories we don't have we have to follow them up."

She is supposed to finish at 10 pm but is still working on her stories at midnight. A taxi driver then rings in to say a big fire has started in stables at Newmarket. She has to ring a photographer and get him out of bed, and they drive to Newmarket. But when they arrive at the scene of the fire, they learn it is only a barn that has caught fire, no horses have been hurt and the owner sends a worker to order the journalists off his land. "So we had no pictures and just two pars in the paper. It was largely a waste of time."

Back in the office at 1 am, she continues working on stories. "I wanted to get the stuff finished so as not miss the first edition. That would not be fair on my colleagues."

3 am: a man rings in and says he has something important to fax over; he also asks for the local radio's fax number. "He then rings off. It's all a bit dramatic."

The fax focuses on a recent paedophile case. She leaves notes for the chief reporter and finally heads for home, arriving at around 3.30 am.

Tuesday

10 am: meets the chief reporter to discuss the faxed "memo". "There was clearly a buzz in the office." She works on "adds" to stories done the previous day, phoning up contacts. "There were many complications with the 'memo' story but we still managed to get a report in the last edition. Everything else I touched that day fell apart big time."

Wednesday

10 am: off to Hitchin for launch of North Hertfordshire policing plan. She stays for lunch. "I find policemen like boasting to women and so I get a lot of stories simply through chatting to them. That's often more profitable than the formal press conferences."

2.30 pm: back in the office and writes up four stories from the assignment.

Thursday

At home, watches television and listens to radio news. 7 am: arrives in office and goes through the routine "calls" to police and fire services. In addition all the nationals and the East Anglian Daily Times are read for any potential follow-ups. Stories left over from the previous evening need working on. "But at this time of the morning it's often difficult finding people for quotes." Work is hectic until first edition at 9 am.

Then drives one of the News' fleet of Minis to Cambridge police station. "It's very important to have face-to-face contact. It does not always provide copy but quite often it does and if they have seen you they are always more likely to help you in the future." She picks up a list of stolen cars and details about a spate of bogus callers harassing elderly people in the area.

Back in the office she rings the Cambridge police tape every hour for any important update. One produces the story that a man out canvassing for the Labour Party has had a finger chopped off in a freak letter-box accident. Helen spends rest of day trying to contact the victim. His number is not in the phone book but through examining the Electoral Register she discovers the names of other people living at the same address and contacts them.

Friday
She has worked the previous Saturday and so has the day off.

Profile

Free to make a "bits and pieces" paper:

● ● ● ● ● ● profile of
the Derby Trader

LIKE many other provincial newspapers, the *Derby Trader* has been through a series of owners in recent years. Originally part of the Trader Group which Lionel Pickering launched in 1966, the group's circulation figures hit a peak of one million in the late 1980s. Then in June 1989 it was bought by Thomson as part of a nationwide trend which saw many of the independents launched in the 1960s gobbled up by the much larger chains. The group's northern region had free titles based on Derby, Burton on Trent, Leicester, Long Eaton, Nuneaton and Bedworth, Hinckley, Ilkeston and Ripley, Nottingham and Loughborough. But by 1993 circulation had dropped to 750,000 and with the centralising of operations some district offices were closed. Finally, Midland Independent Newspapers (MIN, owners of the *Birmingham Post and Mail* and *Coventry Evening Telegraph*) stepped in to purchase the group.

Jeff Humphreys, group editor of the four Trader titles based on Derby, Ilkeston and Ripley, Long Eaton and Loughborough (with a circulation of 238,000), argued that he did not possess the resources to compete directly with the local evenings. Instead, he was aiming to produce more of a "bits and pieces" newspaper "providing something for everyone with local news only a piece of the jigsaw". Thus, comment, columnists, travel, fashion, an agony aunt and gardening were among the all-important elements of his newspapers.

In the area of sport they again realised their competitors had "thrashed to death" the main news and issues over the previous week. To capture the attention of readers they carried prominently an "abrasive, provocative" column by Neil Hallam. In fact, so controversial were his views that his press facilities had been withdrawn at Derby County football ground.

Humphreys' career has been an interesting mix of teaching and journalism. His first job was as a history teacher in Norfolk. Then, having trained on the Thomson journalism course for graduates at Cardiff, he began a spell as a reporter on the *Western Mail*. In 1973 he moved to the *Derby Evening Telegraph* where he became deputy sports editor but then in 1979 moved into training, becoming editorial training officer at Emap.

He was there for four years before returning to the *Derby Evening Telegraph* where he became deputy editor. In 1991 he left to go freelance and then, with the purchase of the Trader group by MIN in 1993, Humphreys took on his current job.

Profile

Still rewarding – despite the salary:
profile of

● ● ● ● ● ● *Sarah Knight, news editor*

SARAH Knight, 31, is enthusiastic about her job. As news editor of the *Derby and Ilkeston and Ripley Traders* she finds it offers her a rewarding challenge – despite the salary of less than £15,000.

She says: "It's so varied most of the time. You're talking to and meeting people. And I like the sense of satisfaction which comes with informing people about something they wouldn't otherwise have known about. I've personally learned so much while reporting. I know the area very well and I love the county."

She began as a trainee reporter in the Heanor office of the Thomson weekly, known then as the *Derby Herald and Post*, moving up to her current job in September 1996. "I guess the main difference is that in the past I would ask for assistance. Now reporters come to me asking for help." And with job cuts in the group, she has found her workload increasing significantly over recent years.

She had always wanted to be a journalist but worked from 1984 to 1990 first for an airline company and then a travel agency. "The Gulf War finished us off." This spurred her to write to local and national papers asking for jobs. The *European* took her on and from June to December 1990 she helped research for news and features.

Her most exciting moment was when she investigated an asteroid which, by the minutest of chances, was due to hit the earth some time in the near future (it didn't) and found the article ending up as a double-page spread in the science section. After three months at Stradbroke journalism training centre she landed the Heanor job.

The most satisfying aspect of her job remains her weekly personal column which she is encouraged to make "as controversial as possible", provoking debate and inspiring people to write in with their responses. "With my usual right-wing views it's not surprising that most of them are anti," she says.

"But it's really hard work composing them. Because I now focus on any issue whether national or local I can spend up to a day and a half reading papers for background and ideas to follow up."

On the necessary characteristics of a reporter, she points to perseverance and tenacity. "A lot of people just don't want to talk to you. They assume that whatever they say will be twisted. You get that an awful lot. You have to have enthusiasm for the subjects you tackle. If you are interviewing someone and you're not interested it will show. And you have to write succinctly in a simple way. It's not something that comes naturally. You have to learn it."

A week in the life of Sarah Knight

Wednesday afternoon
Follows up story about rising council house rents liaising with graphics department and talking to councillors on the phone.

Speaks to one of her regular councillor contacts who is concerned about morale in police force, about the "disgraceful" state of a police station and about the number of police cars in need of repair. This is a "longish", 20-minute conversation.

A photograph is arranged. Police are contacted but they make no comment. Goes through some of her mail.

Thursday

Out for most of the day which is "most unusual". Visits women running a group for mothers suffering postnatal depression, the only one in Derbyshire. "I simply didn't appreciate how bad it was: women committed suicide and even killed children when depressed." Speaks to Derby hospital doctor who deals with only the most acute cases. "Afterwards they said they'd had a brilliant response to the article. At the end of the day, if I can help other people like that, that's all I'm interested in."

Next goes on to meet two women who counsel rape victims or women physically or sexually abused as children. Couldn't print their address since the women could be harassed. Finds the experience "harrowing".

A competition always accompanies her page and she goes out to collect the prizes for that week from a crystal factory.

Friday

In the office all day, 9 am to 5.30 pm (most lunches spent inside eating sandwiches). Compiles news briefs, goes through mail, answers phone and does some of her own calls (which include district and county councillors, Heritage Society, amateur dramatic societies, town clerks, the police).

Weekend

Often works on features on her laptop computer at home. "It's often good to work on features at the weekend. The atmosphere is relaxed and that helps."

Monday

Usually spent in the office, working towards the deadline that day. This week she visits cosmetic surgery clinic in Sheffield. Meets the director, surgeon and woman who had had an operation to shrink her stomach. She has to put on all the proper clothing before going to see an operation in which a woman is having fat removed from her thighs and bottom. "When it comes to blood I'm pathetic. I did feel a bit queasy but I managed to lean on something and got through in the end."

Tuesday

Writes up page. Sorts out competition prizes. Follows up some news stories. Very busy. "Not much scope for relaxing." Writes advertising feature on unusual Valentine presents (such as having a rose dedicated to your name for £600; adopting an ape; visiting a hotel with heart-shaped beds) based on press releases, ringing around and researching.

Profile

From Fleet Street to South African flesh spots:

● ● ● ● ● ●   profile of

Angella Johnson

" **G**ETTING information out of the South African police service is like romancing a virgin in a chastity belt." So wrote Angella Johnson in the provocative, no-nonsense style of reportage she has been developing since leaving Fleet Street for the Johannesburg *Weekly Mail and Guardian* in April 1996.

"I was researching a story and wanted the police to fax me a speech due to be given the next day. They refused. Not only that, the adviser to the Police Commissioner let out a stream of insults and even attacked my supposedly 'colonialist attitudes'. So I wrote up all his insults in a big feature. He had it coming. You see, he thought I was white since I'd only spoken to him on the phone."

As a black Jamaican-born woman with nine years of reporting on the London *Guardian* behind her, Johnson has found moving to South Africa utterly rewarding. "It's the best thing I've done in my life," she says.

"In Britain, racism is prevalent in the media industry; there's classism and cliquism. And the tendency is towards youth. In South Africa experience is appreciated more; ability rather than who you know is all-important. Everyone now has a chance to prove themselves. There is a staleness in Britain while in South Africa there is an opening out. When you write something people tell you: 'That's great; that's good.' In fact, I feel I'm being nurtured by the country."

Yet Johnson, who is the only black woman on her paper, feels journalists in general in South Africa are not "aggressive" enough. "For so many years they've been subservient to the apartheid regime. There's still a tendency to tread softly too often."

And her work as a crime correspondent also revealed the bleaker side to the newly democratic country.

"I was immediately thrust into a world of drugs, taxi crime, car hijacking, child prostitution. It was wild. Yet people I'd meet at parties were so blasé about the violence. I was horrified. For me, one death is too many. And I found the police so bureaucratic, so obstructive when I wanted information. They'd call me 'that Bolshie woman from Britain'." She often faced dangers. "For instance, I was investigating child prostitution in Hillbrow, an area of high-rise buildings and a cesspool of crime, when this man pulled a gun out on me. Fortunately, my driver escort, a woman who looked as cute as a Barbie doll, pulled out her gun too. And the man put his away. In hindsight, I can see it was pretty stupid going so unprepared to such a dangerous area."

After a few months on the crime beat, she was switched to being the newspaper's chief profiler. "I try to empathise as much as possible with my subjects. Many people are incredibly racist. On the phone I obviously sound educated and people talk to me as if I'm not black. It's as if I have two colours. Yet I'll even try and empathise with the racists!"

Johnson has had a colourful career since studying English and History at Leicester University. She took the newspaper training course at City University, London, and then reported on a six-month programme funded by the European Commission in Brussels. After freelancing for Thames News and the BBC World Service, and an 18-month spell on the *Slough Observer* (where she developed an industrial specialism), she did short spells on *The Times* and Robert Maxwell's ill-fated *London Daily News* before ending up on the *Guardian* in 1987.

There, in a home reporting staff of 48, she was one of 15 generalists – with five other reporters based in Manchester, one each in Northern Ireland, Scotland, Yorkshire and Brussels, six acting as Westminster-based political staff and the rest as specialists. Her normal workday was from 10.30 am to 6.30 pm but could often go beyond then and she rarely had time for a lunch break. Given the pressure of deadlines, she could even volunteer to work on her day off.

She plans to stay no more than two years in South Africa. "Any more than that and my face will start to be forgotten on Fleet Street."

A week in the life of Angella Johnson

Friday

The Mail and Guardian *had gone to bed the previous day so she spends a large part of the day scanning the papers to find someone suitable to interview for her profile column. Considers going to KwaZulu Natal to interview a white member of the Inkatha Freedom Party. Then she spots a story about a prostitute who is counter-suing the Minister for Safety and Security (responsible for policing and for law and order) claiming her constitutional rights were infringed when police broke into the brothel where she was working.*

Saturday and Sunday

Days off

Monday

Her editor is interested in the prostitute profile so Angella rings the news agency that compiled the story and they supply the contact numbers. "Journalists aren't so protective of their sources as they are in Britain. There isn't that cut-throat edge as there is on Fleet Street. The agency didn't even ask for any money. Having not been exposed to the rough and tumble of Fleet Street-style journalism South African journalists have a slight innocence and naïveté."

She immediately takes a two-hour flight to East London where the prostitute comes to pick her up at the airport. "Again, she was surprised to see I was black. I don't normally say I'm black. Then when I arrive people are too polite to turn me away."

Johnson spends three hours with her subject and also meets her sister, who works as the brothel's madame. They eat at a steak house and Johnson is shown around the brothel. "She was a dominant mistress type, into S and M but would always say 'I'm not a prostitute'. She stressed she was rather working at an escort agency." *After all that, stays the night at* "a flea-bitten hotel".

Tuesday

Flies back to Johannesburg and transcribes tape recording of interview. "I normally use shorthand for everything and have only taped important interviews. Now after my experiences in South Africa where my quotes have been challenged I'm going to tape absolutely everything." *Works until 2 am on her 1,500-word piece.* "Again, I try to empathise with my subject. OK, I say she is not physically attractive. But that's a fact. On the other hand I can see she's had a hard life. She's not very bright so in South African slang she could have been described as 'poor white trash'. Now, however, she's not doing badly with two houses, one with a pool, and her two children attending good schools."

Competition is fierce for the Mail and Guardian *with the Johannesburg dailies. So she has to be really creative in her work.* "I try to humanise my reporting as much as possible. I do lots of emotional, heartstring-tugging stuff and I feel I'm developing an irreverent, provocative, 'easy-read' style."

Wednesday

Arrives at office at 8.30 am and by noon her piece is finished. Normally the page would be cleared soon afterwards but this week the freelance photographer is late in delivering the picture of the prostitute, so the page has to wait until tomorrow for completion. She normally asks to see the proof of her column and today checks it carefully for literals.

Once her major project for the week is out of the way, she follows up two crime stories on the phone. Work normally ends around 6 pm, but on Wednesdays work is hectic until around 9 pm. "None of us has the time to take lunch breaks. We eat at our work stations. But we take lots of screen breaks so through the day we get our hour."

Thursday
Finishes off the two crime stories and catches up with all the correspondence.

Profile | Why bleepers are not so teething after all:

● ● ● ● ● ● profile of

Richard Garner, education correspondent,
Daily Mirror

ICHARD Garner was at the dentist's for an early morning appointment when suddenly his bleeper sent out its screeching sound. The features desk at the *Mirror* was contacting him. "But I was not inclined to get up when I had all these strange instruments inside my mouth. So I let them wait."

Along with the mobile phone, the bleeper became an indispensable feature of Garner's working life three years ago. And though it means he is on call to his news-paper anywhere – and at any time – he doesn't object. "Once they bleeped me when I was 1,000 ft up on a plane from Manchester to London. But before I had it there was pressure to phone in every couple of hours. Now, when the news or features desks need me they bleep: it saves me having to phone so I quite like it."

One of the longest-serving members of the *Mirror* staff, Garner has seen his £46,000-a-year job of education specialist transformed by the Labour landslide victory in May 1997.

"My biggest problem used to be in fighting to get my stories in the paper. Now it's all changed. During the election campaign our sales went up 25,000 a day and the thinking around here is that the more serious content helped. So we're trying to keep up that seriousness. It certainly keeps me busy. I had lunch today with the health corre-spondent and we agreed that it was our first lunch break for four weeks."

Of his education specialism, he says: "It's obviously political. But you also get the stories about individual achievement and the human interest angles. You see how indi-viduals are faring under the system."

He often finds himself writing through the eyes of a child. "In fact, because I don't have day-to-day contact with children, I feel more nervous talking to them than I do to the head teachers."

The tabloids' reputation among teachers has a mixed impact on his job. "Some heads welcome us, some lump us with the other tabloids and are extremely distrustful. I can understand that."

He particularly identifies with the campaigning thrust of the *Mirror*. One offshoot is the enormous numbers of letters sent to the paper. For instance, an article criticising a prominent educationist who had blamed single parents for virtually all the ills of the day attracted 344 in support and just six against. A double-page spread identi-fying every education authority's cuts and improvements attracted 30 admiring phone calls.

Garner's original decision to become a journalist was heavily influenced by Derek Ingram, former editor of Gemini News Service (coincidentally profiled below). Just as Garner was leaving school, his father invited a number of friends for meals to give him an insight into their jobs. "So I'd meet lawyers and accountants. Derek Ingram was the one professional who didn't put me off."

All the same, he didn't go straight into journalism. In 1967 he became a filing clerk, then a disc jockey at a discothéque, even being auditioned for Radio 1. "They thought I might have a good voice for late night listening on Radio 2. I thought about it for a while but in the end realised that as a career move it was the kiss of death."

He was still pondering journalism, writing poetry and short stories. Eventually he took the plunge, doing the journalism training course at Harlow and joining the *North London Press*, Islington, in 1970. It was his news editor on a later job at the *Camden Journal* who was to have a great impact on his journalistic thinking. "He taught me that reporting was not simply about listening but campaigning on issues."

His path towards becoming *Mirror* education correspondent began in earnest in 1974 when he was appointed local government correspondent on the *Kent Evening Post*, Chatham. Four years later he became education specialist on the *Birmingham Evening Mail*. "It was a right-wing tabloid with a definite slant on its political stories. For instance, they were obsessed with supposed Marxist infiltration of the local trades council. They were always going on about how teachers didn't work hard." He was left devising various ingenious ways for subverting that bias.

In 1980, he moved to the paper's London office as a general reporter and then to Rupert Murdoch's *Times Educational Supplement* the following year where he rose to become news editor. In 1990, to the amazement of many of his colleagues, he left to join the *Mirror*.

He uses shorthand all the time and believes half the *Mirror* staff do the same. "I certainly couldn't survive without it." And he tapes only important interviews, such as with a government minister "when it's important to get the nuances right".

A week in the life of Richard Garner

Sunday

At 11 am he is rung by a contact in the local education authorities who tells him that David Blunkett, the Labour education spokesman, is soon to name 18 schools which had allegedly failed to improve following their Ofsted inspections. "I spent the rest of the day working to stand that up for a Monday paper story. This year, in fact, there have been only three or four times when I have not had to work on Sundays. But it meant a good start to the week for me. I certainly broke the story more accurately than any other newspaper. I'm not bullshitting. One newspaper had it the previous week but said the government would be sending in 'hit squads'. In fact, they were threatening to close the schools down if they did not improve."

Monday

Starts at 9 am. To HQ of the Training and Enterprise Councils with whom the Mirror is organising a competition to find the Modern Apprentice of the Year. Discussions focus on how best to present some case studies, through colour pieces, in the paper.

In the afternoon to Phoenix School in West London. "I'd arranged to go there to do a feature but I was lucky because it fitted in quite neatly into the 'failing schools' story." Phoenix is, in contrast, a success story. Originally Hammersmith School, it was closed down by the local Labour-controlled education authority in April 1995 and

*reopened shortly afterwards with a new name, new head and 50 per cent new appoint-
ments to the teaching staff. Since then, results had improved, absentee rates had fallen.*

Tuesday

*Starts 10 am. Writes 800 words on the Phoenix story for a double-page spread. When
it appears next day there are only 400 words. "But I could see why. There was a lot
of pressure from other stories, particularly the Blunkett announcement, for space."*

*Before heading off to Westminster for the afternoon Blunkett press conference, tries
to gather all the background information (on exam and test results) for the 18 schools.
"This takes much longer than it should have done."*

*After the conference, contacts the usual teacher union spokespersons for their reac-
tions and around 7 pm phones over his story. Then to a restaurant in Upper Street,
Islington, North London, for an off-the-record dinner chat, organised by the Education
Correspondents Group, with Don Foster, Liberal Democrat education spokesman.
Finishes 10.30 pm.*

Wednesday

*On Tuesday, Garner had been rung by Andrew Smith, the Employment Minister, who
was planning to visit a Jobcentre in West London the next day. "He asked me if I
would like to attend. I said fine. So at 9.30 am I was at Kilburn Jobcentre interviewing
the unemployed – and Andrew Smith." Phones over copy.*

*Then has lunch with David Hart, general secretary of the National Association of
Head Teachers (NAHT). "They were due to have their annual conference the following
week and so I had a chat with him on the basis of which I would do a background
piece on the conference, identifying the key items on the agenda."*

*In the afternoon to the Carlton Club. "I hasten to say I'm not a member." During
the recent general election campaign, the* Mirror, *in conjunction with BBC's*
Newsround, *had arranged a number of mock school elections and these were assessed.
Changes for the future were discussed. Finishes around 5.30 pm and heads off to his
Hertford home.*

Thursday

*Garner is due to visit an infant school in Chester which had recorded a "remarkable
improvement" in reading test results. In addition, the head had been appointed by
Blunkett to a national literacy task force. "But on Wednesday evening I'm rung to be
told Blunkett is due to announce the abolition of nursery vouchers the next day so I
hastily have to cancel my trip north."*

*Starts day by writing his column (which appears each Tuesday). Focuses on Youth-
net which is launching an Internet site specially for the young and which has won the
support of newscaster Martyn Lewis.*

*Then to Department for Education, in Westminster, for the Blunkett conference.
Writes that up and then off immediately to a hotel in Paddington for a press conference given by the Schools Curriculum and Assessment Authority which had been given
the go-ahead for the inclusion of moral values in the national curriculum. Phones over
story. Finishes 5.30 pm.*

Friday

*Unusually, stays in the Canary Wharf office all day. One story he writes focuses on
the abolition of the assisted places scheme. Another two stories are written to help tie
the paper over the Bank Holiday weekend. One concerns a scheme to train the 18- to
25-year-old unemployed, the other stems from his lunch earlier in the week with David
Hart, of the NAHT.*

Profile

Tiny outfit with a massive task:
profile of

● ● ● ● ● ● *Gemini News Service*

FROM its cramped offices in north London, Gemini News Service is a tiny operation with a massive ambition – to challenge the anti-Third World bias of the western media.

In some respects it has succeeded. Though largely unknown in Britain, in many Third World countries Gemini is more famous than such giants as Reuters and Agence France Presse.

The agency was founded on 1 January 1967 by Derek Ingram, formerly of the *Daily Mail,* and Oliver Carruthers, a British journalist who had been based in Zambia. A Sri Lankan, Gamini Seneviratne, was the first staff reporter.

Ingram, who remained editor until 1993, commented: "I was particularly concerned to promote reporting about Commonwealth countries from a London base. During the late 1960s, with the end of decolonisation, I saw newspapers in the Third World swamped with material written by British journalists. I wanted to see work about India, say, by Indians, about Zambia by Zambians. Gemini aimed to promote just that."

Significantly, the first piece put out by Gemini was an interview with Indira Gandhi by a prominent Indian journalist. But Gemini has also always used Third World-oriented copy from UK-based journalists.

From its inception the agency has aimed to promote "development journalism" challenging the traditional negative images of Third World countries – famine, violence, poverty, degradation. In their place, more positive images linked to political, cultural and economic achievements are stressed.

During the 1970s the United Nations Educational, Scientific and Cultural Organisation (UNESCO) became embroiled in controversies over development journalism, the New World Information and Communication Order (NWICO) and challenges to the international news system dominated by five leading agencies – the United Press International, Associated Press, Reuters, Agence France Presse and Tass. As Ingram commented: "We were at the nub of the NWICO debate – but before UNESCO had even thought of it."

Ingram watched with concern the decline in interest in the Third World among British papers, both local and national. At one time, local papers in Cambridge, Liverpool, Leicester and Bristol ran Gemini stories. In the early 1970s, the London *Evening Standard* ran Gemini stories three or four times a week. Now a lot of that interest has fallen away.

During the 1970s, Gemini became part of the Guardian Group, operating from the *Manchester Evening News* office in Fleet Street. But in 1982 it became wholly independent again and is currently owned by a foundation (chaired by newscaster Trevor McDonald) whose deed entrenches its editorial independence.

Daniel Nelson, editor since 1 January 1994, has had a vast experience covering Third World issues. After three years on a north London paper he decided he wanted to do "something completely different" and so wrote off letters to every African paper he heard about.

The *Ugandan Argus* took him on in 1963, thus launching him into an impressively varied career. This has included editing the *People*, of Uganda; features editing for *West Africa* magazine, sub-editing for the *Far Eastern Economic Review*, reporting for the *Financial Times* foreign desk from Manila and for the Delhi-based Indian environmental news magazine, *Down to Earth*, launching a radio service, Depthnews Asia, for the Press Foundation of Asia, and being managing editor (news) of Panos, a London-based organisation working with the media on environmental and development issues.

While expressing concern over print coverage of development issues, Nelson stresses that there is some "terrific stuff" in television documentaries.

"While the media in general are more and more obsessed with Europe and North America, some of the stories in the broadsheets on Africa do try to highlight the population, economic and development issues behind the political news."

Gemini distributes six 1,000-word features (plus graphics) twice a week to 145 outlets, mostly in Africa and Asia. "They still go out in little brown envelopes. In time we will be using email. Already, 50 per cent of our reporters are filing via email."

Among its many other activities, the service has developed a "rural reporters" scheme placing journalists in rural areas in 17 countries to find out what is going on in the countryside. Third World reporting is notoriously urban-based: this scheme aims to challenge the sterotypes accompanying that journalistic routine. Over the last 18 years Canadian journalists have joined the Gemini London office on fellowships and attachments while others have come from Africa and Asia.

And Nelson's latest project is the launch of Child Newsline, with the backing of Unicef. Seven features on children in developing countries are distributed all over the world each month.

A week in the life of Gemini

Wednesday

10 am to 6 pm for most of the staff. Daniel Nelson and Glyn Roberts, associate editor, will have to work much later. Rarely a chance for lunch breaks. Work continues on preparing for the Friday transmission of the six features. This week there is a typically wide range of subjects to be covered (elections in Liberia and Guyana, voluntary work in Japan, student butlers in London, Rwanda genocide trials and humanitarian aid for Iraq), most of them far removed from the agendas of the mainstream press.

Roberts, 43, whose experience spans working as a sub-editor for PA, a "polisher of English" at the Xinhua (New Chinese) agency in Beijing during the mid-1980s and seven years on the subs bench at the Daily Telegraph, says some of the copy requires "enormous" amounts of attention. "Because resources are so low here, we have to rely on emails and faxes to contact the writer and that can prove terribly time-consuming and stressful."

Kanina Holmes, 28, at the Gemini office on a fellowship from the Ottawa-based International Development and Research Center, is busy preparing for a four-month stint in East Africa while at the same time subbing stories and preparing her own.

She has been taking a refresher course in Swahili and building up contacts in Uganda and Kenya. A graduate in 1995 from Carleton University, Ottawa, with an MA in International Affairs, she sees one of her challenges as "translating my academic interests into journalism". During her studies she spent 10 months on field work in Tanzania, looking at the issues of gender and environmental change, and plans to return to that country during her East African travels.

She has been a news reporter, current affairs broadcaster and associate producer during her five years at CBC radio and finds significant contrasts between the journalist cultures in London and Canada. "Here the old boys' network is very noticeable. Journalism is a high-paced, heavy-drinking world. And I see lots of egos around. At news conferences, for instance, lots of reporters who ask questions are more keen to let others know how knowledgeable they are than to get at the truth through the answer."

She works closely with artist Paul Slater, 25, in compiling a graphic on the Liberian civil war. "This is quite difficult. I have to go through seven years of Keesing's Record of World Events highlighting the major events." Researching a "think piece" on genetic testing screening also takes up time; she looks at past copies of the Financial Times, Guardian, Sunday Times and Observer for relevant articles and goes back to her notes from a recent conference at the Royal Society on genetic testing.

Thursday

Work begins at 10 am. Again, no time for lunch breaks. Holmes is helping on the revision of a graphic highlighting the achievements of six Third World women leaders who rose to prominence following the deaths of their husbands. An error had cropped up in the original version and so sources at the Sri Lankan embassy and the BBC's Sri Lankan Service are contacted. Slater, who studied technical illustration at Ravensbourne College and Bournemouth and Poole College of Art and Design, works on his cartoon accompanying the butler story. "I actually find cartoons the most difficult. The physical act of drawing provides no problems but it's arriving at the concept which is not easy."

Nelson completely rejigs a story to extract a lively angle buried in the original. Roberts faxes to a reporter a series of questions which are almost as long as the story itself.

Work goes on late into the night.

Friday

Work starts at 9.30 am with all attention focused on the 3.15 pm deadline. Dupe Owodunni, 31, production secretary at Gemini for six years, prepares the features for distribution. In addition she works on developing the service's Web site (http//:www.oneworld.org/gemini) which has links to other news agencies and Third World think tanks and the Childline site (http//:www.gn.apc.org/childnewsline/Index.html). Nelson and Roberts have a final check on copy. The 3.15 pm deadline is missed so the brown envelopes have to be carried up to the post office.

Owodunni prepares the copy for the five email subscribers – in Canada, Uganda, South Africa and Pakistan. Work begins on the next six features. Roberts and Nelson continue working until late.

Monday

10 am start. Staff have been working on stories over the weekend. The six features (on a women's caucus in the Kenyan parliament, child marriage in India, a huge oil project in Chad, the North Korean famine, gold traders in central Africa and feuding between Muslim extremists in Pakistan) again require substantial attention. Each feature is given a lively headline and standfirst; sentences are kept brief and bright. For instance, the Pakistan story is headlined: "Zealots may be barred from dialling M for murder" while the standfirst reads: "Feuding between Muslim extremists has been growing in Pakistan. Following the death of a senior policeman, reports Gemini News Service, the authorities have vowed to get tough with the sects – and with foreign elements believed to be encouraging them."

Holmes comments: "For many of the reporters English is their second, third or even fourth language. And so I have often to read between the lines to figure out what they actually intend to mean. Now that poses some particular ethical questions for me. If the article has got someone's name on it I have to be absolutely clear that I am translating the meaning correctly."

Map graphics are to be attached to the North Korea, central Africa and Chad stories and Holmes and Roberts work with Slater researching the accompanying text. Work continues late into the night.

Tuesday

Another transmission day starts at 10 am. Slater completes the graphic accompanying the Pakistan Muslim story. It shows a young girl reading the Koran while on either side the basic tenets of Islam and the five pillars of the faith are clearly outlined. Roberts wants to contact a reporter urgently. "OK I'll send him a fax but that takes time and he may not even reply. A phone call would be so much simpler but I can't do that." He takes a cigarette break.

Holmes sub-edits copy for the latest Child Newsline service and Owodunni prepares the final version for distribution, both in text form and on the Web. For a graphic illustrating the three Ugandan leaders (Obote, Amin and Museveni) Slater uses photographs of the three faces.

Nelson entertains a group of Third World journalists keen to see the headquarters of such a well-known news service. They are surprised to see how small its offices are.

The 3.15 pm deadline is met. Work starts on the next six features.

2   Efficks – or ethics?

···

JOURNALISTS are often sceptical about the value of ethical debate. As *Financial Times* reporter Raymond Snoddy says: "It certainly sets the British press apart from newspapers in the US where on the whole the word 'ethics' can be uttered without hoots of derision" (*The Good, the Bad and the Unacceptable*; Faber and Faber; London; second edition; 1993).

One journalism lecturer tells of when he invited a prominent Fleet Street editor to talk to his students about ethics. "Efficks. What's that?" the editor asked, bemused, and proceeded to tell a string of stories about his life and times in the industry. A senior editorial manager interviewed by a University of Central Lancashire research team investigating the regional newspaper industry commented: "The reason newspapers are in so much shit is because journalists have been precious with their ethics" (*The Changing Vision*; University of Central Lancashire; Preston; 1993). Most journalism textbooks give only cursory attention to ethical issues.

There are a number of reasons for this scepticism. Many journalists are profoundly idealistic, concerned about ethical issues and determined to improve standards. Yet the dominant attitude prioritises "getting the story" and the demands of the deadline above all else. Ethical and political concerns are secondary, if they are ever considered at all.

Linked to this attitude is the belief that the best way to learn reporting is "on the job" (a belief reinforced by the new National Vocational Qualifications' stress on work-based assessment).

More importantly, many journalists are deeply sceptical about the power they have as individuals to improve media standards. Newspapers seem too committed to entrenched routines and mythologies, too closely tied to the political establishment and to the demands of surviving in a market-led economy.

Most newspaper operations are hierarchically organised with considerable power going to those at the top; many lower down the pecking order often see themselves as impotent (and largely dispensable), tiny cogs in a much larger machine. There is much talk of press freedom but little of the journalist's freedom to influence the organisation for which they work.

Adding to this ethical malaise are the theatrical, unreal elements at the heart of the current debate. A major controversy emerged in 1992 over rights to privacy and journalists' use of telephoto lenses after the publication in several newspapers and magazines of compromising photographs of Sarah Ferguson with her financial adviser. And following the 1992 Calcutt report's call for legal constraints on journalists' use of bugging devices and telephoto lenses the controversy intensified. But these issues confront only a tiny minority of journalists for a small part of their time. Far more significant political issues, such as the impact of advertisers or monopoly ownership on press standards, are marginalised.

The ethical tensions in the industry

JOURNALISTS' scepticism over standards is, in part, a consequence of the ethical contradictions within the newspaper industry. Its central position as a largely monopolistic industry in a profit-oriented economic system means business and entertainment priorities dominate. News becomes, above all, a commodity to be sold.

Yet journalists' rhetoric (prominent in editorial columns throughout the country) promotes notions of the public interest, the right to know and the free press which are often in conflict with the priorities of the market-place.

Moreover, while journalists stress the importance of objectivity and truth (news being a mirror of reality) these notions often conflict with the actual production of bias, myth and propaganda by the press.

The ethics of everyday journalism

JOURNALISTS' widespread scepticism about ethics is strange given the importance of the job's moral dimension. All journalists talk of news "values". Moreover, representations of good and bad, the just and the unjust predominate in the media (see *Folk Devils and Moral Panics*; Stanley Cohen; Robertson; London; second edition; 1980).

Read any popular newspaper and you will see stories about "evil" rapists, "monsters" who attack old ladies, "evil" mums who lead their children into prostitution, "Nazi" Serbs who butcher innocent Bosnians. The 1991 Gulf conflict carried this reporting genre to its extreme with representations of President Bush as "good and heroic", engaged in a personal battle with President Saddam Hussein, the "evil, bully, Butcher of Baghdad".

Jostein Gripsrud relates this moral dimension of newspapers to the emotional excesses of the 19th-century morality play. Today it is the press (and mass media in general) which provide moral tales, stories that give lessons in what is good and bad ("The aesthetics and politics of melodrama", in *Journalism and Popular Culture*; Peter Dahlgren and Colin Sparks (eds); Sage; London; 1992).

The notion of standards is also central to any notion of professionalism which the industry has been concerned to develop. Linked to this process has been the stress on concepts such as objectivity, neutrality, fairness, accuracy, and the separation of fact from opinion. The concern of unions and management since the Second World War to promote journalism training has been closely tied to notions of standards and professionalism.

Some everyday ethical dilemmas

BEYOND these general observations let us identify some everyday ethical issues that can confront journalists:

- Should journalists ever lie or use deceit in the pursuit of a story?

- Should they ever edit a direct quote?

- Is it legitimate to tape a conversation and not inform the interviewee of this?

- Should journalists accept freebies? Should they do so only on certain conditions? Are there any significantly different ethical issues in being offered a book for review, a free ticket to review a play and a free trip to the Seychelles for a travel feature?

- What is the impact of the plethora of awards on standards?

- What considerations should a journalist have when interviewing children?

- Should a reporter contact the parents of a student who has committed suicide at university?

- Should newspapers carry columns by local Christian leaders but not those of other faiths?

- To what extent should newspapers provide readers with the right to reply to inaccuracies?

- What special consideration should a journalist have when dealing with the mentally ill?

- How important is it for journalists to protect their sources?

- Is chequebook journalism (paying sources) justified?

- Is it legitimate to invade someone's privacy for a story? Do different standards apply to public figures and members of the general public?

- To what extent does overt commitment to a political party or campaigning movement interfere with professionalism and notions of fairness?

- Should newspapers carry government misinformation during times of war (and peace)?

- Is it legitimate ever to break an embargo?

- Is it possible to provide guidelines on questions of taste and the use of "shocking" photographs or obscene language?

- To what extent does newspaper language reinforce militarist and ageist stereotypes and how can journalists confront this issue?

- What ethical issues are raised by business sponsorship of newspaper editions?

To relate this ethical discussion to the practicalities of the job, you might talk to journalists from Britain and abroad about these issues. What do they consider to be the five most important ethical issues facing them in their jobs?

A brief history of moves to improve press standards

SINCE the Second World War, press standards have attracted constant concern from governments and politicians. Royal Commissions have reported; surveys into press content have been conducted; committees have pondered such issues as bias, inaccuracy, sensationalism, trivialisation, invasion of privacy, proprietorial intervention. The impact of all this activity is uncertain. Many of the calls for reform have been simply ignored by the industry.

The first Royal Commission (1947–9) arose out of concern over growing monopolies, with Lord Rothermere, owner of the *Daily Mail*, Lord Beaverbrook, of the *Daily Express*, and Lord Kemsley, of the *Daily Sketch*, *Daily Graphic* and *Sunday Times*, coming under particular scrutiny.

Beaverbrook was frank before the commission, saying he ran his paper "purely for the purpose of making propaganda and with no other motive". Yet the commission, chaired by the philosopher Sir William Ross, vice-chancellor of Oxford University, failed to conclude the industry was endangered by increasingly powerful monopolies.

Nor did it discover any concerted efforts by advertisers to influence newspapers. But the commission did express concerns over political bias, inaccuracies and trivialisation. It rejected measures to limit newspaper circulations or profits as well as legislation to halt intrusions into privacy.

Most significantly, the commission recommended a General Council of the Press be set up to safeguard press freedoms and encourage the development of a sense of public responsibility among journalists. It was four years before the council first met on 21 July 1953. Its first ruling was that a *Daily Mirror* poll on whether Princess Margaret should marry Group Captain Townsend was "contrary to the best traditions of British journalism" (how royal reporting has changed!).

A second Royal Commission, set up in 1961, also followed mounting concern over monopolies. Chaired by Lord Shawcross, a former Labour Attorney General, it criticised the industry for its poor response to the 1949 commission's recommendations and stressed the importance of including a lay element on the General Council. Thus, the Press Council came into being in July 1963 with 20 industry representatives and five lay members.

The first commission had predicted no significant trends towards further concentration of ownership. Events had proved it wrong. By 1962 the top three proprietors' slice of the national daily press had risen to 89 per cent, major monopolies were growing in the periodical press and only in local weeklies was concentration "negligible".

To contain this trend it proposed a Press Amalgamations Court. Legislation in 1965 incorporated some elements of this idea, with major takeovers having to be approved by the Secretary of State. But as James Curran and Jean Seaton conclude: "The effectiveness of this legislation may be gauged by the fact that not one of the 50 acquisitions of newspaper companies by major press groups during the period 1965–77 was disallowed" (*Power Without Responsibility: The Press and Broadcasting in Britain*; Routledge; London; fourth edition; 1991).

More significantly, Rupert Murdoch was allowed to purchase the *Sunday Times* and *The Times* in 1981, thereby handing him 30 per cent of national daily circulation and 31 per cent of national Sunday circulation, without any reference to the Monopolies Commission.

The Younger Committee on Privacy was established in 1970 after a Private Member's Bill seeking to introduce a general right to privacy was rejected by the Labour government. It considered a wide range of issues: for instance, how the right to know could conflict with the right to be protected from intrusive reporters; how reporting might cause personal suffering which might outweigh any claims of public interest.

In the end it decided against the introduction of a right to privacy law. A third Royal Commission (1974–7) reported with concern that three owners dominated the national daily and Sunday markets while in the regions morning, evening and weekly papers were being owned by the same group. The commission was also critical of the performance of the Press Council, making 12 recommendations to transform its operating procedures. However, these were largely rejected and the council remained a weak body, lacking the confidence of both the managers and the NUJ (see *Principles of the*

Press: a Digest of Press Council Decisions; Noel S. Paul; Press Council; London. *People Against the Press: An Enquiry into the Press Council*; Geoffrey Robertson; Quartet; London; 1983).

The Calcutt report into privacy and related matters

I N 1989, following a spate of controversies over press intrusions into private grief, the Thatcher government authorised a committee to investigate the possible intro- duction of a privacy law. Earlier, right of reply bills, promoted by Labour MPs Frank Allaun, Ann Clwyd and Tony Worthington, and a privacy bill, introduced by Conservative MP John Browne, had been voted out of the House.

Chaired by David Calcutt, master of Magdalene College, Cambridge, the committee heard evidence from a wide range of people. For instance, the father of an *EastEnders* actor who had committed suicide complained of press harassment. Predictably, the committee's recommendation that privacy laws be introduced to curb the press drew howls of protest from the massed ranks of Fleet Street editors and columnists.

The industry, however, reacted quickly to the call to set up a self-regulatory Press Complaints Commission (PCC) in place of the Press Council and so attempt to ward off legislation. Even though one of its members was Brian Hitchen, editor of the *Daily Star*, one of its first acts was to criticise the *Star* for headlining its front page story on a select committee proposal to admit homosexuals into the army headlined "Poofters on parade".

Most of the national newspapers also appointed ombudsmen to consider readers' complaints. But the campaigning body, Article 19, commented: "So far the evidence suggests that ombudsmen have only a limited influence" (*Press Law and Practice: A Comparative Study of Press Freedom in European and Other Democracies*; London; 1993).

Second Calcutt report on privacy and the press

I N January 1993, Calcutt (by then Sir David) presented a second report focusing on press and privacy issues. The PCC was accused of being ineffective and too domi- nated by the industry. Calcutt singled out its handling of revelations contained in Andrew Morton's book *Princess Diana: Her True Story* (Michael O'Mara; London; 1992), various sex scandals (involving such prominent figures as Paddy Ashdown, leader of the Liberal Democrats, and David Mellor, National Heritage Minister and Chelsea supporter) and the *People*'s contemptuous treatment of the commission after it printed pictures of an infant royal running naked.

In response, Calcutt proposed new offences carrying maximum fines of £5,000 for invasions of privacy and the use of surveillance and bugging devices in certain cases. In defence, journalists could claim the material was obtained for preventing, detecting or exposing crime or anti-social behaviour, or to prevent people being misled by some statement or action of the individual concerned.

The Major government responded positively and later in the year proposed the intro- duction of a privacy law. Yet it was determined not to apply the restrictions to the security services. As the *UK Press Gazette* (6 September 1993) commented:

> The greatest invasion of privacy is carried out every day by the security services, with no control, no democratic authorisation and the most horrifying consequences for people's employment and lives. By comparison with them the press is a poodle.

The government was more sceptical of ideas promoted by the Labour backbencher, Clive Soley, for enforcing a statutory code on press accuracy. Similarly, a proposal from the National Heritage select committee for the industry to set up a voluntary body with powers to fine offending newspapers failed to win support either from the government or prominent journalists.

The PCC responded to all this controversy by introducing new clauses on bugging and the use of telephoto lenses to its Code of Practice and a lay majority to its membership. In addition it appointed Professor Robert Pinker, of the London School of Economics, as its special privacy commissioner.

How the privacy debate hit fever pitch

In November 1993, "peeping tom" photographs taken secretly of a reclining Princess Diana working out at a gym and published in the *Sunday Mirror* and *Mirror* refuelled the privacy debate – though it continued to be focused narrowly on the problems faced by Britain's aristocracy and political elite.

A *Sunday Times* sting operation in July 1994 against two Conservative MPs, Graham Riddick and David Tredinnick, which revealed them accepting £1,000 from a journalist to ask questions in Parliament, provoked more controversy. The newspaper was originally backed by the Press Complaints Commission (PCC) but predictably condemned in April 1995 by the Commons Privileges Committee (with its in-built Conservative majority) for "falling substantially below the standards to be expected of legitimate journalism". But surprisingly, in March 1996, the PCC reversed its decision, ruling that the newspaper did not first gather enough information since an issue of serious public interest was at stake.

In October 1994, the *Guardian* began its own long campaign to expose sleaze among Conservative MPs taking cash handouts from lobbyists in return for asking parliamentary questions. *Guardian* editor Peter Preston admitted that his reporters sent a "cod fax" to the Ritz Hotel in the hunt for financial information about Cabinet minister Jonathan Aitken, using a mock-up of the House of Commons notepaper to protect the source. The privacy debate duly reached fever pitch (*Sleaze: The Corruption of Parliament*; David Leigh and Ed Vulliamy; Fourth Estate; London; 1997).

Preston was summoned to explain his use of the fax to Parliament's Sergeant at Arms and resigned from the PCC, concerned that "too much collateral damage" from the row would damage the reputation of the commission. Soon afterwards, Premier John Major set up a committee, chaired by Lord Nolan, to investigate the ethical behaviour of lobbyists and MPs.

The newly appointed chairman of the PCC, Lord Wakeham, in early 1995 gave a strong warning to editors not to abuse the public interest defence when facing complaints over invasions of privacy. Soon afterwards, the PCC criticised the *News of the World* for publishing pictures, gained through the use of a long-lens camera, of yet another aristocrat: a frail-looking Countess Spencer, sister-in-law of the Princess of Wales, in the gardens of a private health clinic. After her husband, Earl Spencer, complained, Professor Pinker contacted Rupert Murdoch, owner of the *News of the World*, who publicly reprimanded its editor, Piers Morgan. Murdoch described Morgan as "a young man" who "went over the top" in his coverage of the countess's psychological problems. The editor duly apologised (*The Prying Game: The Sex, Sleaze and Scandals of Fleet Street and the Media Mafia*; Christopher Browne; Robson Books; London; 1996).

Then in July 1995, the government published its long-awaited White Paper on privacy. Six years of controversy, since Sir David Calcutt was appointed to chair his committee, ended up with the government retreating from imposing any privacy legislation. Instead, Virginia Bottomley, the new National Heritage Secretary, called for:

- the PCC to pay compensation from an industry fund to victims of privacy intrusion;

- a "hot-line" between the chairman and editors to head off breaches of the code;

- non-industry members to sit on the PCC's code committee;

- and the code to be tightened up to include a clearer definition of privacy.

Tory backbenchers greeted the announcement with jeers; the Labour Party expressed disappointment.

But the Major government did threaten to intervene in the controversial area of "chequebook journalism". Following payments by newspapers to witnesses in the Rosemary West multiple murders trial, the Lord Chancellor, Lord Mackay of Clashfern, in October 1996, proposed to bring in a criminal law to ban such payments. Again the PCC responded by lauding the benefits of "self-regulation" and promising yet another revision of its code to highlight the importance of full disclosure of payments ("Free-ranging rules"; Lord Wakeham; the *Guardian*; 11 November 1996).

Public interest or of interest to the public?

An unprecedented number of political resignations occurred in the three years after John Major's election victory of 1992 and his launch of a "Back to Basics" moral crusade, many of them following "scandalous" revelations in the press.

Such scandals were not confined to Britain. Hardly a country was unaffected by corruption scandals as ruling elites bickered among themselves following the collapse of the Cold War and the demise of the old Soviet enemy. In all, there were 14 resignations on the grounds of scandal in Britain over the three years: this was out of a total government list (Commons and Lords) of about 130. About half the cases involved sexual activities and about half financial irregularities.

The *Independent on Sunday* (23 July 1995) claimed that a five-year period (1990–5) saw 34 Conservative, one Liberal Democrat and four Labour scandals; of these 39, at least a quarter involved sex.

Yet many critics of the press suggest that editors are too quick to hide behind the "public interest" defence cloak when trying to justify blatant and sensational invasions of privacy. It was within this context that Lord Wakeham, in November 1996, outlined seven key public interest tests which he wanted editors to consider before publication.

1) Is there a genuine public interest involved in invading someone's privacy as defined by Clause 18 of the Code of Practice – detecting or exposing crime, protecting public health, preventing the public from being misled – or is this simply a story which interests the public?

2) If there is a genuine public interest, have you considered whether there are ways to disclose it which minimise invasion into the private life of the individual concerned?

3) If you are using photographs as part of the story, which will have to be (or have already been) obtained by clandestine means and therefore compound the invasion of privacy, does the public interest require their automatic publication or are they simply illustrative?

4) Is there a genuine public interest which cannot be exposed in any other way than intrusion; have you considered whether there is any other way to minimise the impact on the innocent and vulnerable relatives of the individual, in particular the children?

5) If you are intending to run a story about someone connected or related to a person in the public eye in order to illustrate a story about a public figure, are you satisfied the connection isn't too remote and there is a genuine public interest in mentioning that connection?

6) Where you are preparing to publish a story seeking to contrast what a public figure has said or done in the past with his or her current statements or behaviour, have you satisfied yourself it is fair to make such a comparison and that the original statement or behaviour was recent enough to justify publication in the public interest?

7) If you are intending to run a story about the private life of an individual where there used to be a public interest, have you applied each of these questions afresh in case such a defence no longer exists?

The PCC Code's clause on intrusion was also altered in November 1996 making it acceptable only when it could be shown to be in the public interest or could be reasonably believed to be in the public interest.

Privacy legislation – by the back door?

The determination of the Major government not to intervene in the privacy issue was reinforced when the Master of the Rolls, Lord Woolf, and two judges upheld a PCC decision that the *Sun* did not warrant censure for publishing a picture of the Moors murderer Ian Brady.

Yet fears were mounting that the Data Protection Registrar Elizabeth France was seeking powers to use the European Union data protection directive (due to be implemented in 1998) to introduce privacy legislation without any parliamentary discussion. In particular there were fears that the directive could be used by individuals to gain access to journalists' notebooks and to stories and obituaries before they were published.

Moreover, the Labour Party, while in opposition, had appeared largely sympathetic to calls for privacy legislation as a way of curbing press intrusions on personal privacy. Yet, following its May 1997 victory, New Labour made clear it was not planning to introduce privacy laws, unless newspapers behaved in an "intolerable fashion". Journalists disguising themselves as doctors was an example given of intolerable behaviour.

To relate this history to the practicalities of the job, why not ask some journalists their views on the introduction of a privacy law? Some prominent journalists, such as Alan Rusbridger, editor of the *Guardian*, Selina Scott, the newscaster (and victim of a 1995 *News of the World* contrived sexposé) and Polly Toynbee, associate editor of the *Independent*, have come out in favour of a privacy law. Do your local journalists (on mainstream and non-mainstream media) agree?

One tabloid journalist told Michael Leapman: "There is no doubt ethical standards have gone down and it affects all of us. If you live in a swamp you get your feet wet"

(*Treacherous Estate: The Press after Fleet Street*; Hodder & Stoughton; London; 1992).
Are journalists you speak to concerned about falling ethical standards?

Have they ever used a bugging device in the pursuit of a story? Or do they find the controversy largely irrelevant? Do newspapers in your area offer readers a right of reply?

The way forward?

CLEARLY there is a need to refocus the ethical debate. Measures to curtail the concentration of ownership in the press remain the major priority. Governments in Austria, France, the Netherlands, Norway and Sweden provide subsidies to publications facing financial problems and to promote diversity: similar measures for this country could be considered. At the same time, mechanisms to protect editorial independence from proprietors need to be introduced. Here, journalists can also gain a certain amount of inspiration from their colleagues on the Continent.

In Germany, for instance, some newspapers have agreed understandings with staffers giving them a voice in editorial decisions and in the editor-in-chief's selection. In Norway, an Editors' Code, drafted in 1953 and revised in 1973, has been recognised by the courts as a statement of custom under common law. It provides the editor-in-chief with sole power to decide what to publish and editorial staff considerable powers to challenge interventions by proprietors. Article 19 (ibid.) records:

> Publishers who have tampered with editorial decisions have found themselves without an editorial staff; in one case a paper went bankrupt when its staff quit following the publisher's order to remove an article about his family business. The strength of journalistic support for the Code and for editorial autonomy has tended to reduce the potentially negative impacts of ownership concentration.

Combating sexism: *is it just old hat?*

THERE are no easy answers to the many ethical dilemmas in journalism. Even when people agree on the importance of certain principles (such as, say, anti-classism, anti-racism) differences may emerge over strategies for implementing them. While certain attitudes and routines predominate throughout the mainstream media, each newspaper still has its own unique culture. What is possible at one will be impossible at another.

Thus in tackling sexism within the industry there are many strategies available. For instance, once you have secured your first job you may choose to lie low on ethical issues and wait until you have established your credibility before speaking out.

You may work on ethical issues through the trade union. Your newspaper may routinely carry Page Three-type images of women and glorify macho images of men. In this context, you may choose to work discreetly, raising issues in discussions with colleagues, using any freedom you have in choosing features and sources to tackle sexist assumptions. Or you may regard the sexism debate as boring old-hat dominated by PC (Political Correctness) fanatics and not worth the bother.

Some journalists even opt out of the mainstream press for ethical reasons. For them, working in the mainstream involves too many ethical compromises. They may see racist, sexist and class biases too firmly entrenched. And constant confrontations over these issues can prove both exhausting and counter-productive. In contrast, they may find a culture in the non-mainstream press more open to progressive ideas and journalistic routines.

Wherever you choose to work, a sense of humour and a willingness to subject your own views to searching criticism will always prove invaluable.

The questioning approach

Since ethical debate remains remote from the dominant journalists' culture, simply raising pertinent questions can become an important first step.

Many ethical questions stem from the unjust distribution of power in society. The focus tends to fall on the "oppressed" – women, children, elderly and disabled people, ethnic minority groups. And the dominant questions focus around how discrimination and stereotyping of these groups can be reduced.

But is there not a danger here of focusing on these groups as victims (of oppression and consequent stereotyping) while the problem groups are really the oppressors – men, adults, the able-bodied, the dominant ethnic groups?

The question of sexism

The 1990s witnessed a few advances for women in the mainstream press. The numbers of female editors of tabloids rose and Rosie Boycott moved from magazine editorship to become the first woman editor of a broadsheet (the struggling *Independent on Sunday*). And at the *Sunday Mirror*, editorial control in November 1996 was in the hands of three women: managing director Bridget Rowe, deputy managing director Pat Moore, and acting editor Amanda Platell. This was significantly the first time in Fleet Street history an all-female executive triumvirate had held power on a national newspaper.

Yet, all the same, research by Women in Journalism pressure group published in 1996 revealed "a pervasive and flexible strand of stereotyping through coverage of women in the news". Newsrooms tended to be male-dominated and traditional sexist attitudes survived unscathed. WiJ concluded: "It seems clear that sometimes news desks go onto autopilot, trotting out clichés and stereotypes when, in fact, the woman in the story before them is unique."

Moreover, Margareta Melin-Higgins found that most of the female journalists she interviewed were concerned that the recruitment system was disadvantageous to women in an industry where an "old boys' network loomed large" ("The social construction of journalist ideals: Gender in journalism education", paper presented at conference "Journalists for a new century"; London College of Printing; 24 April 1997).

Within this context, sexism issues often develop around some of the following questions:

● Do Page Three-type representations of women promote sexist attitudes towards and violence against women? Should they be banned?

● Do sourcing routines marginalise women and feminist perspectives and activities?

● What role do women's pages in newspapers play in either perpetuating or confronting sexism? Should men be prevented from contributing to women's pages?

● Are women too often represented as victims – of violence, rape and so on? Could not this coverage be "balanced" by stories of women challenging the "victim syndrome", tackling, either as individuals or in groups, the consequences of their violent ordeals?

These are all important issues worth raising where and when appropriate. All reporters should be aware of the major feminist texts (for instance, see *Feminist Theorists: Three Centuries of Women's Intellectual Traditions*; edited by Dale Spender; Women's Press; London; 1983) and try to combat the routine marginalisation of women's voices in the media. Reports and features, where possible, should reflect the gender (as well as the race and class) diversity of the culture.

Editors need to be convinced that women's issues should not be confined to special pages and soft features. Just as newspapers have defence and environment specialists, should they not have specialists producing news with a women's focus?

Men and sexism

All these questions "problematise" women. Instead, let's focus on men. To what extent are male roles stereotyped in the press with images glorifying macho firmness, violence, power, militarism, heroism and success? Do not reviewers have a responsibility to challenge such representations in films, plays and books?

To what extent does the press encourage men to question their emotional unease, their career obsessions or their traditional roles away from the home and child-rearing? To what extent are men challenged over their responses to sexual violence towards women or to sexual harassment of women in the workplace?

To add a further complexity to the debate, it can be argued that sexism sometimes works in favour of women. Women foreign correspondents often say the "invisibility" of women in some cultures helps give them access to places where men would be banned or harassed. Editors are sometimes said to favour women as profile writers since men are considered more likely to open up to a female interviewer.

Man-made language

The marginalisation of women in the press and the glorification of macho values does not usually come from any deliberate policy. It emerges within a political culture where certain attitudes are routinely adopted and certain questions are routinely eliminated. One area where sexism is most evident is in language. Very often the male bias of language can render women invisible (see *Man Made Language*; Dale Spender; Routledge & Kegan Paul; London; 1980. *Womanwords*; Jane Mills; Virago; London; 1991).

Challenging this bias is no easy task. Some newspaper-style books avoid all mention of sexism issues except in relation to the use of Ms, Miss and Mrs. Thus *The Times*' comments on Ms: "Use for married or unmarried women where requested in Britain and unless requested otherwise in stories from America." Most newspapers now accept the use of "Ms" where appropriate and avoid using "he" when "he or she" or "they" (as a singular bisexual pronoun) is more accurate. Phrases such as "the common man" and "the man in the street" are also widely avoided.

Discussions over style book changes, then, provide opportunities to raise language issues. But style book revisions are often monopolised by an editorial elite who provide few opportunities for participation by anyone else.

In certain situations it might be appropriate to work with your colleagues in the National Union of Journalists to confront sexist stereotyping in language. To assist such campaigns, the union has drawn up an *Equality Style Guide* suggesting words to be avoided and alternatives such as:

businessman	– business manager, executive, boss, business chief, head of firm etc., businesswoman/people

cameraman	– photographer, camera operator
newsman	– journalist or reporter
fireman/men	– firefighter/fire services staff/fire crews
dustman	– refuse collector
foreman	– supervisor
ice cream man	– ice cream seller
policeman/men	– police officer or just police
salesman/girl	– assistant/shop worker/shop staff/representative, sales staff
steward/ess, air hostess	– airline staff/flight attendant

Even where style books fail to acknowledge these issues, there is often a certain degree of stylistic freedom available to the reporter to use such language.

Not just a black and white issue: *racism and the press*

IT could be argued that the British press is at its worst when engaging in racist, overtly xenophobic rhetoric. Attacks on "Arab rats", "funny Frogs", "boring Belgians", "lazy Irish", are commonplace in the patriotic pops (*Your Daily Dose of Racism*; Chris Searle; Campaign for Press and Broadcasting Freedom; London; 1989. *Daily Racism: the Press and Black People in Britain*; Paul Gordon and David Rosenberg; Runnymede Trust; 1989).

But since racist oppression is historically rooted in Britain's imperial past, is it not inevitable that the press, so much part of the dominant economic system, and its consensual news values should reflect this bias? As Max Hastings, former editor of the *Daily Telegraph*, commented: "We're hideously racist in our approach to news. Because people in Bosnia look like us and speak quite good English we're more interested in what happens to them and we sympathise with them more than we do with the Sudanese."

Most race issues throw up a range of questions. For instance, you are producing a feature about a street in your town where virtually all the sources say the same thing: they want the Pakistanis out. What do you do? Report the racist quotes accurately? Seek out balancing quotes from elsewhere? Would you do the same balancing operation if all the quotes were pro-Pakistani?

Take another case: you are the one black woman on your newspaper. You are tired of being labelled the "oppressed black" by fervent "anti-racists". You just want to get on with your job and succeed. Should you take on the role of an ethnic minorities specialist which is offered to you?

Despite the complexities, reporters have a clear responsibility to tackle the marginalisation of ethnic minority voices in the press. Sourcing routines that reinforce this marginalisation need to be challenged though the scope for doing this will differ from paper to paper.

A major report published in 1995 by the London Institute concluded that less than 2 per cent of British press, radio and television journalists were of black or ethnic minority origin. And out of around 4,000 national newspaper journalists only two or three dozen are black. Moves to increase the number of black journalists through special training grants and other means need to be supported.

Too often newspaper coverage of ethnic minority groups focuses on "problems" – such as "riots", violence, crime and drug abuse. Alongside this representation go media images of Muslim fanatics as mad and threatening global stability. The sensational coverage often given to race issues feeds on people's fears and reinforces them. More newspaper style books need to acknowledge these issues and promote strategies to combat such stereotyping.

Language used uncritically can play a crucial role in perpetuating racism (see *Racism and the Press*; Teu van Dijk; Routledge; London; 1991). Thus, be wary of using "black" in a negative context. When Britain quit the European Exchange Rate Mechanism (ERM) in 1992 it was called "Black Wednesday". Should not journalists have had second thoughts before reproducing that description? Should alternatives be found for blackspot (accident site) and blackleg (strike-breaker)?

The NUJ has drawn up guidelines for race reporting and for covering racist organisations which are worth consulting.

People first? *Handling disability*

D ISABLED people number at least one in ten of the population yet they are marginalised, rendered invisible or stereotyped in the press and throughout the media (see "Disabled lives"; *New Internationalist*; Oxford; July 1992).

Covering the disabled poses a number of ethical issues for journalists which have been highlighted in a campaign "People first" by the NUJ and the Campaign for Press and Broadcasting Freedom (with leaflets available for the partially sighted, in braille and on tape).

The campaign suggests that, as a reporter, you should never assume your audience is able-bodied. When advertising events, newspapers have a responsibility to identify the provisions for access by disabled people. Similarly, traditional news values which marginalise the concerns of disabled people and confine them to specialist columns and publications need to be challenged.

The campaign also raises some pertinent questions: how often are the voices of disabled people represented in the press by able-bodied "experts"? And how much is coverage of disabled people over-sentimentalised? Too often, stereotypes of disability promote the idea that charity can solve their "problems" while marginalising the view that political and economic changes are needed to end the discrimination they confront.

Similarly, disabled people are often associated with being courageous, tragic victims, eternally cheerful, grateful, pathetic and asexual. How often is it recognised they may be black, lesbian or gay?

Language

As a number of style books point out, it is better to refer to "disabled people" rather than "the disabled" which depersonalises them and focuses entirely on their disability. Words such as "cripple", "deaf and dumb" and "abnormal" should be avoided.

Negative words and phrases should not be linked with disabilities as in "lame duck", "blind stupidity" and "deaf to reason". "Physically challenged" is not generally accepted as a substitute for "disabled".

Avoiding the victim syndrome: *handling AIDS stories*

J OURNALISTS face special ethical issues when compiling AIDS-related stories. Reporting of AIDS-related diseases in the early 1980s was minimal, perhaps because those affected – gays, drug users and Africans – were already marginalised by the press. Since then coverage of AIDS-related stories has too often been sensationalised, with the creation of "moral panics" exploiting and perpetuating fears of the fatal condition – and of sexuality in general.

Some style books have identified areas where special care is needed. For instance, on reporting claims for an AIDS cure, the Reuters style book says:

If a story making dramatic claims for a cure for AIDS or cancer does not come from a reputable named source it must be checked with recognised medical experts before being issued (or spiked). If such a story is issued it should include whatever balancing or interpretative material is available from such authorities.

A leaflet produced by the NUJ and the Health Education Authority, *HIV and AIDS: A Guide for Journalists*, suggests stories should not perpetuate myths that AIDS can be spread through casual contact such as kissing. It can only be spread through intimate sexual contact, by the sharing of needles by drug addicts, by blood transfusion or from mother to infant in pregnancy. Some reports about children with HIV, it says, have provoked anxieties among pupils and parents.

Confidentiality about infection by either a child or adult should always be respected. No pressure should be put on people to reveal their identities. Even when names and addresses have been supplied by the police, these should only be revealed with the consent of those concerned.

The NUJ has also drawn up a useful guide for covering AIDS stories. Instead of "carrying AIDS", "AIDS carrier" or "AIDS positive" (which confuses the two phases of being infected with HIV and having AIDS) it suggests "people with HIV". "AIDS test" is to be avoided since the most commonly used test detects antibodies to HIV (Human Immuno-Deficiency Virus). Someone who proves positive, and thus infected with HIV, does not necessarily go on to develop AIDS. A better phrase is "HIV antibody test".

When the distinction is made clearly between HIV and AIDS there is no need to use the term "full-blown AIDS". Nor is it possible to "catch AIDS" like colds or flu. Better to say "contract HIV". People do not "die of AIDS" but of cancers or pneumonia that develop because of a weakened immune system.

Many people with HIV express concern over the way the press has represented them as helpless victims. Reports should avoid phrases such as "AIDS sufferer", "AIDS victim", since someone with AIDS can continue working for some time after diagnosis. Better to say "person with AIDS". Also avoid "innocent victim" since this suggests others are guilty.

The style guide suggests reporters avoid using the term "high risk groups" since there is risk behaviour rather than risk groups. "The fact of being classified a member of any particular group does not put anyone at greater risk, but what he or she does, regardless of groups, may do."

In addition, the NUJ has drawn up a model, nine-point house agreement promoting employment protection for those infected with HIV or who have AIDS. And a leaflet produced by the UK NGO (Non-Governmental Organisation) AIDS Consortium for the Third World suggests strategies to journalists for avoiding racist stereotyping in covering HIV and AIDS stories.

Censorship and self-censorship

IT might seem strange to journalists on a small weekly to raise the issue of censorship. The problem at their newspaper might not be censorship but the opposite: finding enough material to fill the next edition. Proprietorial interference might be non-existent. As for the advertisers, they might take up more space than is ideal but that's reality in a recession-hit economy, isn't it?

Yet, for all journalists censorship issues are relevant. At the most basic level, the dominant news values prioritise certain sources and perspectives and marginalise or eliminate others. In a way, isn't that a form of censorship?

The impact of advertisers

The impact of advertisers on the press is considerable. Occasionally they will put pressure on editors to highlight favourable stories and downgrade or remove others. Free sheets, entirely dependent on advertisers, are particularly vulnerable to this. But, in general, the pressure is far more subtle. Within the general economic environment, advertisers promote the values of materialism and consumerism as well as a conservative respect for the status quo.

Curran and Seaton (*Power Without Responsibility: The Press and Broadcasting in Britain*; Routledge; London; fourth edition; 1991) argue that the emergence of an advertisement-based newspaper industry in the late 19th century helped stifle the development of a radical press. "The crucial element of the new control system was the strategic role acquired by advertisers after the repeal of the advertisement duty in 1853."

Even as late as 1964, the Labour-backing *Daily Herald* closed with a readership far larger than that of *The Times* and the *Financial Times* combined. It had crucially failed to win the support of the advertisers ("Advertising and the media"; James Curran in *Media Culture and Society: A Critical Reader*; Sage; London; 1986).

The impact of proprietorial interference: the Maxwell Factor et al.

The film *Citizen Kane* captured all the mystique and romance that surrounds the media mogul in the cultural history of the West. Men like the American media tycoon William Randolph Hearst, on whom Kane was based, and in Britain Northcliffe, Beaverbrook, Rothermere, Rowland, Murdoch and Maxwell have mostly cultivated images which have made them seem almost larger-than-life: eccentric, egocentric, super-powerful, super-rich.

There are many accounts of these proprietors interfering in the day-to-day operations of their newspapers (e.g. "Owners, editors and journalists"; Bruce Hanlin in *Ethical Issues in Journalism and the Media*; Andrew Belsey and Ruth Chadwick (eds); Routledge; London; 1992).

Editorials have been written or rewritten; layouts have been altered. Partisan politics (largely right-wing and belligerent during crises and wars) have been promoted. Favoured journalists have been promoted; others have been sacked or pressured into leaving (*Barefaced Cheek*; Michael Leapman; Hodder & Stoughton; London; 1983 and *Rupert Murdoch: Ringmaster of the Information Circus*; William Shawcross; Chatto; London; 1992. *Maxwell – the Outsider*; Tom Bower; Mandarin; London; 1988).

Fleet Street's history is often portrayed as a fascinating saga revolving around these figures (*Rise and Fall of Fleet Street*; Charles Wintour; Hutchinson; London; 1990).

Most serious has been the cumulative impact of these devout defenders of the free press on narrowing the consensus in British newspapers. Given the links between the major media throughout the country, that censorship has seriously distorted news values, even in the provinces. Most national newspapers at election times have plumped, predictably and often ferociously, for the Conservative Party and against the Labour Party (though right-wing New Labour has drawn some notable support).

In particular, the integration of the media barons' empires into the worlds of international finance and industry has given rise to a host of potential no-go areas for newspapers. Understandably, newspaper proprietors are reluctant to have reporters probing into their more murky activities. Maxwell managed to keep the scandal of his pension fund rip-off secret during his lifetime through a mixture of intimidation, a merciless use of the courts and libel laws, and through exploiting journalists' desire for the quiet life (*Maxwell's Fall*; Roy Greenslade; Simon & Schuster; London; 1992). As even investigative reporter Paul Foot commented: "When Maxwell was at the *Mirror* I used to have a list on the wall of his friends – and they covered a wide section of British industry. Immediately a story came in about one of those people, I had to be completely on my guard."

Moreover, media moguls have inevitably tended to promote their own financial interests through their newspapers. Tiny Rowland's *Observer* campaigned against the Al Fayeds following their purchase of Harrods (*Tiny Rowland: Rebel Tycoon*; Tom Bower; Heinemann; London; 1993). Maxwell constantly publicised himself and his many "charitable" and political activities. Murdoch has promoted his television interests through his many outlets and opposed the BBC at every opportunity.

There is a danger of exaggerating the power of the proprietors. All have been or are colourful personalities. But virtually every industry today is led at local, national or international levels by a small group of companies. Media moguls are merely the newspaper manifestations of this trend: typical monopoly holders within advanced capitalism. Stressing their power serves to boost their egos while exonerating journalists from some of their worst excesses.

Big brother?

The most powerful factor in journalism has always been the application of the dominant news value system. Censorship by the state has served to create a climate of intimidation and "emergency" at critical moments. But overt interventions by the state into the operations of newspapers have been the exception to the rule. Various other factors, such as the impact of advertisers, the role of the dominant news value system, proprietorial pressures, journalists' self-censorship and the growing number of repressive laws are more important in maintaining conformity and the mainstream press's subtle propaganda (*The Coercive State: The Decline of Democracy in Britain*; Paddy Hillyard and Janie Percy-Smith; Fontana; London; 1988).

The state has, in any case, interfered more with broadcasting than the press, perhaps because the fervent Conservative-backing owners of newspapers have been less independent of the government than the broadcasting companies.

Peter Watkins' *The War Game* film for the BBC about an imaginary nuclear attack on the UK was banned in 1965 and only shown two decades later. Pro-unilateralist views were marginalised in the coverage of the nuclear debate on radio and television in the early 1980s. The BBC was intimidated during the 1982 Falklands conflict and following the US attack on Libya in 1986. The Irish broadcasting ban of 1988 significantly excluded the press from its provisions while the government sought to stop Thames Television's *Death on the Rock* documentary about SAS assassinations in 1988.

In most of these cases, it appeared the government's authoritarianism was running "out of control". Over the Libya attack, Norman Tebbit, Conservative chairman, engaged in an unnecessary personal attack on Kate Adie, one of the most respected (and "loyal") of BBC foreign correspondents. The Irish ban was made to appear ridiculous even before it was removed – with actors speaking the words of the banned.

The most notorious cases of the government slipping on a censorship banana skin followed its long-drawn-out, farcical and ultimately futile attempts to prevent publication of the book *Spycatcher* (Dell Publishing; New York; 1987) by a retired MI5 officer, Peter Wright. In June 1986, the *Observer* and the *Guardian*, which had published some of Wright's allegations of sedition by the secret service in advance of publication, were served with injunctions. Then the short-lived *News on Sunday*, the *Sunday Times* and *The Independent* were each fined £50,000 for having intended to prejudice legal proceedings in the original case through publishing information from the book.

Eventually, these fines were set aside on appeal. Similarly, the injunctions against the *Observer* and the *Guardian* were set aside and the Law Lords ruled that, in view of the world-wide publication, national security could in no way be damaged by publication in the UK.

The wrong arm of the law

David Northmore has calculated that there are well over 100 laws prohibiting disclosure of information (*Freedom of Information Handbook*; Bloomsbury; London; 1990). He concludes, along with many other commentators, that Britain is the most secretive state in the so-called developed world (see also *Secrecy in Britain*; Clive Ponting; Basil Blackwell; Oxford; 1990).

Chris Bye, editor of the *Yorkshire Evening Post*, comments: "It may surprise many people to learn that, in the league table of world press freedom, we are a long way down the bottom, beneath countries like Ecuador and Namibia, and alongside Gambia. So much for our bloated image of ourselves as model guardians of free speech and democracy."

In 1994, the Guild of Editors listed 46 laws restricting disclosure of information of particular relevance to journalists, including the Trade Union Reform and Employment Rights Act and the Young Persons Act, both of 1993. Moreover, the Criminal Procedures and Investigations Act of 1996 gave the courts even more powers to impose reporting restrictions.

Privatised utilities (such as gas, water and electricity), once accountable to Parliament, have been criticised even by the Confederation of British Industry for their lack of accountability and openness in their decision-making. There are an estimated 6,424 quangos in Britain responsible for £63 billion of taxpayers' money yet there is no legal obligation on them to disclose information. Employee contracts often contain restrictive "gagging" clauses (see "The rising tide of shutdown culture", Andrew Johnson; *Press Gazette*, 15 November 1996).

In 1989, the secret state was further strengthened with a new Official Secrets Act (OSA). The 1911 OSA had proved notorious, particularly after civil servant Sarah Tisdall was jailed in 1983 for leaking to the *Guardian* government plans for the timing of the arrival of cruise missiles in England. National security seemed hardly threatened by the disclosure. Then came the acquittal of top civil servant Clive Ponting, charged under Section 2(1) of the Act after he leaked information showing the government had misled the House of Commons on the sinking of the Argentinian ship, the *Belgrano*, during the Falklands conflict.

The 1911 legislation was proving an embarrassment to the government and the 1989 Act was introduced to sort out the mess (*Reforming the Secret State*; Patrick Birkinshaw; Open University; Milton Keynes; no date. *Espionage and Secrecy: The Official Secrets Acts 1911–1989*; Rosamund M. Thomas; Routledge; London; 1991).

In an Orwellian piece of doublethink, the Home Secretary, Douglas Hurd, claimed the Act represented "a substantial, unprecedented thrust in the direction of greater openness". The opposite is nearer the truth. The Act covers five main areas: law enforcement, information supplied in confidence by foreign governments, international relations, defence and security, and intelligence. The publishing of leaks on any of these is banned. Journalists are denied a public interest defence; nor can they claim in defence that no harm had resulted to national security through their disclosures. Clearly, there will be no more *Spycatcher*-like leaks.

As the Conservative government headed for its 1997 humiliation at the polls, the new Home Secretary, Michael Howard, announced plans to give the police extensive powers to bug journalists' homes and offices.

But good news was to come with a landmark decision on 20 December 1996 by the High Court which ruled that a blanket ban on journalists interviewing prison inmates was illegal and an unjustified restriction of freedom of speech. The ruling came after freelance journalist Bob Woffinden and BBC Wales reporter Karen Voisey refused to sign undertakings not to publish material obtained during visits to two prisoner whose life sentences for murder they were investigating as possible cases of miscarriages of justice.

Significantly, the UK remained the only West European country without freedom of information legislation until early 1997. But then, in May of that year, the new Labour government pledged its commitment to a Freedom of Information Act. Dr David Clark, Chancellor of the Duchy of Lancaster, suggested that the legislation would provide a statutory Right of Access to Government with decisions on disclosure subject to judicial review, a statutory mechanism for reviewing complaints against non-disclosure and the appointment of an information commissioner with statutory powers, and the introduction of a "public interest override" setting aside statutes which barred disclosure or made disclosure discretionary.

As another exercise, ask journalists to what extent the "culture of secrecy" impedes them in their work. How many say they enjoy freedom to write whatever they want?

● See *Statewatch* magazine, PO Box 1516, London N16 0EW; tel: 0181-802 1882; fax: 0181-880 1727. See also literature produced by the anti-censorship body Article 19, 33 Islington High Street, London N1 9LH; tel: 0171-278 9292; fax: 0171-713 1356. For a global view see *Index on Censorship* magazine, Lancaster House, 33 Islington High Street, London N1 9LH; tel: 0171-278 2313; fax: 0171-278 1878; email: index-onconso@gn.apc.org; Web: http://www.oneworld.org/index_oc/[.]

Amnesty International has a special network campaigning for imprisoned journalists: Queen Street, Derby DE1 3DX; tel and fax: 01332-290852.

Principled and pointless? *Codes of Conduct*

JOURNALISTS work under many constraints, from proprietors, advertisers, laws and so on. One way in which journalists have regulated their own activities, with the aim of improving ethical standards, is through codes of conduct.

Starting the ball rolling – the NUJ

One of the most enduring is the National Union of Journalists' 12-point code drawn up in the late 1930s (see Appendix 1). It relies on generalised statements of high principle. On the one hand this has clear benefits. As Nigel Harris argues, detailed sets of regulations foster a "loophole-seeking attitude of mind" ("Codes of conduct for journalists"; in *Ethical Issues in Journalism and the Media*; Andrew Belsey and Ruth Chadwick (eds); Routledge; London; 1992).

On the other hand, the code incorporates principles broken every day all over the country by NUJ members. What is the point of having them if they are not backed up by any penalties? Attempts to impose the code through a disciplinary procedure and, since 1986 an NUJ ethics council, have proved difficult. Knowledge of the code by the general public and of possible redress against journalists' unethical behaviour through the ethics council has remained slight.

The Press Complaints Commission's Code of Practice

Following stern warnings from the Calcutt committee in 1992 that the press should clean up its act or face statutory regulation, the PCC (somewhat in panic, very defensively and without any reference to the NUJ) drew up a code of practice. Since then, many newspapers have incorporated it into their style books; some even express commitment to it regularly in their pages though knowledge of its clauses still remains low among journalists.

The code was based on proposals from the Calcutt committee, from the former Press Council and on the existing Newspaper Publishers Association code and amended following later Calcutt statutory threats over bugging and the use of telephoto lenses.

It goes into far more detail than the NUJ's code (see Appendix 2). The section on hospitals was inserted following the mighty row which blew up after *Sunday Sport* "journalists" went to Charing Cross Hospital, London, where the actor Gordon Kaye was recovering from a serious car accident. They entered a room, photographed the actor and even tried to interview him before being shown off the premises. An attempt to obtain a High Court injunction to stop publication failed because English law recognised no right to privacy.

The move to greater detail in the code marks a shift towards the American tradition where codes of conduct can cover a wide range of categories. They can include clauses over conflicts of interest, special privileges enjoyed by journalists (such as freebies), the handling of anonymous sources, plagiarism, or the use of shocking pictures.

To the extent that the code represents a growing concern within the industry to identify major ethical standards it is to be welcomed. But codes in the United States are often used by managements as a disciplinary weapon to remove unwanted journalists and the NUJ has expressed concerns over the similar use by managements in the United Kingdom. Many of the US codes are explicit on conflict of interest issues. The Code of Ethics of the Associated Press Managing Editors Association states: "Involvement in such things as politics, community affairs, demonstrations and social causes that cause a conflict of interest or the appearance of such conflict should be avoided" (*Groping for Ethics*; Eugene Goodwin; Iowa State University Press; Iowa; second edition; 1987. *Playing It Straight: A Practical Discussion of the Ethical Principles of the American Society of Newspaper Editors*; John L. Hulteng; Globe Pequot Press; Connecticut; 1981).

Progressive journalists involved in demonstrations and political campaigning can be removed through this clause. Yet many prominent journalists who are overt in their support for, say, Israel or one of the two main political parties, remain untouched.

As an exercise, you might interview (or simply talk to) journalists about their views on codes of conduct. Are they aware of their existence? What impact do they have on their work? Talk to some NUJ members and ask them about the history of the code; what changes they might want to seek; how it could be more effectively promoted among journalists. Do a survey of newspapers in your region to see how many incorporate the PCC Code into their style books.

You could talk to some foreign journalists based in Britain about the codes and media laws in their countries. Is the taping of interviews without the consent of the interviewee illegal? Do they ban freebies? To what extent are journalists constrained by obscenity legislation?

3

Exploitation, intimidation or co-operation?
Sourcing the news

LEEDS METROPOLITAN
UNIVERSITY
LEARNING CENTRE

A T the heart of journalism lies the source. Becoming a journalist to a great extent means developing sources. As a journalist you need to know a lot: where to go for information, who to ask. And for career development, contacts are crucial.

The contacts book

One of the most treasured possessions of any journalist is their contacts book in which sources' phone numbers, addresses and, increasingly, fax numbers and email details are listed. To be safe, journalists should keep a duplicate in a secure place since the loss or theft of a sole contacts book can be disastrous. Many have contacts on a computer file as a further back-up or use Personal Digital Assistants which, at best, can combine the functions of contacts book, notepad and word processor.

Reporters investigating sensitive areas (national security, spying, the arms or drugs trade, share dealings) tend to keep details of important, exclusive sources in their heads. Police have been known to raid the homes of journalists involved in sensitive areas and thus every step should be taken to protect the anonymity of such contacts.

The importance of the phone to the journalist means that one of the most vital sources is the telephone directory. You are researching a story on Islam. Just go to the directory and see which local and national organisations are listed (and try Muslim at the same time). Telephone directories are also a source for feature ideas. Diamond cutters, chimney sweeps, feminist car repairers, fallout shelters, robots may be listed and worth a follow-up.

Sourcing: *general comments*

Immediacy/newsiness

Sourcing conventions help provide the news dimension of many stories. An issue may be long-running but new information or opinion from a source will bring it into the news. The state of the national economy is an issue of constant concern. The Chancellor of the Exchequer warning of further "inevitable" bankruptcies over the next year becomes news, just as the release of a report by a group of Cambridge University economists highlighting the plight of small businesses is newsworthy.

Elitism and hierarchy

Media research suggests journalists use a remarkably limited range of sources. (A useful overview of research appears in *Media Performance: Mass Communication and the Public Interest*; Denis McQuail; Sage; London; 1992). The components of the hierachy will differ from newspaper to newspaper. Television soap stars and showbiz celebrities feature far more in the national tabloids than in the broadsheets, for instance. Yet there exists a remarkable consensus over news values and sourcing routines throughout the mainstream press. Some sources will be prominent, others marginalised, eliminated or generally covered in a negative way. Elitism is particularly evident in foreign reporting. Moreover, this consensus over news sourcing is reinforced by the growing centralisation and secrecy of government and the ever-narrowing consensus between the three major political parties.

Primary and secondary sources

Many journalists divide their sources into two major categories: primary and secondary (*Writing for the Press*; James Aitchison; Hutchinson; London; 1988). At the local level, councils, Members of Parliament and the European Parliament, courts, police, fire brigade, ambulance service, hospitals, local industries and their representative bodies (chamber of trade or commerce or traders' association), trade unions and trades council and the local football club are defined as primary sources.

Schools and colleges, churches, local clubs and societies, army, naval and air force bases, local branches of national pressure groups and charities are secondary sources. Other contacts in this category in rural areas might include village postmasters, publicans and hotel-keepers, agricultural merchants, livestock auctioneers, countryside rangers or wardens. In coastal areas they include coastguards, harbourmasters and lifeboat stations.

The stress on primary and secondary sources reflects the hierarchical assumptions underpinning conventional news values. Significantly, the definition eliminates a wide range of sources loosely termed "alternative". These might include representatives of religions other than Christian; ethnic minority groups; members and representatives of political parties other than the dominant three; feminist, lesbian and gay groups; pacifist, environmental and animal rights campaigning bodies. And where are the views of the individual (the poor, single father; the harassed commuter) in all this?

Journalists' sourcing routines tend to reflect the distribution of power in society. Representatives of leading institutions and public services dominate, having easier access to the press. Representatives of "alternative" bodies are either marginalised or eliminated from the local and national press which reinforces their relative powerlessness in society. Women and ethnic minorities are marginalised by the political system just as they are marginalised in the press.

Professional routines: on- and off-diary sources

Sources are often defined according to their relation to journalistic routines of news gathering.

Thus on-diary routine sources will include on a national newspaper the government; Parliament and select committees; the major political parties; Confederation of British Industry (CBI) and Trades Union Congress (TUC) conferences; Church of England Synod meetings; prominent court cases; press conferences arranged by prominent bodies such as campaigning groups (e.g. Amnesty International); companies; the police; trade unions; and charities. In one of the few investigations of journalistic practices in this area, Phillip Schlesinger found as much as 80 per cent of BBC news came from routine sources. Off-diary sources are all those which fall outside this routine (*Putting Reality Together*; Methuen; London; 1978). Mark Fishman argues that journalists' routines are closely linked to "bureaucratic idealisations" of the world. Newsworkers will not hesitate to be critical of particular government agencies or specific officials. "But the government bureaucratic structure cannot be doubted as a whole without radically upsetting the routines of newswork. Routine news leaves the existing political order intact, at the same time that it enumerates its flaws." (*Manufacturing the News*; University of Texas Press; Austin/London; 1980).

At the local level a system of "calls" institutionalises this sourcing routine. The news editor, news desk member or specialist correspondent will contact by phone at regular intervals (as often as every hour) such bodies as the police, ambulance station, fire brigade to check on any breaking news. Local reporters will often habitually "call in" for chats to help personalise the contact.

Similarly a local reporter will meet at regular intervals locally important people (such as vicars, business leaders, prominent campaigners and trade unionists) for informal chats from which news angles may or may not emerge. Bob Franklin and David Murphy, in a study of 865 stories in the local press, found local and regional government, voluntary organisations, the courts, police and business accounted for 67.7 per cent of the total (*What News?*; Routledge; London; 1991).

Such groups and individuals are described as "on-diary" sources since details of their activities are listed in diaries, traditionally in book form supplemented by dated files but increasingly now on screen.

Representation

Linked to journalists' sourcing routines are certain notions about representation. A source, other than a celebrity in their own right, tends to assume a significance for a journalist when they can be shown as representing not just their personal views but those of a larger group or institution. Thus, usually accompanying the name of a source is their title or other description. Ms A may believe John Major ought to have resigned over the Iraqgate scandal. But her views will mostly be of interest to a journalist if they can be shown to represent a larger group such as the local Conservative Association, of which she is the treasurer.

Journalists are sometimes tempted, because of sourcing conventions, to invent a title when none exists. During the early 1980s when the Greenham Common women were protesting outside the US airbase, journalists often represented the relatively few people they quoted as "spokeswomen" for the camp. In fact, the women sought to challenge traditional hierarchical notions of representation. Each woman spoke for herself. The group did not have representatives as such. By describing them as spokeswomen, journalists were failing to understand or respect an important political dimension of their struggle.

Credibility and authority

Accompanying journalists' sourcing routines and linked closely to views about representation are notions relating to credibility and authority. The views of party politicians tend to be prominent in the national and local press because they are seen as having been democratically elected to represent certain widely-held views. Along with that representative element goes authority and credibility.

Ms A may have very strong views about abortion. But on what authority does she speak and how credible are those views? Those short titles or descriptive phrases accompanying the name of the person quoted answer that kind of question. Ms B might be described as having "launched a campaign against abortion at her parish church". This immediately identifies her commitment to the cause and her authority as a source. Similarly, when someone is decribed as "an eye witness to the road accident" their authority is established (though they may be mistaken).

Inclusion of such details immediately "hardens" the story. In the same way, the presence of "ordinary people" (without any title or representative function) "softens" the story.

Bias and neutrality

Reporters use sources to distance themselves from the issues explored. Rather than express their views on a subject reporters use sources to present a range of views over which they can appear to remain objective and neutral. The title or descriptive phrase accompanying the quoted person clarifies their bias. But this is the bias of the source, not the reporter.

Sourcing routines also reinforce notions of balance. A campaigning group accuses a local authority of inadequate provision. It is the responsibility of the reporter to contact the authority to balance the report with their response to the allegations. View A is balanced by opposing view B.

But such a process eliminates a range of other views. Indeed, many media theorists question journalists' notion of balance and the existence of an objective reality. Considering the highly-selective process of news gathering, the financial, political and legal pressures on newspapers, and the absence of any neutral language, they argue that objectivity is unattainable and a myth ("Journalism and the critique of objectivity" in *News and Journalism in the UK: a textbook*; Brian McNair; Routledge; London; 1994).

Experts

Experts are often sought by journalists as sources. They play a crucial role since authority and independence are associated with their views. Journalists often use experts such as academics, think-tank members and pressure group campaigners to provide background information, which is not necessarily used in copy, and ideas for future, more newsy contacts. But they can also use them more subtly to add extra weight to a view they (or their proprietors) wish to promote. The *Sun*, for instance, often quotes psychiatric "experts" on the insanity or otherwise of people in the news (for example "madman" Saddam Hussein, Tony Benn of the "loony left" and "barmy" Bernie Grant, Labour MP for Tottenham). But experts can be wrong.

Professional status

(a) Journalists enjoying close contact with people at the top of the sourcing hierarchy tend to have a high professional status. On a national broadsheet the parliamentary correspondent enjoys high status just as the posting as a foreign correspondent (with all the contacts with presidents and other VIPs this will involve) ranks as a journalistic top job. The reverse applies: the reporter who has close contact with the Campaign for Nuclear Disarmament or the Animal Liberation Front enjoys no special journalistic status. At the local level, the journalist whose everyday contacts are councillors enjoys high status; the journalist dealing with Women's Institute reports or the children's page is usually low on the professional ladder.

As Bob Franklin comments: "Journalists are conscious of being sited in a finely graduated hierarchy which influences their access to politicians ... Acknowledging and exploiting to the full the advantages which their position in the hierarchy bestows is a precondition for journalistic advancement" (*Packaging Politics: Political Communication in Britain's Media Democracy*; Edward Arnold; London; 1994).

(b) Journalists' reputations can be built on the ability to extract good quotes from sources. "Did you get any good quotes?" is often asked by colleagues when they return from an assignment. In his appreciation of David Blundy, the Fleet Street reporter killed covering a civil war in Central America, Anthony Holden praises his special "talent to disarm the wariest of interviewees". "From the stepmother of the then Prime Minister, Edward Heath, he elicited the remarkable information that 'Ted is very considerate and never goes out without telling me where he's going. He never forgets birthdays and rings Daddy once a week'" (*The Last Paragraph: The Journalism of David Blundy*; Anthony Holden (ed.); Heinemann; London; 1990).

(c) Professionalism generally implies a certain objectivity and neutrality towards sources. In reality, this is difficult to maintain. Many argue that journalists often get too close to their sources. Journalists' regular contact with elite sources means they are often accused of disseminating a range of conflicting elite perspectives. Journalists tend to be part of the same social milieu as the political elite, they speak the same language, and often come from similar social and educational backgrounds.

Press poachers: *the media as a source*

ALL journalists spend some considerable time each day going through the media. They have to know what is going on, what is being covered and more particularly what is not being covered. They become "media junkies".
Whatever your feelings on the heavy and popular press, it is important to read as many papers as possible. You may despise the pops for their blatant racism and sexism but they are increasingly setting the national news agenda and need to be watched. Similarly, you may find the heavies tedious and long-winded but they carry masses of important national and international news which might even spark ideas for follow-ups. Most newspaper offices stock all the nationals and leading locals. But freelances and staffers will often buy their two favourite papers and a different third paper each day simply to help build up their cuttings files.

Don't concentrate all the time on the nationals and your mainstream locals. They are just one (though the most powerful) ingredient of a diverse range of newspapers and magazines available. Look at the lively ethnic press (*New Nation, East, The Voice, Caribbean Times, Asian Times*), at the religious press (*Church Times, Methodist Recorder, Jewish Chronicle, Catholic Herald, Q News International*), or the left press (*Morning Star, Socialist Worker, New Worker, Tribune, Newsline*) and the gay press (*Capital Gay*).

It's also worth looking at small circulation publications such as *Peace News* (pacifist), *Bad Attitude* (feminist) and *Christian Aid News*.

● They often carry articles by specialists raising issues marginalised in the mainstream press and which can be followed up.

● Their listings of meetings, conferences and visits to this country by potentially newsworthy figures can be followed up.

● Journalists on them are useful contacts and their journals outlets for freelance work (if your contract permits).

Foreign newspapers should not be ignored. The *International Herald Tribune*, carrying a compilation of stories from the *New York Times* and *Washington Post*, is essential reading for anyone wanting an insight into elite opinion in the United States. Most journalists will either speak or want to speak a second language and follow the press in that country. Comparisons with foreign newspapers, on elements such as content, use of pictures, design and questions of taste can all throw up interesting insights into the UK press.

It's impossible to buy even a small sample of these publications on a regular basis. You would end up bankrupt. There are ways round this. Public and university libraries provide a wide range of newspapers and magazines. Most journalists settle for buying on a regular basis a few they consider vital.

The journalist's own newspaper often provides a source for news. Letters to the editor can provide the basis for a follow-up. Similarly, newsworthy letters in other newspapers or magazines can be followed up. National and local newspapers sponsor charity/sporting events which also provide colourful, exclusive coverage.

Cuttings

Most newspapers have their own cuttings library which is a crucial resource. Journalists also create their own filing system. For a freelance without regular access to a cuttings library, it's an essential. Most journalists, particularly freelances, develop specialist areas and tidy filing of cuttings, magazines, photocopies, notes from books and jottings of feature ideas can prove enormously useful and time-saving during research.

But reporters can get details wrong. Unless cuttings are checked, there are dangers of reporters repeating each other's errors.

Follow-ups

The follow-up of an item in the news is a constant feature of newspaper coverage. As *The News Machine* (Thomson Foundation; Cardiff; 1972) comments: "The weeklies poach from the evenings and the evenings poach from the mornings and the national dailies poach, selectively, from everyone."

A controversy emerges in the national press. A local paper will "do a follow-up" carrying the views of relevant local people and providing local information on the issue. Similarly, a story in a local paper, say about an educational controversy considered sufficiently sensational, unusual or with wider implications, will be followed up by a national with new sources and new information.

Newspapers routinely tape selected radio and television news programmes, build up stories from interviews on these media and perhaps do follow-ups on others.

A great deal of coverage in the Sunday heavies comprises follow-ups on the main stories of the previous week. On Mondays (following the relatively dead news day of Sunday) nationals are in the habit of carrying reports on interviews given by prominent politicians on weekend television and radio programmes.

Investigations by Sunday newspapers can be followed up by the national press. Sometimes a reporter will lift a story from another newspaper, rewording it slightly, perhaps adding only a few original pars.

Columnists on both the national and local press often base some comment on an event or opinion highlighted in a national. Journalists will also habitually use fellow journalists as sources. Sometimes a specialist in a field will be contacted by other reporters new to the area for ideas and contacts. It is a matter for the individual journalist how much they co-operate with such requests. The issue is complicated when the question comes from a friend or colleague on a competing paper. Some journalists say no to all such requests. Others supply basic information and contacts but keep to themselves special sources gained only after considerable effort.

Journalists are clearly used as "hard sources" for media-related stories. And often in foreign stories the views of local journalists are considered informed and authoritative.

A survey of 36 British editors by the polling organisation Mori in 1990 found articles in other newspapers were considered the most useful source of information by 86 per cent. Second came their own journalists, with magazines, radio and television all making the top ten. Such is the extent to which the media feed off other media.

Reinforcing the consensus

As competition intensifies between newspapers, pressures to conform to the dominant news agenda grow. Rather than feeling confident and pursuing their own news values, newspapers constantly look over their shoulders to see what their competitors are up to. Consequently, the range of views and experience expressed narrows and newspapers become increasingly predictable (*Manufacturing Consent*; Edward Herman and Noam Chomsky; Vintage; London; fourth edition; 1994).

The media's over-reliance on the media also promotes a passive form of journalism. Investigative journalist Tom Bower has spoken of the "culture of inactivity" (*Maxwell – A Very British Experience*; Sixth James Cameron Memorial Lecture; City University; London; 1992). Reporting becomes a reactive activity, requiring little imagination and courage. Office-based, it becomes a glorified form of clerking.

Disinformation dangers

Histories of secret services show the extent to which newspapers are used for misinformation, disinformation and propaganda purposes (*Writing by Candlelight*; Edward Thompson; Merlin Press; London; 1980. *The Silent Conspiracy: Inside the Intelligence Services in the 1990s*; Stephen Dorril; Heinemann; London; 1993).

For instance, a contrived story alleging various atrocities by a certain anti-US movement might be planted in a foreign newspaper, perhaps financially backed by the secret service. It might then be picked up by the major international news agencies. That first report provides the authenticity and credibility for the ensuing reports.

Media used to combat censorship

Sometimes journalists send copy unsuitable for their own newspaper to another outlet (say *Private Eye*). And media in one country can be used to break through censorship regulations in another. In 1986 the Israeli anti-nuclear campaigner, Mordechai Vanunu, used the *Sunday Times* to reveal details of the secret Israeli nuclear programme which lay hidden behind a rigid censorship regime. (He was later captured by Mossad, the Israeli secret service, and sentenced to 18 years in jail.)

During the lead up to the Gulf conflict of 1991, after details of the "allied" strategy were stolen from a Defence Ministry official's car, a D Notice banning newspapers from reporting the event was issued by a special government committee. News of it leaked to an Irish paper. Thus it became public knowledge and London-based newspapers went ahead and carried their own reports. National security did not appear to be seriously damaged.

On and off the record

On the record

The basis for any good contact between a journalist and source is trust. When that trust is broken the source is lost. Most news is given on the record. A press release is issued; someone talks to you on the telephone or face to face; you report a conference. All this information and opinion you gain on the record.

Off the record

An off-the-record briefing is completely different. Information is given but because of its sensitive nature should not be reported. If the off-the-record undertaking is broken trust is lost. At the same time, such an undertaking leaves the journalist free to try to acquire the same information from another source who might be prepared to go on the record.

Public meetings are on the record. If someone says during one: "Oh, incidentally, that comment was off the record", you have no obligation to treat it as such. Similarly, private conversations are on the record unless otherwise established.

Unattributed/background comments

Half-way between off-the-record and on-the-record comments lie unattributed or "for background only" comments. Reports can carry these quotes but attribution is left deliberately vague to conceal identities.

Take this story from *The Independent* (2 April 1993):

Scott inquiry to hear conflicting evidence
Iraq arms rules 'not changed by Cabinet'

Anthony Bevins
Political Editor

LORD Justice Scott's inquiry into the supply of arms-related equipment to Iraq will be told that a critical relaxation in Whitehall's export guidelines, agreed in December 1988, was never approved by the Cabinet.

According to a well-placed government source, the inquiry will be told that the original guidelines, published by Sir Geoffrey Howe when he was Foreign Secretary in 1985, were maintained right through to the Iraqi invasion of Kuwait in 1990 – when a total embargo was imposed.

But at least one other key government witness is prepared to tell Lord Justice Scott that the guidelines were in fact changed by ministers, and the change was then put into practice by officials. That flat contradiction has emerged as the central issue for the Scott inquiry.

Lord Justice Scott said this week that he wanted to establish the extent to which the government had known of, or had been involved in, exports to Iraq in breach of its guidelines.

The question posed by the *Independent*'s sources – on both sides of the dispute – is whether there was an unofficial, "freelance" set of guidelines, for which senior ministers could deny all responsibility.

John Major has already said that the original Howe guidelines were enforced by Whitehall's inter-departmental committee "with scrupulous care".

But there is no record of Mr Major or any other minister denying that the guidelines were changed in 1988. The *Independent* was told by another source last night that the guidelines were changed at a December 1988 meeting held in a Foreign Office ante-room, attended by three ministers of state – William Waldegrave, Foreign Office; Alan Clark, Defence; and Lord Trefgarne, Trade and Industry – and officials from their private offices.

That allegation conformed with a document presented in evidence at last year's Old Bailey trial of the three Matrix Churchill executives who were acquitted on charges of evading export controls – showing that the wording of a "proposed revision" in the guidelines, dated 20 December 1988, had been "accepted".

Further corroboration of a change in guidelines was given to the Commons Trade and Industry Select Committee inquiry into the supergun affair in January 1992, when John Goulden, a senior Foreign Office official who has since been made ambassador to Turkey, said: "The guidelines set out by Sir Geoffrey Howe in '85 applied until December '88, when the third guideline was amended."

One of those involved in the December 1988 change told the *Independent* last night: "Yes, the guidelines were changed, and it was agreed there should be no announcement."

Menzies Campbell, the Liberal Democrat spokesman, said: "If they are now saying that no such decisions were made, who is telling the truth?"

The journalist has spoken to ministers who, for a variety of reasons, are prepared to have their views recorded but not to have their names attached to them. Identities are clouded by the use of the phrases "a well-placed government source", "another source" and "one of those involved in the December 1988 change".

Background briefings

In Britain, phrases such as "sources close to the Prime Minister", "diplomatic sources", "sources close to the Labour leadership" are constantly appearing in the national press. During the 1992 saga of the Prince Charles/Princess Di split phrases such as "sources close to the Princess" or "sources close to Buckingham Palace" were prominent.

Off-the-record or unattributed briefings hold benefits for both the source and journalist. The reporter can be informed on complicated details of which they may have no specialist knowledge and will learn of the source's bias. Sources often speak more openly at these meetings. And for the source, the briefing provides an opportunity to impress their perspectives on the journalist.

As Rodney Tiffen (in *News and Power*; Unwin Hyman; London; 1989) comments:

Covert manoeuvres are commonly deployed to shape interpretations of public events, of success and failure, of intentions and portents. In complex or technical developments, briefings can highlight the "essential meaning" of the details, to provide what journalists will welcome as a short-cut through the maze, but by doing so affording the briefer convenient scope for convenient selectivity. The meaning of opinion polls and some election results, of economic reports and indicators, of international agreements often pass into the news after the filters of briefings.

Dominant groups, individuals and institutions have the power and access to the press to organise such briefings and the chance to attempt to influence the news agenda. Weaker groups and individuals have much-reduced opportunities for such manoeuvring. Campaigning journalist John Pilger offers this advice: "Beware all background briefings, especially from politicians. Indeed, try to avoid, where possible, all contact with politicians. That way you find out more about them" ("The hidden power of the media"; *Socialist Review*; London; September 1996).

Fact, fiction or faction?

Unattributed comments can also blur the distinctions between fact and fiction. For instance, the *Sunday Telegraph* ran a major story on 10 January 1993, about concern growing in the Labour Party about the supposed lack-lustre performances of the leader, John Smith. Not one critical quote had a name attached to it. Instead, "one senior Labour MP", "one aide" and "his critics" were mentioned. The newspaper can't lose. The damage is done and there is no one there to deny having said those words since no one was specifically named. It could all be fantasy.

There are other occasions when journalists will legitimately want to protect the identity of a source. For instance:

● Given the rise in unemployment, people are increasingly reluctant to criticise employers for fear of the consequences. Nurses may dare not speak out on the impact of the financial cutbacks on the health service – some who have spoken to the press have been intimidated. Teachers may be reluctant to put their names to protests over the radical education changes of recent years. Journalists should respect this reserve and not try to tease out names, simply to harden up their story.

● Interviews with people who talk about intimate aspects of their lives such as sexual problems, illnesses, and domestic violence are often carried with fictitious names. Relevant places, ages and descriptions are either changed or omitted. The newspaper ought to indicate this style at the start of the article. If it is left until the end the reader may feel cheated.

● When an investigative journalist has acquired information without disclosing their professional identity, the newspaper does not then normally carry the sources' names. For instance, Esther Oxford, an *Independent* journalist, explored the world of rent-a-male agencies which provide women with escort and sexual services ("Pay your money and pick your man"; 18 November 1992). She contacted the agencies and described her experiences. Clearly, she could not take her notebook. All quotes and place descriptions had to be written from memory. But the paper left until the end the short disclaimer: "The names of the men have been changed."

Leaking in the public interest

According to Rodney Tiffen, a leak can be broadly defined as the unauthorised release of confidential information (op. cit.):

However, this umbrella covers many variations – that release may come from a dissident but also from someone in authority seeking political advantage, that confidentiality ranges from the very sensitive to the innocuous, from what was intended to be forever secret to the about-to-be announced.

Leaks and the use of anonymous quotations by compliant journalists can be manipulated to launch "trial balloons" or "fly a kite". Government officials may release proposals anonymously through leaks to test responses. If any outcry emerges, the government can denounce the plans they drew up, though only reporters pledged to confidentiality will know this. Leaking can lead to institutionalised lying.

Leaks can also be used to discredit opponents. Histories of the Harold Wilson administrations (e.g. *The Wilson Plot*; David Leigh; Heinemann; London; second edition; 1989. *Smear*; Stephen Dorril and Robin Ramsay; Fourth Estate; London; 1991) show the extent to which secret service leaks to sympathetic journalists in national newspapers were used systematically to smear the Prime Minister and some of his close associates and colleagues.

Because of the aura, glamour and drama surrounding secrecy, information drawn from such sources can be overvalued with an accompanying devaluation of information drawn from other sources. The desire to gain "exclusives" through the privileged access to secret sources can lead to a critical dependency between source and journalist. The lure of the "exposé" can also make a reporter more reluctant to explore alternative perspectives.

Editors' guidelines

Most journalists criticise the over-use of unattributed sources. The *Sunday Express* of 10 January 1993, for instance, carried 11 such quotes.

In the United States, attribution rules tend to be tighter than in Britain. Editors at several national dailies use the following guidelines:

● Identify sources as clearly as possible without revealing their identities. Instead of saying "informed sources" say "a city councillor".

● Explain why the source wished to remain anonymous.

● Try to corroborate the information with at least one other source.

The style book of *The Times* comments:

Unattributed quotes are normally banned. Where they proliferate, for instance in the more pedestrian political reporting, they should be treated with caution. Many readers are inclined to believe they are made up. *The Times* should conform to the code of practice now common in America. An unattributed quote should be used only where confidentiality is clearly essential, not merely to add spice or colour to a story. Even then, the writer should know the source and be prepared to inform the editor of it. Except in extreme cases, unattributed quotes should never be derogatory of individuals or named institutions. Such quotes are cowardly and read as such.
The Times English Style and Usage Guide; Times Books; London; 1992

Unattributed quotes still creep into News International stories. Take a look and check. A double-page spread in the *Sunday Times* (24 January 1993), for instance, included these sources: "an official close to Saddam Hussein", "one former US administration official", "a Foreign Office source", "a recent university graduate [in Iraq]", "one of the [US] officials", "Iraqi officials", "a UN source", "a university professor", "Iraqi sources", "senior officials in the Clinton administration".

Hoaxes

Journalists' over-reliance on unattributed sources can make them more vulnerable to hoaxes. Some hoaxers, such as Rocky Ryan and Joe Flynn, make a profession of fooling the press.

On 17 May 1992, the *Independent on Sunday* revealed that "one of Fleet Street's most prolific sources of information", particularly about the aviation business, was a conman. He claimed to be a highly placed source within British Airways. He was nothing of the sort. One of the most famous hoaxes of all was when the *Sunday Times* printed what it believed to be the diaries of Adolf Hitler. This was only after they were sold to *Stern* magazine by three German businessmen for £2.5m and Sir Hugh Trevor-Roper, author of *The Last Days of Hitler*, said he believed they were genuine.

Then in November 1996, Stuart Higgins, editor of the *Sun*, fell victim to an elaborate hoax involving a video that supposedly showed Princess Diana cavorting with a lover. Earlier the video had been offered to the UK-based *Here!* magazine and the US tabloids, the *Star* and *Globe*. As Jane Ennis, *Here!* editor, commented: "I smelled a rat. The people who came to us were completely shady. They claimed that MI5 or the FBI had left the tape in a studio and they had found it. They couldn't answer any of our questions about when it was filmed or where."

Local papers are by no means no-go areas for hoaxes. New sources, particularly in controversial areas, should be routinely checked and their views and information corroborated by a tested, reliable source. Journalists should be particularly wary of hoaxes just before 1 April and in letters, emails and on the Internet.

The great lobby debate

One of the most famous institutional manifestations of the unattributed briefings sessions is the parliamentary lobby. Every day on which the House sits, Downing Street gives two unattributed briefings to accredited lobby correspondents of which there are around 210 men and 30 women. Membership is restricted to UK and Irish journalists.

The first meeting is at Downing Street at 11 am; the second in the House of Commons at 4 pm. In addition, there are Friday briefings for Sunday journalists, a briefing on Thursdays by the leader of the House on the following week's business and a weekly Opposition briefing.

All lobby members are pledged to secrecy. After they are briefed by the Prime Minister's press secretary, the leader of the House, or the leader of the Opposition, they never attach any name to the information. Instead, such phrases as "sources close to Downing Street", or "government sources" or "members close to the Labour leadership" are used.

In addition, there are briefings by ministers or their mouthpieces to groups and individual journalists under the same conditions or sometimes even on the record.

The lobby was launched in 1884 just five years before the first Official Secrets Act became law. As Michael Cockerell, Peter Hennessy and David Walker say in their study of the lobby (*Sources Close to the Prime Minister: Inside the Hidden World of the News Manipulators*; Macmillan; London; 1984): "The paradox was that as Britain was moving towards becoming a democracy by extending the vote to men of all classes (women still had 40 years to wait) mechanisms were being created to frustrate popular participation in government and to control, channel and even manufacture the political news."

The lobby raises enormous passions, pro and anti. For a number of years while Bernard Ingham was Margaret Thatcher's press secretary (from October 1986) and until October 1991, three high-minded newspapers – the newly launched *Independent*, the *Guardian* and the *Scotsman* – withdrew from the system. Ingham used the lobby for blatant disinformation campaigns on political issues and against individuals both inside and outside the Cabinet (*Good and Faithful Servant*; Robert Harris; Faber; London; 1990). His successors have not adopted similar tactics and by 1995 Christopher Meyer was allowing off-the-record briefings to be attributed directly to Downing Street.

Maurice Frankel, of the Campaign for Freedom of Information, says: "There are good reasons for letting journalists have access to certain parts of the Commons where they can talk to politicians. But what is unacceptable is the mass briefing where spokespeople manipulate the media in an attempt to influence public opinion."

Similarly, Anthony Bevins, of the *Observer*, argues the lobby is popular "because there is a pervasive cowardice about journalism created and cultivated by knee-jerk newsdesks and editors" while, according to Anthony Howard, of *The Times*, "it's almost like Piccadilly with lobby correspondents soliciting for politicians. The MPs treat them like they were clients and in some ways lobby correspondents become instruments for a politician's gratification."

In support of the lobby, Chris Moncrieff, chief PA political correspondent for many years, says: "In any event, lobby meetings occupy only about 30 minutes of every day, so the doubting and high-minded 'searchers after the truth' have the remaining 23 hours or so to engage in the quest."

Another lobby member, Stuart Trotter, argues:

> The government's spokesman's briefing is just a source of information to be assessed along with what the opposition parties, rebel government supporters or anybody else has to contribute . . . Ministers in the process of getting a bad press must wish lobby manipulation was the reality some think it is.

Others argue the lobby system is bound into the culture of secrecy pervading all branches of government and into which journalists are too often sucked. Most of the major decisions affecting national security are decided in secret by a small group of ministers, often without the knowledge of the full Cabinet. The media-consuming public become spectators of a political game played by a tiny group of insiders over which they have no control.

Controversies over confidentiality

Non-attributable briefings are vital to the journalist on many occasions and the Code of Conduct (Clause 7) of the NUJ calls for journalists to preserve the confidentiality of sources. Yet the journalist's right to this confidentiality is not enshrined in law and under section 10 of the Contempt of Court Act 1981 courts have the right to demand that journalists reveal sources. In fact, apart from Norway, Britain is the only European country failing to recognise the right of journalists to protect confidential sources.

Thus Jeremy Warner, of *The Independent*, was ordered in 1988 to disclose the source of a story on insider dealings and shady takeover bids in the City. He refused and was ordered to pay a £20,000 fine and £100,000 costs by the High Court. His paper paid up for him and received good publicity in the process.

In 1990, William Goodwin, a trainee reporter on a weekly trade magazine, the *Engineer*, faced prison for contempt after refusing to hand over notes of a phone call which revealed confidential information about a computer company's financial affairs. He was given a £5,000 fine.

Goodwin escaped becoming the fourth journalist this century in Britain to be jailed for contempt. In 1963, Brendan Mulholland, a *Daily Mail* reporter, and Reginald Foster, of the *Daily Sketch*, were sentenced to six months and three months respectively in Brixton jail for refusing to disclose sources to the Vassall spy tribunal.

Foster had merely discovered Vassall had bought women's clothing at a London store. As he later commented: "So far as I was concerned it all turned on the question of women's knickers. Had I known how precious this titbit was I'd have been round to the Russian Embassy."

In 1971 Bernard Falk refused to tell the court whether one of two Provisional IRA men he interviewed for the BBC was a man subsequently charged with membership and went to prison for his pains.

However, pressure on the government to enshrine in law a journalist's right to protect the identity of sources intensified after Bill Goodwin took his case to the European Commission of Human Rights. In September 1993, the commission ruled that Goodwin's case was admissible and called on the government to negotiate a "friendly settlement".

Three years later, the European Court of Human Rights ruled that Goodwin (who revealed that he had not even seen a copy of the NUJ Code of Conduct before he took the fateful phone call) had been right to protect his source. But still the Lord Chancellor refused to change the Contempt of Court Act. Earlier, Dani Garavelli, then chief reporter for the *Journal*, Newcastle, was threatened under the contempt laws for refusing to name a source after being subpoenaed to give evidence to a police disciplinary hearing. Her 20-month battle ended in 1996 when the High Court ruled against the attempt by two Chief Constables to jail her.

Extra threats

In recent years a number of new threats have emerged to undermine journalists' attempts to keep sources confidential. According to the Police and Criminal Evidence Act (PACE) of 1984 a police officer investigating a "serious offence" can obtain an order requiring the journalist to hand over evidence deemed useful to the court. This can include unpublished notes and photographs.

The first major controversy emerged just eight months after PACE passed into law. The *Bristol Evening News* was ordered to hand over film following a drug bust; it refused, lost the case and had the police take away 264 pictures and negatives. Following violent demonstrations outside the premises of Rupert Murdoch's News International in Wapping, east London, in early 1987, *The Independent*, *Mail on Sunday* and *Observer* newspapers, two television companies and four freelance photographers appealed against an order requiring them to hand over pictures.

On 23 May 1988, Mr Justice Alliot ruled that the pictures should be surrendered on the grounds this would not undermine the freedom and independence of the press. All complied except the four freelance photographers who had earlier taken the unprecedented step of sending their materials, via the NUJ, to the International Federation of Journalists in Brussels. In October 1988, the contempt charges against the freelances were thrown out because they were considered no longer to be owners of the material or to possess it.

Following the poll tax riots of 31 March 1990 the police applied under PACE for access to "all transmitted, published and/or unpublished cine film, video tape, still photographs and negatives of the demonstration and subsequent disturbances which was obtained with a view to being of a newsworthy interest". Some national newspapers complied. Again the NUJ moved fast, sending prints and negatives out of the country.

Jake Ecclestone, of the National Union of Journalists, argues that PACE illustrates the "growth of the big brother state". The courts become agents of the state, the police are agents of the courts while the journalists end up agents of the police. The journalist's job becomes impossible. Increasingly reporters and photographers covering demonstrations, riots and other civil disturbances are being attacked since they are perceived as agents of a repressive state.

The Prevention of Terrorism Act has also been used by the state in an attempt to intimidate journalists into revealing confidential sources. Following a programme by the independent company, Box Productions, in 1991, alleging collusion between loyalist death squads and members of the security forces in Northern Ireland, Channel 4 was committed for contempt for refusing to reveal its source and was fined £75,000.

Subsequently, a researcher on the programme, Ben Hamilton, was charged with perjury by the Royal Ulster Constabulary. Though the charge was suddenly dropped in November 1992, the police retained all the items seized from Mr Hamilton. They included his personal computer, all disks, newspaper cuttings, and notes of telephone calls and meetings with other journalists interested in the programme. Another journalist involved in the programme received death threats and was forced to leave his home and live incognito at a secret address.

The computer-assisted journalist

ONE of the most valuable sources of information for staff journalists is their newspaper library. For instance, News International library, serving *The Times*, *Sunday Times*, *Sun* and *News of the World* is open from 8 am through to 3 am every day and handles up to 700 requests from journalists on a busy day. The Associated Newspapers' London library, serving the *Mail*, *Mail on Sunday* and *Evening Standard*, is open 24 hours a day and contains 80 million cuttings and 12 million pictures dating back to 1910.

As new technology has transformed journalists' work over recent years, so the newspaper library is undergoing a revolution. Instead of just cuttings and reference texts, the most advanced now have CD-Roms and a wide range of computer-accessible databases.

But Gertrud Erbach, reference library manager at News International, says there are still times when cuttings are vital. "For instance, if a journalist was doing an overview of the water industry and needed ideas, it would be most effective to give them the cuttings. However, if they wanted to find information about the suitcase used to carry the Lockerbie bomb, they would not want to look through three shelves of cuttings to find it. An on-line search would find this quickly."

Stephen Torrington, library editor at Associated Newspapers, also feels cuttings still have their role. "Journalists when researching stories tend to ask for both the written and electronic versions. The eye will fix more easily on why a story is important when you see it in its original form. You don't quite get that with the new electronic databases," he says.

One of the most useful databases is *FT Profile* which currently provides access to 28 UK newspapers and Press Association copy (updated four times daily) in its UKNews file. Coverage begins in 1981 with individual papers being loaded at different times over the years. For the American press, *Lexis/Nexis* is unrivalled, according to Erbach. Its Entertainment library is particularly useful since it provides full credits for thousands of films, contacts for celebrities and potted biographies. *Reuters Advertising and Media Briefing* is a new service providing two areas to search: world-wide current news and a news archive going back five years.

At Associated Newspapers journalists make on average 3,000 searches a day of a 17-newspaper database which includes its own titles plus those from News International, the Mirror Group and the *Telegraph*, available on a swap basis from those newspapers.

The regionals have been much slower to join the library revolution. The first to use an in-house database was the *Wolverhampton Express and Star* in September 1985. All journalists had access via their computer split screen, though the newspaper was due by the end of 1997 to have shifted to a new Apple Macintosh system with the database accessible on only a few selected machines.

A number of important issues are raised with the dawning of the computer-assisted journalist. Concern, for instance, has been expressed over the use of newspaper databases by outside bodies. The *Wolverhampton Express and Star* allows bodies such as public libraries and the police access to its database by special appointment. In 1988, use of the database gave the police crucial help in the search for a murderer. And Mark Green, library systems manager, says that current police use of the database is "not infrequent". Jake Ecclestone, of the NUJ, argues that allowing police this access can compromise the freedom of the press. Others say newspapers should in this way assist the community they serve.

CD-ROMs

THESE can serve as vital research tools for the journalist. *UK on CD* carries the electoral roll and details on 37.5 million people. *Hansard* offers House of Commons debates and questions in full (also found on the World Wide Web at http://www.parliament.uk) while *Justis Parliament* gives details on Bills and Acts, short biographies and members' questions (so particularly useful when covering "sleaze" allegations).

The *Oxford English Dictionary*, the *Dictionary of National Biography* and *Encyclopaedia Britannica* are now all available on CD-ROM.

Managing the new information monster: *the Internet*

OVER recent years the Internet has become a vast, almost unmanageable source of information for journalists. The Web was conceived in the USA in the late 1980s. By the mid-1990s, tens of millions of people had access to it via their schools, colleges, places of work and at home. As Wayne Ellwood argues: "Computerisation is at the core of the slimmed-down, re-engineered workplace that free-market boosters claim is necessary to survive the lean-and-mean global competition of the 1990s. Even factory jobs that have relocated to the Third World are being automated quickly" ("Seduced by technology", *New Internationalist*; Oxford; December 1996).

The Web has, in fact, revolutionised publishing. Since anyone with a Web browser can access any Web site; even the smallest of publishers can register their sites with search engines and directories and thus achieve instantly a world-wide audience.

In many newspapers the searches for information will be conducted by librarians though many journalists now have access to Web sites from their homes. Universities and colleges are increasingly being wired up to the Web so providing student journalists all the opportunities to surf the information superhighway in search of sources and information – for free. (Though, as Theodore Roszak argues: "If computer literacy does not include material on what computers can't do and shouldn't do, it is advertising, not education." See "Dumbing us down"; *New Internationalist*; Oxford; December 1996.) Readers now expect to be able to send letters to the editor electronically.

The World Wide Web has, in fact, emerged as the most important new communications medium since television. Randy Reddick and Elliot King argue in their seminal book, *The Online Journalist: Using the Internet and Other Electronic Resources* (Harcourt Brace College Publishers; Fort Worth; second edition; 1997): "It allows journalists to access information from around the world virtually instantly. It also allows reporters to find information from sources that they previously would never have found. It allows journalists to be more thorough, more accurate and more complete. And it allows people to publish information for an international audience in a cost-effective, efficient way. The Web is profoundly changing the practice of journalism."

But investigative reporter John Pilger offers these words of caution: "Beware celebrating technology until you find out who controls it. The Internet is brilliant, but its most fervid bedfellows are the American government and a cluster of multi-national companies whose message posting is outstripping all others" ("The hidden power of the media"; *Socialist Review*; London; September 1996).

National and local newspapers such as the *Huddersfield Daily Examiner*, the *Leicester Mercury*, *Lancashire Evening Telegraph*, *Surrey Advertiser*, *Sunderland Echo* and *Cambridge Evening News* (along with magazines and television and radio stations), in Britain and throughout the world, have also been rushing to go online – with varying degrees of success.

Many online newspapers encourage their journalists to become "interactive" with readers, engaging in discussions and stimulating new story leads. Moreover, new auditing tools are allowing journalists to check who's reading their stories, when and for how long. According to Washington-based computer expert Brock N. Meeks, the Internet is giving birth to a new kind of journalist. "It takes nerve to publish and write for an interactive crowd. Every word, every phrase, even your damn syntax will be picked apart a thousand times over by people more expert than you on any given subject."

In response to these developments, journalism training courses are increasingly incorporating units on the Internet and electronic publishing. This new media sector has the potential to provide considerable job opportunities in the future – all the more significant since traditional newspapers appear to be in decline and are cutting staffs.

Internet: *the journalist's vital resource*

DIANA Clement, personal finance editor of *Sunday Business*, is one of the many journalists for whom the Internet has become an indispensable working tool. She says that almost every story she composes is researched to some degree on the Internet. "As well as a quick scan of the dailies each morning, I use the Web to check out the latest electronic versions of trade magazines from *Insurance Age* to *Euromoney*, *Offshore Financial Review* and *Forbes*, and Internet-only 'e-zines' such as *MoneyWorld* – a source of personal finance news."

She particularly values the *Profound* database since it provides an "alerts" service whereby the system automatically emails her when articles arrive on a pre-defined subject area. The *FT*'s site also has a bulletin board where readers can discuss subjects of mutual interest which she finds useful ("Online advantages for journalists"; *Press Gazette*; London; 18 April 1997).

The Internet has also opened up for journalists information which was previously inaccessible or difficult to find. For instance, in December 1996 the Inland Revenue placed on the Internet its register of "conditionally exempt works of art". This lists people who have, following an agreement with the Revenue, escaped inheritance tax by agreeing to provide public access to important private art collections. According to journalist Tim Weeks, this is "a genuine breakthrough for public access to information and a useful source for features and listings for journalists" (http://www.dpr/gov.uk).

Companies House permits online searches of its database on directors of limited companies at seven city sites in the UK. It was through this database that John Birt, BBC director-general, was discovered not to be an actual BBC employee. And according to a government green paper on the Internet, *government.direct*, published in November 1996, this information would soon be available on PCs. Weeks comments: "As *government.direct* begins to come into action, it will be even harder for journalists to ignore the Internet."

Some useful sites for harassed hacks

- Two sites where you can find all (well, almost all) newspapers on the Web are Steve Outing's online directory, *Editor and Publisher's Online Newspapers*, at http://www.mediainfo.com/ephome/npaper/nphtm/online.htm and Eric Meyer's directory at *AJR Newslink*, http://www.newslink.org/news.html

- A number of sites have been created specifically to aid journalists to navigate the Web. For instance, Odd de Presno has launched an online guidebook to the Net, the *Online World Resources Handbook*, at http://login.eunet.no/~presno/index.html. It includes advice on electronic conferencing, job hunting by modem and working from home.

- The *Journalistic Resources Page*, at http://www.algonet.se/~nikos.journ.html includes links to newspapers and magazines, to journalism schools in Austria, Denmark, Canada, the USA, Africa and Asia, and to such journals as the *American Journalism Review* and the *Canadian Journal of Communication*.

- The *Internet Journalism Resources* site at http://mhd2.moorhead.msus.edu/~gunarat/j/creation/res/ provides links to resources providing tips on writing news and feature articles and CVs. In addition it has links to sites offering dictionaries, encyclopaedias and style manuals.

- Worried about your grammar? Want to know more about the present past perfect continuous tense? *An Elementary Grammar* site at http://www.hiway.co.uk/~ei/intro.html aims to answer most of your queries.

- The *Reporters' Internet Guide* at http://www.cfc/rig/ allows searching of online newspapers and magazines world-wide and provides links to sites of interest to specialist journalists.

- *David Cracknell's HomePage* at http://www.warwick.ac.uk/guest/cracknel/index.html includes a lively discussion of whether online newspapers sound the death knell of traditional papers and links to a wealth of sites invaluable for reporters and difficult to find elsewhere.

- The UK-based *Future Events News Service* can be found at http://www.hubcom.com:80/fensnews/

- Interested in investigative journalism? A special site including guides, sources, contacts and story ideas is at http://www.vir.com/~sher/julian.html

- *FACSNET* at http://www.facsnet.org provides journalists with useful backgrounders and reporting tutorials together with a specialist subject Internet browsing resource.

- A fascinating site providing a database of journalistic ethical codes from around the world can be found at http://www.uta.fi/ethicnet/ethicnet.html while http://www.journalism.sfsu.edu/www/ethics.html is also worth visiting.

- Another good place to start searching is *World Wide News Sources on the Web* (www.discover.co.uk/NET/NEWS/news.html) since it provides links to newspapers, news agencies and broadcasters.

- The *Electronic Telegraph* (www.telegraph.co.uk) was the first to be set up and is still regarded as one of the better sites. The *Guardian*'s site (www.guardian.co.uk) includes a searchable database of MPs' interests while *The Times*' online (www.the-times.co.uk) provides for keyword searching.

- *Roget's Thesaurus* is available online at http://wilma.cs.city.ac.uk/text/roget/thesaurus.html

- *No 10 Downing Street online* provides an illustrated tour of the State Rooms, biographies of recent Prime Ministers and current Cabinet ministers, PM speech transcripts, notes on legislation and press releases (http://www.coi.gov.uk/coi).

- An online dictionary of computer terminology can be found at www.whatis.com

- Strunk and White's seminal *Elements of Style* is at http://www.columbia.edu/acis/bartleby/strunk

- An insider's guide to computer magazines in the UK and a listing of IT events throughout the UK is available at www.thesource.dwpub.com

- *Feminist.Com* at http://feminist.com/ includes sections on activism, health issues and a wide range of speeches and articles. It also provides links to sites on self-defence, reproduction rights and women's culture elsewhere on the Web.

- *Switchboard* Web page at http://www.switchboard.com provides telephone numbers of more than 90 million people.

- New York University's site at http://solar,rtd.utk.edu/~aboyle/grm.html takes a serious look at many issues surrounding armed conflicts around the world.

Taking the slog out of surfing: *the joy of search engines*

WITHOUT search engines journalists would find tracking down information nearly impossible, according to Nigel Whitfield ("Search me", *Internet World*; London; May 1997). They do all the hard work, trawling through Web information, indexing it and providing access to sites through keyword searches.

Most of the early search engines (such as *Alta Vista* at http://altavista.digital.com[,] *Metacrawler* at www.metacrawler.com[,]; *Webcrawler* at www.webcrawler.com; and *Lycos* at http://lycos.cs.cmu.edu) were US-based. But in recent years a number of UK sites have emerged. Indeed, they have become big business: the rate card for *Global Online Directory* (www.god.co.uk) quotes monthly charges ranging from £125 to £14,000 depending on the online placement of the advertisement.

One of the most popular search engines is *Yahoo UK & Ireland* (at www.yahoo.co.uk), an offshoot of its US parent (http:www.yahoo.com). *UKPlus* at www.ukplus.co.uk was launched in January 1997 by Associated Electronic Publishing, an offshoot of the media group that publishes the *Daily Mail*. Using journalists to review all the featured sites, it offers a wide range of subject-area links including arts/humanities, business, computing, education, environment, health/medicine, kids, money/investing, news, science and technology, shopping, sport and travel.

SavvySearch (http://guaraldi.cs.colostate.edu:2000/form), one of the most powerful search tools, is able to query many search engines at once, as does All4One (http://all4one.com/).

Yell at www.yell.co.uk has an A–Z of business sites, a film guide and access to the Electronic Yellow Pages. Other search engines worth visiting include *UK Search* at www.uksearch.com and *Apollo* at www.apollo.co.uk

In addition to search engines there are "casting programmes" which can be personalised to search the Web for specific subjects. PointCast is a free service (funded by advertising) which can continuously search, say, CNN, the *New York Times* and *Los Angeles Times* for international and business news.

The joy (and pain) of email

WITH more than 30 years of development, email is one of the most sophisticated tools for the computer user and can prove a vital aid for the reporter. Increasingly journalists are using email for filing copy. As Bill Thompson, of the *Guardian*, commented: "I have never submitted copy to my newspaper other than electronically. I can file five minutes before the deadline via email and even see a copy of the subbed piece before it goes to print." But he added: "Obviously, this relies on the publication having the capability to receive copy in this way. It is not unknown for emailed material to be printed out and re-keyed into the editorial system because of the lack of any proper gateway."

Journalists are engaging in discussions with readers via email while it is being used increasingly as a tool for interviewing. According to Thompson, it is easy to get people to reply to email. "The medium is fresh enough for most people and many of the barriers we have put up to block unwanted contact have not yet been developed for email. It may be impossible to reach the chief executive by phone, but an email may well get a response; a researcher may be travelling but will probably be checking email daily."

But Thompson is also careful to stress the limitations of email: "An email 'conversation' is more like an epistolary novel than a live interview and while it does allow some space for reflection, the outcome cannot be compared to a real interview."

Diana Clement, of *Sunday Business*, argues that email is the single most useful Internet tool for the journalist. At one click of a mouse she can send off the same message to 30-odd PR companies. "If I'm planning a feature, I can send a short outline to every PR company in my organiser in less than the time taken for a single phone call."

There is a serious downside to the email explosion. A journalist can arrive at the desk in the morning to find 30-odd messages requiring some kind of response. Thus email constitutes yet another form of communication for the journalist to cope with (in addition to internal written memos, readers' letters, press releases, radio and television broadcasts) adding to the demands and stresses of the job.

Moreover, viruses that can wreak havoc on computer systems often arrive via email ("Keys to the plague"; Adrian Mars; the *Guardian Online*; 8 May 1997). And always remember that it is relatively easy to snoop on emails, as secret services around the world are only too well aware.

Chatting on the Web: *email discussion lists*

R ANDY Reddick argues that reading or participating in a discussion list can be extremely useful to the journalist. "It puts reporters in contact with people who generally know a lot about a specific topic. The reporter can then follow up with those people, ask where more information can be found or ask who would be a good source to interview."

The principle of the discussion groups is simple: an individual sends a message to a specific address for a particular discussion list and that message is automatically distributed to all subscribing to that list. The address of the list distribution software is known as the Listserv.

Discussion lists of interest to journalists include:

FOI-L, on freedom of information issues at listserv@listserv.syr.edu

CARR-L, on computer assisted research and reporting at listserv@ulkyvm.lousville.edu

NEWSLIB, on researching news stories at listserv@ripken.oit.unc.edu

COPYEDITING-L, on grammar, punctuation and style issues at listserv@cornell.edu.

How to get the discussion ball rolling

I F you wanted to subscribe to JOURNET-L, a list which deals with issues relating to journalism education and research, you would send an email message to listserv@American.edu and in the message text area you would write simply:

sub JOURNET-L your first name your surname (so for me it would be sub JOURNET-L Richard Keeble)

Once accepted on the list you would send messages to JOURNET-L@American.edu You would also receive details on how to end the subscription (unsubscribe in the jargon) and you should file these in a safe place. You never know when you may need them.

There are dangers here, however, of your email basket being packed with up to 70 messages a day from fellow list subscribers. Fortunately there are procedures available for restricting messages to one a day and for turning off mail for a period (while perhaps away on holiday).

Indiana University has produced a database of more than 65,000 discussion lists at http://www.listz.com while the site at http://tile.net/ helps locate email lists. Paul Gilster's book *Finding It on the Internet: The Internet Navigator's Guide to Search Tools and Techniques* (John Wiley & Sons; London; 1996) offers an excellent guide to other email search tools while a visit to *Yahoo!* or *Alta Vista* can often reveal information about a relevant mailing list.

In addition, online service providers often offer services of particular value to journalists. CompuServe, for instance, offers the Fleet Street Forum which includes jobs listings, a discussion group on ethics and a newsdesk. Its UK Newspaper Library contains selected articles from leading UK and European newspapers, updated daily, while the UK News Clips collates news from the wires.

LineOne provides on-line editions of the *Sun*, *The Times*, *News of the World* and *Sunday Times*, encyclopaedias, and phrase books from HarperCollins while the search directory is *UK Plus*, compiled by UK journalists.

Some ethical issues

SINCE Internet technology has developed at such a rapid pace over recent years, it is not surprising that journalists have found it difficult to establish the precise implications for their working routines and ethics. No clear rules have emerged. For instance, how free is a journalist to report comments made in email discussion groups? How does a newspaper credit an online source? Should journalists always identify themselves as such when joining a discussion group? Should journalists allow their news sites to be linked to promotional or advertising sites? Issues relating to copyrights associated with Internet material and emails remain unresolved.

Journalist Andrew Bibby certainly advises Web users to include a copyright notice on every item. His reads: "Copyright held by Andrew Bibby. Use for commercial purposes prohibited without prior written permission from the copyright holder. This text has been placed here as a facility for Internet users and downloading is permitted for the purposes of private non-commercial research. The text must not be modified nor this copyright notice removed."

Online newspaper discussion groups could face legal problems if they carried material considered defamatory, grossly indecent, or offensive. In these cases, the Web site providers could find themselves the subject of a civil action for defamation or might be committing an offence under the Telecommunications Act 1984. Further legal complications could arise from the Internet's global reach since material could be legal in Britain but against a law in some other country. A disclaimer of liability could accompany all text. This would not necessarily prevent problems but it would at least demonstrate a responsible approach by the Web site provider.

According to Reddick and King: "Journalists should almost always identify themselves as such if they plan to use information from discussion lists. In most cases, journalists have the ethical obligation to allow people to choose to go on-the-record or not. To lurk in a discussion list, then quote people who did not know that what they wrote would be used in a different context is as deceptive as posing or going undercover to report a story."

When virtually anyone with the right technology can publish on-line, publishing suddenly acquires a distinct "democratic" element. At the same time, journalists' claims of special skills and ethical concerns are thrown into question. In the anarchic, frenzied world of Web publishing what is to distinguish "professional journalism" from entertainment, advertising, overt propaganda or simply "ego-tripping"? A number of non-journalistic agencies are also moving into the news business, again throwing into question the special skills of traditional media institutions. For instance, there is AT & T's magazine *Lead Story* (http:/www.leadstory.com) and IBM's *Infomarket Newsticker* (http://www.infomkt.ibm.com). How can journalists respond to these dilemmas?

Pressure to cut costs while making news more attractive, which only intensifies on the Web, is already eroding journalistic distinctions around hard news, according to Wendy Swallow Williams ("The death of objectivity"; *Internet Newsroom*; Glen Echo, Maryland; 1 July 1997). She argues: "The Web is instantaneous, limitless, interactive and jittery, all qualities that could militate against careful, accurate and balanced reporting if journalists get caught up in the glitz and gadgets. For example, most online news includes links to sources outside the news organisation, but readers may not be aware that they have stopped reading the newspaper and moved to reading a promotional message."

Researchers at the Poynter Institute, in St Petersburg, USA, have published guidelines for determining the reliability of online content (available at http://www.poynter.org/me/nme/jvn1.htm).

New media: *new (cyberhack) journalist*

A CCORDING to Milverton Wallace, Internet specialist at City University, London, online publishing carries the potential to revolutionise journalistic practice, opening it up to public scrutiny in dramatic new ways. He comments: "Journalists must develop new conventions and new ways of seeing. And in the process, slay some sacred cows."

The print media are good at relating the latest news events but readers can be left with no clear understanding of the deeper issues involved.

"But why shouldn't we get the latest news and the in-depth background at the same time? In a hypertext Web publication, readers are only a mouse click away from the source of the story. With access to the primary source or the full text of the report, they can weigh the evidence and come to their own conclusions. Such a procedure will not sit well with journalists who are jealous of their source material or those who believe that readers are incapable of analysing and synthesising supporting material.

"This is short-sighted. Among the professional classes, journalists are among the least trusted by the public. What better way to show a clean pair of hands than by letting them examine the bases on which the story is constructed."

Wallace also argues that the flexible online services which take no account of the 24-hour news cycle of the print media can help transform journalistic routines. "Most print journalists would recoil in horror at the notion of the death of the deadline. But this is what an online medium does: it eliminates the fixed news deadline. Stories are updated as and when required. This means that the shelf life of the news content is greatly extended, allowing journalists to offer more in-depth information, to craft stories more carefully, to tease out relevant links and provide supporting data." (See also "Death of the Deadline"; *Press Gazette*; London; 12 April 1996.)

Reference texts

M OST journalists will need to consult libraries and reference books constantly throughout their working life. Amongst those commonly used are: *Encyclopaedia Britannica* and *Chambers Encyclopaedia*; the *Guinness Book of Records*; *Keesing's Contemporary Archives* (for comprehensive round-ups on the news globally); *Who's Who* (particularly useful for profiles, obituaries or contacts addresses and phone numbers); *Who's Who in the Theatre*; *TV and Radio Who's Who*; *Who Owns Whom; International Who's Who*; *Vacher's Parliamentary Companion* (for MP details); *The Times Atlas and World Gazetteer* (to check spellings of foreign places); *Social Trends* (annually up-dated) HMSO; a dictionary; a dictionary of quotations; *Halliwell's Film Guide*; a dictionary of scientific and medical terms; *Dictionary of Art and Artists*; *McNae's Essential Law for Journalists*. And most newspaper libraries will contain copies of these.

In the case of their specialist areas, journalists will purchase copies of the important texts for their own libraries.

Further sources

Internet Resources Made Simple; Peter McBride; Butterworth-Heinemann; Oxford; 1996.

Netscape Navigator in Easy Steps; Mary Lojkine; Computer Step; Southam, Warwickshire; 1996.

The Internet and World Wide Web: The Rough Guide 2.0; Angus J. Kennedy; Rough Guides Ltd; London; 1996.

Research for Writers; Ann Hoffman; A & C Black; London; fourth edition; 1992.

The Search: Information Gathering for the Mass Media; Lauren Kessler and Duncan McDonald; Wadsworth Publishing Company; Belmont, California; 1992.

The Media Guide 1998; Steve Peak (ed.); Fourth Estate; London; 1997 (annually updated).

Press Gazette; 33–39 Bowling Green Lane, London EC1R 0DA. Tel: 0171-505 8214; fax: 0171-505 8220; email: pged.media.emap.co.uk[.] Carries weekly list of useful news contacts.

Environmental Information: A Guide to Sources; Helen Woolston and Nigel Lees (eds); British Library; London; second edition; 1997. One of a series of specialist source books published by BL. Invaluable for journalists.

War and Order: Researching State Structures; Celina Bledowska (ed.); Junction Books; London; 1983.

Freedom of Information Handbook; David Northmore; Bloomsbury; London; second edition; 1991. An indispensable resource for all journalists.

A Guide to Library Research Methods; Thomas Mann; Oxford University Press; Oxford; 1987.

Encyclopaedia of the British Press 1422–1992; Dennis Griffiths (ed.); Macmillan; London; 1992.

● Campaign for Freedom of Information; 88 Old Street; London EC1V 9AR; tel 0171-253 2445; fax: 0171-608 3325.

● Campaign for Press and Broadcasting Freedom; 8 Cynthia Street, London N1 9JF; tel: 0171-278 4430, fax: 0171-837 8868.

4 The long, short and enthralling art of interviewing

THE dynamics of every interview are different. They may be short or long; in a pub, in an airport lounge, in a sauna. They may be friendly or occasionally confrontational. They may be about someone's sex life or high matters of state. Many interviews are unpredictable. Sometimes an interview can change your life. This happened to Fenner Brockway, the late Labour peer, peace activist and journalist, who was converted to socialism following his interview with Keir Hardie.

How then to write about such imponderables? One of the most eminent Fleet Street interviewers, Lynn Barber, of the *Observer* and formerly of the *Independent on Sunday* and *Sunday Times*, admits: "I've made various attempts at instituting a system for organising interviews, but have come to the conclusion that, in journalism, panic is the system" (*Mostly Men*; Viking; London; 1991).

Here then are a few tips to help you traverse the fascinating territory of the interview. The best way to learn is to go out and do it. But always go about your journalism with a critical hat on. Watch colleagues, see interviewers on the television, listen to them on the radio. Notice how they can differ in their techniques. Seek all the time to improve what you are doing.

Why interview?

AN interview is intentional conversation. But, as a journalistic convention, it has to be seen in its historical context. It is easy to imagine the interview as a "natural", unproblematic activity. Christopher Silvester shows, however, in his seminal history (*The Penguin Book of Interviews: An anthology from 1959 to the present day*; Penguin Books; Harmondsworth; 1994), that the interview, as a journalistic genre, had to be invented. In fact, the interview between Horace Greeley, editor of the *New York Tribune*, and Brigham Young, the leader of the Mormon Church in 1859, lays claim to being "the first fully-fledged interview with a celebrity, much of it in the question-and-answer format familiar to modern readers", as Silvester comments.

Journalists should always be aware of the interview's specific purposes: they may be seeking information, opinion or evidence of someone's state of mind. They may be investigating a subject and seeking to expose a lie or a wrong-doing.

For the source the interview has a purpose, too: they are seeking to convey an opinion or information, hide a secret, or merely articulate their mood. But beware:

- The source may be confused, yet afraid to admit this.

- They may be afraid to speak their true opinion; they could lose their job; they could face social or professional isolation.

- The source may be lying; conveying misinformation, propaganda.

- They may be intimidated by the presence of the reporter and so not express their true feelings.

- The source may be flattered by the interest of the journalist and be more extrovert and "colourful" than they normally are.

- They may forget or hide important details.

- They may be speaking in a foreign language and so unable to express what they mean.

- The reporter's personality and bias, even their body language, is likely to affect the relationship with the source and the kind of responses solicited. A different reporter might draw different answers. Someone may respond more openly to a woman reporter, another may feel more relaxed with an older man. Research has shown that interviews by black and white people draw different kinds of responses.

The quickie/grabbed interview

Many interviews are short. You may be covering a parliamentary select committee and want to follow up something said by an MP. You have time to ask just a few questions. You have a clear idea of your angle and need extra information and/or quotes to support it. You go to the MP, pen and notebook in hand (tape recorders are not permitted). There are just a few minutes before the MP is off on other business.

Vox pop

This is not about interviewing Jason Donovan or Madonna. It's the jargon word for the short interviews journalists have with people on a given subject (vox pop being derived from the Latin "voice of the people"). Do you think a law should be introduced to restrain the press from invading people's privacy? That sort of thing.

Newspapers often build a story around a series of short quotes drawn from street interviews or ring-arounds. A subject is identified and there follows a list of people with direct quotes attached to them. Or a vox pop can constitute part of a feature. The main story can dwell on the news, background and important details. A series of quotes highlights the range of views in an easy-to-read format.

Phones and phoney journalism

Phoney journalism is on the increase. Speed is the essence of journalism and the phone provides the easiest and quickest way of contacting a source. It helps in the pursuit of a reluctant source. Journalists have to develop their own "phone personality"; special "phone relationships" emerge between reporters and sources.

The phone is coming to dominate the journalist's life far too much. As Christopher Brown comments (*The Prying Game*; Robson Books; London; 1996): "The speed and frequency of deadlines mean that instead of meeting their sources face to face, an increasing number of today's reporters and correspondents rely on mobile and standard telephones, faxes, pagers, teleprinters and computers to get their stories. This creates an artificial barrier between the newsmen and the news leading to errors, misunderstandings and reports that lack the inimitable freshness of human contact." In fact, a dominant "phone culture" has grown throughout Western industry. Proprietors like phone journalism because it's relatively cheap. But lots of people don't possess a phone or have access to one at work. They are to a certain extent denied access to the media. There is something discriminatory about the phone.

The advice is clear: whenever you have an opportunity to see a source face to face take it. If you are to develop that source you will need to meet them.

Phone interviews tend to be shorter than face-to-face contacts. Reporters have to be clear about the questions they are to put and the information they need. There is little time for waffle.

Profiles are rarely conducted by phone; the contact between reporter and source is too superficial and impersonal. At the same time, reporters conducting phone interviews have to be extra sensitive to the nuances of speech; a hesitancy, an abruptness, a quivering in the voice all carry meanings which the reporter should be quick to note or respond to.

A reporter should try to confront the impersonality of the phone and respond emotionally to the conversation. Facial and arm gestures can all help; if you are stressing a point move your hands about; if jokes are made, laugh. Standing up can help provide extra confidence when making a particularly difficult call.

Some journalists lodge a phone on their shoulder while typing up a conversation they are having on the phone. This can be intimidating to the source and the reporter may have to return to note-taking with a pen if no other solution is possible.

Interview phobia: *a solution*

I T is common for people new to journalism to find first contact with sources difficult. It is a challenge to ask a stranger questions (maybe in a foreign language) and maintain a coherent conversation while taking a note. Some find the "distance" provided by the phone reassuring; others find face-to-face interviewing less intimidating. If you find the phone intimidating you are not alone. According to Dr Guy Fielding, a communications specialist, 2.5 million people in Britain suffer telephone anxiety ("Don't call me, please, and I won't call you"; Barbara Rowlands; *The Independent*; 24 August 1993).

In your first few months' reporting it is good to join up with a colleague during assignments. While journalism is an individualistic job, it can only succeed through people working well in a team. Joint reporting in no way conflicts with journalistic norms. One of the most famous scoops, the exposé of the Watergate break-in, was the result of a joint effort by Carl Bernstein and Bob Woodward, of the *Washington Post*. Investigative reporters often work in pairs. It's safer and while one asks the questions the other can observe reactions and the environment closely (*Investigative Reporting and Editing*; Paul N. Williams; Prentice Hall; New Jersey; 1978).

If you are alone on an assignment in those early months, or at any other time, it is fine to ask someone to slow down in their talking. Don't hesitate to ask the interviewee to spell out a difficult word, to repeat a strong quote or important information. Figures, names, titles are worth particular attention. Don't hesitate to ring back to check or extract new information. That merely reflects painstaking efficiency rather than incompetence.

Phone tip-offs

Sometimes journalists are rung at their homes or offices with some news. The journalist has no time to prepare questions. They have to think quickly. Information drawn from an unknown source in this way has to be checked and the source's contact number sought so they can be rung back if necessary.

The role of PROs

If you are contacting pressure groups, political parties or professional bodies you are likely to come into contact with their Press Relations Officer (PRO). It is important to establish good relations with this person.

They can be a vital source for background information and sometimes good for a quote. They can provide contact numbers for other sources and help in setting up meetings and interpreters if deaf people or foreign language speakers are being interviewed. But PROs expect a certain amount of background knowledge from reporters. A local government PRO would not expect to have to explain the intricacies of the council tax to an enquiring reporter.

Official spokespersons are generally not referred to by name. They are described as "a spokeswoman for such-and-such body". They might also refer you to someone else in the organisation with a specialist knowledge and responsibility in the area you are investigating.

In case of intimidation

Some people may feel intimidated by a phone call from a journalist. It might be their first contact with this awesome and seemingly powerful institution, the press, so capable of destroying reputations.

You may decide to give them time to think about their responses. You could give them a few basic questions which they can respond to when you ring back in say 20 minutes. You have established some trust and they may be more inclined to respond openly to other questions. If the source is a racist attacking Pakistani homes in the East End of London you will adopt a different strategy. As so often in reporting, political and ethical issues merge.

Arranging a face to face

BE polite, relaxed and sound efficient. It's important straight away to establish the likely length of the interview. The source is likely to have their own diary of engagements to complete. And the time-length provides a shorthand indication of the likely depth of the questioning. Most interviews aiming to extract specific information can last for around half an hour; for a profile of any depth at least three-quarters of an hour to an hour is required.

Give a brief indication of the purpose of the interview (whether for a profile, as part of a feature or an investigation) and, in general terms, the kind of questions to be put. Identify clearly the newspaper you are working for and, if you are a freelance, the target publication you are aiming at. In some cases a subject will be interviewed by a group of reporters. In that case, it is a good idea to spell out briefly how your approach is intended to be different. Indicate if you are to be accompanied by a photographer.

Fixing time and place.

There are a range of potential locations:

- *your territory* (newspaper office if you are a staff writer; your home/office if you are freelance; college if you are a student). This is rarely adopted by reporters; offices lack the privacy and relative calm needed for interviews and can appear intimidating to members of the public.

- *their territory* (home, particularly likely if the person is unemployed, office or shop floor). Journalists often visit the source's home when writing a profile. People tend to feel relaxed there and talk most freely. The home is an expression of their personality; the source might wish to display it. The reporter can certainly use their observations of it and the source's behaviour within it to provide colour in their copy.

The reporter might also visit the home when conducting an interview the source might consider too sensitive to hold at their workplace.

Visiting homes is not without its problems. The source is extending their hand to the reporter, inviting them into their private territory. The reporter might find it more difficult criticising the source after developing this kind of contact.

The source's office is a common site for an interview (factory shop-floor workers are rarely profiled). The environment can be made relatively free of distractions and relevant information and documents will be at hand.

- *neutral territory* (a pub or restaurant). Useful sites when you are building up contacts. Their informality promotes fruitful contacts. The source is being "entertained" and that helps conversation flow. The journalist will always go with a specific intention but the informality allows time for digressions, small talk, gossip and jokes. All this helps in the development of the relationship. The journalist can express their own knowledge of and views about the subjects discussed and that, too, helps trust develop.

Sometimes a source will need reassuring they are not opening themselves to attack by agreeing to be interviewed. Members of progressive groups such as peace activists, feminists, trade unionists, gays, lesbians, have been pilloried in the media and their fears are understandable. Even in today's democratic Britain, a large number of people are afraid or unwilling to express their views to the media.

In these situations it is important to explain whom you are writing for, what you hope to extract from the interview. Never speak to someone on the basis you are writing for one media outlet which they are happy with and then send the copy elsewhere without consulting them. Student journalists might win a difficult interview on the understanding it is not for publication. They should resist the temptation to betray the trust and send the copy off to a newspaper.

Someone might speak to you only on the condition they see a list of questions beforehand. Many politicians and showbiz stars are now adopting this line. It is a practice that, in general, should be challenged. Journalists can end up clerical poodles pandering to the whims of politicians and media celebrities.

But it is wrong to call for a blanket ban on this request for questions. A journalist might be aware of the interviewee's views; they are more important as a source of information. Since speed is of the essence in journalism, the source might plead ignorance and essential information may go missing. They might need to do some research, consult colleagues before answering. At least the sending of questions gives them time. They cannot plead ignorance during the face to face.

It might be legitimate, when a crucial source is sought and no other way appears possible, to agree to send a list of questions. At least some response is gained and there is the possibility the source will be impressed with your questions and invite you in for a face to face.

At the opposite end of the scale from the media-shy person is the self-publicist. Every newspaper office will be harassed by someone desperate for coverage. Reporters need to guard against this kind of person.

Preparing for an in-depth interview

Preparation is essential for interviews. If you are well informed, you are more likely to extract new and interesting information and to be sensitive to the source's bias. Read the cuttings, do the research, talk to friends and colleagues about the subjects likely to be raised. An uninformed reporter becomes a pawn in the hand of the source; they can lie, they can hide crucial information, they can misinform; they can steer the conversation away from tricky subjects.

Most professions have their own stock of jargon and a bewildering array of acronyms with which the reporter should have some familiarity. But sources used to handling the press have different expectations of journalists. The specialist is assumed to have more knowledge than the generalist. Both should not be afraid to express ignorance. Better to clarify a point than flounder or convey inaccuracies to readers.

The question of questions

Journalists differ on the extent to which they prepare specific questions. Some argue it is best to write down most of the crucial questions in a logical order and tick them off as the interview proceeds.

Many find this can impede free-flowing conversation. Talk moves too fast usually to allow this "ticking off". If the detailed list of questions is used it should be on a separate sheet of paper and not buried in a notebook. In any case, interviews can often move in unpredictable directions, making it absurd to stick to any pre-planned outline.

Another approach is to think through the interview beforehand listing detailed questions in a logical order. The act of writing helps the memory. For the interview, three or four vital headings are listed and around this skeleton the flesh of the interview can be spread.

Dress sense

A journalist should be conscious of the messages put out by their dress. Informal dress will be appropriate on some occasions such as when interviewing members of progressive campaigning groups or think-tanks, formal dress when meeting white-collar professionals or politicians. A journalist will always have at the back of their mind: "If I dressed differently would the source be more open to me and trusting?"

Preliminary courtesies

First contact is crucial. The reporter should be calm and relaxed, polite but assertive. The greeting should be pleasant with a firm handshake and some eye-to-eye contact. The reporter might need to make clear again the purpose of the interview (though during some investigations the real purpose might be hidden).

If the interview is for some reason off the record or unattributable this needs to be established. Politicians and most PROs will be aware of the attribution conventions of newspapers. Many people are not. They might begin to answer questions and then try to designate them as off the record. A journalist should not be willing to permit that kind of arrangement automatically. A source may say something on the record which, in print, could damage them or someone else unnecessarily. In this case the journalist will operate self-censorship.

If you are planning to use a tape recorder, make sure this is fine with the source, who might choose to set up their own taping device, after all. You might not wish to bring out your notebook until you have relaxed into the conversation and passed the preliminary courtesies. The notebook should never be over-prominent.

The actual interview: *general points*

Note-taking

In your first weeks as a reporter you might find it difficult keeping a conversation going while making notes at the same time. Don't feel self-conscious about that. You might even say: "That's an important point. Would you remind repeating that?"

Picking out the useful information and quotes becomes an art. Sometimes all the notes will be used; usually just a part will be used. The writer, confident in their powers of memory, might add more details or comments they remember but did not take down. This has to be handled carefully, particularly if the views are contentious and potentially libellous. Without any note or tape recording, the journalist has little defence in court.

Presenting your personality

It is impossible to deny your personality in the meeting as some journalists suggest (*The Journalist Interview*; Hugh C. Sherwood; Harper & Row; New York; second edition; 1972). The selection and bias of your questions, your manner, your dress all carry the stamp of your personality. The extent to which your personality more overtly intrudes on the interview will differ according to the circumstances.

In most interviews where the focus is on extracting views and information the reporter's intervention is likely to be limited. An exchange of views, a joke or two are useful for varying the mood and helping conversation flow.

In profile interviews your own personality can come more to the fore. Someone confronted with a reporter who is nothing more than a blank sheet of a personality merely uttering concise questions can hardly convey their own. But you should never come to dominate the meeting. Your views and experiences are of secondary importance and should be revealed only to entice more out of your subject. Displaying some of your knowledge on the subject can also impress the interviewee and help build up trust. Never show off.

Pacing the interview

Most journalistic training manuals advise reporters to begin always with the non-threatening questions establishing basic information and views. This helps create trust after which more sensitive questions can be raised. In practice, reporters respond in many different ways to the shifting dynamics of the interview. Some suggest it is best to throw in a difficult question near the start. As Lynn Barber comments (*Mostly Men*; Viking; London; 1991): "The subject's relief at having survived it so quickly and painlessly may pay dividends for the rest of the interview." Yet there is always the danger the interviewee may call a stop to the conversation early on if this strategy fails.

Raise sensitive issues delicately: "I hope you don't mind me asking this but what is your salary?" Barber says that at the start of interviews she makes a point of stressing the interviewee's right to refuse: "Please don't be offended by my questions. If you don't want to answer them, just shake your head and I won't even put no comment" (*Press Gazette*; London; 18 October 1996). Questions should be concise. But the interview is not likely to be all questions. It may be fruitful to exchange ideas. Formulate a mix of open-ended questions and specific questions avoiding those which give a yes/no answer.

Active listening

Most interviewers stress active listening is one of the most crucial skills. Journalists can often be surprised at how open and talkative people are when profiled. Their vanity may be flattered. Here is someone taking an interest in them; however fleeting, a little fame is assured by the coverage.

In some respects the press (and the media in general) has taken over the role of the Church as being the site of the confessional, where personal secrets are revealed. Every day the press carries the revelation of some secret: the secrets of so-and-so's sex life; a secret memo of one Cabinet minister to another; a secret arms sale. Paradoxically, this is happening in a society where government and industry are becoming increasingly secretive and remote from democratic accountability.

Given this willingness to talk, the journalists' role is to listen intelligently and help the conversation along with concise, clearly focused questions.

The flexible approach

Reporters should be relaxed and flexible, ready to abandon their list of questions and follow up more interesting issues as they emerge.

They should always be clear about what they want from an interview. It is dangerous to go into an interview with a vague brief hoping something will come out of it. It rarely does: the reporter will end up with lots of waffle. In contrast, continual evasive responses to key questions suggest to the reporter they are on to something important.

There is a place for unstructured chat, say over a meal, between journalist and source. Contacts are being maintained and maybe something of interest will emerge. But chat is very different from an interview.

Power games people play

The distribution of power in many communication processes is complex and fluctuating. A source may seek to exploit the reporter to transmit their views; their misinformation, their propaganda. The reporter exploits the source as a "quote-giver" or "information-giver". In this light, interviews can be seen as a contest. The journalist must be aware as far as possible of the dynamics of the interview and try to be in control, determining the flow. The interviewee should never take over. If they do, by rambling on some irrelevant point, for instance, the journalist should reassert their authority with a pointed question.

Body talk

Eye contact is important but continuous contact is likely to appear intimidating. During profile interviews, other aspects of body language and non-verbal communication such as sighs, shrugs, silences, grins, coughs, shrugging of shoulders, will be closely observed by the reporter.

Dealing with the difficult ones

The hostile interviewee

An interviewee may be hostile for any number of reasons. They may have a poor opinion of the press in general or have been criticised in the press. They may feel threatened or insulted by a particular line of questioning; they may simply dislike the sound of your voice or the colour of your jacket. As a result, you may have to reassure them about the standards you and your newspaper follow. You may have to reassure them you understand their sensitivity about a particular issue.

Whatever happens, keep cool. Never argue with an interviewee. Try to steer the conversation towards calmer waters. If the source is particularly important and reacts nervously to your questions you may agree to show them the copy before publication. Sometimes they might walk out on you. That's their privilege.

The over-hasty interviewee

This is the person who says: "I don't have time to talk to you." A good response is to say something like: "I won't take up much of your time but this is an important matter and I want to get it right." Be sympathetic and straight to the point. They should thaw.

The silent interviewee

You don't seem to be getting anywhere. They answer in dull, monosyllabic tones. Give them time to warm up, open-ended questions and lots of encouraging head-nods. If all else fails fall silent and see what happens.

The "no-comment"

They need to be told this looks bad in print. Stress you don't want to write a one-sided story and need their comments, perhaps to correct inaccuracies. Ask why they can't comment. Someone may try to delay you until the following day. Suggest the story is going to print and will be unbalanced without their quotes.

The dodger

They may claim ignorance of some major detail but be simply trying to avoid controversy. You need to be well briefed to cope. They claim to have been absent at a crucial meeting. "Ah, but I have looked in the minutes of the meeting and noticed you were present." That sort of response should jog their memory.

The waffler

They might habitually be a raconteur and stray away from main conversational issues. Or they may be trying to evade a delicate issue. Don't let them take command of the conversation. Keep it focused.

Ending the interview

- Sometimes it's worth asking: "Is there anything else you wish to mention?"

- Appropriate courtesies should be made: thanks for time etc.

- Arrangements for checking and future contact (perhaps also by a photographer) can be made. If you have interviewed them at their office, it might be useful to have their home number.

- An interviewee might ask to see copy before it is published. You will then have to deal with that issue.

After the interview

This is another crucial period. You might need to ring back to clarify some points. They might well ring you back. Often after profile interviews, it's courteous to write back thanking them for their time. Also, try to compile your article as soon as possible after the event. If you wait you are more likely to forget details, distort others and find your notes incomprehensible.

When the interview is part of a feature investigation, it should similarly be written up as soon as possible and ideas for new interviews and issues to examine should be noted.

Quotes checklist

Direct quotes

- These are best reserved for expressions of opinion. For instance: "She said: 'Margaret Thatcher was the outstanding Prime Minister of this century.'"

- Direct quotes add newsy elements to stories and provide colour, immediacy, authenticity and a crucial human dimension to copy, hence their prominence. They can add humour.

- Quotes help personalise the news. It is always better to have an individual express a view than an impersonal, institutional voice. Instead of "The British Medical Association claimed . . . " say "a spokeswoman for the BMA claimed". When using a press release, a phone call may be necessary to add this detail.

- Lengths of direct quotes will vary. But take any book of quotations and see how short the majority are. Some of the most famous are a matter of a few words. Just as the heavies use longer sentences than the pops so their quotes tend to be longer. But do people speak in shorter sentences to tabloid journalists?

- It is a vexed issue among journalists as to how much freedom they have to edit a direct quote. Most will agree such phrases as "you know", "like I said" and "er, er" slipped into conversations can easily be cut. Beyond that, some argue a direct quote should never be changed.

However, there is a case for editing when someone speaks ungrammatically. Nothing is served by leaving it other than showing the source is stupid. Thus, particular care should be given when quoting people for whom English is not their first language.

- Nonsense is worth quoting when the subject of the piece requires it. For instance, newspapers have focused on the ungrammatical language used by a series of prominent US politicians (Reaganspeak, Haigspeak, Bushspeak), often in off-the-cuff remarks to journalists. As here, from *The Independent* of 14 October 1990:

Read my lips: no new syntaxes

From John Lichfield in Washington

PRESIDENT BUSH made five attempts to define White House policy on taxation of the super-rich last week. This weekend, many people are still baffled. In part, it is a political confusion caused by conflicting pressures in the Republican Party. But in part, it is down to Mr Bush's celebrated inarticulacy.

He was in especially opaque form at Tuesday's press conference, which started the rot. This was what he said about his campaign support for Senator Jesse Helms, who had then failed to support his budget deal: "But – so we're talking about the broad principles that unite us, and urge you vote not just for Jesse, but for others who – let's see

how I get this properly – grammar, you know, the grammar – if we had more of whom we had – would – we wouldn't be in such a problem."

Mr Bush's bizarre patterns of speech are a mixture of sports *patois*, technical jargon, acquired Texan, upper class New England nursery slang and a casual acquaintance with the traditional rules of grammar.

President Eisenhower, sometimes compared with Mr Bush, employed similarly baffling language. Once, a White House correspondent attempted revenge: he wrote, and circulated, a version of Abraham Lincoln's Gettysburg Address, as if spoken off the cuff by Ike.

- Peculiar speech mannerisms and dialect can be quoted to convey the source's typical speech patterns. This has to be done sensitively, mostly in features.

- Particular kinds of cliché, jargon and rhetoric do not make good quotes.

    Thus: "The President said: 'This historic meeting of the world's leading industrial states has achieved a lot and we have reason to be proud of what we have done this weekend.'"

    "She was 'very pleased' with the takings from the raffle for handicapped children."

    These are examples of cliché and rhetoric which can be easily cut.

Reported speech

The conventions of reported speech are simple. Following verbs such as "said", "informed", "claimed", "warned", "demanded", "alleged", "hinted", "added", the tense of the verb in reported speech takes one step into the past.

Direct speech	Reported speech
am/are/is	was/were
shall	should
will	would
may	might
was/were	had been
have been	had been
must	had to
could	could have

"Aneurin Bevan said: 'I read the newspaper avidly. It is my one form of continuous fiction'" is using the direct quote. In reported speech it becomes: "Aneurin Bevan said he read the newspaper avidly. It was his one form of continuous fiction." It is wrong to say: "Aneurin Bevan said he reads the newspaper avidly. It is his one form of continuous fiction."

Thus: "He said: 'The trade union movement has been crippled by the Tory government's punitive legislation'" becomes: "He said the trade union movement had been crippled by the Tory government's punitive legislation."

● Pronouns are affected by reported speech conventions. "She said: 'We may decide to emigrate to Iceland'" becomes: "She said they might decide to emigrate to Iceland."

"She told the council: 'Your attempts at promoting equal opportunities in this county are pathetic'" becomes: "She told the council their attempts at promoting equal opportunities in the county were pathetic."

● Adverbs are also affected:

Thus: "He said: 'We shall all meet here soon to plan next week's agenda'" becomes: "He said they should all meet there soon to plan the following week's agenda." (For a longer exposition of reported speech rules see *Writing for the Press*; James Aitchison; Hutchinson Education; London; 1988 and *English for Journalists*; Wynford Hicks; Routledge; London; 1993).

Notice the use of reported speech in this article from the *Independent on Sunday* (20 December 1992):

Yeltsin is fighting for his political life

Helen Womack in Moscow reports

BORIS YELTSIN appeared to be fighting for his political survival yesterday after he cut short a visit to China, saying he was needed in Moscow to "restore order" and save reform. The Russian capital was quiet and it was not immediately clear what prompted Mr Yeltsin's hasty departure.

Speaking to reporters at Peking airport, Mr Yeltsin suggested that Russia's new conservative Prime Minister, Viktor

Chernomyrdin, was trying to dismantle the reformist cabinet assembled by his predecessor, Yegor Gaidar. "Someone has started fighting for portfolios too early, to pull the government apart, so the master must return to restore order," the President said.

Although he had to sacrifice Mr Gaidar last week because of pressure from the Congress of People's Deputies, Mr Yeltsin was hoping to keep the rest of his circle of reformist economists.

However a claim by Mr Yeltsin's spokesman Vyacheslav Kostikov that things "could have been worse" suggests that other candidates even more conservative than Mr Chernomyrdin might have been foisted on the President. One was Yuri Skokov, a shadowy figure from the unelected Security Council, who won more votes than Mr Chernomyrdin in the first vote in Congress. Mr Yeltsin said later he would take advice on foreign affairs from Mr Skokov, which was a bad sign for the liberal Foreign Minister, Andrei Kozyrev, and could be just as bad for the West, which may find Russia taking up positions less to its liking.

Mr Chernomyrdin, 54, was the best compromise Mr Yeltsin could hope for after losing his struggle with the turbulent assembly.

Now Russian business people and Western investors alike can only wait and see how the man who has been described as a "dark horse" will handle the Russian economy. At his first press conference, Mr Chernomyrdin gave little away. He said he would continue the course of reform, but would not say how. He also hinted at more state intervention. His priority, he said, was to support industry, since a great country like Russia could not achieve a free market by "becoming a nation of shopkeepers".

Par. 1: following verb saying – reported speech "he was needed . . ."

Par. 2: following verb suggested – "was trying to dismantle".

Par. 4: following verb said – "would take advice".

Par. 6: following verb said – "he would continue the course of reform but would not say how".

"My" becomes "his", "is" becomes "was" and "can" becomes "could" in:

"His priority, he said, was to support industry, since a great country like Russia could not achieve a free market."

- Beware of making reported speech, say in a press release, into direct speech. A release that says: "Nelson Mandela accused the South African government of ruthlessly suppressing black rights," cannot be changed into: "Nelson Mandela said: 'The South African government has been ruthlessly suppressing black rights.'" There is no proof he said those words. The indirect speech might have been the paraphrase of a longer sentence or combination of sentences.

- Reported speech within a direct quote cannot be converted into direct speech. Thus: "He said he would ask his wife if he should resign tomorrow" cannot become: "He asked his wife: 'Should I resign tomorrow?'"

- Most reports of speeches will combine direct and indirect speech. A report concentrating too heavily on indirect speech will lack immediacy and colour; a report almost exclusively in direct quotation conveys the impression the journalist has surrendered their role of selection and interpretation to the source.

Partial quotes

These are used to highlight particular words in sentences. Thus, the *Evening Standard* reported (16 December 1992):

> Police investigating the murder of a Cardiff prostitute "bullied and hectored" one of the suspects during a "travesty of an interview", the Lord Chief Justice said today.

Journalists use partial quotes sparingly. They are most commonly used in intros but become confusing if used throughout a story.

Quotation dangers

● Two or more people rarely speak in unison. When reporting a public meeting it is strange to have two people identified with the same direct quote. Thus: " 'The BBC should be privatised immediately,' two Conservative councillors urged yesterday" is wrong.

People can agree on an issue and be linked to an indirect quote without any problem. Thus it is perfectly feasible to say: "The BBC should be privatised immediately, two Conservative councillors urged yesterday."

The *Independent on Sunday* reported (27 December 1992):

> PRESSURE for intervention appeared to increase yesterday after Muslim forces accused the Serbs of defying the no-fly zone by using helicopters to reinforce Jradacac, a northern Bosnian town under attack by Muslim forces.
>
> But in Geneva Andrei Kozyrev, the Russian Foreign Minister, and the UN Secretary-General, Boutros Boutros-Ghali, both said they were opposed to any foreign intervention to stop the war in former Yugoslavia. "The peace process must prevail," Mr Boutros-Ghali said.

Notice how the speakers are linked to the same view in reported speech but the name of only one accompanies the direct quote.

● Be careful not to distort reports by over-selective quoting. Someone may devote part of a speech to conveying the pros of an issue, the other part to the cons. One side of the argument may be highlighted; it is irresponsible to eliminate all reference to the other side.

● Journalists can let their imaginations take over when quoting. The Press Complaints Commission has gone so far as to censure journalists for too frequently resorting to invention in the use of quotes. One of the most famous instances was the *Sun*'s invented interview with the wife of a Falklands war "hero" killed in battle. (The woman journalist involved went on to edit a national newspaper.)

- A variation on the invention theme is the "words in the mouth" technique. When an interviewee remains unresponsive the journalist is tempted to feed them quotes. They might ask an interviewee: "Do you think this scheme is outrageous and should never have been backed?" When the hesitant interviewee replies: "Er, yes" the journalist is able to report: "She said she thought the scheme was outrageous and should never have been backed."

Such a technique should be used sparingly. Some Fleet Street newspapers use it quite often. Former *Sunday Mirror* hack Wendsley Clarkson (in *Confessions of a Tabloid Journalist*; Fourth Estate; London; 1990) tells of when he met ex-Beatle Paul McCartney in his car, with his wife alongside him, as he drove out of his country estate. Merely on the basis of a few grunts of the "Yep, sure do" variety Clarkson invented an "exclusive".

- Along with invention can go exaggeration and sensationalism. Two residents are quoted as being opposed to plans for a shopping complex on a school sports site. The story reads: "Residents are protesting etc." The report gives a false picture of the strength of opposition for the sake of journalistic hyperbole. If one of the residents was a spokesperson for the residents, then you could intro.: "Residents are protesting etc."

- When opposing views are expressed "rows" have not necessarily broken out, nor have "wars", nor is one side necessarily "up in arms".

- There is a danger of placing direct quote marks around a phrase and not making clear the source. Such "hanging" quotes confuse. Always make the attribution of any quote clear.

- Be careful not to run two sections of a direct quote together when they were separated by sentences. End the first sentence with double inverted commas. Begin the next sentence with, say: "She added: 'Etc . . .'"

Quotes punctuation

- Most newspapers adopt the following style. They will say:

She added: "I intend to vote for the Raving Loony Party." Notice the colon followed by a space, then double inverted commas and a capital letter. At the end of the sentence the full stop is followed by the inverted commas.
   Variations on that model are considered wrong. Avoid:

She said, "I intend to vote for the Raving Loony Party".
and:
She said that "I intend to vote for the Raving Loony Party."

- When a partial quote is used, the punctuation at the end should fall outside the quote marks. Thus:

He described the Allied attacks on Baghdad as "unnecessary and barbaric".
or:
The rail strike is "outrageous", according to Prime Minister Tony Blair.

- Normally double quotes are used, with single quotes within quotes. Thus:

  He said: "The Gulf conflict is best seen as a 'barbaric slaughter' of thousands of innocent Iraqi conscripts."

- Hybrid sentences mixing direct with indirect elements as in: He said of the allied attacks on Baghdad: "They were unnecessary and barbaric" are generally to be avoided.

- First words in partial quotes are not capitalised. Thus: Barbara Tuchman said war was the "Unfolding of miscalculations" is wrong. It should read: Barbara Tuchman said war was the "unfolding of miscalculations".

- Square brackets are used in direct quotations around words inserted by the journalist to make the meaning clear. Thus:

  "He [Mr Bush] was quite obviously involved in the covert strategy to sell weapons to Iran in the mid-1980s."

- Put an ellipsis (. . .) in a direct quote to indicate irrelevant words are missing. Used more than once it looks as if the reporter is struggling with a poor note or indulging in over-zealous editing. Simpler to change the quote into indirect speech and remove the offending ellipsis.

Attribution verbs

"Said" is most commonly used to convey attribution. It is short, neutral and for these reasons is rapidly read over. To use "said" on every occasion would be dull and words such as "replied", "commented", "pointed out", "protested", "warned", "indicated", "explained", "added", "hinted", "revealed", "claimed", "alleged", which have specific meanings, are used, always carefully. They are most often placed in intros where they convey extra emphasis and drama. They should never be used simply to provide colour.

"Claimed" should only be used for controversial statements of alleged fact when there is some reasonable doubt over them. When evidence is undisputed the use of "claim" throws up unnecessary doubts. When a newspaper reports: "In its report which follows a detailed review of the operation of the 1976 Race Relations Act, the commission claims ethnic minorities continue to suffer high levels of discrimination and disadvantage," it is using "claim" in a subtly racist way to dispute the fact of widespread discrimination.

"Admitted" should only be used when a source is confessing to an error, a failing, a limitation, charge or crime. For instance, the *Cambridge Evening News* (19 December 1992) reported:

AN ambulance chief has admitted the Cambridgeshire service is short of funds after an inquest was told a woman died on a day a crew took hours to arrive.

"Added" should be used only after a source has already been quoted. It is wrong to introduce a new source with the words "She added: 'Etc . . .'"

"Revealed" should only be used when significant new information is being relayed. "Stated" is archaic and generally avoided. "Quipped", "joked", "chuckled" are clichés and are best avoided.

An effective way of conveying attribution is to use the phrase "according to . . .". It is most commonly used in intros as here (from the *Evening Standard*, 16 December 1992):

> COMMERCIAL radio has received a ratings drubbing at the hands of the BBC, according to secret figures leaked from the first-ever joint audience survey.

Getting the quotes down: *recording techniques*

Shorthand

One of the essential skills of the journalist is recording notes effectively. The National Council for the Training of Journalists and the newspaper National Vocational Qualifications require 100 words per minute from successful candidates. Many training courses devote considerable time to shorthand and most provincial papers will require good shorthand from applicants.

The two most popular systems with journalists are Pitmans and Teeline, the latter invented primarily with trainee journalists in mind.

During the 19th century, the emergence of shorthand as a special journalistic skill helped in the development of the notion of professionalism. As Anthony Smith argues: "It meant that a man could specialise in observing or hearing and recording with precision . . . it gave the reporter an aura of neutrality as he stood between event and reader" (*The Politics of Information*; Macmillan Press; London; 1978, orig. 1972).

Today there is a paradox that the higher up the greasy pole of journalistic success you go the less likely you are to find shorthand competence. Not all Fleet Street writers possess it. Very few other journalist cultures give shorthand the kind of importance British provincials attach to it.

Yet it is important for all aspiring journalists to do shorthand to at least 100 words a minute. Nobody regrets the effort put into the learning. For certain jobs, such as covering Parliament, select committees, courts and coroners' courts where tapes are banned, and council meetings, good shorthand is essential. If reporters had better recording techniques fewer errors would crop up and the habit of inventing facts and quotes would diminish.

Alternatives

- *Personal shorthands*: the most commonly used abbreviation system is Astbury's and you may want to develop your own based on the idea of cutting out vowels. "Between" becomes "btwn, "against" "agst" and so on.

- A new shorthand system, *AgiliWriting*, has been invented by Anne Gresham, which she describes as "ezy t rd, ezy t wrt and ezy t lrn". The outstanding feature is that it is accompanied by a computer program allowing the writer to type in shorthand copy and transform it into longhand. (For more information: 39 Totteridge Lane, London N20 0HD; tel: 081-446 0086.)

Thus, it is possible that in the near future journalists will attend press conferences with their laptop computers, type notes in shorthand form, then send them via a modem to the office for conversion into longhand.

● Acquiring the skill of *selective note-taking* is crucial. It is not essential to record everything said. Over-detailed note-taking prevents profitable contact in interviews. The best shorthand writers are not necessarily the best writers.

The good journalist knows when something of interest is being said. Their ears prick up and all attention is paid to getting down those facts, those views, that feeling. If you are not certain you have the quote correct either double check or paraphrase the general meaning (if you are clear about that) and put it in reported speech.

In some cases, journalists don't take down notes at all. During an investigative exercise a journalist may keep their identity hidden. At a particularly sensitive interview a journalist may consider the presence of a notebook impedes conversation and over-formalises the meeting. A source may be prepared to talk but find the notebook intimidating. On these occasions the reporter has to rely on memory. Only those with a good memory should adopt this approach.

● *Tidiness*: reporters usually use easy-to-handle notebooks that slip easily into pockets and whose pages flip over quickly. Notes should never be made on odd sheets of paper. These can easily be mislaid.

A tidy system of keeping used notebooks is essential since back-referencing is sometimes needed. When complaints are made to newspapers over coverage, easy access to the relevant note is essential. One of the Press Complaints Commission's warnings to newspapers was over their increasing habit of losing important notes. When complaints were made newspapers had little ground on which to base a defence.

Note-taking from written sources

For developing background knowledge of people, events and issues written sources are vital.

For work in libraries (with CD-Rom, cuttings and other written sources) you may work with a quiet laptop or more usually with pen and paper. Always make clear the title of the book or article, full name of author, publisher, place and year of publication. These details are usually in small type on a page before the contents list.

It's also advisable to identify the page number as you note the document. This can be important if you go on to write a project or book on the subject. Many journalists work on books in their spare time or on sabbaticals. So it is a useful habit to develop.

Make clear the distinction between a direct quote from a work and a paraphrase. To lift someone's words directly and not attribute them can lead to allegations of plagiarism.

Learn to use books, reports, articles selectively. You will only rarely read from cover to cover. There is not the time. Sometimes you will rapid-read a work and take detailed notes of the conclusions or recommendations. There may be a vital book or article which is worth three readings to digest. Use book indexes to go straight to the material you need. Look at the bibliographies for other useful sources.

Tapes: pros and cons

Many journalists are relying increasingly on tape recorders. Their prices range from around £30 up to £200 and beyond. They are small and unobtrusive and few people are intimidated by their presence. If a source challenges a reporter over a quote nothing is better at ending the controversy than a tape providing the evidence.

You should always inform a source you are using a tape. Some newspapers have phones set aside for taping while a few journalists have devices on their phones at home.

Taping always requires careful handling. Never rely entirely on the tape. You may lose it or you may have forgotten to press the vital "on" switch. Many a journalist has had this sad tale to tell. The battery may run low; the microphone may pick up unwanted noises such as the tapping of fingers on a desk. If you put it on the centre of a table during a panel discussion it might not register the voices at the end of the table. Always take a back-up note.

For copy needed quickly tape recorders can be a positive nuisance. There is not time to wade through the tape to find the relevant quotes and information. Tapes are best used for features and profiles when you have time to note and digest their contents.

It is very rare that journalists transcribe all the tape. Take down the most important sections as soon as possible after the interview; then return to it for a more thorough run-through when writing up your story.

Bugging

Bugging devices are available at relatively cheap prices and a few journalists have used them during investigative exercises. Various bugging devices, and not scanners as was originally thought, were used to reveal the private conversations of various romantic royals towards the end of 1992, the Queen's self-declared "annus horribilis". But it appeared journalists were not involved in these buggings. In South Africa, the *Weekly Mail* which is published with *The Guardian Weekly*, hired a firm of private investigators in September 1992 in a controversial attempt to bug an agent of the security forces.

Investigative reporter Gerry Brown highlights the fact that bugging is illegal under the Interception of Communications Act 1985. But recording your own end of a two-way telephone conversation is legal ("Fines are just fine by me"; the *Guardian* 24 July 1995) He says: "Quite simply, newspaper reporters who tap people's phones are already breaking the law. I've been doing sneaky investigations for the tabloids for 20-odd years and I've never tapped a phone or been asked by a newspaper to tap a phone. What I do is monitor and record phone calls.

"The difference is simple. When you hook up to a phone line and listen in to two people without either of them being aware you're eavesdropping, then that's 'tapping' and you're breaking the law.

"But if you or your contacts are simply recording your own end of a two-way conversation, that's 'monitoring'."

And he continues: "Hide a radio microphone in a room and crouch behind the bushes in the garden to snoop on what's being said, and that's bugging, an offence under Section 1, the Wireless Telegraphy Act 1949. But if you're in the room yourself with the microphone running to a micro-tape recorder stuffed down your underpants, again, perfectly legal." (See also *Exposed! Sensational True Story of Fleet St Reporter*; Gerry Brown; Viking; London; 1995.)

The PCC Code of Practice advises against bugging bar exceptional cases. However, the use of bugging by the state and its secret services and by industrial spies is far more widespread (see *Bugging: A Complete Survey of Electronic Surveillance Today*; John Wingfield; Robert Hale; London; 1984. *On the Record: Surveillance, Computers and Privacy*; Duncan Campbell and Steve Connor; Michael Joseph; London; 1986).

The law is currently confused on scanners. Possession is not illegal and they can be bought for around £300 in the high street. People use them for listening to Citizens

Band Radio and the weather report from ship to shore. There is even a UK scanning directory listing such sensitive frequencies as airport security, USAF bomb disposal units and Ministry of Defence Tactical Communications. But it is illegal to listen in to official or private conversations and mobile phones are particularly vulnerable to scanning.

5 Learning the language of news

∙∙∙

THE language of news today is the product of centuries of linguistic evolution. It is not a "natural" form of writing. It is a particular discourse with its own rhythms, tones, words and phrases (*News as Discourse*; Teu A. van Dijk; Lawrence Erlbaum Associates; New Jersey; 1988. *Language in the News: Discourse and Ideology in the Press*; Roger Fowler; Routledge; London; 1991). It has to be learnt.

Kiss and tell

MANY young reporters from academic backgrounds, where writing essays 2,000 words long might be the norm, find writing news difficult. Compose a story of 300 words and every word has to count. The sense of news values has to be sharp and that only comes with practice.

"Kiss (Keep it short and simple) and tell" could be the journalist's motto. Complex sentences overloaded with long subordinate clauses should be avoided. Short, precise sentences are best.

George Orwell advised:

> A scrupulous writer, in every sentence he writes, will ask himself at least four questions, thus: "What am I trying to say? What words will express it? What image or idiom will make it clearer? Is this image fresh enough to have an effect?" And he will probably ask himself two more: "Could I put it more simply? Have I said anything avoidably ugly?"
>
> ("Politics and the English language"; in *The Penguin Essays of George Orwell*; Penguin; Harmondsworth; 1984)

The Independent even begins its style book with that quote.

You don't need to count words all the time. But think in terms of a maximum of around 32–5 for a news sentence. The tabloids and many local papers have around 16–20 maximum limit.

Take these three examples:

This *Guardian* report (24 January 1992) has 28 and 32 words in its opening pars.

David Beresford in Johannesburg

CONCLUSIVE evidence has emerged in South Africa of the existence of a conspiracy initiated by the security services to foment township violence in order to influence political developments.

Two young black gangsters have told how they were encouraged, equipped and trained by the security forces to carry out murderous acts of violence against targets linked to the African National Congress.

David Beresford © the *Guardian*

These pars from the *Nottingham Herald and Post* (11 February 1993) have 11 and 15 words.

Garage thieves targeted

POLICE have launched a campaign to beat garage thieves in Nottingham.

Crimes committed on commercial garage premises cost over £2 million in the county in 1992.

These from the *Socialist Worker* (27 March 1993) have 14 and 15 words.

Unions must fight back

"QUITE HONESTLY the unions aren't much good. They've gone along with racism for years."

That's how an active trade unionist in Huddersfield described the trade unions' response to racism.

Economic base of economical writing

Many factors lie behind the creation of this concise news language. The arrival of the telegraph and telegram during the last century put a clear cost on elaborate language (*The Politics of Information*; Anthony Smith; Macmillan Press; London; 1978). With the competition today between advertisers and editorial for space in newspapers, every reported word involves a cost. Economic language helps provide economies in production.

Speed is the essence of newspapers. Sentence structure and page design are influenced by the need to help readers move through the newspaper quickly. As the speed of everyday life increases, the average concentration span narrows. Sentences become shorter; headlines end up just a few "punchy" words. Acronyms proliferate. Words made from acronyms become standard ("yuppie", "yummie", "AIDS"). Phrases that compress complex meaning into a few words are everywhere ("the silent majority", the "new world order").

Newspaper design also influences language and sentence lengths. As Fred Fedler comments:

> Newspapers are printed in small type, with narrow columns, on cheap paper. Long paragraphs – large, gray blocks of type – discourage readers. So reporters divide stories into bite-sized chunks that are easy to read. Also, the white space left at the ends of paragraphs helps brighten each page.
> (*Reporting for the Print Media*; Harcourt Brace Jovanovich Publishers; Florida; fourth edition; 1989)

Boil it down

Never use two or three words when one will do. Words and phrases such as "in order to" (use simply "to"), "at the present time" ("now"), "in the region of" ("about"),"despite the fact that" ("even though"), "in view of the fact that" ("because"), "on the subject of training" ("on training"), "strike action" ("strike") are all cuttable.

Prefer short to long words: "about" rather than "approximately", "show" rather than "demonstrate", "after" rather than "following". Avoid the over-wordiness of adjectives and adverbs: "totally destroyed", "root cause", "important essentials", "past history", "invited guest", "best ever", "broad daylight", "close proximity", "considerable difficulty", "initial beginning", "final outcome".

"Very", "quite" and "rather" are meaningless modifiers, eminently cuttable. Beware unnecessary prepositions as in "divided up", "circled around", "fell down".

Try not to repeat a word in the same sentence or any striking words close together unless a specific effect is intended.

The word "that" can often be cut, as in: "He admitted that he was guilty of stealing a pen from his office." Also be careful when using the small word "of". Usually you can make a phrase more precise. "In the northern part of Iraq" is better written "in northern Iraq".

Use language precisely. Don't confuse discrete/discreet, dependent/dependant, decimate/destroy, less/fewer, luxurious/luxuriant, affect/effect. Generally try to avoid using "thing". It's vague and ugly. (For useful sections on wasteful and commonly-misused words and redundancies see *Newsman's English*; Harold Evans; Heinemann; London; orig. 1972, and *Newspaper Language*; Nicholas Bagnall; Focal Press; Oxford; 1993. *The Elements of Style*; William Strunk Jr and E.B. White; Macmillan; New York/London; third edition; 1979 is an essential aid on grammar and punctuation.)

Be active

Rather than: "A meeting will be held by TUC leaders next week," it is better to say: "TUC leaders will meet next week."

Fun with puns

Puns are extremely important in newspapers. They play with language and its multi-faceted meanings. Some can be forced. But their contrivance is part of their appeal. A certain wit is needed to construct them just as they can convey a certain humour (*Understanding Popular Culture*; John Fiske; Unwin Hyman; London; 1989).

Take, for instance, the *Ilford Recorder* (11 March 1993), a typical local where puns are important. The intro. of a front page picture caption reads: "This talented art student has designs on selling to top London stores after winning a textile competition." Another caption story reads: "A group of friends hit the right note in a Jewish song competition." An intro. reads: "Lifeguards are taking the plunge in a bid to swim twice the width of the Channel for charity." Elsewhere: "Marathon man Peter House ran up £1,700 in sponsorship money when he competed in the Chicago race," and "A young artist drew on her skills to come out tops in a competition."

Puns feature particularly in the pops. Their humour contributes to their overall appeal. For instance, the *Sunday Mirror* (7 March 1993) carried this intro.: "Lord Jamie Blandford, heir to the £100 million Blenheim estate, slipped off his bathrobe to reveal his true aristocratic colours – a white suspender belt and navy blue stockings." Without the pun "to reveal his true aristocratic colours" the sentence would be missing that crucial extra sparkle.

The heavies are more likely to reserve puns for soft news stories and headlines. But many of the parliamentary sketch writers, such as Matthew Parris, of *The Times*, build their copy, often, on a single pun idea.

Clichés: avoid them like the plague

Clichés, for Fleet Street columnist Keith Waterhouse, count as his No. 1 sin among his "seven deadly sins" of writing (*English our English (and How to Sing It)*; Viking; London; 1991). There are thousands of clichés and they come in many guises. For instance, there are alliterative phrases such as "safe and sound", "slow but sure", "chop and change", "share and share alike", "petticoat protest", "followed in the footsteps", "few and far between".

They appear as meaningless, over-dramatic adjectives such as in "driving rain", "miraculous escape", "tragic accident", "brutal murder", "coveted title", "sudden death", "horrific injuries", "sweeping reforms", "heated argument", "proud parents", "bare minimum", "shock/major/hard-hitting report", "mercy mission".

There are metaphors gone stale with over-use: "blanket of snow", "pillar of strength", "tower of strength", "tip of the iceberg", "sweep under the rug", "local boy made good".

Some single words, such as "fairytale", "viable", "on-going", "crisis", "situation", "scandal", "tragedy", "disaster", "fury", "fuming", "angry", "shock", "outrage" amount to clichés.

One of journalism's biggest clichés is "exclusive" which has been devalued through over-use. The *Sunday Mirror* of 7 March 1993, for instance, carried an "exclusive" logo on 16 stories. *Lynn News*, of 27 August 1993, had four "exclusives" on pages four and five.

Newspapers clearly live on clichés. For instance, every day the popular press in these post-heroic times (when machines and technology have taken the place of humans in so many fields – scientific exploration and military strategy to name but two) recreates clichéd images of heroism.

During the Gulf conflict of 1991 the press was full of images of "Top Gun heroes": the British hostages (sudden "victims" caught up in the drama of history) were all transformed into heroes. The same process is at work during periods of peacetime. Thus, on 25 March 1993, the *Daily Star* reported: "British helicopter heroes told last night how they braved shellfire to rescue wounded war victims from a Bosnian hell-hole." And: "Hero schoolboy Simon Dunne sang and joked as he and seven schoolmates struggled for their lives in the freezing sea." And: "Hero bobby Mark Toler spoke of his grief yesterday as he visited the flower-strewn spot in Warrington where three-year-old Johnathan Ball died in an IRA bomb blast."

One of the most prominent clichés revolves around metaphors of violence and warfare. "Hit out at", "(bitter) battle", "under siege", "fight", "massacre", "blast", "axe", "(vicious/cowardly) attack", "mount a defence" are everywhere. There are many factors behind this militarisation of language. It reflects the militarisation of culture with the enormous expenditure on the weapons of war and the industrial importance of the arms trade. In addition, there is the high social status enjoyed by the military, the ever-presence of war toys and computer games and the media's glorification of violence and macho "firmness". Just as the culture is brutalised, so is the language of news.

Many stories are built around the drama of conflict and warfare is an obvious metaphor for this. Moreover, as the media are driven to extremes to capture attention, constantly "bombarding" readers with sensationalised trivia, so the language of violence is used to carry out this "bombardment". Geoffrey Hughes comments: "Generally speaking, the more colourful the metaphor of antithesis, the more it is favoured by the press; the metaphor prevents the analysis from being too exact, while allowing it to remain suggestive" (*Words in Time: A Social History of the English Vocabulary*; Blackwell; Oxford; 1988).

Politics and sport are the two areas most afflicted by this form of cliché. Thus, the *Daily Telegraph* (25 March 1993): "The Government secured a breakthrough last night in the gruelling parliamentary battle to speed progress on the Maastricht Treaty through the Commons." The *Sunday Mirror* (21 March 1993) carried these intros: "County plunged back into the First Division relegation dogfight after being overwhelmed at St James's Park." And: "Ronny Rosenthal plunged the relegation knife into arch-rivals Everton with a last-gasp winner . . ." A report of the England–Turkey football international in the *Daily Mirror* (1 April 1993) had Nigel Clarke reporting "from the front line" with accompanying headline: "Brave England win battle of Turkey". It wasn't an April Fool.

To simplify the historical record and highlight its confrontational dimension, the press often resorts to categorising. Doves and hawks, hardliners, wets and dries, loony/soft/cuddly-left, hard-left, unilateralists and multilateralists, militants, chattering classes, West and East, conservatives and reformers/radicals (in the reporting of Russia) are constantly "doing battle" in the press.

The modern mass media also create a whole new genre of cliché. A film, pop song, catch-phrase, television programme, or vogue words emerge and suddenly they are everywhere. After the Queen uttered the phrase "annus horribilis" (translation: bum year) in 1992, for at least a month hardly a newspaper could appear without a play on those words.

Euphemisms: how job cuts became rationalisation

Journalists stress their commitment to writing plain English and so it is not surprising euphemisms (bland expressions) are considered out. Thus never write so-and-so "passed away" or "slipped away calmly" – they died.

Philip Howard describes euphemism as the "British linguistic vice" (*State of the Language*; Hamish Hamilton; London; 1984): they are part of the air we breathe. It is impossible for journalists to avoid them.

Instead of the emotive sounding "slump", we have the euphemistic, abstract Latinism of "recession". In business, "rationalisation" and "restructuring" mean job cuts. Hospitals often describe people seriously hurt as "comfortable". The "spikes" for the tramps of Orwell's day are now the (equally appalling) "rehabilitation centres" for down-and-outs.

"Wars" today are no longer declared. And people are no longer killed in them (except "by mistake"). "Targets" are "hit" by "precise", "clean", "surgical" missiles. A whole lexicon of euphemistic nukespeak (such as "independent nuclear deterrent", "flexible response", "collateral damage", "strategic sufficiency") has emerged to acclimatise the mind to the unspeakable horror of the nuclear holocaust (see *Nukespeak: the Media and the Bomb*; Crispin Aubrey (ed.); Comedia; London; 1982).

Jargon: getting rid of gobbledegook

One of the biggest challenges young journalists face is to cast aside the academic trappings of their backgrounds and the jargon that accompanies it. Each social grouping (local authorities, education, the military, law, computers, librarians, Trotskyites, New Conservatives) has its own in-language/jargon as a communication aid and "shorthand". Academics are in no way peculiar. For instance, General Norman Schwarzkopf contributed this piece of military gobbledegook during the 1991 Gulf conflict: "It's not yet possible to get clear BDA in this area of the KTO. The continued presence of Triple A means a constant risk of allied personnel becoming KIA or WIA."

With jargon such as this, language becomes a kind of fetish not serving the act of communication but reinforcing the group's special identity – and excluding uninitiated outsiders.

The reporter's task, often, is to learn rapidly the jargon of a group and translate it into terms comprehensible to a mass readership. It's not easy, particularly when spoken at speed.

Journalism has its own jargon. Not only is there its own vocabulary (see Glossary). Many of the clichés of journalism (journalese) amount to a form of jargon. "Probe", "axe", "boost", "jibe", "hit", "shock", "blast" all have a currency in journalism which bears no relation to their use in conversations.

Times: they are a-changing

ONE way to examine the newspaper language of today is to see how *The Times* style has changed over the years just as it will, no doubt, change in the future.

JAN 1   **On This Day**   1855

Joseph Sturge (1793–1859) played an important part in the fight to abolish slavery. He was also a member of a deputation from the Society of Friends which went to Russia in 1854 to carry their protest against the Crimean War to the Tsar

The "Friends" on the War

THREE notable members of the Peace Society, and of the Society of Friends, spoke at a Christmas meeting of workmen at Glocester, on Thursday night, on the subject of the war. Mr Joseph Sturge, one of the deputation from the Society of Friends to the Czar, Mr S. Bowly, the peace and temperance advocate, and Mr T. M. Sturge, of Glocester.

Mr Joseph Sturge, after alluding to his mission to St Petersburg, with the view of bringing about a termination of hostilities, expressed his firm belief, notwithstanding all that had been said against the Emperor of Russia, or whatever might be the evils existing in his Government, that there was no man in Europe who more earnestly desired a return of peace than that monarch, provided it could be done consistently with what he regarded as the honour of his country.

He also alluded to certain accusations which had been made against himself in a letter that had been published, he having been accused of a desire to promote the war because it kept up the price of grain, and, in another part of the same letter, he said he was charged with wishing to put an end to the war, simply because it interfered with his trade.

Providence had, however, placed him in such a position that personally he should not feel the effect of the war further than being now unable to obtain grain from where he could formerly procure it; but he was unable now to give employment to as many men as formerly, and he feared matters in this respect would grow worse.

At the present time wheat was, in England, worth about 10s a bushel, whereas in Russia it could be bought for 2s; and thus, as a pecuniary question, it was desirable that the war should be terminated, apart from higher ground of the Christian duty of putting an end to such fearful scenes of bloodshed as were now taking place in the Crimea. He did not wish to say on whom the blame of the war rested, but he was desirous that each of his friends would use his influence to promote peace, should an opportunity of so doing present itself.

Mr Thomas Sturge recalled to mind the horrors of the wars of the French empire, during which period it was computed by the most credible historians that 5,000,000 human beings were slaughtered. During the seven years of the Wellington campaigns 70,000 British lives were destroyed; and at the battle of Waterloo, where there were under 40,000 British engaged, no less than between 800 and 900 officers, and upwards of 10,000 soldiers, were destroyed. And he was of opinion that if the war in the Crimea continued there would be an equal loss of life.

© Times Newspapers Ltd, 1 January 1992; orig. 1 January 1885

Notice how the language is influenced by the news sense applied. "Spoke . . . on the subject of the war" is too generalised and carries no dramatic weight according to today's news values. The second sentence fails to carry a verb, merely listing the "three notable members" of the first sentence.

Current newspaper style would be stricter on the coverage of the names: Mr Joseph Sturge carries the necessary first name while Bowly and the other Sturge are only given their initials. Today this would be considered an unfortunate disturbance of style. The repetition of Society of Friends is unnecessary.

The second par. is a monster by modern standards – 80 words with five subordinate clauses. There is an over-expansive, literary feel to the par. "Alluding to", "with the view of bringing about a termination" and "notwithstanding" today have an archaic air.

The third par. is also long – 68 words with repetitions of "war", "letter" and the awkward "accusations"/"accused". As well as being cluttered with subordinate phrases, it has such unnecessary embellishing words as "certain" and "simply" and phrases such as "a letter that had been published" (better to say "published letter") and "to put an end to the war" (better "to end the war"). The letter is contradictory so hardly worth reporting.

Par. 4 has 59 words – still long by today's standards. The next sentence has 63 words. The following two are short in comparison, 38 and 32. The final two are 41 and 21.

● It is interesting to see that though the report covers a speech there are no direct quotes.

Converted into the news language of today, the report would read something like:

The Russian Emperor urgently desires peace in the Crimea, Mr Joseph Sturge, who has just returned from a meeting with the Czar, said on Thursday.

But any peace for the Czar had to preserve the honour of Russia, he told a meeting of workers in Gloucester.

Mr Sturge, who met the Czar in St Petersburg on a peace mission for the Society of Friends, said the war had interfered with his buying of grain and he had been forced to lay off some workers.

In England, wheat cost 10s a bushel against just 2s in Russia. So it was not only his Christian duty to seek an end to the bloodshed but such a move was needed for financial reasons.

No side could be blamed for the war, and he urged everyone to do their best to promote peace.

Mr Thomas Sturge, also of the Peace Society, said 5m people had been slaughtered during the wars of the French empire.

Some 70,000 Britons had died during the seven years of the Wellington campaigns while at the battle of Waterloo between 800 and 900 British officers and 10,000 soldiers had been killed.

He feared there would be an equal loss of life if the Crimean War continued.

This *Times* report (18 January 1940) shows how language and sentence structure were becoming shorter though the copy still lacked the directness of journalism today.

On This Day

January 18 1940

Finland was invaded by Russia in November 1939, and in spite of heroic resistance was compelled to surrender in March 1940.

FINNS' NEW SUCCESS
UNEQUAL STRUGGLE IN THE AIR

From Our Special Correspondent

Helsinki, Jan. 17

ALTHOUGH the weather is the coldest for 35 years, the Finnish ski patrols are still active and are distinguishing themselves in the Salla area, where the Russians have been driven back some 12 miles, and are still retreating, pressed by the Finnish troops. Today's communiqué states that there was patrol activity north-east of Lake Ladoga between forces of similar strength, in which the Finnish troops routed an enemy company, which lost 70 killed, two tanks, and about 100 rifles.

While the strictly military results of the Russian air raids have been comparatively small, even when attacks were made with 400 machines, the sufferings of the civilian population have been great. Although most of the houses in the provincial towns are still standing, bomb explosions have smashed thousands of windows over wide areas, so that each day more and more houses become uninhabitable in this Arctic winter with temperatures which are exceptional even for Finland.

In the village of Ryttyla, where there are no military objectives, Soviet airmen machine-gunned a funeral procession.

The size of Finland is such that it is impossible to keep the whole of it, or even the more densely populated southern and central districts, adequately supplied with anti-aircraft guns and bomb-proof cellars; but considering that even now Finnish airmen, with rather slow machines, have been able to bring down a good number of enemy aircraft is evidence that a sufficient force of quick, modern fighters is the best means of checking and ending the attacks on civilians. This need for aircraft from abroad is at present the most urgent and decisive issue, the Finns declare.

One example will show the spirit in which the nation is meeting the horrors of air warfare. In a large industrial centre, where there have been frequent air raids, the management of a certain factory asked the employees whether they would be willing to continue to work during air-raid alarms to save time and increase the output of this important factory. The men were offered an extension of their summer holidays in exchange. They answered that they agreed to work during the raids, but would not accept the reward offered them. "We are doing this," they said, "because the Russians must be beaten."

© Times Newspapers Ltd 1940

Of the first five sentences, four begin with subordinate clauses. Newspapers now adopt the opposite style, starting with the main clause except occasionally for variety. Sentence lengths are still long: the first six have 43, 37, 31, 44, 17, 79 words.

The first par. opens without any impact on a subordinate clause about the weather. If the Russians have been pushed back the phrases "are still active" and "are distinguishing themselves" are redundant.

The second sentence focuses on the communiqué "stating" rather than on the more dramatic "routing" of the enemy. The next par. also reflects the passive, low-key coverage. Rather than the active "400 planes attack" it says "attacks were made with 400 machines". Similarly, instead of "civilians have suffered greatly" it says more passively "the sufferings of the civilian population have been great".

The next sentence repeats the point about the winter coldness made at the start.

● Note the bias of the coverage. The Finns, fighting the Nazis, are represented as heroic and the sufferings of innocent civilians are highlighted. In contrast, the enemy Soviets are portrayed as ruthless warriors even machine-gunning a funeral procession. Coverage of the Soviets was to change dramatically once they changed sides following the Nazi invasion of their country.

Fifty-three years after the Second World War report, Britain was again at war, backing the United States in its attacks on Iraq. Notice how the language and sentence structure have changed.

AMERICA last night launched a second military strike against Iraq, firing 40 Tomahawk cruise missiles on a nuclear weapons facility near Baghdad.

Pentagon officials said that the computer-guided missiles had been fired from warships in the Gulf and Red Sea. The attack was made on the second anniversary of the start of the Gulf war and followed the shooting down yesterday of an Iraqi MiG fighter in the northern air exclusion zone.

In an eerie replay of January 1991, the skies over Baghdad were lit up dramatically by Iraqi searchlights, anti-aircraft fire and surface-to-air missiles, and three people were reported to have been killed in the centre of the capital. One building damaged was the al-Rashid Hotel, which was full of foreign visitors.

Marlin Fitzwater, the White House spokesman, said the attack had been designed to show President Saddam Hussein that "non-compliance with UN resolutions would not be tolerated". He said America had targeted the Zaafaraiyah plant 13 miles from the city centre, which made components for Iraq's nuclear enrichment programme, but he did not know if it had been destroyed.

Mr Fitzwater added that he did not believe an American missile had hit the al-Rashid Hotel; it was more likely to have been damaged by Iraqi anti-aircraft fire. He emphasised that the strike was primarily in response to Saddam's continued refusal to allow UN inspection planes to land in Iraq without imposing conditions that are unacceptable to Washington.

He said that "Iraq's weapons of mass destruction must be destroyed", indicating there would be further strikes if Iraq continued to defy UN resolutions. Last night the International Atomic Energy Agency said that the Zaafaraiyah plant had already been destroyed by the United Nations.

At least three civilians were killed and sixteen injured when two residential areas and the al-Rashid Hotel received direct hits. Hundreds of Islamic conference delegates and scores of foreign journalists were staying at the hotel when a missile struck the side, gutting most of the marbled lobby area and killing a manager.

Dr Abdel al-Mansouri, at the Yarmuk Hospital, said: "Most of the casualties have been admitted suffering abdominal and facial injuries from shrapnel. It is a great disappointment to me that this is happening to our people."

Amar Ismail, a survivor, from the Karada district of Baghdad, said that a missile hit his street without warning, destroying four homes. "My mother was killed in the attack, but I managed to get my neighbour out of the rubble and bring her to the hospital," he said, pointing at a young woman writhing in agony on a hospital bed.

The Iraqi government reacted angrily to the large civilian toll and accused the Americans of striking a civilian plant south of Baghdad, rather than a nuclear facility.

The Kuwait government announced after the raid that Iraq had started to dismantle six Iraqi border posts inside Kuwait territory in compliance with United Nations demands. Iraq had previously ignored all UN ultimatums for it to do so.

The attack took place after a day of growing hostilities between Iraq and the UN. Saddam said he would guarantee the safety of UN inspectors' flights into Iraq only if the UN ceased all its air operations in the air exclusion zones, but Washington said the condition was unacceptable. Later, an Iraqi soldier was killed and a second was captured after three Iraqi soldiers crossed the Kuwaiti border, where they were challenged and shot at by a Kuwaiti patrol. The third Iraqi escaped.

The Iraqi MiG was shot down in a skirmish with an American F16 yesterday morning. The Bush administration said the accident happened when Iraqi anti-aircraft guns fired at two American F16 warplanes at about 10 am, Baghdad time. Iraqi MiG aircraft began to fly in the UN-imposed exclusion zone and, shortly after 11 am, an Iraqi missile battery locked its radar onto an American F16 plane, which fired a missile at the battery. At 12.38 am an American F16 fired an air-to-air missile at an Iraqi MiG 23 inside the exclusion zone.

In a defiant 90-minute televised speech marking the second anniversary of the Gulf war, Saddam challenged both the no-fly zones. He also stated that the Iraqi MiG had not been flying in a no-fly area at all. He criticised his Arab neighbours for their "treacherous" alliance with the West and said: "Iraq will remain steadfast and will inevitably come out of the present confrontation victorious."

The attack followed intensive consultations between President Bush, John Major and President Mitterrand, his coalition partners. Mr Clinton was also kept fully informed. He said last night that Saddam Hussein's "continuing provocation has been met by appropriate and forceful response". Mr Major said Saddam had been "courting trouble – he has had trouble".

© Times Newspapers Ltd 1993

Focusing on the first pars of the front page lead story (the splash) of 18 January 1993 for analysis, sentences can be seen to be much shorter than the previous examples: 22 words, 18, 32, 38, 13, 26, 32.

Precise language and structure

Most sentences begin with the main clause, the language precise and dramatic. The intro.'s verbs are active. The opening sentence does not say: "A second military strike was launched last night by America against Iraq with 40 Tomahawk missiles being fired on a nuclear weapons facility near Baghdad."

The second par. expands on the point made in the intro., attributing the information to "Pentagon officials". Next comes a brief contextualising sentence explaining the first military strike.

Adjectives and adverbs are used sparingly in the "heavies"; different criteria apply in the tabloids. In par. 3 the adjective "eerie" is precise and carries a lot of meaning. Most sentences carry no more than one subordinate clause.

Language tone and contrasts in human interest bias

The human interest angle appears matter-of-factly here, buried in a sentence. The impact of the killings is further reduced by the use of "reported". The implication is that those reports may have been wrong and none may have died. The dramatic (rather than highly emotive and sensational) tone of the article is influenced by the focusing on the American firepower ("40 Tomahawk cruise missiles") rather than the human conse-quences of the attack (the deaths of innocent civilians). Clearly, the human interest bias of the press is not applied constantly. Different criteria apply when "our" people or "they" ("our enemy") are involved. Different language tones emerge.

The next sentence focuses on the building damaged; the people injured and killed come second. Opposite criteria would apply if "our" people had been involved.

Absence of overt comment

No overt comment is inserted into the article by the reporters. There is no relaxed, subjective, conversational element to the article. As van Dijk argues (*News as Discourse*; Lawrence Erlbaum Associates; New Jersey; 1988) the language of hard news is impersonal because, though it may be by-lined, it is essentially an institutional, bureaucratic voice. At the same time, it becomes clear that a specific bias affects the selection and arrangement of sources and facts.

Language and the impact of dominant sources

The language of the news is profoundly affected by the language, biases, jargon, tones and rhythms of the sources quoted. Here, the opening pars are based on the perspec-tive of the leading source, the White House spokesman. No attempt is made to present an alternative perspective in this crucial opening section nor embellish the phrases conveying attribution in the opening pars: "said" (par. 2), "were reported" (par. 3), "said" (par. 4, twice), "added, emphasised" (par. 5), "said" (par. 6, twice).

In contrast, the Iraqi government is said to have "reacted angrily" and "accused" (par. 10). Other "balancing" pars giving Iraqi viewpoints are confined to pars 8, 9 and 14.

Language and the personalisation of news

News often over-personalises events. But in this the press are also reflecting the bias of the politicians. Here, Fitzwater says the attack was designed to show "Saddam Hussein" that "non-compliance with UN resolutions would not be tolerated". During the Iran–Iraq war of 1980–8 Iraq (then an ally of the West) was generally referred to simply as "Iraq" or "Baghdad". The equation of "Saddam Hussein" with Iraq is histor-ically-determined. Here, *The Times* has unproblematically adopted the language of the military/government elite.

Language and the simplification process

The language of news also seeks to simplify events, to make the complex dynamics of history intelligible. The personalisation of news is part of this process. Here the traditional "who" (the Americans), "what" (attacked targets), "where" (in Iraq) and the "how" (with Tomahawks) are clear. The "why" factor is always more problematic. For instance, the origins of the US war with Iraq lie deep in the history of the Middle East with responsibilities on many sides. Fitzwater provides a dominant US perspective: it's because of "Saddam Hussein's non-compliance with UN resolutions". That is accepted uncritically by the reporters. But there are many other perspectives and language tones eliminated from this coverage. For instance, the dangers and possible illegality of attacking nuclear weapons sites are nowhere explored.

News language is concrete and non-abstract

On a more fundamental level there simply is not the space to explore the complexities and abstractions of historical factors. News language, as here, is concrete and only rarely abstract.

Just watch it, guys: *Americanisms*

G IVEN the Hollywoodisation of culture, American spellings, meanings and grammatical structures are forever seeping into our language. Many American usages have been adopted into the English language. Caucus, mass meeting, squatter, commuter, executive, teenager, can (for tin), mail and know-how, scoop, hype, mothballed, lookalike and the verbs jeopardise, corner, itemise, enthuse, engineer, bulldoze and boom all came from across the Atlantic.

But today some words and phrases still have distinctly American meanings and spellings which should not be adopted for the British press. Confusions would only arise. Special care has to be applied when computer spellcheckers provide American versions.

Most style books highlight words and phrases to avoid. The Reuter book lists 38 including:

to agree something – to agree on something	to meet with – to meet
to author – to write	ouster – dismissal
clout – influence	presently – currently
downtown – central	proponent – supporter
facility – military base, factory	rhetoric – language
fall – autumn	to sanction – to approve or to penalise
gasoline – petrol	to slate – to criticise
to gun down – to shoot	straight – successive
to hand someone a defeat – to beat	to stump – to campaign for
heist – robbery	to table – either to put forward or to propose discussion of
pay hike – pay rise	to talk with – to talk to
to hospitalize – to enter hospital	to task with – to ask to
to host a dinner – to give a dinner	to throw rocks – to throw stones
	to visit with – visit

Word play: *word invention*

ONE of the most fascinating features of journalism is the way it records society's complex language shifts and at the same time creates new words, new
meanings. Take a look at the *Longman Register of New Words – Vol. Two*
(John Ayto; Longman; Harlow; 1990) and see how many hundreds of new words are
recorded and invented every year in newspapers and magazines. Pick up any newspaper, look closely and you will see a reporter (or sub-editor responsible for the
headlines) playing with words and often inventing them. For instance, the close political links between President Bill Clinton and his wife, Hillary, gave birth to the word
"Billary".

Many new words emerge from play with well-known prefixes or suffixes. Thus the
"Euro" prefix might provoke "Euro-wimp" or "Euro-chic". The suffix "mania" has
already given birth to "Gorbymania" and "Raisamania". It could lead to talk of the
absence of "Nainamania" (Naina being the wife of President Yeltsin of Russia) or
maybe, even, Haguemania (and its absence, too).

The suffix "ite" has provoked Trotskyite, Thatcherite and even given birth to
"Clintonite", "Majorite". But "Smithite", for a supporter of the former Labour Party
leader, never emerged. Following Watergate, "gate" has given birth to "Irangate",
Iraqgate", "Squidgygate", "Bastardgate" and so on.

Just as George Orwell coined the words "doublespeak" and "newspeak", so they
have spawned endless variations: "nukespeak", "massacrespeak", "quangospeak",
"Reaganspeak". In *The Times* (3 March 1993), Benedict Nightingale, in a theatre
review, spoke of "shrinkspeak".

Many inventions come from linking two or more words together. For instance, in
his *Independent* theatre review (30 March 1993), Tristan Davies wrote: "In this tale
of girl-dates-dorks, girl-wins-loses-and-takes-back-dreamboy . . ." In her *Mail on
Sunday* column of 26 January 1992, Julie Burchill talks of a "certain insouciant watcha-
gonna-do-about-it daring".

Trade names

THERE is a long list of registered trade names which journalists can easily mistake
for generic terms. For instance, it is tempting to think that Hoover is a general
and accepted word for vacuum cleaner; but whenever it is used, the first letter
must be capped.

Other such trade names include: Aspirin, Aspro, Autocue, Band-Aid, Biro, Burberry,
Calor, Catseye (road studs), Dettol, Dictaphone, Duffel, Dunlopillo, Fibreglas
(note one "s"), Gillette, Horlicks, Jacuzzi (whirlpool bath), Jeep, Jiffy, Kleenex, Lego,
Marmite, Martini, Meccano, Plasticine, Polaroid, Portakabin, Scotchtape, Sellotape,
Tampax tampons (the two words should always be used together, and with a lower
case "t" for tampons), Tannoy, Teflon, Thermos, Vaseline, Yellow Pages.

Doing it in style?

ALL newspapers have a view about good journalistic style. This is outlined in a
document called the style book (occasionally editorial handbook or sheet) though
it is increasingly carried on screen. It will tend to focus on such elements as
spellings, punctuation, abbreviations, the use of capitals, titles, Americanisms to avoid,
the handling of quotations. That is the theory. The reality is very different.

As Keith Waterhouse notes, style books are unfortunately "often peppered with the random idiosyncrasies of editors and proprietors past and present". Moreover, there is an enormous variation in approaches to style throughout the industry. *The Times* has gone so far as to publish its own style book (*The Times English Style and Usage Guide*; Times Books; London; 1992). *The Economist* magazine has also published its style as *Economist Style Guide*; Economist Business Books; London; 1991.

The international news agency Reuters (*Handbook for Journalists*; compiled by Ian MacDowall; Butterworth–Heinemann; Oxford; 1992) and *The Independent* (*The Independent Style Book 1992*) have published theirs. Keith Waterhouse's *The Mirror's Way with Words* (Mirror Books; London; 1981) is a lively critique of the tabloid's style.

The Times style book opens with some brief general comments on brevity, abstractions, punctuation, paragraphing, quotations and headlines. It lists some "essential tools": *Collins English Dictionary* (usefully published by Rupert Murdoch's HarperCollins, of which Times Books is a division); the *Complete Plain Words*, by Sir Ernest Gowers, *A Dictionary of Modern English Usage*, by H.W. Fowler, *The Oxford Dictionary for Writers and Editors* (ODWE), *The Times Atlas of the World* (also published by Times Books); *Webster's New Geographical Dictionary* and *Who's Who*.

The bulk of the book comprises an alphabetical listing of items over 150 pages from a, an ("the fundamental rule is to use a before consonants and an before vowels"), through leper ("do not use as a metaphor or as a term of abuse") to Zambezi ("is spelt thus") and -zed ("in almost all cases use -ise ending, not -ize").

The *Guardian*'s handbook comprises 16 sections including English grammar, objectionables, capital rules, titles and personal names, terms and usage, religion, scientific terms, trade and place names, foreign, computer language and sport.

In its opening section it suggests avoiding the following:

● Ornate words and phrases: convey (take), pay tribute to (praise), seating accommodation (seats).

● Needless prepositions tacked on to verbs; check up, try out, face up to.

● Chatty style in news stories, e.g. "the Princess Royal went home to Mum last night" . . . "Maggie Thatcher had the kids round to tea."

● Conspiratorial language with its dossiers, secret files, meetings behind closed doors and leaks to the *Guardian*.

● Vague words like considerable, substantial, quite, somewhat.

● Verbiage: vast majority of, in a number of cases, in connection with, as regards.

● Unnecessary Americanisms: to contact, to pressure, to pressurise, to appeal (a verb omitting "against"), to meet with, through (as in Monday through Friday). Retain useful Americanisms, e.g. maverick.

● Foreign tags: idée fixe, raison d'être, en masse etc.

● Clichés: acid test, shambles, he hails from, crystal clear . . .

● Occupations as titles, e.g. playwright John Mortimer, barrister Lord Gifford.

● Political comment in news stories and headlines. People must be able to rely on the objectivity of our reporting.

Among the "objectionables" are charisma, due to (because of), en route, finalise, fruition, grassroots, hail from, hospitalise, inversion (such as "said Mr Blair"), nigger in the woodpile, nitty-gritty, object of the exercise, prior to, sang-froid, swoop, up till (until), upturn, walked free, wildcat strike, Xmas.

At the *Cambridge Evening News*, editor Robert Satchwell stresses the importance of all his editorial staff sticking to the style. All new recruits to the paper are sent a copy on appointment.

A response from a group of readers to a story in the paper prompted a change in the style book. Following a report on an accident involving disabled children, a number of teachers contacted the paper suggesting the coverage had presented a negative image of disability. Satchwell visited the school to meet the teachers and afterwards a section on handling of disability (on the lines of the NUJ recommendations; see page 35) was added to the style book.

In the foreword to the 58-page stylebook, Satchwell comments: "A newspaper style, like its content and design, is set with the reader firmly in mind. Coupled with continuing efforts to produce copy that is comprehensive yet concise, anything that makes the paper easier to read and understand makes it more acceptable. Anything that stops the reader in his or her tracks, raises questions, or irritates, must be bad news."

And he continues: "That is why this style book must be carefully studied and strictly followed by everyone."

On "adjectives", the style book comments: "Use sparingly. Often they import comment or inaccuracy into an otherwise factual story." On "ages" it begins: "Get them. Use them. They are an important element in most stories." On "attribution", the section includes this comment: "Only where a degree of non-attribution is a condition of getting the story is the vague 'sources' permitted and then it must be pinned to a group or body: 'Government sources . . . defence sources . . . Whitehall sources . . . security sources'. 'Sources' alone is never enough."

"Banned words" include: aggro, bonk, climaxed, hospitalised, kids, gravy train, forked out, love nest. On "contacts" it says: "The newsdesk maintains a permanent contact list which can be read by every journalist. It is vital that reporters regularly add to our records with names and home and office phone numbers of any contacts who may be useful."

On "four letter words", it comments: "Where four letter and other abusive words are germane to the story (in court cases, ill-tempered outbursts on television, etc.) they should be given as part of a directly quoted statement. Each case needs to be decided on merit so consult your department head and above."

The item on "love" advises: "Do not use 'made love' as a euphemism for sexual intercourse except where the couple involved clearly had intercourse as a physical expression of their love. The phrase is sometimes used with grotesque inappropriateness where the intercourse was forced or unnatural and where 'had intercourse' or 'had sex' is correct."

In contrast, at the *Ham & High*, in north London, production editor Sam Syres said he deliberately kept his eight-page style guide short. Journalists would not tend to remember anything longer and so much had to be made "on the hoof" in response to changing events. But the guide begins: "Some things don't change fundamentally, however, such as pleas to reporters: No misspellings, please. Incorrect renderings of accommodate, amenity, exercise, humorous, liaison, independent or any other words could result in your appointment as milk monitor."

It goes on to carry sections on "addresses", "government", "other titles", "courts", "anglicisation", "singular, plural", "hyphens", "quotation marks", "measures and numbers", "last week, this week, next week", "full points" and "acronyms" before concluding with a list of frequently misspelled words (such as "axeing", "convener", "manifestos", "protester", "supervisor" and "Zimbabwean").

While style books differ in length and focus many newspapers seem to manage without one. A sub on the *Sun* said they didn't have a style book but each sub had a manual giving advice on potential legal problems. Many local papers rely on memos from the editor and chief sub rather than a style book. A number of local papers rely on the Press Association style, with local additions included through memos from the editor.

Charles Wilson, *Daily Mirror* managing director, says style books "have ceased to be the vogue". "We all used to have one but now industry experience and reading the paper count far more. If people have any problem they speak to the chief sub."

Presentation of copy

IT is vital that all copy, whether for your college, newspaper or freelance outlet, is immaculately tidy and follows basic rules. Untidy copy is simply spiked. Freelances should particularly bear this in mind.

Copy layout rules differ slightly from newspaper to newspaper but the essential principles remain the same throughout the industry.

Copy is usually written on screen, transferred to sub-editors working on screen and only appears in "hard" form when printed out in the newspaper. When "hard" copy is presented, as by freelances without a computer disk or modem link-up arrangement with the publication, it is always typed on one side of a white A4 sheet. Hand-written copy is never accepted unless from a big Fleet Street "name" who can get away with such archaic eccentricity.

All freelances should work on personal computers where possible. PC facilities for providing corrections and clean copy are invaluable as are their easy filing systems. Always give stories file names which immediately identify them. Don't call them Document 1, Document 2 and so on. Searching through such files can be extremely time-consuming.

By-line

On the top, left-hand side of the first page goes your name. Unless otherwise stated, this will be the name on any by-line accompanying the story. Then comes an oblique stroke followed by the name of the publication.

Dateline

In the centre goes date of publication, not the date of writing. This is particularly important for weeklies or monthlies. When using words such as "yesterday" or "tomorrow" it is advisable to put the day in brackets afterwards to avoid confusions.

Catchline

At the top, right-hand corner goes the catchline. This will usually be one word that clearly identifies the story. Page one of a story about press cards will be catchlined "Card 1", page two "Card 2" and so on. Avoid using such words as "kill", "dead", "report", "story", "must", "spike", "flush", "hold", "splash", "header", "leader" which have specific meanings in newspaper jargon (see Glossary for other words to avoid).

When covering a crash, council meeting or fire don't use obvious catchlines such as "crash", "council" or "fire". Other such events may be covered by other journalists and to avoid duplication, words identifying the story's uniqueness should be used.

Copy

Your copy will begin some way down the first folio. This leaves space above the start for any sub-editorial marks. Copy typed on newspaper computers will be formatted appropriately but freelances should normally present copy with double-spaced lines. Leave wide margins on both sides of the copy and clear spaces at the top and bottom of the page. Leave a clear space between pars and never hyphenate words between lines. Never let a sentence run from one folio to another.

At the foot of each folio except the last should be "more" or "mf" (short for "more follows"), usually centred. This will normally be carried in the headers and footers/ document set-up section of the computer's page layout but freelances should reproduce this style in their copy. The story finishes with "end" centred.

By-lines, publication, date of publication and catchline will be produced at the top of each folio. Normally no large space is needed between the headers and copy on the second and any subsequent pages.

Copy should always be double checked before submission. As many corrections as possible should be done on screen but it is still possible to insert corrections on the final copy if necessary. Better that than to include mistakes. Never delete the file of your story on disk. Copy can be lost or mislaid. Sometimes you might need to refer back to a previous story. If you send a disk through the post always make a copy.

Whenever there is an unusual spelling, such as Smythe instead of Smith, or a name with possible variations, such as Dennis or Denis, put "correct" in brackets afterwards. The sub should then delete it. Convoluted foreign names should be treated similarly to make clear to the sub you were aware of the spelling issue and confirming its correctness. The sub may still double check.

● If submitting copy as a freelance, add daytime details: address and phone number along with home details. In some cases, a brief outline of your special credentials for writing the story might be appropriate. A word count is also invaluable to editors.

Example of copy

Mike Reid/ Guardian	31.08.89	Medellin 1

Colombia yesterday (Wednesday) imposed a curfew on the drug capital, Medellin, after a series of bombings and a foiled rocket attack on a fuel tank.

The municipal government imposed a 10 pm to 6 am curfew in the city that is home to the most powerful cocaine cartel.

Soldiers patrolled city streets yesterday, stopping pedestrians, searching for weapons and checking identity cards.

Medellin, Colombia's second biggest city, has been rocked by 17 bomb attacks since a group known as the Extraditables, believed to be financed by drug lords and opposing extradition to the US, declared war on the government last Thursday.

more

| Mike Reid/ Guardian | 31.08.89 | Medellin 2 |

The latest bombings early on Tuesday blew up six drink stores operating under government concessions. Police said guards at a state-owned liquor factory foiled an attack on a fuel tank by firing at three men who pulled hand-held rocket launchers from a suitcase.

Colombian leaders have firmly rejected renewed calls for talks with drug traffickers and said that President Virgilio Barco's government will continue its offensive against the cocaine trade.

"The government has not considered the possibility of a dialogue with people who have committed drug-related crimes," said Mr Carlos Lemos Simmonds, the Communications Minister who is temporarily in charge of the justice portfolio.

Mr Pablo Escobar, believed to be the richest and most powerful of the traffickers, is reported to have said this week that he is prepared to end his war with the government immediately in return for an amnesty. Otherwise, he would wage "total war . . . to the end".

The ultimatum came in an alleged conversation by radio telephone between Mr Escobar and an unidentified caller, published by the Paris newspaper Liberation on Tuesday.

End

6

Hitting them hard
News reporting

∙∙

FOR the purposes of simplicity, let's say hard news is the reporting of issues or events in the past or about to happen. It's largely based on selected details and quotations in direct or indirect speech.

Hard news begins with the most striking details and thereafter information progressively declines in importance. Some background details may be needed to make the news intelligible but description, analysis, comment and the subjective "I" of the reporter are either excluded or included only briefly.

Hard news differs from a range of newspaper genres which include:

- *soft news*: the news element is still strong and prominent at or near the opening but is treated in a lighter way. Largely based on factual detail and quotations, but the writing is more flexible and there is likely to be more description and comment. The tone, established in the intro. section, might be witty or ironic. Notions of hard and soft news emerged in the last century: the first, linked to notions of accuracy, objectivity, neutrality, was for conveying information; the second was more an entertainment genre.

- *news feature*: usually longer than a straight news story. The news angle is prominent, though not necessarily in the opening paragraph/s, and quotations are again important. Can contain description, comment, analysis, background historical detail, eye-witness reporting and a wider/deeper coverage of the issues and range of sources. A "timeless" feature, in contrast, has no specific news dimension (for instance, it might be about mending holes in roofs).

- *backgrounder*: emphasis here not so much on the news but on explaining the news or setting the scene for an event about to happen. Might focus on historical background and/or seek to explain range of issues and personalities involved. A retrospective is a similar feature looking back at an event.

- *colour feature*: an article of feature length concentrating on description, eye-witness reporting, quotations, and the build-up of factual details. Can also contain historical background material. Need not have a strong news angle.

Going straight to the point

Intro.

The intro. (known in America as the lead or nose, and in France as the attaque) is the most important par. since it has to draw the reader into the story by creating a sense of urgency and exciting their interest. It should highlight the main theme or angle of the story and set the tone.

When a reader surveys a newspaper page there are a few major foci for attention: pictures, headlines, intros, and picture captions. Their grammatical style and content set the tone and character of the whole paper.

Choosing the best angle (or news peg in America) is one of the biggest challenges for a journalist. Reporters often find once the opening angle has been "bashed out" the rest "writes itself". A good intro. also helps the sub-editor to think of a suitable headline more quickly.

The famous five Ws

"Who", "what", "where", "when", and "why" are the famous five intro. Ws. In addition, some stories have a "how" element. But the intro. should not seek to answer all of these questions: it would be overloaded with words. Usually the intro. defines the news angle by selecting two or three of these questions. The rest of the story may go on to answer some of the others.

Take this story from *The Voice* (13 April 1993):

> **A** 15-year-old schoolboy drowned in a swimming pool while he was on work experience at a leisure centre.

Who: A 15-year-old schoolboy

What: drowned

Where: in a swimming pool

When: while he was on work experience at a leisure centre.

Here is an intro. from *The Times* (15 April 1993):

> **P**RISONERS are being routinely handcuffed and chained when they visit the lavatories at one of London's busiest crown courts because security is so inadequate.

Who: Prisoners

What: are being routinely handcuffed and chained

When: when they visit the lavatories

Where: at one of London's busiest crown courts

Why: because security is so inadequate.

Here is an intro. from the *Daily Mirror* (20 April 1993):

> R AMPAGING youths hurled rocks and firebombs at police yesterday during the funeral of black South African leader Chris Hani.

Who: Rampaging youths

What: hurled rocks and firebombs at police

When: yesterday during the funeral of black South African leader Chris Hani.

Main clause

Most news stories begin with the main clause as in these three examples. This is because the "who" and the "what" tend to be the most important. Readers don't want to wade through dull details, background or comment before arriving at the main point.

Thus, the *Mirror* journalist did not write:

> The murder of ANC leader Chris Hani has provoked fears of mass unrest in South Africa as blacks confront police across the country. Yesterday the crisis escalated when youths hurled rocks and firebombs at police during Hani's funeral.

Such an intro. delays the impact of the news opening with an unnecessary scene-setting sentence.

People

News often tends to focus on the human angle. Thus, if you were a news agency reporter covering the IRA attack on the Conservative Party conference in 1984 it would have been poor to write:

> The Grand Hotel, Brighton, was rocked today by a Provisional IRA bomb attack during the Conservative Party conference but Mrs Thatcher escaped unhurt.

The focus needed to be on the fate of the Prime Minister. The angle could not wait until the end of the first sentence:

> Premier Mrs Thatcher narrowly escaped an assassination attempt today after the Provisional IRA bombed the Grand Hotel, Brighton, where she was staying for the annual Conservative Party conference.

Given the choice between the structural damage to a hotel and the fate of the Prime Minister, the second provides the better angle.

Descriptions/titles

People in the news are always accompanied by a title or description. The reader needs to know on what authority or on what basis they are speaking. Thus a story might begin "President Clinton last night criticised . . .". Or "PLO chairman Yasser Arafat yesterday condemned . . .".

People with long titles provide problems for intros. They can clutter them up with words. For instance: "Mr Doug McAvoy, general secretary of the National Union of Teachers, yesterday claimed . . .". One way round this problem is to use a phrase such as "The leader of a teachers' union yesterday claimed . . .". Then in the next par. or sentence you might give the name and title.

The description of the person in the news does not have to be a formal title such as secretary, MP, councillor, director. It can be looser, for instance "of the Green Party", or "who witnessed the rail crash", or "author Nadine Gordimer". Here, the *East Anglian Daily Times* (2 April 1993) intros on a descriptive phrase, delaying the name until par. 2:

A N INTERPRETER for the deaf and dumb who spent her lifetime campaigning on behalf of charity has died.

Mabel Palmer, 61, of St Martin's Street, Bury St Edmunds, was honorary secretary of the West Suffolk Deaf Association for 45 years, regularly organising fund-raising events and charity outings.

Timing

(a) News is rooted in time, the more up to date the better. Thus the "when" element ("yesterday", "last night", "earlier today", "earlier this week" etc.) is crucial in many hard news intros. Morning newspapers, through their various editions, mostly focus on the events of the previous day and plans/warnings/forecasts of future events. Weeklies mix a review of the previous week's events with up-to-date news and pointers to the future. Dailies tend to focus on the latest "hot" news and can change stories through editions as the day progresses. "Stop press" columns give the news just before the paper is printed.

This emphasis on "newness" is commercially driven. The hotter the news the more sellable it is. As the new technology of satellites and video cameras brings "as-it-happens" news to the television screens, expectations for "newness" of the media-consuming public increase.

Intros hardly ever begin with the basic "when" words such as "last night", "yesterday", "earlier this week". Occasionally when the timing is significant it should be highlighted, as here, from *The Independent* (15 April 1993):

> TWENTY months after the hardline coup attempt in Moscow, the trial of the 12 main figures behind it finally began yesterday and immediately the defendants challenged the validity of the court and the probity of the prosecutor, Valentin Stepankov.

Usually, it is not necessary to be precise over the "when" in the intro. Do not say: "Mrs Gandhi, the Indian Prime Minister, was assassinated by Sikh bodyguards at 2.59 am today." Sufficient to report "earlier today". The precise detail can be added later. (b) Another, popular way of conveying news urgency is used here in *Q News* (16–23 April 1993):

> A BBC programme depicting British Muslims as pimps, drug dealers and criminals has provoked nationwide response from community leaders and activists. Five solicitors and a barrister in Huddersfield are suing the BBC over its Panorama programme *Underclass in Purdah* which was screened on 29 March.

and in the *Ilford Recorder* (11 March 1993):

> **By Caroline Jones**
>
> A DESPERATE mother is appealing for help to find her 30-year-old mentally ill daughter who disappeared nearly two weeks ago.
>
> Joy Hounsell, 60, of West Road, Chadwell Heath, said her daughter Tracey usually phoned every day and had never gone away without telling anyone before.
>
> Tracey suffers from schizophrenia and needs regular medication. Without it she becomes very confused and starts hearing voices.
>
> She disappeared from her home in Oglethorpe Road, Dagenham, in the early hours of February 28 with only £5 in her purse. Three days earlier she skipped her vital fortnightly injection.

This eliminates the specific "when" element from the first sentence. It can be carried later on in the story. But weeklies often eliminate specific "when" references since phrases such as "last Wednesday" and "early last week" reduce the news impact.

Where

Local papers will often include the "where" element prominently in the intro. since it stresses the local angle. Thus the *Stamford Mercury* (19 February 1993) had this among numerous examples:

> PENSIONERS are becoming too scared to open their doors and are demanding more police on the beat after the latest in a series of "despicable robberies" in Stamford and Deeping.

National papers may sometimes delay mention of the "where" to add an element of vagueness and encourage everyone from all over the country to read on, as here in the *Sun* (31 March 1993):

> COP Alistair Shields stole £870 from a Christmas party fund meant for colleagues' kids.
>
> He got two trusting civilian staff to sign blank cheques from the fund, of which he was treasurer.
>
> But the PC, based in Aylesbury, Bucks, was caught when he tried to pay back £120 with a bouncing cheque.
>
> Married father-of-two Shields, 39, escaped jail at Aylesbury Crown Court yesterday.
>
> The judge heard he had quit the force, lost his police house and faces a reduced pension. He was sentenced to three months suspended.

Most foreign stories carry the "where" prominently as here in the *Guardian* (20 April 1993):

> **Simon Tisdall in Waco and**
> **Martin Walker in Washington**
>
> A VAST funeral pyre whose smoke spread darkly over the Texas plains brought a violent end to the 51-day siege of Waco yesterday, as the Branch Davidian cult of David Koresh died in a biblical holocaust of fire.
>
> Simon Tisdall and Martin Walker ©
> the *Guardian*

When the "where" element is particularly significant it is worth starting the story with it, as in this report in the *Observer* (4 April 1993):

Bonn
Tony Catterall

I N A book that has broken publishing records, former Chancellor Helmut Schmidt castigates German politicians for "inadequate leadership" after reunification and warns his fellow countrymen in the West that they must accept lower incomes for years to come.

Tony Catterall the *Observer* ©
Published by permission of the *Observer* ©

Brevity

As the chapter on language identified, intros should be written as concisely as possible. The maximum number of words you should be thinking about for the first sentence is 30, though intros in the broadsheets will tend to be longer than in the populars and local papers.

The average wordage in the 16 news stories in *The Independent*'s first two pages was 29 (though the longest had 48 words and the shortest 10). In the *Daily Express* of the same day, the average in the 13 stories on the first two pages was 21 (but one had 10 and the longest had 30). The 16 stories in the *Cambridge Evening News*' first three news pages averaged 16 words (shortest 11, longest 32).

Brightness

While always remaining true to the style of your publication, be as bright as possible. Try to use active verbs and strong nouns.

Take this intro. from the London *Evening Standard* (14 April 1993): a "deluge of criticism", "descended", "call to arms", "slaughter" all carry impact.

A DELUGE of criticism descended on Baroness Thatcher today as the Government warned that her call to arm Bosnia's Moslems would only be a recipe for yet more slaughter.

Popular papers tend to heighten the sensational, emotional content by adding adjectives and adverbs. Take this par. from the *Sunday Mirror* (21 March 1993):

KINKY Howard Smith last night boasted of his sex games with the beautiful wife who wanted him dead.

"Kinky" and "beautiful" are clichés, aiming to add to the sexy, sensational element. But adjectives and adverbs often carry strong ideological value judgements. Here from the *Mail on Sunday* (26 January 1992):

> GLENYS KINNOCK will stand the General Election heat better than Norma Major, Labour chiefs believe.
>
> So in a high-risk move, they will effectively focus their campaign on personalities.

The adjective "high-risk" reflects the paper's political bias.

Quotations

Lively and controversial comments provide material for many intros. But hard news hardly ever begins with direct quotes. There is a "softness" about a direct quote which is felt more appropriate to "soft" news, news features or profiles.

Such a convention is not universal. In France, hard news stories commonly begin with direct quotes, as here from *Le Monde* (23 April 1993). Two other hard news stories in the same edition began in a similar way.

> **Belgrade**
> **de notre correspondante**
>
> *" Il s'agit d'une mission sérieuse à un moment très difficile (. . .) où les hommes politiques doivent prendre leur décision."*
>
> Lord Owen, le médiateur européen qui copréside la Conférence de paix sur l'ex-Yougoslavie, est venu, mercredi 21 avril, à Belgrade pour tenter une nouvelle fois de convaincre les Serbes de signer le plan de paix pour la Bosnie. En cas de refus, les sanctions votées dimanche par les Nations unies et visant à isoler totalement la nouvelle Yougoslavie (Serbie et Monténégro) deviendraient effectives le 26 avril.

Notice, too, how French newspapers often highlight direct quotations by using the italic, sloping typeface. There is no such convention in Britain.

Now look at this article from the *Herts and Essex Observer* (25 February 1993):

> COMMUTERS in Bishop's Stortford this week called the Government's plan to privatise British Rail "a recipe for disaster."

The reporter did not write: "'A recipe for disaster'. That's how commuters in Bishop's Stortford this week described the Government's plan to privatise British Rail." Such copy separating the quote from the attribution would be too disjointed.

Direct quotes are often reserved for a second or third par. which makes a strong back up to the first par., expanding the opening theme.

But quotation marks are inserted around words and phrases to highlight them and indicate attribution as here, from the *Evening Standard* (12 March 1993):

> THE great institutions of Britain – the monarchy, parliament, church and the judiciary – are being damaged by "a fierce wind" of criticism and abuse, Douglas Hurd warned today.

Sometimes individual words or short phrases have inverted commas around them without being attributed. This happens usually with colourful/significant words or phrases conveying opinion which the inverted commas imply will be later attributed. Inclusion of the attribution in the intro. would overload it.

Take this intro. from the *Cambridge Evening News* (18 March 1993):

> A MAN stabbed a teenager four times after he was "goaded" into a fight, a court heard.

That quote "goaded" is later attributed to the assistant recorder at Peterborough Crown Court, Stephen Tomlinson.

Attribution

Opinion is nearly always attributed clearly in the intro. par. Thus *The Independent* (27 March 1993):

> ANTI-MAASTRICHT Tories should either cease their filibustering or form their own party, Sir Edward Heath, the former Conservative prime minister, said yesterday, writes Patricia Wynn Davies.

And look at these pieces from the *Liverpool Echo* (15 May 1992):

> THE Royal Family's reputation with the public is at an all-time low, a BBC poll claims tonight.

A NEW £28m youth training plan will be a surefire hit with young people, said Radio One DJ Simon Mayo.

This attribution rule is particularly important when covering allegations and counter claims in court cases. But it is occasionally broken, most often when the views or findings are considered uncontroversial and amount to "fact" in the eyes of the paper. As here from the *Sunday Mirror* (21 March 1993):

E ACH day in Britain, an astonishing 52,000 men, women and children suffer some form of sports injury.
The staggering total – 19 **MILLION** injuries a year – costs the hard-pressed National Health Service £240 million to put right.
The shock findings, to be announced by the Sports Council on Tuesday, come as the rugby world is reeling from the death of player Seamus Lavelle.

Tenses

B RITISH Rail is being manipulated by the Government in the current dispute, the Rail, Maritime and Transport union claimed last night.

The *Guardian* report (19 April 1993) begins with the present tense "is". Normally with such words as "warned", "said", "declared", "indicated", "criticised", the accompanying clauses follow the rules of reported speech and move back one tense into the past. An intro. is one place where these rules are often ignored. This gives an extra sense of urgency to the report. Similarly, headlines are usually in the present tense though they report events which happened in the past.

Magnitude

Wherever possible stress the magnitude of any event. The numbers of people, objects, buildings, or amount of money involved will often be highlighted in intros. Here is an example from *The Independent* (2 April 1993):

O NE OF the country's longest serving prisoners alleges that file documents have been stolen from the Director of Public Prosecutions Office and passed to him in an attempt to help prove his innocence.

Some errors to avoid

Questions

Hard news intros do not start with questions just as question marks hardly ever occur in news headlines. Intros are for informing readers, not interrogating them. Occasionally questions can open features and "soft" news stories.

The "There is" cliché

Avoid beginning stories "There was" or "There is" or "There will be". This is dead copy delaying the appearance of the real news.

So don't report: "There was a riot in Bow, East London, last night in which four policemen and two youths were injured."

Better to say: "Two youths and four policemen were injured in riots in Bow, East London, last night."

Label intros

These are drab sentences showing no news sense. A good intro. will do more than say "a meeting was held", "a speech was given", "a report was published". "Mr Yeltsin gave a long speech at the United Nations in New York yesterday covering issues as diverse as the threat to the rain forests and nuclear disarmament," is too vague.

A better angle would be more specific: "President Yeltsin yesterday called on the world community to introduce a 50 per cent arms trade tax to fight poverty in the Third World.

"In a wide-ranging, 50-minute speech to the United Nations in New York, he said . . ."

Present participles

Intro. sentences starting with present participles are to be avoided e.g. "Referring to the Ethiopian famine, Bob Geldof . . . " or "Criticising the government for 'monumental ineptitude', Mr William Hague . . ." Better to say: "Millions face starvation in Ethiopia, Bob Geldof warned . . . " and "The government was accused of 'monumental ineptitude' by Mr William Hague . . ."

Unidentified pronoun

Opening with a subordinate clause is particularly poor when there is an unidentified pronoun, as in: "With what his colleagues described as a clarion call to the party, Paddy Ashdown . . ."

Negatives

There is always a way to avoid using negatives. For instance, instead of: "The Foreign Office would today neither confirm nor deny that two British pilots had been released," say: "The Iraqis are reported to have freed two British pilots but the Foreign Office is non-committal."

Numerals

Sentences never begin with numerals. Don't say: "5 people were injured after a Rolls-Royce collided with two stray pigs in Oakdown last night." Instead: "Five people were . . ."

Varieties of hard news intro.

OME of the 68 – and more – varieties of intro. include:

"Clothesline" intro.

So-called because everything is hung on it. For instance: "Lady Godiva rode naked through the streets of Coventry today in an attempt to cut taxes." This contains the six basic ingredients: "who", "what", "where", "when", "why", and "how".

Immediate identification intro.

Used where the person concerned is so important or newsworthy that their presence is the main part of the story. For instance: "Mr Blair made a sponsored jump from a plane at RAF Brize Norton today and wrecked a three-ton truck after his parachute failed to open." It would be wrong to say: "A three-ton truck was wrecked after Mr Blair's parachute failed to open while he was making a sponsored jump at RAF Brize Norton today."

Delayed identification intro.

Used where the person involved is not inherently newsworthy but has become so because of what he or she has done or said. Thus the *Ilford Recorder* (11 March 1993) reported:

MAN accused of murder told a court he had no memory of stabbing to death the woman he loved after finding her in bed with another man.

Clifford Chester, 33, stabbed Mrs Susan Brix through the heart after catching her with a work colleague at her flat in Fullwell Avenue, Barkingside, the Old Bailey heard.

Mr Roger Tyack, from Swindon, only survived the savage onslaught after emergency surgery, it was said.

The prosecution claims Chester had yelled at his mistress: "If I can't have you, nobody's going to."

"Summary" intro.

This is used when the reporter, faced with a number of competing angles none of which stands out, settles for a generalised angle.

Thus: "President Clinton presented a revolutionary package of disarmament proposals to a historic session of the United Nations General Assembly yesterday."

"Single element" intro.

This contrasts with the summary intro. and is used when one angle is particularly strong and needs highlighting.

Thus: "President Chirac, of France, called the arms race a 'crime against humanity which must be halted' at a meeting of the United Nations General Assembly yesterday (Monday)."

"Bullet" or *"staccato"* intro.

This is used when the main point can be covered very briefly. For instance: "The New World Order is dead – and that's official."

"Personalised" intro.

Generally news excludes the "I" of the journalist. It suggests too much subjectivity. The personalised intro. subverts that convention and places the "I" at the centre of the action. The journalist witnessing the event carries its own newsworthiness. Thus, the *Daily Mail* reported (5 September 1990):

From the Mail's
DAVID GARDNER
on the escape convoy

I JOINED the weary convoy of British women and children on their trek from Kuwait to Baghdad last night.

The 148 women and 155 children arrived in the Iraqi capital exhausted from a 15-hour journey through the blistering desert heat.

There was no jubilation at the prospect of being one step nearer to freedom. Only despondency at having to leave their men behind in Kuwait.

I stopped one of the seven coaches on the last leg of its journey to Baghdad, heading for the three hotels where the families spent the night before trying to fly home today.

Gruelling

Despite the air-conditioning, the coach was appallingly stuffy. Drink cans littered the floor. The children were silent after the 750-mile journey, where no-one was able to use the toilet for 12 hours at a time.

© *Daily Mail*/Solo

"Comment" intro.

News often has the appearance of objectivity when, in fact, it is the journalist commenting. From the *News of the World* (19 April 1992):

By Political Editor
IAIN MACASKILL

N EW Employment Secretary Gillian Shephard has only been in the hot seat a week – but already she looks just the job to ensure bosses give youngsters a fair deal.

The phrase "she looks just the job" is opinion reflecting the bias of the paper.

"Punning" intro.

This is found particularly in the "pops" and some local newspapers (see also Chapter 5). It provides brightness to the copy. Names of television programmes, stars, or films and well-known vernacular phrases are often used. As here from the *Sunday Mirror* (21 March 1993):

> THE beautiful young wife of 'Allo 'Allo creator Jeremy Lloyd is threatening to say "G'bye G'bye" to him.

Narrative intro.

This is used when the unusual aspect can best be conveyed through a brief chronology of events. Here, *The Independent* (23 October 1991) begins with a staccato summary (showing a legitimate use of the "There is ..." opening) and then moves quickly on to the narrative:

> BONN – There were red faces among Germany's police yesterday. First they allowed four armed and dangerous criminals to cruise out of their high-security prison, having placed a car at their disposal, as well as DM2m (£689,000) in used notes. Then they lost all trace of them, writes John Eisenhammer.

Intros – soft news

SOFT news stories have the news element at or near the opening. But the news is treated more colourfully and some of the "rules" of hard news reporting outlined above are broken to provide a "softer" feel to the copy.

Direct quotation

Starting with a direct quote "softens" the story as here, from *The Independent* (2 April 1993):

> "WE MIGHT have to fix that. I think John Knox is marginally higher up than St Patrick." This was one of the final worries of staff putting the finishing touches to a new £6m museum of religious life and art which opens in Glasgow today. The city is claiming the new museum to be the world's first based solely on humanity's struggle to find a meaning for life.

Questions

Beginning with a question mark "softens" the story as here from the *Daily Mirror* (24 April 1993), crudely exploiting the racist anti-Irish joke syndrome:

Cops see through hold-up

HEARD the one about the Irish bank robber who wore his bala-clava mask back to front?

When he pulled it down he couldn't see to point his dummy gun at the cashier and nearly died laughing.

It's no joke really . . . it happened at a branch of Lloyds in Luton, Beds.

But police were lying in wait and nabbed John Hegarty and accomplice Edward Copeland, both 23.

Yesterday both men admitted robbery and possessing an imitation firearm. Ringleader Copeland was jailed for 13 years. Hegarty got nine.

Delayed drop intro.

Delaying the main angle is difficult to achieve and needs to be handled with caution. It works by arousing the reader's sense of curiosity and will fail if the reader is not curious to know how it all ends. It is best used when something unusual has happened and the reader is kept in suspense before being let into the secret. Here from the *Guardian* (1 April 1993) a colourful human interest background section precedes the news which comes in par. 4 ("Today . . .")

GWILYM Lewis's father was a man of few, prophetic words. "Very dangerous, young man," he said when Gwilym announced that he intended to join the Royal Flying Corps and fly its open-cockpit contraptions of Irish linen and braced wire. So it proved. But the boy survived to shoot down 12 enemy aircraft, which qualified him as an ace.

When the first world war ended, his father had another forecast. "You've been the cat's whiskers, rightly so," he said, "but you'll be forgotten so quickly it will hurt."

Gwilym took the point and never flew again, unlike others of his generation who tried to prolong the excitement with civilian flying. And he and they were largely forgotten, until people began to make films about those magnificent men in their flying machines.

Today, he and his one-time generation of 25,000 young men are remembered and honoured as 21 of the 50 still alive are saluted by the Queen at RAF Marham in Norfolk. The event – commemorating the 75th anniversary of the formation of the RFC's successor, the Royal Air Force – marshals 148 aircraft in a great flypast.

© the *Guardian*

"Eye-witness" human interest

As here, from the *Guardian* (3 February 1992) where the reporter focuses on "a small blonde child" before looking in more detail at the educational project:

Lesson in playing safe at schools

David Ward, Northern Education Correspondent

A SMALL blonde child with an angelic expression starts to skip and everyone chants:

"*Cinderella dressed in yeller,*
Went upstairs to kiss her feller.
How many kisses did she get?"

The rope keeps the child's enthusiasm under control and trips her at the fourth kiss.

It's a quiet day in the playground and Ann Broughton looks on with some satisfaction. She has helped turn lunchtime play at Newall Green infants' school in Manchester from mayhem to innocent frolic, and now stars in a training video to help other schools do the same.

The video and a training pack, launched this week, is the work of Gill Fell (sole proprietor of Strategies for a Less Violent Environment), who was financed mainly by the Rowntree Trust and Manchester city council's education committee. "As a frequent visitor to primary schools ... I felt some form of training for lunchtime staff could help

reduce playground violence and raise the status and self-esteem of lunchtime organisers."

Teams of organisers were created after the 1980s disputes when teachers withdrew lunchtime cover. Non-teaching staff took over, and so the dinner lady often became lunchtime organiser.

"There are now 150,000 of them," said Gill Fell. "They are not well paid. Most have had no training and were being asked to do the impossible. In some schools they were treated as nobodies whose role was to stop the children killing each other."

Ms Fell has worked in 14 Manchester schools, giving up to five hours training in each. She suggested ways to make school mealtimes more bearable for all, for introducing peaceful playground activities and for dealing with the ultimate school nightmare: a wet playtime.

"All this works best when there is a whole school approach, with lunchtime organisers and teachers working together," said Ms Fell.

That's how they do it at Newall Green, where Ann Broughton has been senior lunchtime organiser for more than two years. "We have been teaching the children to play and part of Gill's work was to get the team of ladies who work with me to remember games they used to play," she said.

"Wet days are a delight now," said the head, Marsha Grime. "We have switched from containment to a constructive use of time."

David Ward © the *Guardian*

Keep it flowing, keep it clear: *structuring a news story*

NEWS stories, whether of 5 or 35 pars, are formed through the linking of thematic sections. The reader progresses through them in order of importance, except on those few occasions when the punch line is delayed for dramatic reasons. The journalist's news sense comes into operation not only for the intro. but throughout the story.

Who is the most important person to quote? Who is the next most important person? What details should be highlighted and which left to the end or eliminated? How much background information is required and where is it best included? All these questions are answered according to a set of news values held by the reporter.

Thematic sections

SPEED is the essence of news reading just as it is of news gathering. Information should flow logically and easily through copy, the structure being so refined it is invisible to the reader. Only when a story is badly organised, with confusing chronology, say, or jumbled up quotes, does the reader become aware of any structure.

Opening section

Intro. pars tend to highlight the news angle. Second and often third pars can expand on intro. angles giving extra important information. There is an urgency about hard copy which should be maintained throughout the story but particularly in the opening pars. Unnecessary background information, comment and description should not be allowed to delay the dramatic flow of the copy.

Take these opening pars from the *Evening Post*, Nottingham (25 January 1992):

Labour 'dig own grave'

ATORY minister claimed that two Labour marginal seats in Notts would fall – through job losses resulting from their own election pledges.

> Employment Secretary Michael Howard said Nottingham North and Mansfield would both be hit by an average 3,750 job losses because of Labour policy pledges.
>
> He said Labour plans to introduce a minimum wage and a "job tax" of 0.5% of payroll levied on all employers would cause widespread unemployment.
>
> He added their plans to introduce the EC Social Charter – which the government rejected at Maastricht – would also hit jobs.
>
> "Those three policies would have an appalling effect on Britain's economic performance – and on people's employment prospects."
>
> Nottingham North MP Graham Allen, who has a majority of 1,665, immediately invited Mr Howard to address the unemployed in his constitutuency to debate the matter.

The intro. highlights the claim of a "minister". The second par. gives the name and title of the minister, identifies the two seats and the precise figure of job losses mentioned in the intro.

> A BURY ST Edmunds RAF widow has slammed the BBC for showing a programme which she says is an insult to the memories of the men killed in the Gulf War.
>
> Mrs Deborah Bowles has joined with 16 other recent RAF widows to condemn the BBC's new series "Friday on My Mind".
>
> The second episode of the programme, about a war widow who has a relationship with an RAF grief counsellor, will be shown tonight.

These three pars from the *Bury Free Press* (22 May 1992) show similar news values at work. The first par. summarises the story, with references to "a Bury St Edmunds RAF widow" and "a programme". The next par. continues the dramatic news flow adding the precise information "Mrs Deborah Bowles" and the title of the programme "Friday on My Mind". It adds to the news impact by reporting the widow was joined by 16 others in her complaint.

Par. 3 gives important background information before the reporter launches into a substantial section of direct quotes. To have placed par. 3 as par. 2 would have disturbed the dramatic flow.

● The second par. can be used to introduce a new, though connected item rather than expand the intro. The report needs to return quickly to the opening angle to save it from being left hanging in the air. For instance:

> **B**ILL CLINTON has completed his selection of the most diverse Cabinet in U.S. history by appointing the country's first woman law chief.
>
> The President-elect also picked a fourth black and a second Hispanic to join his top team.
>
> Zoe Baird, currently general counsel for the insurance company Aetna Life & Casualty, will be his Attorney General.
>
> Black representative Mike Espy was named Mr Clinton's secretary for agriculture while former major of Denver Federico Pena, a Hispanic, will be responsible for transport issues.

This report from the *Daily Mail* (26 December 1992) shifts to a new but linked angle in par. 2. The third par. expands on the intro. while par. 4 fills in details relating to the second par.

Later sections: the inverted pyramids concept

Traditional analysis of news stories stresses the notion of the inverted pyramid with the most important elements at the top and the least important (often defined as background) briefly at the bottom.

This notion is useful for stories based in the main on one source. For the vast majority it oversimplifies the writing process. News values operate throughout the individual sections while background can occur anywhere in a news story. Sometimes when a story is unintelligible without background information it will occur high up.

News stories are usually made up from a mix of quotes (in direct and indirect speech), factual details, background information and occasionally brief analysis, comment, description. Each of these elements usually comprise separate thematic sections. Within each section news values apply: the most important comes first, the least important last.

Instead of a single inverted pyramid it is more useful to think of a series of inverted pyramids within an overall inverted pyramid (see Figure 6.1).

Section structure

Each section will tend to begin with its main subject and most newsy elements associated with it. This could be the most important quote (in direct or indirect speech) or detail.

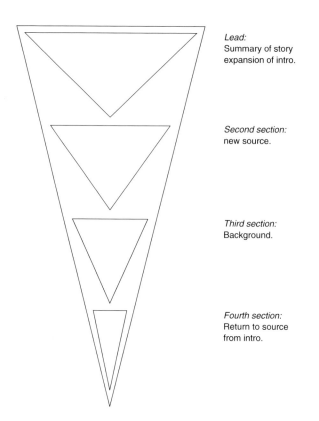

Lead:
Summary of story
expansion of intro.

Second section:
new source.

Third section:
Background.

Fourth section:
Return to source
from intro.

Figure 6.1 The inverted pyramids concept

Section structure

Each section will tend to begin with its main subject and most newsy elements associated with it. This could be the most important quote (in direct or indirect speech) or
detail.

Take this report from the *News of the World* (19 April 1992):

3 held over Julie killing

ARMED police yesterday arrested three men for the murder of English tourist Julie Stott.

One of the men tried to grab a gun as the undercover cops swooped on their hideout in a run-down New Orleans housing estate.

Last night Julie's body was being brought back to Manchester by her grieving parents Ray and Margaret. When she was told of the arrests, Mrs Stott said: "Thank God. But it will not bring our girl back."

Robert Jones, 19, was charged with

first degree murder – which carries the death penalty in Louisiana.

Christopher Border, 18, and David Oliver, 19, were charged with being accessories.

Jones also faces kidnap, rape and armed robbery charges arising from separate incidents.

Cocaine

Design director Julie, 27, was shot by a mugger on Tuesday when she and boyfriend Peter Ellis, 27, were held up in the city's French quarter.

New Orleans police spokesman Barry Fletcher said reward offers – including $10,000 from our sister paper The Sun – attracted vital information.

Detectives believe the motive for the robbery to get cash to buy crack-cocaine.

A policeman who took part in yesterday's raid said: "We have three scared punks and they could be executed for this."

Lieutenant L.J. Canal, who led the raid, said: "This crime fills the criteria here for a death sentence.

"If they're found guilty then they would be executed by lethal injection."

The sectional structure is clear:

Section 1: pars 1 and 2 – details of arrest

Section 2: par. 3 – response of parents, news element being stressed with "last night" reference.

Section 3: pars 4–6 – details of the three men charged.

Section 4: par. 7 – background detail on mugging.

Section 5: pars 8–12 – police reaction. First par. identifies source ("New Orleans police spokesman Barry Fletcher") and highlights newsy element of money given by "sister paper" to the reward offer.

Notice how this conforms to hard news conventions, built around factual details, dramatic content ("arrested", "murder", "tried to grab", "swooped", "shot by a mugger") and quotes. Comment, description, analysis are missing.

Take this report from the *Liverpool Daily Post* (23 May 1992):

By David Rose
Political Editor

JUNIOR Health Minister Tom Sackville yesterday raised hopes of a reprieve for a Liverpool hospital's casualty department which is threatened with closure.

He told MPs Liverpool Health Authority was reviewing the future of the unit at Broadgreen.

And the minister said they were bound to take account of the views of local family doctors and the community health council.

His announcement came after Liverpool Broadgreen's new MP, Jane Kennedy, used her maiden speech to plead the case for the casualty department to remain open.

While Liverpool's population was still in decline, she said the numbers living around the hospital were stable and would be increased by new housing.

And the Labour MP said that after the Government's health reforms, which has seen Liverpool hospitals opting out to become independent trusts, there was a need for a period of stability.

She said: "Staff are tired and worn out

by constant reorganisation the uncertainty is undermining morale."

Mr Sackville said a study on the future of the casualty department had been ordered and would be considered by the health authority.

Alan Doran, chief executive of the Liverpool Health Authority, said a paper had been prepared outlining plans for all local hospitals.

"We are now following that up by looking at the detailed implications of that report.

"We will be talking to everyone and there will obviously be full public consultation," added Mr Doran.

The thematic sections are clear:

Section 1: Pars 1–3 – views of Junior Health Minister.

Section 2: Pars 4–7 – views of Labour MP Jane Kennedy.

Section 3: Par. 8 – return to views of Health Minister.

Section 4: Pars 9–11 – views of Liverpool Health Authority chief executive.

The story has a simple structure built around quotes, in direct and indirect speech, from the three people, reported in order of news value. A more detailed analyis will highlight other aspects of story structure.

Par. 1: intro. sets the hard news tone. The emphasis is on factual detail (who, what, when); on concise, dramatic language and an absence of descriptive colour, analysis and background.

Who – Junior Health Minister Tom Sackville (his ministerial status gives extra authority and news value to his comments).

When – yesterday.

What – raised hopes of a reprieve for a Liverpool hospital's casualty department which is threatened with closure.

The use of the phrase "raised hopes of a reprieve" stresses the positive angle and is more colourful than "said a casualty department could be saved from closure". The local angle is stressed with the reference to Liverpool. The phrase "which is" might have been cut but its inclusion does not grate.

Par. 2: expands opening par.: par. 1 is dramatic but vague. This par. flows naturally from the first explaining why hope has been raised.

"He told MPs", in effect, provides the "where" to the story. The minister was speaking in Parliament but the reporter has written this in shorthand form.

After the verb "told" reported speech conventions are followed with "was reviewing". "Unit" avoids repetition of "casualty department" while "Broadgreen" spells out its name.

Par. 3: this par. finally clarifies the intro. angle on "raising hopes" since local views, presumably opposed to closure, will be taken into account in the review. It also identifies the story as being the latest in a series focusing on the threat to the casualty department. The reader has to presume local opinion is opposed to the closure plans – background filling in this detail might have been included but the emphasis is on the news of the Labour MP's House of Commons plea and the minister's response. Background information is, accordingly, eliminated. Notice there is no need for the word "that" after "said".

Par. 4: "His announcement came after" is a useful link phrase to introduce a new source. It shows how news values often disturb chronology. The minister spoke after the Labour MP but his views are considered more newsworthy and come first. The link phrase indicates the chronological connection.

This par. opens the second thematic section and news values are applied carefully. The fact that this was the MP's maiden speech is newsy and so comes high up in her opening par. The Liverpool angle is reinforced.

Rather than say "said the casualty department should remain open in her maiden speech" the reporter has used the more colourful phrase "used her maiden speech to plead the case for the casualty department to remain open". Having used "unit" in par. 2 to avoid repetition, the reporter is free to use the more specific "casualty department" here.

Par. 5: when a news report consists of a series of quotes in reported and direct speech there is a danger of starting every par. with similar syntax: subject followed by verb "said" or variations on that. Par. 2 begins "He told"; par. 3 "the minister said"; par. 6 "the Labour MP said"; par. 7 "she said"; par. 8 "Mr Sackville said"; par. 9 "Alan Doran . . . said". This repetition tends to dull the story. In par. 5, the writer attempts to create variety by starting with the subordinate clause "While Liverpool's population was still in decline" which delays the introduction of the "she said". Reported speech conventions are used with "were stable and would be increased". No need for "that" after "said".

Par. 6: after the first reference to "Liverpool Broadgreen's new MP Jane Kennedy" in par. 4, she is next referred to as "she" (in par. 5 and in this par. 6) as "the Labour MP" ("the MP" would have been adequate since no other MP is mentioned).

"That" is needed after "said" since it is followed by a subordinate clause. There is a literal with "has" which, following reported speech conventions, should be "had".

Par. 7: simple introduction to direct quote which concisely conveys strong opinion. It is obvious Jane Kennedy is the source since she was the last person mentioned. Thus "she said" could be cut.

Par. 8: return to minister as a source so his identity is established at the start. But the par. adds no new information and inserting it between the Kennedy and Doran quotes causes confusion.

Par. 9: new source, with title, is established at the start. The reporter has used the exchange in the House as the basis for his report but followed it up with a discussion (probably on the phone) with the health authority chief to gain official confirmation of the minister's statement. After the use of "said" (no need for over-dramatic words such as "revealed", "disclosed" or even "pointed out") comes reported speech "had been prepared".

Pars 10 and 11: direct quotes, each paragraph conforming in length to the average already established. The style of the *Post* is clearly to give first name and surname on first mention, then title plus surname thereafter. It is also obvious Mr Doran is speaking those last two pars so the "added Mr Doran" is unnecessary.

Transitional words and phrases

To help the flow between sections, transitional words or phrases can be used. Given tightness of copy, these phrases have to be precise and used sparingly. The *Post* report used the phrase "His announcement came after" to link two sources and show the chronological order. The use of "And" twice at the beginning of sentences for transitional purposes was unnecessary.

Stabbed WPC Lesley fights for her life

By Stephen Thompson

Brave policewoman Lesley Harrison was fighting for life last night after being seriously injured for the fourth time in her short career.

Her heart was punctured by a blow from a screwdriver as she grappled with a suspected burglar.

The man also stabbed the 29-year-old former Wren in the arms as she tried to arrest him.

Vigil

Despite her injuries, the superfit sportswoman chased the man 50 yards before collapsing with blood streaming from her wounds.

As flowers and cards poured in from well-wishers, Lesley's parents, three of her five brothers and her boyfriend – a former policeman – kept a vigil at her bedside in intensive care.

A senior police chief paid tribute, saying: "We are proud of you."

Three times before Lesley has suffered serious injuries while on duty. They have kept her off work for almost one year of the five she has served.

In one she was beaten by a thug, in another she dislocated her shoulder while chasing a burglar and in the third she was hit on the head by a brick.

Earlier this year when Lesley returned to duty after five weeks off following one of the incidents, she said: "I love the job.

"There's no question of me quitting."

But the former secretary and casino croupier admitted: "Some officers go through their whole service without a single injury."

This story from the *Daily Express* (29 December 1992) uses a variety of transitional phrases. In par. 4, the short subordinate clause "Despite her injuries" helps maintain the flow; in the next par. "As flowers and cards poured in from well-wishers" serves the same function as does "Earlier this year" and "But" in later sentences.

Transitional words and phrases fall into a number of categories:

● *contrasts*: e.g. "but", "however", "nevertheless";

● *comparisons*: e.g. "similarly", "likewise";

● *chronology*: e.g. "meanwhile", "earlier", "later", "at a previous showing", "in conclusion/concluding", "the incident followed", "the review was launched after", "in a separate development", "it was the latest in a series of clashes";

● *geographical situation*: e.g. "addressing a London press conference", "in Nottingham Council House";

● *thematic development*: "on the government's plans to privatise British Rail", "on the global environmental crisis", "also".

Sentences rarely serve as useful links between thematic sections. For instance: "He also spoke on the media's handling of the royal separations." This is too bland, delaying the dramatic flow of copy. Better to use "also" as the prime transitional word and incorporate some specific detail as in: "He also highlighted the media's 'absurd hyping' of the royal separations."

Questions similarly serve to delay the flow of hard news stories and should be avoided as transitional devices. Thus: "What did she think of the US plan to bomb Iraqi targets? 'It is totally inappropriate and will only serve to escalate the crisis,' she said." Better to say: "On the US plan to bomb Iraqi targets, she said: 'It is totally inappropriate. . .'"

Background

The amount of background information included will differ from story to story. Some will need it to make the report intelligible; often pressures of time and space mean such information is eliminated. Placing of background can occur anywhere: in some it will occur at the end, in others it may occur near the start.

Warlords lift 'green line'

Agencies in Mogadishu

MOGADISHU'S two main rival warlords embraced yesterday at a peace rally on the "green line" that cuts through Somalia's bombed out capital and said they would work to unite their devastated country.

Ali Mahdi Mohammed, Somalia's self-styled interim president, and General Mohammed Farah Aideed led more than 10,000 people waving branches as tokens of peace to celebrate their agreement to lift the Beirut-style dividing line between their forces.

"We are demonstrating today our unity, peace and reconciliation," Gen Aideed, wearing pink flowers in his shirt, told reporters. "We are friends."

But a gun battle in which US soldiers killed a Somali gunman showed lawlessness still stalks Mogadishu's streets.

The shoot-out erupted after three Somali gunmen held up a Visnews television news agency camera crew in sight of a Marine post at the entrance to the US-controlled airport.

Gen Aideed and Mr Ali Mahdi agreed on Saturday to lift the green line and halt clan fighting so as to implement a seven-point peace accord the two men struck on December 11, two days after the US-led task force began arriving in Mogadishu.

The two turned on each other after joining forces to oust the former dictator, Mohammed Siad Barre, in January 1991. Their power struggle caused much of the bloody chaos behind the famine which has killed more than 300,000 Somalis.

President Bush will visit American troops in Somalia on New Year's Eve, a Marine spokesman said yesterday.

Colonel Fred Peck said Mr Bush would also visit a relief site some 12 miles out of Mogadishu and would fly to the inland town of Baidoha to visit an orphanage.

© the *Guardian*

This report from the *Guardian* (29 December 1992) carries background detail in pars 6 and 7. This is sandwiched between the opening pars concentrating on the peace moves and the gun battle and the final two pars looking to the future and President Bush's visit to Somalia.

Dentists vote for deadline on NHS

DENTISTS in the area have voted by a massive majority to impose a three month deadline for people to register with them – or lose their right to National Health Service treatment.

The move was backed by 49 dentists at a special meeting of the Wakefield Local Dental Committee – with only one voting against.

The decision is part of the dentists' on-going battle with the government over the amount they are paid.

Last week the Department of Health introduced a seven per cent cut in fees, slicing £6,000 to £7,000 at a stroke off their average salary of around £35,000 per year.

The latest action means people not on a dentist's list by October 1 will lose their entitlement to NHS care and be forced to go private. After the cut-off date they will have to find the full fee, rather than 75 per cent of the first £225 they pay at present.

However, dentists say fees won't be anything like those quoted in the national press and that they are considering banded charges to keep costs broadly similar in the 94 practices in the area.

Since news of the then likely move broke last week, surgery telephones have been buzzing with patients asking if they are entitled to NHS care.

Now the step is official, dentists are urging people to check and make sure they are not left out in the cold when the change comes into force.

Local dentists are keen to stress that their action is less extreme than that taken in some other areas, where dentists have already shut the door on all new NHS patients.

"We felt it was unfair to penalise patients who had been having health service treatment for a long time. That's why we set the deadline giving people the chance to register for NHS care.

"However we still wanted to make it clear we are protesting about what the government is doing," said Mr John Milne, vice-chairman of the local dental committee.

"The message we want to get across to people is that anyone who hasn't had a check-up for more than a year must make sure they are listed with a dentist, because their registration could have lapsed."

Mr Milne emphasised that patients entitled to completely free care –

● **Turn to page 2**

This front page story from the *Wakefield Express* (17 July 1992) integrates background details effectively in par. 4 (on the Department of Health's fees cut "last week") and par. 7 (on patients' confused response).

7

Some common news assignments
Accidents, fires, demonstrations and human interest stories

··

Planning for the unforeseen: *covering transport accidents and fires*

R EPORTS of transport accidents and fires feature regularly in local papers. Indeed, while journalists stress the "newness" of the news, sociologists often highlight its "endless repetitiveness".

The more serious the consequences the more prominent will be the coverage. Nationals are likely to cover accidents and fires only if they involve a serious loss of life (and thus amount to disasters) or if some "celebrity" is involved.

Journalists will only rarely witness an accident. News comes through tip-offs from the public or more usually from routine calls by reporters to police, hospitals and fire services. In contrast, a major fire might be witnessed by reporters.

Readers relate ambivalently to the coverage. They are drawn in, somewhat voyeuristically, to the tragedy, the human suffering, the drama of any rescue attempts. They are relieved they are not involved. At the same time they are repelled by the event's awfulness, the terrible unpredictability of fate that strikes down one person and leaves another (the reader, for instance) unscathed (see "Beyond the consensual paradigm"; Jock Young in *The Manufacture of News: Deviance, Special Problems and the Mass Media*; Stanley Cohen and Jock Young (eds); Constable; London; ninth edition; 1988).

Coverage of transport accidents and fires falls within a dominant genre which presents news as a series of disconnected "bad" events and individuals as victims of forces beyond their control. Ideological, economic, cultural, religious factors are more difficult to identify and report though their historical impact is considerable. An accident, in contrast, can be reported as an isolated event with a beginning and an end. Coverage can slot easily within the dominant routines of journalistic research.

The accumulation of details is always important in accident reports. Yet research suggests readers remember little of it. Instead, the coverage contributes to the representation of a powerful, ever-present, symbolic world of tragedy, suffering and potential heroism ("Myth, chronicle and story"; S. Elizabeth Bird and Robert W. Dardenne; in *Media, Myths and Narratives: Television and the Press*; James W. Carey (ed.); Sage; London; 1988).

Details to stress

The human interest angle

The most important focus for any report will tend to be on the consequences to human life. The impact on property or means of transport is secondary to this.

Thus it is wrong to intro.: "An engineering factory was gutted by a fire in Birmingham yesterday (Monday) in which four employees were seriously injured and two died."

Better to say: "Two engineering workers died and four were seriously injured in a fire which gutted a Birmingham factory yesterday (Monday)."

Similarly, in an accident coverage it would be poor to intro.: "A Rolls-Royce driven by a Birmingham man was seriously damaged in an accident with an Austin Maestro in Molesworth yesterday (Thursday)."

Be specific

Hospitals are usually well prepared to deal with media inquiries following fires and accidents. Spokespersons are available (either in face-to-face or phone interviews) to provide regular bulletins on the conditions of any casualties.

Go for specific details when covering casualties. Thus rather than "Many people were injured after a fire swept through a night club in Bognor Regis last night (Friday)" it is better to report: "Twelve people were admitted to hospital with serious burns after fire swept through a Bognor Regis night club last night (Friday)."

In fast-breaking fire and accident stories hospital and ambulance authorities are often unclear about the exact number of casualties. A fire breaks out in a hotel; 12 people are pronounced dead either at the scene or in hospital and three other people are unaccounted for. In this case it is possible to say "Some 15 people were feared dead after fire swept through a hotel overlooking Brighton's promenade yesterday (Monday)."

Names of people involved, their ages and home addresses are supplied by the police but in cases of fatalities only after the nearest relatives have been informed. Sometimes details of work status are provided or can be gathered from friends or relatives.

In accident reports, it's important in local papers to identify where the accident happened and at what time. The number and type of vehicles need to be identified.

Use the past tense

In covering fires and disasters, there is a temptation to use the present tense to convey the drama. For instance: "Seven people are feared to have died in a fire which gutted a factory in Doncaster earlier today (Friday). Ten fire appliances are at the scene trying to bring the flames under control." But by the time the paper appears (and almost certainly by the time the reader sees the copy) the situation may have changed. The fire might have been contained. All details have to go in to the past tense. "Seven people were feared dead after a fire gutted a factory in Doncaster earlier today (Friday)."

By "News" Reporters

MORE than 30 people were reported hurt today after a passenger train and articulated lorry crashed on a level crossing in Cambridgeshire.

The accident happened in thick fog at Dimmock's Cote, at Wicken, near Ely. Visibility near the crash scene was said by the emergency services to be down to 50 yards.

One coach left the track and finished up in a field. The other coach of the two-unit Sprinter was derailed.

First reports said five of the injured, passengers on the train, were seriously hurt.

The train was the 8.48 Stansted Airport to Liverpool Lime Street service.

A Cambridgeshire fire service spokesman said the incident happened at about 9.40 am.

The train was said to have collided with the trailer of the articulated lorry on the level crossing.

It was not known if the lorry driver was hurt.

But passengers on the train did suffer injuries, many of them caused by flying glass, the fire service spokesman said.

He added: "There are no persons trapped. All have been removed from the train, and both vehicles have been made safe to prevent an explosion."

Cambridgeshire Ambulance Service sent four ambulances to the scene and dealt with scores of minor injuries to passengers from the train.

A Magpas doctor also attended.

The line in both directions was expected to be closed for some time.

This front page story from the *Cambridge Evening News* (8 February 1993) says: "First reports said five of the injured, passengers on the train, were seriously hurt" rather than "are seriously hurt". And the last par. says: "The line in both directions was expected to be closed for some time" rather than "is expected".

Drama

Concentrate on the drama high up in the story. Any rescue attempts, activities by fire-fighters and ambulance crews need highlighting. Eye-witness reports can often enhance the dramatic content of the report.

Highlight any uniqueness

Try for a specific intro. angle to identify the uniqueness of the fire or accident. Rather than: "A fire gutted a hospital in Birmingham last night (Tuesday)," better to say: "A fire caused damage estimated at £2 million at a Birmingham factory last night – just two weeks after its opening."

Similarly, the accident may have happened at an infamous site for crashes. You may need to consult the cuttings files or database for background details in this case.

The causes

Always after a tragedy like a fire one of the first questions to be asked is why did it happen. Thus the "why" element will be prominent in most fire stories. Even if the authorities have no explanation at the time of going to press this is still worth carrying: "Police were unable to determine the cause of the blaze."

Also be careful if the police refuse to confirm or deny rumours that arson took place. They may say: "We have heard rumours that the fire was started deliberately. At the moment we have no evidence to support that theory. At the same time we are not ruling out the possibility." You may afterwards look at your note and see "we have no evidence to support the arson theory". But the police spokesperson went on to qualify that statement. It would be possible to intro. strongly on "Two elderly women died in a fire in Birmingham yesterday (Monday). Afterwards police refused to rule out the possibility of arson."

Similarly, in transport accidents, one of the major issues to be addressed high up in the story is why it happened. Theories can be explored (failure of warning lights at the crossing, for instance) but no individuals should be identifiable in the criticisms.

The leading sources

Police: examine the causes of the blaze, time of outbreak and how it was discovered; often provide details of casualties. After accidents, the police are often able to describe the accident, perhaps on the evidence provided by street surveillance videos. Be careful here not to impute blame to a particular driver. Better to say "The cars were in collision" than "Car A collided with car B" or, even worse, "Car A hit car B".

Ambulance services: provide details of number of ambulances (and sometimes helicopter ambulances) sent to scene, number of people sent to hospital.

Hospitals: give casualty details, conditions of those in hospital, kinds of injuries suffered; numbers of those in intensive care; numbers pronounced dead. It's important to avoid such clichés as "fighting for her life". Better to say "in a critical condition". Remember injuries are not "received" but "suffered" or "sustained". "Lacerations" and "contusions" are medical jargon words to avoid. Instead, "cuts" and "bruises" respectively. Skulls can be "fractured" but bones are "broken".

Depending on the time available before your deadline, you may be able to follow up friends and relations of anyone killed in an accident for their tributes. Sensitivity will be required here, too.

Fire-fighters: supply details of number of appliances at scene; accounts of any rescue operations and specific difficulties encountered. Might also conduct own investigations into causes. Provide warnings and advice to avoid repeat of tragedy. Avoid using "firemen" (they may be women). Many style books suggest "fire service spokesman" or "spokeswoman".

Eye-witnesses/survivors: often provide dramatic accounts of how people reacted and, in cases of fires, how buildings and contents were affected. But be wary of using any quotes which blame the fire or accident on any person. Formal inquiries are held to determine that. Eye-witnesses can be mistaken.

You may visit the scene of the fire or accident, perhaps accompanied by a photographer, which might prove harrowing. In no way disturb the work of the rescue services in your efforts to secure your story. Be sensitive to the feelings of anyone involved in the fire or accident or any eye-witnesses. They may not be prepared to talk. However, eye-witnesses might want to talk since it could help release some of their anxiety.

Owners of property: following fires they are sometimes able to provide an estimated cost of the damage and details of whether the property was insured.

The Automobile Association (AA) provides details about the impact of accidents on traffic flows. Rail companies similarly provide information about the impact of rail accidents on train timetables.

Follow-ups

Follow-ups are often possible. Casualty lists may change over time and need up-dating. Emergency services may be criticised for their alleged inefficiency or praised for the speed of their reaction. Coroners' inquiries and sometimes public inquiries are held to determine the reasons. Calls may come for safety improvements at junctions or to trains or planes. Political parties and campaigning groups are good sources here.

The emotional trauma of accident and fire victims and of those who witness them generally goes unrecognised, not only by the media but by health professionals and their families and friends. A feature could highlight their plight and the ways they are overcoming it. For example, Headway, the National Head Injuries Association, of 200 Mansfield Road, Nottingham NG1 3HX (tel: 01159-584084) has 90 groups around the country helping accident victims ("Survivors who come round to a nightmare"; Penny Lane; *Guardian*; 24 January 1992).

Analysis of "Morris dancer dies in road crash";
Matlock Mercury (26 February 1993)

Morris dancer dies in road crash

A WINSTER morris dancer was killed in a car smash last Monday – the second from the group to be involved in a tragic road accident in four months.

Dave Bathe (48) of Barncliffe, East Bank, Winster, was killed outright when his Vauxhall Nova saloon was in collision with a Peugeot 205 on the B6012 at Edensor, Chatsworth, at 7.50 pm.

Last October William Roy Witham (59) of Elton Road, Winster – the chairman of Winster dancers – lost his right leg in an accident at Stanton-in-the-Peak and was in intensive care for a week.

A police spokesman said the two cars were travelling in opposite directions when they collided.

Mr Bathe – who worked for Derbyshire County Council in the planning department – was certified dead at the scene and taken to High Peak Mortuary at Buxton.

Mr Witham said Mr Bathe would be greatly missed.

"It's come as a shock to us all, it's really sad," said Mr Witham.

Mr Bathe had been a member of the Winster Morris Dancers since 1978 and he was planning to go to Monterubbiano in Italy this May with the group and his young son.

Driver of the Peugeot Joanna Cannon (25) from Ashbourne suffered facial injuries and was taken to Chesterfield and North Derbyshire Royal Hospital.

Police are appealing for witnesses to the accident to contact the road traffic department at Matlock station on 580100.

Par. 1: focus on the human tragedy. The reference to the previous accident provides the angle, the use of the dash highlighting this point effectively. To avoid repetition, the reporter says "car smash" and then "tragic road accident". There is journalistic licence here. "Tragic accident" might refer to a second death. As becomes clear later, the accident victim lost a leg, not his life. But "tragic accident" is not inaccurate and adds to the drama of the intro.

Par. 2: development of intro. telling who was killed, which vehicles were involved, where and more specifically when. The use of "outright" alongside killed is redundant. Better to say simply "died".

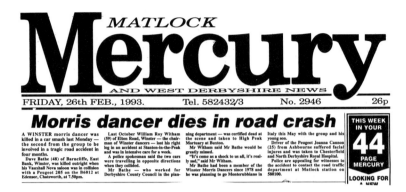

Courtesy *Matlock Mercury and West Derbyshire News*

Par. 3: development of second part of intro. after the dash. Use of dashes here, instead of commas, does not follow normal newspaper style.

Par. 4: police quote on the "collision".

Par. 5: more details on the dead man. Commas rather than dashes would have been better.

Pars 5 and 6: quotes, first in reported speech, then in direct speech, from morris dancer who survived accident. Both are rather predictable.

Par. 7: more touching details about the dead man, particularly developing the morris dancer theme.

Par. 8: details of the other driver involved in the crash.

Par. 9: police appeal for witnesses. Significantly, no eye-witnesses are quoted in the story.

This report appears as a hamper on the front page. On page 10, the *Mercury* carries a story ("Morris dancer vows to perform again") about Roy Witham, the man who lost his leg. Clearly this was prepared before the front page but a cross reference from the death crash story to the inside story was called for.

Analysis of "Woman dies in blaze"; *Weekly Post and Recorder, Nottingham (21 January 1993)*

Woman dies in blaze

By Tom Tanner

AN elderly woman died in her bedroom when fire swept through her Chilwell home despite desperate attempts to save her.

Her 40-year-old son tried several times to get into the house to reach his mother but later had to be restraine from rushing back into the house by fire-fighters from Beeston and Dunkirk.

He was taken to the Queen's Medical Centre suffering from shock and the effects of smoke inhalation.

Cigarette

Neighbours called the emergency services after the smoke alarm in their two-bedroomed home on Oak Acres was activated. The property was severely damaged in the blaze.

The fire had spread to neighbouring lofts before firecrews brought it under control.

Firefighters wearing breathing apparatus found the woman in the front bedroom after a search of the house.

Police believe the fire was caused by a lit cigarette and firemen have carried out an investigation into what they described as a "very serious fire."

They were waiting for relatives to arrive from Southampton to identify the woman formally.

Neighbour and friend for seven years, Ann Pickering, was woken in the early hours by banging on the window.

It was the son of the woman living opposite and he was shouting: "The house is on fire, the house is on fire."

Mrs Pickering said: "We ran out and the house was engulfed in flames coming right out over the roof. It was an inferno."

"She was a jolly little soul. She would do anything for anybody."

Mrs Pickering plans to lay flowers under the charred home in memory of her friend.

Notts Fire and Rescue Service stressed that a smoke alarm can give householders the vital seconds they need to escape.

Theme 1: death of woman and failure of son's rescue bid

Par. 1: focus on the human consequences, the tragedy and the drama. Death of elderly woman and failure of desperate attempts to save her. Perhaps the human drama would have been heightened further if a reference to the son had been included in the intro. Thus: "An elderly woman died in her bedroom when fire swept through her Chilwell home despite desperate attempts by her son to save her. The 40-year-old man tried several times . . ." No dateline in story: the newspaper, a free weekly, rarely dates its news stories.

Par. 2: focus on the drama of the son's attempts to save mother.

Par. 3: consequences for son.

Theme 2: chronology of fire drama

Par. 4: begins with details of how alarm was raised, then moves on to describe kind of property affected and extent of damage.

Par. 5: further details on extent of fire before being brought under control.

Par. 6: chronological section ends with the fire-fighters' discovery of body.

Theme 3: police on possible cause and identification procedure

Par. 7: police quoted on cause of fire. This is important detail and might have made par. 4 in a rearranged story.

Par. 8: continues the "dead woman" theme. With par. 7 moved up this would flow nicely after the par. on the discovery of the body.

Theme 4: eye-witness

Pars 9 and 10: dramatic story of son banging on window and shouting.

Pars 11 and 12: direct quote from eye-witness.

Par. 13: her plans for paying tribute to her friend.

Theme 5: follow-up advice

Par. 14: warning from fire and rescue service.

No picture was possible since that would identify the dead woman and the police were not disclosing this until relatives had been informed.

Analysis of intro. of "Baby burned by petrol bomber"; *Daily Telegraph (5 March 1993)*

Baby burned by petrol bomber

By Tim Butcher

A SEVEN-month-old baby was badly burnt when two petrol bombs were thrown into a terrace house in Coventry.

Sean Long, who lives with his mother in Charles Street, near the city centre, was being looked after by neighbours, Mr Norman Loach and his wife, Ann-Marie, on Wednesday night.

As he played on the floor of the Loaches' front-room the window was broken and two petrol bombs were thrown in, landing on the sofa.

Sean's clothing caught fire and he suffered 12 per cent burns before Mr Loach, 52, extinguished the flames.

Mr Loach suffered slight burns to his hands. The fire was quickly extinguished and the house suffered only minor smoke damage.

A spokesman for West Midlands Police said they believed the petrol bombs were a "grudge attack" after a quarrel between a member of the Loach family and a local young person.

Last night police were questioning a youth in connection with the attack.

Mr Loach's daughter, Anette, 13, said her brother, Wayne, 15, had had a row over a girlfriend.

"A lad turned up with a group of others. They were shouting abuse from the top of the street.

"I was sitting by the fire when there was a smash and flames everywhere. The baby was in the middle of the floor and flames leapt from the settee and set fire to his clothes.

"Everyone was screaming. My dad picked up baby Sean and ran to the kitchen and put him under the tap so the cold water would put out the flames."

Sean was taken to the burns unit at the Birmingham Accident Hospital where his condition was described last night as comfortable.

Firemen called to the scene found that the fire had been put out by local people including Father Giles Harris-Evans, minister at the local church of St Peter's.

A neighbour said: "There was a group of lads arguing with Norman and his son Wayne. They left after a while. About half an hour later I heard an almighty bang; I rushed out and saw Norman's house on fire."

Intro. focuses on the tragedy of a baby injured by petrol bombs. No dateline appears because the event occurred two days before publication. Mention would date the story which derives its impact from the drama of the attack. The language is deliberately factual with no over-emotional adjectives and adverbs (e.g. "in a callous attack", "heroic rescue bid by neighbour").

Notice the sentence structure: the baby comes first. The reporter did not write: "Two petrol bombs were thrown into a terrace house in Coventry badly burning a seven-month-old baby." Even worse would be: "A Coventry terrace house was hit by fire after two petrol bombs were thrown into its front room. Playing there was baby Sean Long, who was badly burnt after the petrol bombs landed on a sofa."

Par. 2: chronological section begins with baby playing in neighbours' house.

Dealing with demos: *covering marches*

PRESS and political strategies increasingly overlap. Though demonstrations were held long before our mass media age their media dimension is now crucial. People carry banners with simple slogans, they wear eccentric costumes, they chant, they play music, they choose routes often heavy with symbolism, they distribute leaflets, they attract prominent speakers. They do all this for political reasons. But they also do it hoping to attract media attention.

A demonstration serves many purposes. For the participants and organisers, it represents a public statement of solidarity for a cause. When people are angry or concerned they may demonstrate. It's as if more traditional avenues for debate and political action – the smoke-filled committee room, media, parliament, the protest meeting – are incapable of containing the feelings involved. They then break out into the streets.

Demonstrations and vigils are regular occurrences in London and, not surprisingly, the vast majority are ignored by Fleet Street. Even well-attended ones (with numbers in the thousands) often suffer the same fate or are marginalised in various ways. Coverage of a political march may be confined to an aesthetically-pleasing picture or over-personalised with stress on the presence or speech of a "celebrity".

The tone and prominence of coverage is often influenced by the attitude of the newspaper to the event. The massive CND demos during the early 1980s received largely negative coverage because of the papers' almost universal opposition to unilateral nuclear disarmament. In contrast, the London march in support of the miners following the government's sudden announcement of pit closures in 1992 was given generally positive, front-page coverage.

A demo on which violence breaks out is almost always given negative coverage, even though the violence may involve only a tiny fraction of the participants and last for a matter of minutes and may even have been started by the police (see *Demonstrations and Communications*; James Halloran, Phillip Elliot and Graham Murdock; Penguin Books; Harmondsworth; 1970). Sometimes newspapers intro. on the absence of violence: "The CND demo in London yesterday passed off peacefully with the only problems coming to police in the form of massive traffic jams."

When violence breaks out the blame is often explicitly or implicitly put on the demonstrators. Sometimes a demonstration can be covered neutrally in the news columns but is attacked or supported in features and/or editorial comments.

For local papers a demonstration (even the peaceful variety) can usually provide good copy. Advances are often compiled outlining plans of the organisers and police.

Guidelines for demo reporting

- It's important to report numbers of people involved. There can often be significant differences between figures given by the organisers and the police. Figures should, then, always be attributed. Sources might also have views about the numbers attending. They may be delighted at the turn-out or disappointed and blame the weather. Do not take the word of an organiser that the demo is, say, the biggest ever in the town. Claims like that need to be double checked.

- If the demo includes a march indicate its route. Observe the responses of passers-by.

- It's always worth joining the march. Chants and slogans can often provide useful "eye-witness" colour. In some cases it is not advisable to identify yourself as a journalist. Some reporters and photographers have been attacked by demonstrators suspicious of the bias of most newspapers. The compliance of some editors with police demands for incriminating photographs following demo violence has not helped protect journalists on such assignments.

- Participants can be drawn from a variety of groups, local and national. These are worth identifying. Prominent participants, not necessarily speakers, can also be identified.

- Demos usually end with rallies at which speeches are given. Coverage will depend on space available. Local papers, operating as "journals of record", will often cover as many speeches as possible in order of news value.

- Response of audience to speakers (applause, jeers, heckling, for example) are worth carrying to convey eye-witness colour.

- Background often essential. For instance, when the demo is part of a nation-wide or European-wide series of protests, that needs to be mentioned to place the local or London action within its proper context.

- If violence breaks out or if arrests are made, be careful not to sensationalise these elements. Try to convey any conflicting views on causes of violence from police, organisers, participants, eye-witnesses.

- Police are increasingly detaining journalists covering demonstrations. For instance, Simon Fairlie, associate editor of the *Ecologist*, was arrested at Twyford Down in March 1993 and held in custody for almost two days. He later accepted damages of £1,000 from the Hampshire Police in an out-of-court settlement.

- At the same time, demonstrators are becoming increasingly hostile to journalists. You should always assess the risks involved before covering a demo. It might be more appropriate to cover it from a vantage point, high above the demonstrators; if you decide to walk with the protestors it might be sensible to be accompanied by a colleague and with a mobile phone. Always be aware of "get-out" routes in case violence breaks out and protesters are pinned into a confined space by the police. As the safety manual *Danger: Journalists at Work* (International Federation of Journalists; Boulevard Charlemagne 1, Bte 5, 1041 Brussels, Belgium) stresses: "No story is worth your life. You are more important than the story. If you are threatened, get out fast."

- Journalists covering demonstrations should be aware of the 24 January 1997 High Court judgment. This ruled that, under the offence of trespassory assembly aimed at curbing road protests, police can ban groups of 20 or more meeting in a partic-ular area if they fear "serious disruption to the life of the community", even if the meeting is non-obstructive and non-violent. The ruling related to the cases of two people who were the first to be convicted of trespassory assembly under the contro-versial 1994 Criminal Justice Act after taking part in a peaceful demonstration at Stonehenge in 1995.

- Reporters covering marches should also be aware of the provisions of the Public Order Act 1986. This gave police unprecedented new powers. Organisers must give police seven days' notice unless it is not reasonably practical to do so. Police can impose conditions on a march or ban it. Moreover it becomes an offence if the date, time and route differ from that notified to the police. Road blocks are now routinely used by police to stop people from attending major demonstrations. More than 300,000 people were estimated to have been stopped by police road blocks during the coal dispute of 1984–5. Peace campaigners and travellers aiming to hold their traditional mid-summer festival at Stonehenge have also faced road blocks. (*The Coercive State: The Decline of Democracy in Britain*; Paddy Hilliard and Janie Percy-Smith; Fontana; London; 1988).

Analysis of "Protesters mount dole demo"; *Herts and Essex Observer (25 February 1993; page 13)*

Protesters mount dole demo

Report by Kathryn Donachie

DEMONSTRATORS took to the streets of Bishop's Stortford as part of a nationwide protest against the number of unemployed going beyond three million.

Statistics for Bishop's Stortford and Hertford constituency show a 350 per cent increase in people without work since March 1990, and a 374 per cent jump for the same period in the Saffron Walden constituency.

About 50 members of the Manufacturers Science Finance union, mainly from Whitehall College, Bishop's Stortford, marched on Thursday from Dane O'Coys Road to the town, giving out leaflets in protest.

Spokeswoman Tina Mackay said: "Along with the local Labour party, we are expressing our anger and concern about the level of unemployment.

"There has been a staggering increase and now there are over three million out of work – and more, unofficially, which is terrible.

"People right across the spectrum are concerned about it and we have got strong support in the town."

The Department of Employment figures showed that 3,722 people in Bishop's Stortford and Hertford, and 3,747 people in Saffron Walden, were out of work last month.

This compares with 827 unemployed people in Bishop's Stortford and Hertford in March 1990, and 789 unemployed in Saffron Walden at the same time.

As part of the countrywide demonstration, John Edmonds, the general secretary of the GMB union, called for an emergency package to end the economic "catastrophe".

"This economy needs a boost of at least £10 billion. John Major is insulated from the misery of ordinary people – hearing nothing and doing nothing."

The burying of the story on page 13 is significant. Had violence broken out it would probably have made page one.

Thematic structure

Section 1: general view of demo placed within national (but not European) context (par. 1).

Section 2: local unemployment details (par. 2).

Section 3: detail about march (par. 3).

Section 4: speech by Tina Mackay (pars 4 to 6).

Section 5: return to par. 2 theme. More jobless details. (pars 7 and 8).

Section 6: John Edmonds' speech (pars 9 and 10).

PROTESTERS MOUNT DOLE DEMO

Report by KATHRYN DONACHIE

DEMONSTRATORS took to the streets of Bishop's Stortford as part of a nationwide protest against the number of unemployed going beyond three million.

Statistics for Bishop's Stortford and Hertford constituency show a 350 per cent increase in people without work since March 1990, and a 374 per cent jump for the same period in the Saffron Walden constituency.

About 50 members of the Manufacturers Science Finance union, mainly from Whitehall College, Bishop's Stortford, marched on Thursday from Dane O'Coys Road to the town, giving out leaflets in protest.

Spokeswoman Tina Mackay said: "Along with the local Labour party, we are expressing our anger and concern about the level of unemployment.

"There has been a staggering increase and now there are over three million out of work — and more, unofficially, which is terrible.

"People right across the spectrum are concerned about it and we have got strong support in the town."

The Department of Employment figures showed that 3,722 people in Bishop's Stortford and Hertford, and 3,747 people in Saffron Walden, were out of work last month.

This compares with 827 unemployed people in Bishop's Stortford and Hertford in March 1990, and 789 unemployed in Saffron Walden at the same time.

As part of the countrywide demonstration, John Edmonds, the general secretary of the GMB union, called for an emergency package to end the economic "catastrophe".

"This economy needs a boost of at least £10 billion. John Major is insulated from the misery of ordinary people — hearing nothing and doing nothing."

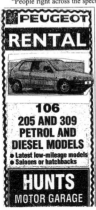

PEUGEOT

RENTAL

**106
205 AND 309
PETROL AND
DIESEL MODELS**
● Latest low-mileage models
● Saloons or hatchbacks

HUNTS
MOTOR GARAGE

Courtesy *Herts and Essex Observer*

Detailed analysis

Par. 1: local angle stressed along with national news of jobless figure going beyond three million. No dateline given because reference to "last week" would detract from the news impact. "Thursday" is delayed until par. 3.

Par. 2: local details about unemployment stress leap since March 1990. Rest of details follow later. If pars 7 and 8 had been placed here, the news urgency surrounding the demo would have been buried under the weight of factual details.

Par. 3: "About 50 members" is neutral (and contrasts with the loaded "barely 100 people" in the *Matlock Mercury* report of their local demo on the same day). Not sourced. Outline of route.

Pars 4 to 6: first speaker identified along with title. Quotes rhetorical, the 3m merely repeating detail in the intro. And the reference to "strong support" does not seem to tally with the turnout of just 50 people. Perhaps it is meant to be read ironically.

Pars 7 and 8: details from DoE. Repetition of "people" unnecessary.

Pars 9 and 10: "As part of the countrywide demonstration" is unclear (while demonstrations were organised on a European-wide basis, also). "GMB union" has not been referred to before and so needed spelling out. Strong quote.

Picture rather posed and should really have a caption.

Analysis of "Not one"; *Morning Star (8 February 1993; page 1)*

Marchers demand: Not 31 . . .
NOT ONE

By Isolda McNeill

NOT 31, not, 21, not 10, not one, was the battlecry of over 10,000 demonstrators who marched in defence of the nation's pits at the weekend.

The demand to save all the 31 collieries threatened with closure and to reject any compromise offering echoed through the streets of London.

The Women Against Pit Closures demonstration was led by a bevy of children from the mining communities, each bearing a placard representing a hit-list pit.

Miners' banners – many from pits now closed – turned out in force to take pride of place behind the women's support groups and the children.

And the heart of the Labour and trade union movement was there as well, with a galaxy of banners from every union in the TUC.

A discordant note was struck by the Socialist Workers Party whose members refused to carry placards bearing the slogans agreed by the women of the coalfields.

Despite repeated pleas from the women organisers – and a previously given pledge – they insisted on their own slogans and placards.

But the day belonged to the women who created the demonstration and who are the backbone of the coalfield resistance.

This was clearly highlighted by the banners from the women protest camps which have sprung up outside threatened collieries.

An all-woman platform addressed the rally in Hyde Park, miners' leader Arthur Scargill being the only male speaker.

"Not for the first time, it falls to miners and the mining community to provide the focus of the hostility of the people to this dogmatic government," said Labour deputy leader Margaret Beckett.

Stressing the need to defend our manufacturing base, AEEU women's officer Maureen Rooney emphasised "the reality is that we are losing jobs day in and day out."

Labour MP Ann Clwyd hailed the fact that the demonstration took place 75 years to the day since British women got the vote.

"We have 1,000 years of coal underground – we do not have 1,000 years of oil," she declared, recalling how since she was elected to Parliament, Wales had lost seven of its eight pits.

In a moving interlude NUPE representative Margaret Dunn called Ann Scargill on to the stage to receive a cheque for £1,000 "from the low paid women of NUPE to aid your struggle."

Condemning the "obscenity" of government attacks on public sector workers, Ms Dunn said to applause: "Let us see the City make the sacrifices – let us see this government make the sacrifices.

"We want to save the pits, not out of charity to the miners, but because it makes economic sense and is in the interest of Britain as a whole," declared Labour MP Diane Abbott.

There was a huge ovation for a Burnsall woman striker, whose young sister translated her speech from Punjabi and finished with the call: "Victory to the Burnsall strikers, victory to the miners."

For the TUC women's committee chairwoman Margaret Prosser linked "the struggle being waged on many fronts," with the fight to save wages councils.

NUM leader Arthur Scargill said that it was "entirely fitting" that men should march behind the women's banners on the anniversary of the gaining of the vote by women.

"I would be failing in my job and betraying my principles if I did not say that there comes a time when marches are not enough," he declared.

"There comes a time when we have to understand that in the face of the most reactionary government in living memory we have to respond."

That response must be industrial action, Mr Scargill stated, asking "the TUC and the whole of the labour movement" to join the miners in strike action.

"Let us learn what people power is all about," he urged.

THE tone of this piece in the daily paper of the Communist Party of Britain contrasts with that of the previous report. It is far more partisan in support of the demonstrators and prominently displayed even though the march is peaceful. The words associated with the march are all positive and combative: "battlecry", "echoed through the streets of London", "turned out in force", "pride of place", "heart of the Labour movement", "galaxy", "the day belonged to the women", "moving interlude", "huge ovation". Along with the simple "said", as people are quoted, dramatic words like "declared" (three times), "condemning", "hailed" and "urged" are used.

The piece gives close attention to various speakers, highlighting a range of political points to emerge from the demo.

Par. 1: identification of the story with the aims of the march is sealed when a slogan is used to provide the intro. angle. It provides a striking opening. Immediately the turnout is established though the source of the figure is not identified together with the dateline "at the weekend".

Par. 2: a repetition of intro. but in more colourful language.

Par. 3: eye-witness reporting of striking detail giving a clear picture of the event. The focus on the children adds to the emotional tone of the piece.

Par. 4: solidarity between miners, their wives and children highlighted.

Par. 5: solidarity theme maintained with (slightly questionable) reference to "every union in the TUC".

Courtesy *Morning Star*

Pars 6 and 7: the positive note stressed throughout the piece is broken only by this reference to the Socialist Workers Party. The importance of sectarian conflict on the left is reflected in the high positioning of this observation.

Par. 8: return to the positive with the reference to women "creating the demonstration" and being the "backbone of coalfield resistance".

Par. 9: symbolic importance of the presence of banners already seen in par. 4 stressed again here.

Par. 10: first reference to speakers at the rally; Arthur Scargill identified as the only male speaker.

Par. 11: quote from Margaret Beckett; but as a new speaker her name should have come at the start of the sentence.

Par. 12: good use of present participle ("Stressing the need . . . ") to vary the syntax as speakers are being quoted. "Our" is used rather than "the country's" as it links with later reference to "we" in direct quote.

Not 31, not one, say marchers

From p1

community to provide the focus of the hostility of the people to this dogmatic government," said Labour deputy leader Margaret Beckett.

Stressing the need to defend our manufacturing base, AEEU women's officer Maureen Rooney emphasised "the reality is that we are losing jobs day in and day out."

Labour MP Ann Clwyd hailed the fact that the demonstration took place 75 years to the day since British women got the vote.

"We have a 1,000 years of coal underground — we do not have 1,000 years of oil," she declared, recalling how since she was elected to Parliament, Wales had lost seven of its eight pits.

In a moving interlude NUPE representative Margaret Dunn called Ann Scargill on to the stage to receive a cheque for £1,000 "from the low paid women of NUPE to aid your struggle."

Condemning the "obscenity" of government attacks on public sector workers, Ms Dunn said to applause: "Let us see the City make the sacrifices — let us see this government make the sacrifices.

"We want to save the pits, not out of charity to the miners, but because it makes economic sense and is in the interest of Britain as a whole," declared Labour MP Diane Abbott.

There was a huge ovation for a Burnsall woman striker, whose young sister translated her speech from Punjabi and finished with the call: "Victory to the Burnsall strikers, victory to the miners."

For the TUC women's committee chairwoman Margaret Prosser

Back the MINERS

linked "the struggle being waged on many fronts," with the fight to save wages councils.

NUM leader Arthur Scargill said that it was "entirely fitting" that men should march behind the women's banners on the anniversary of the gaining of the vote by women.

"I would be failing in my job and betraying my principles if I did not say that there comes a time when marches are not enough," he declared.

"There comes a time when we have to understand that in the face of the most reactionary government in living memory we have to respond.

That response must be industrial action, Mr Scargill stated, asking "the TUC and the whole of the labour movement" to join the miners in strike action.

"Let us learn what people power is all about," he urged.

HONORARY WOMAN: NUM president Arthur Scargill, the only man on the platform in Hyde Park on Saturday.

Pars 13 and 14: striking intro. to the Clwyd section.

Par. 15: emotional content of the piece is maintained with the reference to the "moving interlude" and the generosity of the low paid.

Par. 16: continuing high emotional level and contrasting with the generosity of the poor, the Dunn section highlights her call for the City and government to make sacrifices. "Said to applause" maintains the tone and provides succinct eye-witness colour. Quote marks missing after "sacrifices".

Par. 17: Abbott direct quote, but the source's name should have come at the start of the sentence.

Par. 18: "Huge ovation" provides more eye-witness colour. Good observation here together with a fighting slogan which captures the mood of the gathering.

Par. 19: Prosser introduces a new link with the campaign to save wage councils.

Pars 20–24: the one man on the platform comes symbolically last in the report. But he is privileged with the longest quote over five pars just as he features on two of the poorly reproduced pictures.

Consensual concerns: *the "human interest" story*

HUMAN interest angles predominate in all sections of the press. Not in just the obvious areas: profiles, biographical extracts and reviews, showbiz features and throughout the popular press – but also in the heavies, local press and in all the specialist areas (see "The political economy of the human interest story"; James Curran, Angus Douglas and Paddy Whannel; in *Newspapers and Democracy*; Anthony

Smith (ed.); MIT Press; Cambridge, Massachusetts; 1980. "Press and popular culture"; Colin Sparks and James Curran; in *Media Culture and Society*; London; April 1991).

Politics coverage, just as much as sport and the arts, is dominated by the human interest focus. Many issues are represented as being duels between two people: Blair against Hague; Bruce Kent against Thatcher; Reagan against Gorbachev or Gaddafi; Maxwell against Murdoch; Bush against Noriega or Saddam Hussein and so on.

Pick up any paper and human interest angles are everywhere. Take, for instance, a selection from the *Liverpool Echo* of 15 May 1992. The front page has a preview of the wedding of world boxing champion Paul Hodkinson ("a fairytale ending to an incredible six months for Paul"), and a former rugby player who asked for Monty Python's "Always look on the bright side of life" to be played at his funeral ("Ray has last laugh"). Page two has a story of a Merseyside man's trip to war-torn Yugoslavia to rescue his mum and two nephews ("Agony and joy of son's mercy mission to Sarajevo").

Elsewhere there is a story about a father whose son died at Hillsborough seeking a meeting with Liverpool manager Graeme Souness ("Tragedy dad's fury over surgery story"). Another story is about a family of a Royal Marine Commando killed 26 years previously seeking a burial with full military honours ("Final salute for lost soldier son"); another focuses on the death on holiday of a local race relations campaigner ("Tragedy of city race crusader"). And there is a story about the families of two brothers ready for kidney transplant surgery anxiously waiting for news of the postponed operation ("Anxious wait for kidney swop").

This human interest consensus is rooted in the journalists' culture which stresses the importance of human sources as opposed to abstract ideas. In stressing the human interest, newspapers are responding to a curiosity people have about others. Amidst all the complexities of modern living, the human interest bias serves to explain the evolution of history in comprehensible terms. At the core of all human interest stories (as the *Echo* selections show) is the representation of basic emotions: love, lust, hatred, anger, tragedy, sadness, pity, joy. People can relate and identify with these emotions and the dramatic narratives structured around them. Interestingly, many of the *Echo* selection focus around family dramas.

Economic factors are fundamental. Since the emergence of the mass selling press in Britain at the turn of the century, proprietors have been well aware human interest stories sell. As competition has mounted so have the numbers of human interest stories.

The human interest bias can often end up representing people's biographies as being untouched by the dynamics of history. Newspapers are said to provide the first draft of history. But it is often a distorted, elitist history. Exaggerating the power of a few individuals serves to eliminate so many other people and their struggles from the historical record.

Alongside this elitist feature of the human interest story runs a significant "democratic" element. The dramas, hopes, fears, tragedies of "ordinary" people feature every day in such stories – just as the press's tendency to seek to bring the powerful down to size (through scandals and revelations) promotes this "democratic", "subversive" dimension.

Analysis of "They're in the money: John and Jeff scoop pools win"; *Ripley & Heanor News (26 February 1993)*

They're in the money
John and Jeff scoop pools win

CRICKET is John Hardwick's first love, but it's football which has put a smile on his face this week, with a £196,945.75p win on Littlewoods Pools.

John would rather be listening to the sound of leather on willow, but in winter he has to settle for the rattle of the teleprinter putting out the football results on television at his home in Inns Lane, South Wingfield.

Last Saturday it was music to his ears as he watched seven of his score draws print out and waited for the eighth which meant he was in the money.

"When it came up it was incredible. I was rather hoping I wouldn't have a heart attack and that I would survive until payday.

"I didn't sleep for two nights worrying if the coupon had got there OK. Now I know it has, it's quite amazing, delightful, I can't say better than that," he said.

John knew the numbers as they came up, without checking his coupon. He's been using the same ones every week for 18 years, so he was on the phone to Littlewoods Office as soon as it opened to make a claim.

Pools partner

His first call though, was to his pools partner Jeff Harris who shares the win. Jeff's a keen Derby County supporter and was at the match on Saturday, but when he got the message to ring John he knew straight away it was a pools win.

The pair first started doing the pools together when they were workmates at the Alfreton firm Exchem.

Jeff, who lives at Birchwood Lane, Somercotes, left about ten years ago to set up business as an insurance broker, but John stayed on as a stores supervisor.

They still keep in touch and do the pools using a system they devised when they first started, based on permutations on three lines of eight from ten. Their weekly stake is £3.24 and the winning line cost them just 54p. They've had eight draws up before, but it netted them just £120.

John, 44, who is married to Val and has four children Steven (18), Robert (16), Paula (14) and Paul (12) said: "I don't think we'll be going mad with the money. It's not enough to give up work or anything like that, but it will give us security.

"I am researching a history of South Wingfield, so probably the first thing I'll buy is a decent computer to help me with that. But apart from that I haven't really had time to think," said John.

Jeff, 40, is married to Andrea and has two young children Emma two and six week-old baby Tom.

He'll be spending some of his share on doing up the farmhouse he's just bought.

The pair are also looking ahead – they've already filled in a coupon for this Saturday's matches when Littlewoods Pools will be introducing a new points system aimed at increasing the number of people who win jackpot prizes.

RIPLEY & HEANOR

news

CHOOSE
RENT **JVC** BUY
TELEVISION + VIDEO
VIDEOMOVIE + HI-Fi
FRANK BUTLIN
1 West Street, Riddings Tel: 602242 (see page 2)

FRIDAY 26th FEBRUARY, 1993.   Vol. 105 4417   Tel: RIPLEY 742133/4, 747395   **Price 26p**

THEY'RE IN THE MONEY

CRICKET is John Hardwick's first love, but it's football which has put a smile on his face this week, with a £196,945.75p win on Littlewoods Pools.

John would rather be listening to the sound of leather on willow, but in winter he has to settle for the rattle of the teleprinter putting out the football results on television at his home in Inns Lane, South Wingfield.

Last Saturday it was music to his ears as he watched seven of his score draws print out and waited for the eighth which meant he was in the money.

"When it came up it was incredible. I was rather hoping I wouldn't have a heart attack and that I would survive until payday.

"I didn't sleep for two nights worrying if the coupon had got there OK. Now I know it has, it's quite amazing, delightful. I can't say better than that," he said.

John knew the numbers as they came up, without checking his coupon. He's been using the same ones every week for 18 years, so he was on the phone to Littlewoods Office as soon as it opened to make a claim.

Pools partner

His first call though, was to his pools partner Jeff Harris who shares the win. Jeff's a keen Derby County supporter and was, as the match on Saturday, but when he got

John and Jeff scoop pools win

the message to ring John he knew straight away it was a pools win.

The pair first started doing the pools together when they were workmates at the Alfreton firm Exchem.

Jeff, who lives at Birchwood Lane, Somercotes, left about ten years ago to set up business as an insurance broker, but John stayed on as a stores supervisor.

They still keep in touch and do the pools using a system they devised when they first started, based on permutations on three lines of eight from ten.

Their weekly stake is £3.24 and the winning line cost them just 54p. They've had eight draws up before, but it netted them just £120.

John, 44, who is married to Val and has four children Steven (18), Robert (16), Paula (14) and Paul (12), said: "I don't think we'll be going mad with the money. It's not enough to give up work or anything like that, but it will give us security.

"I am researching a history of South Wingfield, so probably the first thing I'll buy is a decent computer to help me with that. But

apart from that I haven't really had time to think," said John.

Jeff, 40, is married to Andrea and has two young children Emma two and six week-old baby Tom.

He'll be spending some of his share on doing up the farmhouse he's just bought.

The pair are also looking ahead — they've already filled in a coupon for this Saturday's matches when Littlewoods Pools will be introducing a new points system aimed at increasing the number of people who win jackpot prizes.

Celebrating — Val and John Hardwick (Picture Brian Eyre)

Courtesy Ripley & Heanor News

THIS front page lead story captures many of the ingredients of the human interest story. The emotional element is strong, here it's joy. How it shows on the faces and body language of the couple in the picture! Other human interest stories in the same edition included "a dream turning into reality" for two local musicians soon to "hit the high note" at the Tower Ballroom, Blackpool (joy); nearly half a page of local weddings (joy); a page of obituaries (sadness); a page of golden weddings (joy); the winning of a Duke of Edinburgh Gold Award by a Ripley man (pride).

A local man achieves the seemingly impossible and is prepared to talk about it. What a talking point; what a good local story. And good publicity for the pools company, too.

Much news represents people as subject to forces beyond their control. In this case, fate was kind to two lucky men. This is "good news". Pools, and in recent years the national lottery, in any case, play a crucial symbolic role in the culture. They symbolise the power of luck and money to offer "solutions". In one respect, the article symbolically celebrates the system which has provided these two men with their "fortune". The thousands of disappointed pools players are in no way newsworthy.

First section – par. 1: success

An opening twist. The drama lies in the paradox of his love for cricket but finding fortune (luck originally meaning "good fortune") through football. The crucial facts (the amount of the win, the name of the pools company) and the newsy "when" angle ("this week") are highlighted. Local angle avoided since it would overload the sentence already 26 words long.

Second section – pars 2 to 6: the narrative drama

Par. 2: continuation of the "paradox" theme. The local angle is cleverly introduced with the colourful reference to the "rattle of the teleprinter". The intimacy of the human interest story is reinforced by the use of "John". "Mr Hardwick" or "John Hardwick" would be too formal.

Par. 3: copy flowing nicely. The "rattle" now becomes "music to his ears". And there is an element of dramatic narrative and suspense as we hear of his seven score draws.

Par. 4: the short narrative ends in joy. A colourful direct quote captures all the excitement.

Par. 5: the emotional intensity can carry the quote over this second par. Words such as "amazing" and "delightful" continue to convey the drama.

Par. 6: copy shifts swiftly and cleverly over the chronology. Background detail (he's been using the same numbers every week for 18 years) quickly shifts to the newsy narrative (he's quickly on to the phone).

Third section – pars 7 to 10: the pools partnership

Par. 7: the crosshead "Pools partner" has been inserted by a sub-editor to clear a space amidst the block of grey type or to help make the story fill the space available. It is serving essentially a design function: crosshead words should not be irrelevant to the story but they usually carry no great significance.

Shift in focus to the pools partner. The writing is informal and maintains the pace well: "Jeff's" instead of the more formal "Jeff is" and "got" instead of "received".

Par. 8: background to the formation of the partnership. The "first" in "first started" is redundant.

Par. 9: biographical background on Jeff and John focusing on jobs.

Par. 10: outline of winning pools system. Specific details about stake all intriguing.

Fourth section – pars 11 and 12: focus on John

Pars 11 and 12: married status and age of John and names and ages of children. The separation of the subject "John" from the verb "said" is awkward. Perhaps it would have been better to have split the sentence into two: "John is married to Val and has four children . . . He said . . ."

Obvious question: "What will you do with the money?" Here is the reply. The "said John" at the end of the par. is grammatically incorrect since the attribution for the quote ("John . . . said:") came in the previous par.

Fifth section – pars 13 and 14: focus on Jeff

Par. 13: human interest details: age, marriage partner and children (echoing coverage of John). Perhaps brackets were needed around "two" to maintain style. Normally it would read "six-week-old" with two hyphens, but styles do differ on this.

Par. 14: reply to question "What are you going to do with the money?" in reported speech.

Final section – par. 15: look to the future

Par. 15: slightly quirky finish. Despite their success the men are continuing to do the pools. And there is a nice puff for Littlewoods.

Sexploitation of the human interest

S EX sells. At least that's what national press proprietors believe. So day after day stories about sex fill pages of the nationals.

Extra-marital affairs, prostitutes, sex-changes, bedroom secrets, ministerial and royal "scandals", love-children of Catholic bishops, randy vicars, nights of passion, naughty schoolgirls, full-frontal nudity on TV, Hollywood starlets who do or don't (strip for the cameras); how to do it; where to do it – the list of subjects seems endless.

The sex lives of virtually everyone, from former FBI chiefs and Presidents through media celebrities and royalty to truck drivers, seem fair game for the press. Nor is this sex-obsession confined to the pops. The "heavies" are equally interested though in more discreet ways, of course. Serialisations of biographies will usually focus on the bits about sex; photographs accompanying reviews of plays or operas in which nudity occurs will often be far more explicit than anything in the pops.

Take any tabloid and see how many stories are built around the human interest sex angle. In the *News of the World* of 19 April 1992, they included a story about "Fergie's dad" and his alleged affair with a 33-year-old woman ("Major Ron and his bogus 'lady'"); a caption story about topless "saucy Sarah Jaffer"; a double-page spread showing paintings of the royal family in the nude ("We are not a nude!"); an investigation into prostitutes at Euro Disney ("Hookers sell sex at Euro Disney kids' parade").

Another "exclusive" focused on a man turning into a woman ("My lost dad's turned into a woman"); a feature introed on how the husband of "stunning movie star Jane Seymour" called out her name during a "sexy clinch with a Texan beauty" ("Oh Jane! He opened my blouse and shouted my wife's name"). There was a profile of "agony uncle" Phillip Hodson ("People even tell him their sex problems in stores"). The television preview "exclusive" focused on *Home and Away* new boy having an affair with a sexy schoolgirl ("Guy's new love is just a schoolkid"). And so on.

On one level this is all escapist, titillatory trash. Significantly, when Rupert Murdoch bought the *News of the World* in 1969 and his mother expressed unease at his association with the scandal sheet, he explained that the poor Brits had to have such entertainment as their lives were so wretched (*Murdoch*; William Shawcross; Pan Books; London; 1992). But what lifts a lot of the sex coverage is its humorous tone. There is, moreover, often a subversive element running through the coverage often overlooked by outraged critics (see "Popularity and the politics of information"; John Fiske; in *Journalism and Popular Culture*; Peter Dahlgren and Colin Sparks (eds); Sage; London; 1992).

Stories of randy royals, blushing bishops and corrupt politicians expose the hypocrisy at the heart of the body politick. In a sophisticated way, the pops reflect the underlying contempt for authority figures which lies deep in the heart of British culture. The pops are virulent supporters of the status quo, usually rushing to support right-wing parties, whether Conservative or New Labour, by all means (fair or foul) at election times and other critical moments. At the same time, they subtly tap some of the anti-establishment feelings held by many people. Satirical shows such as *Spitting Image* tap it in different ways.

This tone of "subversive laughter" is peculiar to many of the tabloids and accounts for much of their popularity. A lot of their contrived humour is built on down-right lies. But in a complex way, people want to be lied to, to be seduced into a fantasy world while at the same time seeing through the lies. Ask someone why they read a paper like the *Sun* and they may well say: "It's a larf, isn't it?" That humour, that blend of fact and fiction is not easy to achieve.

Analysis of "Builders' bums are out"; *Sun (4 March 1993)*

Council bans lotsa bot

Dear Mr A. Breeze

ROADWORKS

Thank you for your letter dated 21 January.

The matter you raise is a subjective one. Generally, I would agree with you that the majority of the travelling public would find the sight of a workman's backside obscene. There are, of course, others who may not.

Therefore, erring on the side of the majority, I have asked those responsible for site operations in this authority to ensure that offensive behaviour of this nature does not occur in future.

Yours

Assistant County Engineer

BOTTOM LINE . . . the Breezes' letter from East Sussex council boss.

Builders' bums are out

**Exclusive by
Paul Hooper**

HOUSEWIFE Sandy Breeze has won a ban on council workmen showing their bums. Mum-of-two Sandy, 30, was horrified by the sight of building site workers with their bottoms showing over their trousers.

She got husband Alan, 32, to write to four councils – Kent, East Sussex, Hampshire and Essex – asking them to order a cover-up.

The only reply came from East Sussex whose Assistant County Engineer Chris Walker sent a memo to its 300 workers and contractors ordering them to keep their bots under wraps.

He said: "I suppose some might find the sight of a workman's backside obscene – but maybe there are whose who don't.

"However, it can't be the most pleasant picture in the world.

"Our first consideration is always that the workmen wear clothes to ensure their safety.

"But I pointed out that if they could wear things that won't cause offence it would be appreciated."

Eyesore

Sandy, from Sandwich, Kent, said: "The letters were a bit light-hearted – but I'm glad something is being done.

"It's a problem wherever you go. Every time a workman bends down he displays part of his backside.

"It's fairly obscene, enough to put you off your shopping.

"I felt the only way to make it more enjoyable was for workmen to wear a pair of braces."

Courtesy the *Sun*

THIS story is built on the smutty, cheeky humour associated with holiday post cards and bare bottoms. It's guaranteed to provoke a giggle.

The headline sets the tone, playing on a pun. The bums are out (banned); but they are also subverting the ban, showing out as in the picture. That "subversive" element is so crucial to the story. An authority bans the showing of bare bums (a petty problem, after all) and the *Sun* pictures a man happily flouting the ban. The paper is sticking up for the "ordinary man" and putting two fingers up to dowdy authority. Why should "they", the faceless bureaucrats, stop us having our fun, is the underlying message.

The humour is maintained with the punning captions: "behind in his work" and "Bottom line". The structure of the "exclusive" is simple. The first section (pars 1 to 3) focuses on the protest of "housewife Sandy Breeze". Section 2 (pars 4 to 8) takes in East Sussex's response with a direct quote from the assistant county engineer. The last section (pars 9 to end) quotes the protester.

The "straightness" of the story is interesting. East Sussex was at the time a Conservative-controlled council. Had it been a Labour council, coverage might have been different, with stresses placed on the "fun-hating, loony-lefties" and "faceless council chiefs" issuing "boring ban-the-bums" diktats.

Analysis of "What's a mice girl like you doing in a job like this?"; *News of the World (19 April 1992)*

What's a mice girl like you doing in a job like this?

Hookers sell sex at Euro Disney kids' paradise

By Mazher Mahmood

CHEEKY vice girls are taking the Mickey out of the new Euro Disney complex.

As dreams come true for children in the fantasyland east of Paris, randy dads are being offered their own private fantasia in plush Disney hotels.

The tarts' business is completely unknown to Disney bosses who would never sanction anything of the sort. The girls advertise as £300-a-day freelance guides to show clients around the fun park.

But they also offer sexy extras. One told News of the World investigators: "Most of our customers are businessmen, but maybe we'll also get single fathers.

"First we'll put the children to bed – and then we'll put their daddies to bed too."

Last week as the Disney hotels filled with bank holiday revellers, our men met blonde Innes and Flora.

At the Newport Bay Club hotel – one of six within the Euro Disney complex – Innes said: "We'll accompany you around the site. We'll have lots of fun and it won't stop in the park.

"We'll do full sex and oral sex, but it must be with a contraceptive."

Flora, who arrived in a green designer jacket over a saucy black camisole, said: "The charge will be £300 a day.

"You can have a sexy show with us both if you wish. We'll do anything for your pleasure."

Innes, a leggy German in a black mini skirt over white lace undies, is training as an interpreter.

She polishes up her English as a guide for UK businessmen by day. At night she becomes their sleeping beauty.

"All of us have been looking forward to the opening of Euro Disney," the 27-year-old said.

Pictures

"It will do our business a lot of good. We were getting bored with tours of the Eiffel Tower, Louvre and Moulin Rouge."

Flora, 38, who lived in London's Knightsbridge for several years and is now a Paris antique dealer, added: "I only do this type of business when I feel like it.

"I like sex and sexy Englishmen. Besides we're both Disney fans. We love Mickey Mouse."

The girls put on Mickey Mouse ears and posed for pictures for our reporters, who were posing as businessmen.

"You'll be our first Disney customers," went on busty Flora.

"It'll be great fun. All the agencies are getting busy because of the crowds expected here in the holiday season."

Many of the girls work for Paris agencies. None has any connection with the Disney organisation.

Flora and Innes work for IBS International Top Lady Guides, run by French madame Angelica.

It advertises in Paris entertainment guides, including Parisscope and Allo Paris – available at newsagents and hotels in the Disney complex.

But competition among guide agencies is fierce. Another agency, Lady Guides, offered a £400-per-day-per-girl deal.

Our reporters declined her offer but she plagued them with cut-price deals.

Katrina, of the Paris Guide Agency, also offered saucy guides for £400 a day. We declined all the girls' services but paid for their time.

EURO Disney is a world of fabricated fantasy and this "investigation" seems more fiction than fact. But it's a larf, isn't it? The "vice girls" appear in the pic to be enjoying themselves with their funny hats and coy attempts to expose a breast. From the start it all seems too contrived.

It gets off with a giggle. The girls with their Mickey Mouse hats are said to be "taking the Mickey" out of the new Disney complex, thus making an archetypal punning intro. Also central to the main angle is the construction of an archetypal moral tale, contrasting innocent children in their Disney fantasyland with the "vice girls" luring randy dads to play out their rather different fantasies.

Significantly, sex (of an extramarital kind) is associated here with "vice". As so often in tabloid representations of sexuality, the coverage is ambivalent. There is a hedonistic stress on fun and laughter. But the reporting reflects the puritanism and sexual repression lying deep in the culture by identifying sex (usually outside marriage) as something naughty, fearful and done in secret. The penultimate par. expresses this dimension – using the word "plagued" (with all its disease associations) in connection with offers of sex.

This moral ambivalence underpins the piece. On the surface, the puns maintain the light-hearted tone, the reference to fantasia, for instance, cleverly playing on the title of Disney's famous film.

There is a secret element to add further spice to the story. Par. 3 tells us "The tarts' business is completely unknown to Disney bosses."

The story is built around direct quotes from the "vice girls" but all of them are so stilted they hardly ring true. An unidentified "girl" is quoted as saying "First we'll put the children to bed – and then we'll put their daddies to bed too." But doesn't that seem too perfect a quote to be credible?

Adding to the drama of the piece is the fact that the investigators ("our men") are working "undercover" to acquire the story.

Par. 7 quotes "tart" Innes but she does not appear to have an enticing way with words. She is a rather direct proponent of safer sex: "We'll do full sex and oral sex but it must be with a contraceptive." It is intriguing how the story mixes titillation

Courtesy *News of the World*

with a matter-of-fact bluntness ("The charge will be £300 a day" "Flora" says in a no-nonsense sort of way but we've already been told that in par. 3.)

The descriptions of the women, of course, only focus on their "sexiness", on their potential for providing men with sexual gratification. "Flora" has a "green designer jacket over a saucy black camisole", the other woman , "a leggy German" is "in a black mini-skirt over white lace undies".

Much of the article is based around moral contrasts: in par. 12 "Innes" is described as a guide for UK businessmen by day. Then she is being "good". In contrast, at night she becomes "their sleeping beauty". In the dark of the night she becomes "bad". Then, the fun of Euro Disney ("All of us have been looking forward to the opening") is contrasted with the boredom of ordinary Paris tours.

Par. 15 focuses on an English angle: "Flora" has lived in London for several years. And there is something banal about her bluntly saying she likes sex (surprise, surprise), sexy Englishmen (ditto, ditto) and Mickey Mouse (giggle, giggle) all in the same breath.

A quote that follows from "busty" Flora seems strange. "You'll be our first Disney customers," she tells our intrepid reporters. But isn't the story built around the notion that these "girls" have been having their Disney fun for some time? It's all getting too complicated. "It'll be great fun," she adds but it's hard to imagine any "vice girl" uttering those immortal words. One is almost expecting her to say "And jolly hockey sticks, what?"

Par. 20 stresses the absence of any connection between Disney and the "vice girls". Par. 3 has stressed exactly the same point. Clearly the paper is worried about the legal implications of the story and protecting itself as best it can.

Next follow some pars about two "escort agencies" operating at the Disney complex. In a way, the reporters declining the services serve to articulate the moral condemnation of the vice girls' activities which lies at the heart of the story. We are left with an image of the reporters' moral uprightness, compared with the girls' moral degeneracy: "We declined all the girls' services but paid for their time." But the reader also ends with a giggle. Since so much of the story appears a fiction so too could be that final claim.

8

Some more news assignments
Meetings, press conferences, reports, speeches and eye-witness reporting

....

Meeting the challenge: *reporting meetings and conferences*
....

PUBLICITY is a crucial dimension of the public meeting. Such meetings provide a forum where controversies can be aired and decisions made. Information and views can be disseminated to those present and through the press to the public beyond.

Every day there are scores of meetings throughout Britain. Many are private, many are open to the public, but only a relative few are covered. An underlying news value system operates to determine which meetings are covered, which are ignored.

Some meetings, such as those of Parliament, local councils and their various committees, occur on a regular basis and are covered routinely. Details are logged in news desk diaries and they are often covered by specialists.

Many organisations such as Friends of the Earth or Amnesty International hold regular public meetings (and occasional conferences) throughout the country but these are not usually covered on any routine basis given their relatively low status in traditional news values.

There is also a category of non-routine public meetings and conferences which draws press attention. Organisations will invite either a prominent speaker or panel in the hope of raising issues, promoting a cause, highlighting a controversy. Adverts may appear in the press, bills might be stuck up and leaflets distributed.

In other cases, the organisers might not be so publicity-conscious or may simply be sceptical of any attendance by the press. An advance notice may appear in a small circulation newsletter or magazine. In fact, the news potential may be considerable. This kind of event is particularly worth looking out for, whether you are a staffer or a freelance.

In addition, there are meetings and conferences which are private but to which the press is invited. The CBI may hold a conference on building European exports, the TUC may call a meeting on the government's privatisation plans. Unions, campaigning bodies, charities and professional associations may hold their annual conferences. All these events can provide a rich source of news to the press.

Be prepared (a useful journalist motto)

The issues to be covered, the backgrounds of the speakers, the views of the organ-isers: these are some of the areas worth looking into before attendance. If the meeting is focusing on a running issue, the cuttings should be consulted.

Because you are not faced with the demands of confronting a source face to face, as in an interview, there is a danger of thinking you can bluster through a meeting without any serious preparation. But just as with an interview, you may be confronted with some major issue you may be unprepared to tackle. Your note is untidy, you don't follow the subtleties of the debate, so a news angle goes missing or is carried inaccurately.

All that said, news-making is a hectic business and preparation is not always possible. General reporters can be assigned by their news desk to cover a meeting at short notice. They have a lot of rapid thinking to do. Practice certainly helps here. So does constant immersion in the news.

If the meeting or conference is considered of major importance, a backgrounder, or advance story may be written highlighting the issues, personalities, any power strug-gles and possible decisions and outcomes.

Meeting strategies

- Reporting strategies will depend on the length and news quality of the meeting. Covering all-day meetings and three-day conferences can be exhausting, given the degree of concentration required over such a period. Journalists might elect to cover all the contributions. Otherwise they might choose those they consider the most important and make inquiries about the others to make sure nothing was missed.

  If the meeting lasts more than three hours, a reporter on a daily will tend to leave it for certain periods while they alert the news desk over developments and send over copy for specific editions. An evening meeting lasting for, say, two hours is generally covered from start to finish.

- Never feel obliged to cover all the speakers in your copy. Some small local paper might routinely cover all the speakers irrespective of news value. But then jour-nalism is turning into a form of PR (for which, it may be argued, there is a place in small communities). Your news desk is likely to have briefed you over the kind of wordage required. If the story turns out to be worth far more or far less you should argue your case. If there is no hard news (mere platitudes, rhetoric or esoteric waffle) you should not feel obliged to provide any coverage.

- Similarly, never feel obliged to cover the speakers chronologically. A report of a meeting by a non-journalist often begins with the first speaker and "concludes" with the last. News values tend to subvert chronology. The most important point in your intro. might emerge from the last words spoken. It might come from a brief aside.

- Never feel obliged to reproduce the priorities of the organisers or the speakers. Some 95 per cent of a speech might be devoted to some un-newsworthy topic. You might consider just 1 per cent newsworthy. That 1 per cent might be the focus for your copy, the rest may be eliminated altogether.

- The most newsworthy item may come from the floor rather than the platform or in response to a question from the floor. In this case, it's worth trying to contact that person to check the spelling of their names and their title. Sometimes it's difficult to hear a speaker from the floor so go to them afterwards to check any quote and maybe get more information and views from them.

- Some of the most difficult meetings to cover are those when the speeches are funny. You are tempted to sit back and enjoy it rather than engage in the mundane task of recording the joke. Your body tends to shake in laughter which adds to the note-taking problem. Incorporating the joke in a hard news story (which, by definition, is an "unfunny" genre) is stylistically difficult too.

  One solution is to "soften" the story carrying a witty, light tone throughout. Another is to carry the main report as straight hard news and contribute a second, wittier story for an existing diary column or a special one created for the event.

- Responses from the audience are always worth noting. Including references such as "was greeted with laughter/boos/jeers/applause/silence" adds a small but telling "eye-witness", colourful dimension to your copy.

- Even the dullest meeting or conference can be useful to the reporter. Contacts can be made, ideas for follow-up stories can emerge. National conferences can draw people from all over the country. Someone from northern Northumbria may talk to you and reveal a wonderful story you may otherwise have missed. Afterwards you will follow it up.

- "Dullness", in any case, is a subjective notion. What is dull to you might be fascinating to someone else. One of the many challenges for a journalist is to report the "dull" in an interesting way.

- Many public meetings contain informal discussions rather than set-piece speeches. Often a more "feature-ish" approach is suited to this event, where you might incorporate some comment and descriptive elements. While the meeting itself might not produce hard copy, a talk with one or more of the participants afterwards might.

After the meeting

A lot of meetings covered in the press are never attended by the reporter. The spread of "phone journalism" means they are often simply "picked up". A journalist will contact either one or more people present for their account of the decisions made and for their views on any possible consequences. Or a reporter might compile a retrospective, looking back at the meeting/conference, or write an opinionated feature on the meeting and its implications.

Events or pseudo-events?: *covering press conferences*

PRESS conferences often provide important sources of news for journalists. Take a look at the back page of any edition of *Press Gazette*, the journalists' trade journal, with a selection of items from PA's diary for the forthcoming week and see how many press conferences are listed.

Press conferences are useful for both the organisers and the journalist. For the organisers it marks an attempt to influence the news agenda. Journalists will be given a chance to look in depth at issues from the perspective of the organisation and to meet some of their important representatives.

For the journalist, the event can provide the basis for a news report, for gathering background information and views, for developing contacts.

Organisations tend to send out press conference details three or four weeks in advance. If the news editor considers it possibly worth attending details will be noted in the diary for the day. Any accompanying literature containing, for instance, addresses, contact numbers and names will be filed. If there is likely to be a photo-opportunity ("pic op") linked to the event, the picture desk will be notified.

Organisations often contact the newspaper again by telephone a few days before the event as a reminder. They can also send a press release (embargoed until after the likely end of the conference) giving an account of the event as if it had already occurred but not enough information to discourage journalists from attending.

Conferences can be held at any time. EC leaders may meet for a day and at around 4 pm give a press conference to outline the decisions made. But the most popular time is around 10.30–11.30 pm. Journalists have had time to go into their offices, check their mail, their timetable for the day, write up any copy from the previous evening or a short report for that day's paper.

Mondays and Fridays are considered bad days for press conferences. Mondays are often out because it is the Sunday newspaper's day off; Fridays because local Saturday papers tend to be read by fewer people.

When you arrive at the conference venue, you are usually asked to add your name and that of your newspaper (or to indicate freelance) to a list. You may be given an agenda: for instance 11 am start with chairperson's introduction and welcome; 11.05 first panel speaker, 11.15 second panel speaker, 11.25 questions, 11.45 drinks/coffee. Sometimes you are given a badge to identify yourself when meeting others afterwards.

Transcripts of one or more of the speeches to be made and other background information on the organisation and relevant issues may be provided. It is important to compare the transcript with the actual speech. Occasionally, small changes appear and there can be a story behind those alterations. For instance, there may have been a last-minute compromise to delete some controversial comments.

Equally, non-scripted asides can provide the most interesting quotes and angles.

It is important to establish, soon after arriving, the names, spellings and titles of the people on any panel. Contributions can often move rapidly among the speakers and, without notes giving attributions to the various quotes clearly, writing a story afterwards can prove nightmarish.

Conferences usually begin on time or at the most five minutes late, so it is important to arrive on time. In any case, it reflects badly on your organisation if you arrive late.

● An organisation might spend most of the conference on an issue it considers important but which the journalist may regard as only marginally newsworthy.

For instance, an organisation may use the press conference to spell out its "14-point charter for green consumerism". A passing comment by a speaker may be more newsworthy. A prominent environmentalist may claim a BBC documentary the previous night had "seriously misrepresented the environmentalists' case" and that her organisation was planning to protest to the corporation. That angle might then dominate the intro. with references to the 14-point plan coming later. Or it might take over all the story with the reporter following up with calls to the BBC and other environmental groups. No mention at all for the 14-point plan, the whole *raison d'être* of the press conference.

Question of questions

● It is often important to raise questions, particularly if you think later opportunities will be denied you. Perhaps an important source has indicated they will have to leave immediately after the conference.

Sometimes journalists, as a group, co-ordinate on a series of questions to extract particularly complex and sensitive information. Sometimes, operating as a pack, they will swap around ideas for angles and quotes afterwards. When questions are asked out loud it becomes difficult for the journalist to identify an "exclusive" angle. Press conferences can promote a culture in which conformist, consensus news reporting is accepted too uncritically.

On many occasions, the most important part of the press conference for the reporter is during the informal questioning afterwards. This provides the chance for following up individual angles and delving into an issue more deeply. It provides the reporter with a chance to check any details, quotes and spellings. Never feel embarrassed to ask for clarification of a complicated point. People tend to admire rather than despise you for this. Better to get it right than botched up. Ideas for further follow-ups and contacts can emerge from these informal meetings. In addition to the speakers, other people from the organisation often attend who can prove useful sources of information.

Different circumstances will demand different strategies on handling the notebook during this informal period. Sometimes you will approach people with your notebook and pen clearly visible. At other times it will be more appropriate to chat on in a relaxed way perhaps with a drink in one hand but aiming to remember everything said and only after a time bringing out your notebook (if at all).

Stage-management and manipulation

● All press conferences should be treated carefully. Sociologists have called them the archetypal "pseudo" news event (see *The Image – or What Happened to the American Dream?*; Daniel Boorstin; Harper & Row; New York; 1962). It's not a "real" event like a football match, a car accident, a court case. It's artificially contrived, aimed at gaining publicity. It has no status other than in relation to the media coverage it is seeking.

An organisation calling one has a message to sell. It has gone to the trouble of sending out the details to the press, maybe booking a room, laying on drinks (and sometimes a meal) for journalists. It expects something in return. Namely publicity and preferably good publicity.

There is the danger that the journalist will be used as a glorified PR officer for the organisation. Press conferences are attempts to stage-manage the news.

● Since they are tightly managed affairs you should be thinking all the time: What are they trying to tell me and, more particularly, what are they trying to prevent me from knowing?

The experience of Australian war correspondent Wilfred Burchett is pertinent here (see *Burchett: Reporting the Other Side of the World*; Ben Kiernan (ed.); Quartet; London; 1986). At the end of the Second World War, following the bombing of Hiroshima and Nagasaki, 600 allied journalists covered the official Japanese surrender aboard the battleship *Missouri*. Only Burchett subverted the dominant news values and went, with great difficulty and courage, to Hiroshima. From there he filed one of the most famous scoops of all times.

His description of the devastation of the Japanese city after the nuclear bombing and the suffering and dying of people from radiation sickness was carried in the *Daily Express* of 5 September 1945 under the headline "The atomic plague: I write this as a warning to the world". His reporting of radiation sickness was to be ferociously denied by the allies for years afterwards. But he was right about radiation sickness – and right to report it (*Shadows of Hiroshima*; Wilfred Burchett; Verso; London; 1983).

Reporting reports

REPORTS constitute an important source for news stories and features. They can appear in book or leaflet form, as press releases, in specialist journal articles or in the agenda papers or minutes of meetings.

Their value comes from the deep research which normally underpins them. Reports from such bodies as Shelter, the International Institute for Strategic Studies, Amnesty International, the Joseph Rowntree Foundation, the Low Pay Unit, the Child Poverty Action Group, Oxfam and other prominent charities provide a body of "authoritative" details which journalists can use as the basis for their articles. Reports usually argue a case or come to some conclusions which can then lead on to recommendations for action. These provide good copy.

Clear attribution becomes the critical task for the journalist in handling the report. The most striking views can be covered in direct speech; other important views and details can be summarised in reported speech.

Press conferences can accompany the publishing of reports. These provide the journalist with the chance to "humanise" their coverage, presenting views through the voices of spokespersons as well as the impersonal report. Background details can also be established.

When press conferences are not held reporters often ring up the writers for comments. In all cases they might contact others for follow-up responses.

People with mortgages are the 'new poor'

By Rosie Waterhouse and Colin Brown

WORKING families with mortgages and the struggling self-employed are the "new poor" to emerge from a select committee report on poverty during the Thatcher years.

The report, *Low Income Statistics: Low Income Families 1979–1989*, published by the Social Security Committee yesterday, shows a striking new trend in the type of people classified as living below the poverty line.

The figures, which the Government did not want published, show the number of families that have a full-time worker living on incomes of less than the basic unemployment benefit rate has doubled from 470,000 to almost one million over a decade.

Researchers from the Institute for Fiscal Studies revealed that about half the 970,000 families with a worker living below this poverty line were self-employed and two-thirds of them – 620,000 – had mortgages. In 1979, of the 470,000 working families below the poverty line, fewer than half – 200,000 – had a mortgage.

Home owners on low incomes have been ensnared in the poverty trap because of benefit rules. If they were unemployed and receiving Income Support, the Department of Social Security would pay the mortgage. But interest will not be paid for those in full-time work – defined as working over 16 hours a week.

Also, people on low incomes who live in rented accommodation are entitled to Housing Benefit, which pays a substantial proportion of the rent, but working people with mortgages get no such assistance.

Steve Webb, an economist who conducted the research, said that if the DSS paid building society interest for employed people with mortgages, almost 500,00 of the 620,000 would not be below the poverty line.

He said: "The groups we have traditionally thought of as being poor, such as pensioners, are tending to get better off and their place is being taken, in part, by a new poor such as lower paid workers with mortgages and the self-employed."

Charities working with families living below the poverty line, such as the National Association of Citizens' Advice Bureaux and the Children's Society, confirmed that the biggest increase in poverty was among people with mortgages.

Ian Sparks, the Children's Society director, said: "Unlike families on Income Support, those in low-paid work get no help with mortgage interest repayments. They get into extreme difficulties and this often leads to the repossession of their homes."

Ministers believe the Government will have to tackle the plight of house-owners who cannot afford their mortgage repayments as a priority for winning back wavering Tory voters.

They fear the collapse of confidence in the housing market has undermined support for the Tory party among many home-owners who purchased their homes under the Thatcher right-to-buy legislation.

One former ministerial policy adviser said the Government should consider replacing mortgage tax relief – no longer regarded as a taboo area – with a new benefit directed at the low-paid facing difficulties in paying.

Peter Lilley, Secretary of State for Social Security, is believed to be preparing a wide-ranging review of benefits.

Launching the report, which showed that the number of people living on incomes even lower than state benefit rose by almost 50 per cent to three million, Frank Field, the committee chairman, called for a review of the effectiveness of the welfare state, which spends £80bn on benefits a year.

❏ *Low Income Statistics: Low Income Families 1979–1989;* HMSO; £10.

Home-owning family living in poverty trap

Sue Thompson and Ray Smith, her partner for 20 years, are a classic example of the new poor, low earners living in the mortgage trap, writes *Rosie Waterhouse*.

The only way they have staved off repossession is by cutting down on food and other essentials and running up debts that reached £3,000 last year.

The couple and their three children, Leon, 16, Rebecca, 15, and Lesley, 12, cannot afford to pay for the funeral of Mr Smith's mother, who died this week.

Their three bedroom cottage near Corton, four miles outside Lowestoft, Suffolk is heated in one room only by an open fire fuelled by wood collected by Mr Smith and the children from the nearby forest at weekends.

The family have one joint of meat a week and fill up on bread and home grown fruit and vegetables. All Ms Thompson could afford to buy the children for Christmas were stocking fillers.

She is still paying off debts to catalogues for presents from three years ago.

Their formerly comfortable life in a cottage, worth about £60,000, which was bought with a £20,000 mortgage in 1984, ended two years later when the coach-building company that Mr Smith had worked for for 25 years closed.

He has had menial, low paid jobs ever since. As a father of three taking home £130 a week from his job, and with Family Credit and child benefit, he would be £40 a week better off unemployed. He would get about £20 less in Income Support, child benefit and family premium, but the state would also pay his mortgage interest payment of £60 a week. But "he couldn't bear to be thought a parasite", Ms Thompson said.

If he was in rented accommodation he would also be better off because, even if he was working, he could claim Housing Benefit of almost £57 a week.

Notice how this report from *The Independent* (15 January 1993) uses responses from various sources. Par. 7 focuses on the compiler of the report. Par. 9 refers to the National Association of Citizens' Advice Bureaux (the use of "x" there following *Independent* style) and the Children's Society (CS). The next par. focuses on the views of the CS director.

Unnamed ministers are next referred to, as is "one former ministerial policy adviser", for some reason afraid to come clean and speak on the record. Finally, reference is made to the committee chairman speaking at the official launch. In the chronology of the research, that last comment could easily have come first. That doesn't mean it leads the report.

A popular device to brighten coverage of reports is to accompany them with follow-ups looking at the human interest aspects.

The Independent report above ("Home-owning family living in poverty trap") follows this approach, focusing on a couple as "a classic example of the new poor" highlighted in the main report. A photograph of the couple would have helped give this human interest angle still more life.

National reports are also given local follow-ups, as here in the *Derby Evening Telegraph* (25 February 1993) which follows up two NSPCC reports with the views of a local campaigner with a final par. response from the society.

MUM ATTACKS ABUSE REPORTS

CAMPAIGNING mum Julie Boniface has criticised a national charity's call for extra measures to protect disabled children from abuse.

The Derby mother-of-four says two NSPCC reports published this week were a "waste of money" because moves to tackle the problems are already under way.

The NSPCC studies uncovered a wide range of physical and sexual abuse of handicapped youngsters

by Claire Lumley

who, it says, are less likely to speak out.

The findings prompted officials to call for better training for care workers to spot signs of abuse.

But Mrs Boniface says her two-year campaign for the same measures is already seeing success and has caught the attention of Government ministers.

She says other studies have drawn the same conclusions.

"Of course, it's a good thing to highlight the terrible things that go on but I am staggered that the NSPCC has the money to waste on finding out what was already known," she said.

"They would have been better using the money to help train care workers — one of the measures they are calling for."

Mrs Boniface set up the self-help group Voice to help victims of abuse in

1991, with husband Ivan, after their 24-year-old daughter was sexually abused in a Derby Mencap charity home.

A care worker was later jailed, but the couple were appalled to discover staff had no formal qualifications and no training in identifying signs of abuse.

They have campaigned for police vetting of all care workers and are holding a meeting at the House of Commons on March 23, with health minister Tim Yeo.

Mrs Boniface was also asked last year to help adapt a Government report on child sex abuse.

The NSPCC reports, conducted in the last three years, found evidence of abuse including rape and forced injections.

A spokeswoman said: "We know Mrs Boniface is doing very good work and we think our reports will add to increasing awareness."

● Staggered ... Julie Boniface, with husband Ivan.

Courtesy *Derby Evening Telegraph*

Mum attacks abuse reports

By Claire Lumley

CAMPAIGNING mum Julie Boniface has criticised a national charity's call for extra measures to protect disabled children from abuse.

The Derby mother-of-four says two NSPCC reports published this week were a "waste of money" because moves to tackle the problems are already under way.

The NSPCC studies uncovered a wide range of physical and sexual abuse of handicapped youngsters who, it says, are less likely to speak out.

The findings prompted officials to call for better training for care workers to spot signs of abuse.

But Mrs Boniface says her two-year campaign for the same measures is already seeing success and has caught the attention of Government ministers.

She says other studies have drawn the same conclusions.

"Of course, it's a good thing to highlight the terrible things that go on but I am staggered that the NSPCC has the money to waste on finding out what was already known," she said.

"They would have been better using the money to help train care workers – one of the measures they are calling for."

Mrs Boniface set up the self-help group Voice to help victims of abuse in 1991, with husband Ivan, after their 24-year-old daughter was sexually abused in a Derby Mencap charity home.

A care worker was later jailed, but the couple were appalled to discover staff had no formal qualifications and no training in identifying signs of abuse.

They have campaigned for police vetting of all care workers and are holding a meeting at the House of Commons on March 23, with health minister Tim Yeo.

Mrs Boniface was also asked last year to help adapt a Government report on child sex abuse.

The NSPCC reports, conducted in the last three years, found evidence of abuse including rape and forced injections.

A spokeswoman said: "We know Mrs Boniface is doing very good work and we think our reports will add to increasing awareness."

Publication of reports can help provide a strong news angle to a feature. You may be researching pre-menstrual tension and have a number of interesting quotes and details. The publication of a new report on the subject could provide the vital news angle.

You may build up close contacts with an organisation or individual who may entrust you with an exclusive release of an important report. Otherwise, you may contact an exclusive source for a response to a report.

Though reports are often covered after their publication the journalist puts their story in the present tense. It is perfectly acceptable to write "says a report published yesterday" and continue in the present tense. The report's findings are still current "today" as they were "yesterday" on the day of publication: using the past tense and reported speech can date the piece unnecessarily.

The publication of the report does not normally constitute the news. It would be dreary to begin "A report highlighting the dangers of excess television watching was published yesterday by a group of eye specialists." This is too general. A more specific intro. is required: "People who watch television for more than five hours every day can suffer serious damage to their eyes, according to a new report."

● Notice there the attribution in the intro. It would be wrong to begin: "People who watch television for more than five hours a day can suffer serious damage to their eyes." That is not a fact. It is drawn from the research that might be faulty. It is only opinion and must be attributed.

● Where information emerges from a report which is clearly fact and not opinion, it appears strange to attribute it. A report might say: "Next month, four new national newspapers are to be included on the FT Profile database." This could prove the basis for an intro. but it would be wrong to attribute it, say, to a report on newspaper libraries by the chief librarian of a university. Inclusion in the FT Profile database is not a matter of opinion, it's a question of being factually right or wrong.

It would have been better to intro.: "Four national newspapers are to be included next month on the FT Profile database, a move which has been welcomed by the chief librarian at Blanktown University."

● Reports often provide the journalist with the chance to internationalise their coverage from a UK base. A report by one of the many solidarity groups (such as the Burma Action Group, Nicaragua Solidarity Campaign, Philippines Support Group) can provide the basis for a detailed, authoritative report. Follow-ups with local representatives of the groups can help add the local angle. Think internationally, act locally is a slogan worth remembering as a journalist.

● It's often useful to end the story with details of the report: full title, publishers, cost and maybe even address where available.

Analysis of "400 deaths a day"; *Liverpool Echo (22 May 1992)*

400 deaths a day

New survey shows that one-third of regular smokers will be killed by their deadly habit

By Echo reporter

MORE than one-fifth of people in developed countries will die from smoking-related diseases, according to a new report.

In the UK, 400 people die every day as a result of tobacco – on average one every four minutes.

Rising

While smoking among men in the UK

has decreased substantially, deaths among women are rising to make a total of about 150,000 deaths a year.

A study by The Imperial Cancer Research Fund Cancer Studies Unit in Oxford, published in the Lancet, shows out of a total world population of just under one and a quarter billion, 250 million will die from smoking-related diseases – equivalent to the population of the United States.

The report shows there are already two million deaths a year from tobacco in the industrial nations, and during the 1990s about 21 million will die from the habit.

Of these, five to six million will be in the EC, five to six million in the USA and 10 million in other developed countries, with further increases likely in subsequent decades.

Cancers linked with tobacco include those of the lung, mouth, pharynx, larynx, oesophagus, kidney and bladder.

Other conditions related to smoking include coronary, artery and cerebral and other cascular disease as well as chronic lung and respiratory conditions.

ICRF Professor of Medical Statistics at Oxford and head of the Cancer Studies Unit, Richard Peto, said: "Most people already know that smoking is dangerous, but most people don't realise how enormous the risks are.

"The new American study that we have used indicates that more than one-third of all regular smokers will be killed by the habit and about half of those killed will still be only in middle age.

Stopping

"Those killed by tobacco in middle age lose about 24 years.

"In many countries teenage smoking is still rising and it's those who start when they are still in their teens who will have much the greatest risk of death from tobacco in middle age.

"About the only good news is that stopping smoking works remarkably well.

"Obviously, if you wait until you've got lung cancer then it may well be too late."

Par. 1: details from the report are more important than the publishing of the findings. It does not begin: "A new report, published today, highlights the fact that more than one-fifth of people in the developed world will die from smoking-related diseases." The coverage goes straight to the most striking information which is attributed: "according to a new report".

The reporter has gone for striking details relating to the "developed countries" rather than the more predictable British angle which still comes prominently in the next par.

Par. 2: newsy UK details reported succinctly. No need for attribution. It's clear from the previous par.

Par. 3: UK focus continues, contrasting male and female trends. Again, no attribution necessary.

Par. 4: source finally identified. It's a bit of a mouthful ("A study by the Imperial Cancer Research Fund Cancer Studies Unit in Oxford, published in the *Lancet*") which, placed any higher, would detract from the impact of all those striking details. An intro.: "More than one-fifth of people in developed countries will die from smoking-related diseases, according to a new study by the Imperial Cancer Research Fund Cancer Studies Unit in Oxford" highlights a body little known in Liverpool.

Par. 5: "The report shows . . ." clearly attributes the following details. It is tempting to begin sentences with a similar construction. Here, the reporter avoids that temptation.

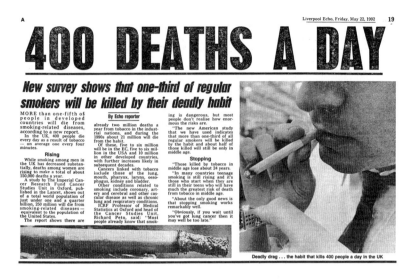

A
Liverpool Echo, Friday, May 22, 1992 **19**

400 DEATHS A DAY

New survey shows that one-third of regular smokers will be killed by their deadly habit

By Echo reporter

MORE than one-fifth of people in developed countries will die from smoking-related diseases, according to a new report.

In the UK, 400 people die every day as a result of tobacco — on average one every four minutes.

Rising

While smoking among men in the UK has decreased substantially, deaths among women are rising to make a total of about 150,000 deaths a year.

A study by The Imperial Cancer Research Fund Cancer Studies Unit in Oxford, published in the Lancet, shows out of a total world population of just under one and a quarter billion, 250 million will die from smoking-related diseases — equivalent to the population of the United States.

The report shows there are already two million deaths a year from tobacco in the industrial nations, and during the 1990s about 21 million will die from the habit.

Of these, five to six million will be in the EC, five to six million in the USA and 10 million in other developed countries, with further increases likely in subsequent decades.

Cancers linked with tobacco include those of the lung, mouth, pharynx, larynx, oesophagus, kidney and bladder.

Other conditions related to smoking include coronary, artery and cerebral and other cascular disease as well as chronic lung and respiratory conditions.

ICRF Professor of Medical Statistics at Oxford and head of the Cancer Studies Unit, Richard Peto, said: "Most people already know that smok-

ing is dangerous, but most people don't realise how enormous the risks are.

"The new American study that we have used indicates that more than one-third of all regular smokers will be killed by the habit and about half of those killed will still be only in middle age.

Stopping

"Those killed by tobacco in middle age lose about 24 years.

"In many countries teenage smoking is still rising and it's those who start when they are still in their teens who will have much the greatest risk of death from tobacco in middle age.

"About the only good news is that stopping smoking works remarkably well.

"Obviously, if you wait until you've got lung cancer then it may well be too late."

Deadly drag . . . the habit that kills 400 people a day in the UK

Courtesy *Liverpool Echo*

Par. 6: "Of these . . ." provides a useful, concise link phrase. Again the emphasis falls on hard, factual details.

Pars 7 and 8: specific focus on cancer-linked details drawn from the report.

Pars 9–14: new source so they are mentioned at the start of the sentence. The acronym ICRF was not identified when the Imperial Cancer Research Fund Unit was first mentioned in par. 4 and so might confuse the rapid reader here. Better to have placed ICRF in brackets after the first mention in par. 4.

It's not clear if Peto was speaking on the phone, at a press conference, or even in a foreword to the report. But that kind of detail is not essentia!. The reporter allows Peto to speak freely. The information buried in par. 10 that one-third of regular smokers will be killed by the habit could have been included in par. 2. Significantly, the headline writer used that strong angle for the subordinate deck.

The article is well illustrated.

Analysis of "Aquino blamed for 'country of widows' "; *socialist (5 November 1991)*

THE writer has a number of sources to consider: comments by Carlos Allones and reports by Amnesty International and Oxfam. Details from all these have to be selected and placed concisely in order of importance.

Aquino blamed for 'country of widows'

REPRESSION of Philippine trade unionists is worse under president Cory Aquino than under Ferdinand Marcos, according to National Federation of Sugar Workers representative Carlos Allones.

He was in Britain earlier this month to gain support from unions following an Amnesty International report which said security forces and semi-official death squads are believed to have killed "dozens of union members".

The government equates industrial action with armed opposition, so trade unionists become targets of counter-insurgency campaigns. Sugar workers have been the main victims, Amnesty says.

Since Aquino came to power in 1986, 250 members of the NFSW have been unlawfully detained, 40 killed by government forces and seven have "disappeared". In May, 11 NFSW national leaders were charged with subversion.

"Mrs Aquino fought an election as a tragic widow," Allones said. "But under her government, our country is becoming a country of widows. There are more death squads, more disappearances, and more executions of vigilantes.

"When we demand our basic rights, we are labelled communists. That is like a death sentence. What we had hoped could be a liberation in February 1986 has turned into a nightmare; what was people's power is now murder gangs."

Amnesty cites several official killings of NFSW workers and members. On 26 January 1990, 16-year-old Hernando Pelaro and Pablito Labrador were drinking coffee with other farm labourers in the village shop. A police unit and paramilitary gunmen arrived and without warning sprayed the shop with bullets.

The shop's occupants, some wounded, were lined up in the street. A soldier picked out Pelaro and Labrador as NFSW members and shot them dead.

In another incident, 100 soldiers arrived at a village in a sugar plantation and demanded to know who were members of the union. The soldiers then shot and killed Eduardo Lazona, an NFSW organiser.

An Oxfam report published this month says: "The development strategy [in the Philippines] inspired by the IMF and World Bank is inherently anti-union ... because the maintenance of a pool of cheap, productive and docile labour is necessary for the strategy to work."

The strategy is needed to pay the massive £20,000 million debt run up by Marcos. Much was for useless projects promoted by transnational corporations. The interest payment on debt for the Bataan nuclear power plant, never used because it is in an earthquake zone, is £200,000 per day.

● *The Philippines: Debt and Poverty*, £7.44 from Oxfam, PO Box 120, Oxford OX2 7AF.

Philippines Human Rights Violations and the Labour Movement, Amnesty International, 1 Easton Street, London WC1X 8DJ.

socialist 23 October - 5 November 1991

Aquino blamed for 'country of widows'

REPRESSION of Philippine trade unionists is worse under president Cory Aquino than under Ferdinand Marcos, according to National Federation of Sugar Workers representative Carlos Allones.

He was in Britain earlier this month to gain support from unions following an Amnesty International report which said security forces and semi-official death squads are believed to have killed "dozens of union members".

The government equates industrial action with armed opposition, so trade unionists become targets of counter-insurgency campaigns. Sugar workers have been the main victims, Amnesty says.

Since Aquino came to power in 1986, 250 members of the NFSW have been unlawfully detained, 40 killed by government forces and seven have "disappeared". In May, 11 NFSW national leaders were charged with subversion.

"Mrs Aquino fought an election as a tragic widow," Allones said. "But under her government, our country is becoming a country of widows. There are more death squads, more disappearances, and more executions by vigilantes.

"When we demand our basic rights, we are labelled communists. That is like a death sentence. What we had hoped would be a liberation in February 1986 has turned into a nightmare; what was people's

■ Sugar cane workers are threatened by death squads. PICTURE: BELINDA COOTE

power is now murder gangs."

Amnesty cites several official killings of NFSW workers and members. On 26 January 1990, 16-year-old Hernando Pelaro and Pablito Labrador were drinking coffee with other farm labourers in the village shop. A police unit and paramilitary gunmen arrived and without warning sprayed the shop with bullets.

The shop's occupants, some wounded, were lined up in the street. A soldier picked out Pelaro and Labrador as NFSW members and shot them dead.

In another incident, 100 soldiers arrived at a village in a sugar plantation and demanded to know who were members of the union. The soldiers then shot and killed Eduardo Lazona, an NFSW organiser.

An Oxfam report published this month says: "The development strategy [in the Philippines] inspired by the IMF and World Bank is inherently anti-union ... because the maintenance of a pool of cheap, productive and docile labour is necessary for the strategy to work."

The strategy is needed to

pay the massive £20,000 million debt run up by Marcos. Much was for useless projects promoted by transnational corporations. The interest payment on debt for the Bataan nuclear power plant, never used because it is in an earthquake zone, is £200,000 per day.

● *The Philippines: Debt and Poverty*, £7.44 from Oxfam, PO Box 120, Oxford OX2 7AF.
Philippines Human Rights Violations and the Labour Movement, Amnesty International, 1 Easton Street, London WC1X 8DJ.

Courtesy *socialist*

Thematic block 1: repression in the Philippines, according to Allones and Amnesty

Par. 1: highlights a claim that contradicts expectations. Hence its news value. Aquino was supposedly installed as Philippines President in 1986 at the head of a "people's revolution" that hoped to throw off the repressive apparatus of the US-backed dictator, Ferdinand Marcos. According to the newspaper's source, the reverse is the case. Notice how the controversial comment is attributed in the intro., thus following normal newspaper convention.

Notice, too, the source. For national and local newspapers he is unusual: a trade union representative in a country which had largely dropped out of the mainstream news since the "revolution". The newspaper, operating its own political bias, attaches high news values to Allones's comments. The mainstream press, with their own biases, either eliminate or marginalise the views of such people.

Allones's opinions have also been highlighted because there is an element of the "exclusive" about them. The reports from Amnesty and Oxfam carry strong views and details but the mainstream media are likely to have received them. Journalistically, too, the spoken word is also stronger and more colourful than the written word. A speaker injects a vital, human dimension into the news. A written report, in comparison, has none of that immediacy.

Par. 2: spells out a "when" element in the story ("earlier this month . . . following . . .") which helps the copy flow on to the Amnesty report which supports the opening claim.

Par. 3: adds more evidence to support the opening allegation, being clearly attributed to the Amnesty report.

Thematic block 2: background

Par. 4: "Since Aquino came to power. . ." is a transitional phrase leading up to a concise detailing of facts which support the "repression" theme.

Thematic block 3: back to main source for direct quotes

Pars 5 and 6: Allones's comments are concise and yet emotionally charged. Words and phrases like "tragic widow", a "country of widows", "death squads", "liberation", "nightmare", "murder gangs" carry considerable dramatic power.

Thematic block 4: back to Amnesty

Pars 7–9: now that Allones has been given his two pars, the writer can devote two pars to expanding the Amnesty evidence. "In another incident" is the transitional phrase linking the Pelaro/Labrador case to the Lazona incident.

Thematic block 5: Oxfam introduced

Pars 10 and 11: the news value of the Oxfam report is stressed in the phrase "published this month". Since *socialist* was a bimonthly that reference still has strong news credibility. The direct quote is strong, further supporting the original claim. The final par. is strong on factual detail and paraphrases sections of the Oxfam report concisely.

Thematic block 6: final two pars: information service to readers

These spell out information for anyone wanting to acquire the Oxfam or Amnesty reports. Too often national newspapers miss out these details. *socialist* clearly sees its role as educational, with the article aiming to spark further involvement in the issues raised.

The report shows how foreign stories can be written effectively from a UK base. Campaigners, politicians, writers, academics, refugees from all over the world are arriving in Britain every day and many are potential news sources. National newspapers often complain how financial constraints impede foreign reporting. Imaginative use of sources in Britain can, to some significant degree, offset those problems.

Whilst using UK-based sources, the article in no way patronises the plight of the Filipinos. News of foreign countries often appears in UK newspapers and magazines when the policies of the governments in London or Washington focus on them or when there are clear UK angles. A British businessman may be arrested on charges of spying in a foreign city, UK trade with a country may be affected by a particular development. This story, in contrast, focuses on the Philippine angle.

Covering speeches

A SPEECH constitutes a perfect event for news coverage: it has a tidy beginning, middle and end. A chosen speech will usually provide some copy so attendance makes economic sense. A complex and controversial issue may be usefully simplified through the voice of one person.

The Bosnian civil war may have been a complex, on-going process with origins buried deep in the ethnic divisions of the former Yugoslav republic. A report of a speech on the war by a celebrity or major politician provided a focus for news coverage, reducing the complexities to a comprehensible event rooted in the "now" of news.

Many covered speeches are not attended by the press. Publicity departments (of political parties, companies, campaigning organisations and the government, for instance) distribute a regular supply of press releases giving verbatim or edited accounts of speeches.

A journalist attending a speech will often, then, attempt to incorporate some "eye-witness" feature to indicate their presence. They may report the responses of the audience or the mood of the speaker.

A report will tend to combine direct quotes with reported speech. The direct quotes are reserved for the most colourful expressions of opinion.

As in conventional news stories, it is normally important to carry the "who", "what" and "when" in the intro. section.

See how this appears in the *Liverpool Daily Post* (27 November 1992):

Get behind Eldorado Grade tells BBC chiefs

By Rob Scully
Daily Post Correspondent

CHANNEL 4 chief Michael Grade last night accused the BBC hierarchy of failing to support the much-maligned Spanish-based soap opera Eldorado.

"You can't spend that sort of money without top level approval," he told the International Television Festival in Edinburgh.

"A public message of support from the top would not come amiss – it would also give the hierarchy some credibility.

"As and when the show does come good, they will be the first to say 'we always knew it would'," said Mr Grade, a former programme director at BBC TV.

"Second guessing is second nature at the top of the BBC.

"But what has been forgotten, or not understood, is that the BBC has always prided itself on the record of staying with shows that weren't instant successes, like Dad's Army and, yes, EastEnders.

"It must never look like a place where safety first is the rule, where instant success is demanded of popular entertainment," said Mr Grade, who has been criticised for taking Channel 4 down-market since assuming control.

He also attacked the BBC Board of Governors, accusing them of ignoring popular taste in favour of highbrow programmes.

The future of the BBC was in doubt amid debate about licence fees, political interference from the government and a lack of support from the top for programme-makers, he said.

"The high ground policy is simplistic nonsense. It will marginalise the BBC, reduce choice and erode the public's willingness to pay."

Mr Grade was delivering the James MacTaggart Memorial Lecture which opened the festival.

Howell James, BBC Director of Corporate Affairs, later described Mr Grade's contribution as "spirited and stimulating" – but wrong.

"Nowhere in his speech does he recognise the considerable changes that have occurred in broadcasting since the current BBC Charter was issued in 1981 – changes which will accelerate in the coming year.

"New services on television and radio will dramatically change people's viewing and listening habits," he said.

First par.:

Who – Channel 4 chief Michael Grade

When – last night

What – accused the BBC hierarchy of failing to support the much- maligned Spanish-based soap opera Eldorado.

The second par. follows a conventional approach for reporting speeches, with a succinct direct quote supporting and expanding the intro. In addition, the par. neatly conveys the "where" of the story, "the International Television Festival in Edinburgh".

The more detailed description of the speech being "the James MacTaggart Memorial Lecture which opened the festival" is important for the organisers but only of secondary news value. Hence it appears at the end of the Grade section, in the eleventh par.

Thatcher blasts West on Bosnia

LADY Thatcher has delivered a savage attack on the West's "paralysis" over the Yugoslav civil war.

In a speech which will enrage Downing Street she virtually called for armed force to impose peace on the warring factions bringing strife to Bosnia.

Addressing a meeting of German business leaders, the former premier said scornfully: "How much better it would have been if the West had not only given humanitarian aid but had struck at this problem's very root by preventing the terrible atrocities which have occurred.

"Alas, we tried to act on the basis of consensus and, as so often happens, consensus led to paralysis, when effective leadership was needed.

"The contrast with the Gulf War is all too apparent, for then we had the United States willing to take the lead and the aggressor was stopped.

Poet

"In a new world order Europe must have the courage to show conviction."

She quoted the words of a German poet describing the old Habsburg monarchy: "This is the curse of our old house – halfway means and halfway steps warily treading to halfway aims."

In her speech, at Frankfurt on Wednesday, Lady Thatcher also vigorously stirred the Maastricht pot, just when the Government was hoping the furore was dying down.

She heaped scorn on European ministers who, she claimed, had failed to recognise the growing doubts throughout the European Community about the treaty.

She said: "Scepticism is on the increase. People feel that their governments have gone ahead too fast – and they are not sure about the direction, either.

"The trouble is that European ministers spend so much time in each others' company they get out of touch with the people and too much in touch with themselves.

"People do not want to become citizens of a European superstate."

© *Daily Mail*/Solo

The Thatcher report in the *Daily Mail* (27 November 1992) carries the undated "has delivered" and, in typical tabloid style, the more emotive "savage attack". This approach continues throughout with the use of "said scornfully", "vigorously stirred the Maastricht pot" and "heaped scorn".

It transpires that the "undated" approach has been used because the speech was given on Wednesday, late for a Friday newspaper. The "undated" approach obscures this, with the Wednesday reference coming only in the eighth par.

The second par. launches into comment and interpretation. In contrast, the *Liverpool Daily Post* report nowhere interjects overt comment or analysis. "In a speech which will enrage Downing Street" is presented as fact but is comment. Downing Street probably had lots of other matters to worry about that day. And the section "she virtually called for armed force to impose peace on the warring factions . . ." is more interpretation.

The *Mail*, at the time, was calling for armed intervention by the West into Bosnia. Lady Thatcher did not explicitly call for it but she said sufficient for the newspaper to suggest she "virtually" did. Thus this interpretation comes higher up the story than the report of the content of the speech.

The "where" comes in the third par.: "a meeting of German business leaders". The town is not mentioned until par. 8 since its news value is not high.

Both reports use mainly Lady Thatcher/she or Michael Grade/he. Grade is only once referred to as "Channel 4 chief" and once as "a former programme director at BBC TV", significant because he is shown here to be criticising his former employers. Lady Thatcher is only once described as "the former premier". Other descriptive phrases or the repetition of the titles would be over-wordy.

The structures of both stories are clear. The Lady Thatcher piece divides into two sections. The first, up to par. 7, focuses on Bosnia. The second, from par. 8 to the end, shifts to Maastricht. The crucial phrase linking the two sections is "In her speech, at Frankfurt on Wednesday, Lady Thatcher also . . ."

The Grade piece also divides into two. The first section ends at par. 11; the second, from par. 12 to the end, carries a follow-up quote from the BBC. The first section could also be subdivided into two with the first subsection focusing on Eldorado, the second on the Board of Governors' "high ground" policy.

The *Mail* report carries no by-line. Certainly the report appears as a blatant "plug" for Lady Thatcher, with long stretches of direct quote and no attempt to "balance" the piece with quotes from someone warning of the dangers of military escalation in Bosnia.

One explanation could be that the report was based on a press release. Writing up in *Mail* style was perhaps considered a mundane task by the sub-editors and so not worthy of a by-line.

All in the eye of the beholder: *eye-witness reporting*

Journalists are the observers of history. When the Berlin Wall falls, they are there describing the tumultuous events. When the Americans invade Grenada and ban journalists from the island, the brave ones take to boats in an attempt to evade the censorship regime and see the attacks at first hand. More mundanely, a local journalist attends a football match and reports what he or she sees.

This "eye-witness" dimension (also known as "direct observation") is one of the crucial distinguishing features of journalism.

Reporters cannot possibly witness all the events they report. They have to rely on others for their accounts. Editorial cutbacks of recent years have further reduced the eye-witness element in the news. Meetings, for instance, are often no longer attended but "picked up" afterwards.

But when reporters are present at significant events, that witnessing can be used to dramatic effect, providing an immediacy and an appearance of authenticity to copy.

Even a straight report of a meeting can be enlivened by the inclusion of an eye-witness element such as descriptions of participants' appearance, accounts of questions from the floor and responses from the audience.

Notice how in this report in the *Independent on Sunday* (31 January 1993), the writer describes the response of the audience as "tumultuous applause". Of the "guests" he says they are "a strange mixture of very old and very young Tory faithful. Staff from Conservative Central Office kept a low profile . . ." Castle was there: he wasn't just bashing out another press release. He saw and heard and he makes use of that experience in his copy.

Who could Lady Thatcher have been talking about?

By Stephen Castle
Political Correspondent

NOT once in the blistering, hour-long demonstration of oratorical bombast was *his* name mentioned. But the audience at the London dinner given by the National Association of Conservative Graduates did not need their degrees to work out who was in

Lady Thatcher's firing line.

In the week when John Major sued two magazines, she gave short shrift to the idea that politicians should care about what is written about them. Without referring to any libel actions she said: "Goodness me, I didn't read the papers. I just got on with the job."

Adopting a mariner's metaphor, she spoke of a government's need for ideals and principles: "If you do not have stars to steer by, a fixed point in the heavens and a compass to guide you, you will then become merely the slave of your in-tray. There are new stars in the firmament . . . shooting stars. They are called Compromise and Consensus."

Could these errant stars be guiding British government economic policy? Lady Thatcher did not quite say so, although she knew the course to navigate: "We knew we had to cut expenditure; you only get into difficulties, financially, when you depart from orthodox financing [huge applause]. You don't garner the respect of the people if you say 'yes' to every request only to land them in terrific debt."

And on defence, at a moment when the armed forces are at full stretch, she observed: "At no time did we ever have to think 'do we have the correct defence equipment?' We knew we had."

Lady Thatcher had taken her text from Theodore Roosevelt: "Far better is it to dare mighty things, even though chequered by failure, than to dwell in that perpetual twilight that knows not victory or defeat." Strangely, my dictionary of quotations substitutes "grey" for "perpetual".

The 600-strong audience at London's New Connaught Rooms on Thursday had expected a rousing speech from the former prime minister, and they were not disappointed. Besides the coded baiting of Mr Major's government, there was a tribute to Churchill; thoughts on foreign policy ("pragmatism is never enough"); and a heartfelt demand for more Western aid for Russia.

Then on to Europe. Lady Thatcher, whose position on the Maastricht Bill will gain increasing significance as it passes to the Lords, defended her decision to sign the single European Act but attacked the notion of a single currency. The Maastricht Bill, she said, "goes further than before". The process, she said (to more tumultuous applause) would mean "surrendering more and more to bureaucracy and that less and less is done by democracy in our own elected Parliament".

The guests were a strange mixture of very old and very young Tory faithful. Staff from Conservative Central Office kept a low profile, and the one member of the Cabinet who was due to introduce the main speaker – the very dry Chief Secretary to the Treasury, Michael Portillo – sent his apologies. He had to cancel, due to a three-line whip on the Maastricht Bill.

Eye-witness reporting plays a significant role in this *Sunday Express* report (3 January 1993). As the Czech and Slovak republics split, McAlpine describes what he sees in Prague: people milling around the Palach memorial and wandering in the streets, the packed bridge, the fireworks. Playing on contrasts, he writes: "They drank, but were not drunk. They celebrated, but were not happy. The Velvet Divorce had become absolute."

Till death us do part
After a 74-year marriage two nations go it alone

from Alistair McAlpine in Prague

ROLL up that map, it will not be wanted these 10 years. Prime Minister, William Pitt, said these words at the beginning of the 19th century.

At the end of the 20th century a new map is needed almost every week. Europe is constantly changing its shape.

Amidst the confusion of the Russian empire's disintegration, the warfare of Yugoslavia and the threatening danger in Macedonia, a divorce has been taking place between the republics of Czech and Slovak.

At the stroke of midnight on December 31, Czechoslovakia became two nations.

I watched the crowds in St Wenceslas Square as they milled around the memorial to Jan Palach, the brave student who stood before a tank in the name of freedom. Flowers were strewn on the spot where he died.

Champagne

The people wandered in the streets as dusk came. Fireworks began to explode. There seemed to be no great enthusiasm, no real joy. Do the people want this divorce, arranged by politicians?

Through the autumn, the opinion polls suggested they did not.

The shops are filled with goods – goods for tourists.

The night was very cold, the people seemed poor. The prosperity only skin-deep.

I walked over the Charles Bridge. I could see the floodlit castle and Prague's many spires. The river Vltava was black and freezing.

The bridge was packed with people as the New Year approached. The fireworks exploded in volleys.

Through the crowd, towards the old town square, it was jammed with people, many drinking Russian champagne straight from the bottle.

As the town's clock struck 12 there was no great cheer, no patriotic singing, no shouts of hope, just a barrage of explosions and a sky filled with the coloured lights from scores of exploding rockets.

I walked home through the vast crowds. They drank, but were not drunk. They celebrated, but were not happy. The Velvet Divorce had become absolute.

There only remains the division of the minor spoils. The contents of museums, the objects belong to the histories of these new countries.

In this "Eyewitness" feature from the *Guardian* (4 January 1993), Hella Pick, being part of the small journalistic group accompanying the UN secretary-general, became part of the news story. What she saw she recorded. The story has many ingredients: drama, danger, the threat of violence and farce.

UN chief forced to flee Somalia by angry mob

Eyewitness

**Hella Pick
in Mogadishu**

THE United Nations was dealt an ignominious blow yesterday when supporters of General Mohammed Farah Aideed, one of Somalia's faction leaders, forced the UN secretary-general, Boutros Boutros-Ghali, to cut short his visit to the capital, Mogadishu.

As an angry crowd pelted the UN headquarters with stones and rubbish, Mr Boutros-Ghali took refuge with United States Marines and shifted a scheduled press conference to the city's airport.

As he flew out he left two senior UN staff and a small group of journalists besieged in the UN compound, where they were used by the American military commanders as decoys until the secretary-general's plane had taken off.

Mr Boutros-Ghali went to Mogadishu on the eve of a conference in Addis Ababa of Somali faction leaders, which he has convened to try to promote national reconciliation. Despite yesterday's violence in Mogadishu, Gen. Aideed and his rival faction leader, Ali Mahdi Mohammed, said yesterday that they plan to send delegations to the meeting.

And in spite of the resurgent lawlessness he had seen on the streets of the capital, Mr Boutros-Ghali said that he believed the conference would be the beginning of the solution to the Somali crisis. "1993 will be the year of reconstruction, reconciliation and rehabilitation," he promised.

He had planned yesterday's brief visit to demonstrate support for the small band of UN staff in Somalia. "These people are risking their lives. They must be supported," he said on his flight in to the capital yesterday morning.

How true that was we soon found. When we landed in Mogadishu the secretary-general was first taken by helicopter to visit an aid station at Afkoi while the rest of us, UN under-secretary for African and Middle Eastern affairs, James Jonah, a senior assistant, Lisa Buttonheim, and four journalists, were driven off without military escort in white cars bearing the UN flag.

But as we turned a corner towards the UN compound in southern Mogadishu, a hail of large stones greeted us. A crowd of about 200 Somalis, supporters of Gen. Aideed, had gathered to denounce the secretary-general's efforts.

The windscreen of the first car, in which the UN's resident Canadian security officer, Colonel Michael Parr, was travelling, was smashed as we drove past.

Outside the iron gates of the compound the mob grew to around 1,000 and became angrier. A man tore down the UN flag, hoisting the Somali flag in its place. The crowd believed Mr Boutros-Ghali was in our procession, but he never reached us, and for several hours we feared the mob would break down the gates.

"Boutros-Ghali is responsible for death and starvation," Gen. Aideed's supporters screamed from the road outside. "We want no UN trusteeship, no UN-sponsored troops."

Mr Boutros-Ghali had been told by the Americans that they could not get him to the compound, and he took shelter in the former US embassy, now headquarters to the 20,000 US Marines in Somalia.

"The incidents which happened around the UN headquarters do not represent the feeling of the Somali people," he said later at a chaotic airport press conference. "They represent just the position of those who do not want peace and who are interested in maintaining chaos and continuous confrontation."

Meanwhile, when Mr Boutros-Ghali had safely left the country, Col Parr announced that an American rescue mission was being mounted to extricate our small group at the UN compound.

The earlier drama now turned into farce. With a flurry a back gate opened and amid clouds of dust six open military lorries arrived, each with a complement of GIs.

As we screeched out at speed a handful of women in the street outside waved and children smiled. The mob had gone. There was no ambush, no shots, no stones.

Hella Pick © the *Guardian*

Eye-witness elements often appear in profiles. Here Caroline Phillips, in the London *Evening Standard* (1 February 1993) describes what she sees of her subject, Mary Wesley.

The Caroline Phillips interview

Eighty-year-old novelist Mary Wesley explains how she learned about life and why she's looking forward to death

IT HAS been a good decade for Mary Wesley. The best-selling author of The Camomile Lawn, who wrote her first book aged 70, has sold 1.5 million books in paperback. "I'm always terrified when I've finished a book that it'll be a disaster," she says. "I used to think, 'What am I trying to do? I can't write.' Now I still think each book will be my last."

Her books have been described as like Jane Austen with sex: witty and racy, they are well-mannered English novels about upper middle-class people with a workaday knowledge of adultery and illegitimacy. They line one shelf (including Japanese and Danish translations) in her cosy cottage in Totnes, Devon.

This week sees the publication in paperback of A Dubious Legacy (for which film discussions are under way), and Harnessing Peacocks will be on television this spring. "I'm really pleased with Harnessing Peacocks," she says emphatically. She advised the director and went on set for a couple of days – "terribly boring and repetitive" – but once they were filming "wouldn't have dreamed of interfering".

Wesley, a spritely 80-year-old, is elegant in her favourite black cashmere jumper and trousers. She is weeny, with silver hair and a face that expresses strength and timidity. Seemingly brisk, tough and upper-class on the phone (it transpires she doesn't like talking during "office" hours), she now seems mischievous and her acerbic intelligence shines through. She is remarkable for her age.

But what journalists report on the basis of direct observation is not necessarily "true". The act of witnessing is always subjective. The reporter comes to the task with all their personal, cultural, psychological and political baggage and biases. The experience of a white or black person, a man, woman or child may well be different at any event. It is psychologically and physically impossible for the reporter to see everything. At best they must be true to their own experience.

In wars, for instance, a reporter might report what they see at the battle front (though in major UK/US wars today they are likely to be part of a tiny pool kept well away from any serious action). This is only a tiny (and probably censored) part of the story. What is happening down the road ruled out of bounds? Seeing that might place their witness in a different light. And warfare exists on so many different levels, though the media tend to prioritise the military. There are the social, diplomatic, economic, psychological, mythical, rhetorical aspects. The battle front witness of the reporter can provide only a tiny "truth" – but an important one all the same (*The First Casualty: The War Correspondent as Hero, Propagandist and Myth Maker*; Phillip Knightley; Quartet; London; third edition; 1982).

9 Powerful information
Reporting national and local government
John Turner

···

POLITICS is about power and information is power. Journalists are part of the information business and are crucial in a political process which involves the exercise of this potent force. People with power, whether they be Cabinet ministers, senior civil servants or chief executives of local councils, have a vested interest, not only in protecting their own power, but in obscuring the extent of their authority in the first place. The journalist occupies a pivotal position between those who make and implement important decisions and those who are often forced to comply with such decisions. Any democratic system depends on people being well informed and educated about politics by a media which give a full and accurate account of news, encompassing a wide and varied range of political opinions.

The media in general have a large and growing significance on politics. However, there is unclear evidence regarding the nature and extent of this influence. The political impact of the media, and the press in particular, is difficult to assess because:

- it is difficult to isolate the effect of the media from other influences like family, education, work and economic circumstances.

- there is a complex myriad of mutually-influencing factors which complicate the relationship between newspaper and reader. The political impact of a paper will depend less on what is being read than on who is doing the reading and their level of knowledge and experience about politics in general.

- the media are fragmented, with television, radio and the national press having different effects compared with local coverage. A direct relationship between any media's influence on a political issue is therefore confused.

- similar messages are received and interpreted in different ways by different people, hence a claim that the media are being used for propaganda purposes cannot be verified because one cannot be sure of the effect intended.

Before turning to aspects of local and national politics it is important briefly to outline three ways in which the impact of the media has been assessed.

- *Agenda-setting and primary definers*. Here the media are accused less of telling people what to believe, than in providing a more pervasive influence on what people think about and how they make judgements about different issues. Agenda-setting involves a constant interaction between a newspaper and its readers. Newspapers also tend to take on board sources of information which control and establish initial definitions of particular issues. As such, a great deal of news coverage reflects the interpretations initially created by official sources.

● *Reinforcement and hegemony.* Here the media are not so much creating attitudes, but are involved in strengthening and reinforcing existing beliefs and prejudices. This can be linked to the notion of hegemony whereby consent is sought for those ways of making sense of the world which fit with the perspective of those in power.

● *Independent effects.* There is a growing view that the media have a more direct and independent effect on beliefs and behaviour. Again evidence for such a view remains controversial. New media technologies have as much of an influence on attitudes and behaviour as the uses to which they are put.

Newton has pointed to a paradox in the media's impact on political awareness ("Mass media"; K. Newton; in H. Drucker *et al.*, *Developments in British Politics*; Macmillan; London; 1986). Whereas political information is delivered faster to more people, nevertheless the mass tabloids contain only a little political content and what they report is personalised, trivialised, sensationalised and biased. Consequently, a large proportion of the public is provided with restricted news and knowledge of current affairs. This contradiction has been discussed by Seymour-Ure in his distinction of levels of readership between a mass public and informed political public (*The Political Impact of the Mass Media*; C. Seymour-Ure; Constable; London; 1974). An information gap has been created with a small, well-educated public who use the media to become better informed and a mass public who mainly read gossip columns and sports pages and are therefore more readily influenced by biased news.

Local papers do not work in a vacuum. They are as much a part of the political system and process as anyone, and journalists working for them have assumptions about the way in which the political system operates. There is far less of a division between local and national politics today. Local government has increasingly become simply an arm of central administration and, as in the case of education policy, it is difficult to disentangle separate national and local agendas. Equally, there is nothing inherently local about local newspapers. Much of what is considered to be national news is local in nature and source. Indeed, Britain's tradition of a dominant national press has imposed a kind of artificial parochialism on the local press which has led to a number of criticisms about the rather narrow way in which local papers have covered local politics. The homogeneous and national nature of the British political system and political culture must not be underestimated in this respect. They have had an important effect on the way in which politics is reported by the local press.

The British political system

PREVIOUS studies of the British political system have pointed to its strong civic culture, supported by a stable and cohesive system of politics (*The Civic Culture*; G. Almond and S. Verba; Princeton University Press; Princeton; 1963. *Politics in England*; R. Rose; Faber & Faber; London; 1965.) Power in Britain is centralised and, according to the traditional view, is concentrated in the Cabinet in Parliament and Whitehall, supported by political conventions, the cohesiveness of political parties, Treasury control, ministerial responsibility and the Crown prerogative. This strong and cohesive model of British government has been accentuated by a period of Prime

Ministerial dominance, without the safeguards of accountability which might be imposed by a Bill of Rights or Freedom of Information Act. Before considering aspects of these institutions it is important to consider the underpinning nature of Britain's political culture.

The culture of deference

Deference and tradition

People in Britain have a remarkably deferential attitude towards the dominant political institutions (*Political Science and Political Behaviour*; D. Kavanagh; Allen & Unwin; London; 1983). An appeal to tradition is used as a way of defending many of the institutions which have become a stable part of the political system. The monarchy, the House of Lords, the dominant role of the Prime Minister and pervasive secrecy are the ingredients of a political culture which has not been up-ended by revolution or war. Leigh has referred to the system as a huge mountain with abandoned monuments, with some still powerful and others forgotten (*The Frontiers of Secrecy: Closed Government in Britain*; D. Leigh; Junction Books; London; 1980). An example is the role of the royal prerogative. It is no longer abused by monarchical power but has been transferred to the hands of the Prime Minister and executive. Before MPs protested in 1993, the government considered denying Parliament the right to vote on the Maastricht Treaty. The Prime Minister's press office attempted to argue that under the Crown prerogative such treaties did not need the vote of Parliament, but could be ratified by the Prime Minister on behalf of the Crown.

Political participation

Such deference has made Britain a relatively law-abiding country. There is a general respect for authority and the law which complements a low level of political participation. Many social scientists were surprised that there were not greater social disturbances as a result of mass unemployment in the 1980s. Some 75 per cent vote in general elections, the figure falling to around 50 per cent for local elections. However, only about 5 per cent are members of a political party, with only about 2 per cent becoming party activists.

Centralisation and concentration of power

Based in London, decision-making and political institutions are highly concentrated around government, Parliament and the administration. The unitary, national state has failed to develop any notion of federal-style devolution of powers for local government. Local administration is tightly controlled from the centre, reinforced by the political parties which are similarly organised on national and centralised bases.

Politics at the periphery

In the past ten years there have been more than 50 pieces of legislation concerning local government. Significant parts of the local government system have been abolished, the Greater London Council and six metropolitan authorities in 1986, the Inner London Education Authority in 1990 while a Commission's findings could streamline the system further. Many services have been taken away from the direct responsibility of authorities – competitive tendering has meant private companies now provide many services like bin collection and cleaning. The financial system has been overhauled, with the rates replaced first by the poll tax and then by the council tax, while charge capping has been introduced to restrict spending still further. Internal procedures have also been reviewed with the 1986 Widdicombe report warning of the greater politicisation of local government (*Report of the Committee of Inquiry into the Conduct of Local Authority Business*; D. Widdicombe; HMSO; London; 1986). In addition, there has also been significant legislation changing the nature of services in the areas of housing, social services, education and planning.

Quango state

In recent years there has been a tendency to distance areas of administration from direct political control and public accountability. This quasi-government operates in a no man's land, occupying an increasingly crowded territory between central and local government. Quangos, or quasi-autonomous non-governmental organisations, include public, private or voluntary organisations, or combinations of each. In Britain, examples include the Independent Television Commission set up as a statutory body by Parliament; the BBC established by Royal Charter; the University Grants Committee set up by the Treasury; and the National Consumers' Council which is a non-profit-making company. A key issue for these bodies is the degree to which they are accountable to the public or to the political process of election. A further problem with the growth in quangos has been the process of patronage and the process of appointment to such bodies by ministers. Many posts involve some financial benefit and a large proportion of them have been filled by appointees supportive of the government. The *Guardian* (11 April 1996) reported that the chairman of the London Ports Authority received a payment of £4,000 a day for 12 days' work a year. In 1996 the Nolan Committee on Standards in Public Life recommended that there should be an end to payments for those sitting on public bodies.

Privatisation

The process of privatisation has seen public utilities which were formerly nationalised industries sold off to the private sector. These private companies, like British Telecom, British Gas and the electricity and water companies, are now huge monopolies which have been able to make very large profits for their senior managers and shareholders. In a number of cases the problem of delivering public services in an efficient and cost-effective way has raised issues of accountability. The water companies, for example, have been criticised for failing to deliver services in Yorkshire and British Gas executives were criticised for paying themselves large increases in salary. In all these cases it has been difficult for politicians to regulate the activities of these bodies. Regulatory bodies like OFWAT and OFGAS have been powerless to interfere with their activities.

Secrecy

Linked to this centralisation is the secrecy which pervades British politics and the patronising assumption that government knows best. There is no public right of access to information and no Bill of Rights. The courts are left to interpret such matters, while the government proscribes openness through a restrictive Official Secrets Act and D Notice system.

Party politics

Since the 1880s Britain has been dominated by political parties and politics is still organised around a two-party system. In the 1980s some 80 per cent of people still identified with one of the two main parties and just over 50 per cent of the electorate voted for them in the 1992 general election. Parties control the political agenda through professional party machines and discipline, while party managers, through the Whips, dominate in Parliament.

The emphasis of laissez-faire

Britain has a strong state and free economy. There is active state intervention to ensure law and order and social control, but little to ensure full employment and increased social justice. In the past decade the trend since 1945 towards collectivism and corporatism has been halted and the Keynesian rationale for state intervention has been undermined by free-market philosophies.

Language and symbols of politics

The use of particular forms of language defines political identities and reassures supporters. On the right terms are used like "freedom of choice", "patriotism", "individuality", "efficiency"; the left is labelled "extremist", "communist", "red" and "unpatriotic". For the left, terms like "equality", "socialism", "class" and "the state" are used, and the right is labelled as "uncaring", "capitalist", "Fascist" and "selfish". Such terms have tended to highlight differences between the parties which have not in policy terms existed.

Consensus

Even despite the radical policy shifts of Thatcher there has been a high level of agreement on the main areas of policy in British politics. Over a range of policies, like foreign affairs (Iraq and Bosnia), Northern Ireland, race relations, economic management, there has been agreement between the parties, with governments being prepared to negotiate and compromise with pressure groups.

Authoritarian populism

A more populist politics under Thatcher in the 1980s placed a new emphasis on self-reliance, individualism, market economics, curbing trade union immunities and encouraging private enterprise. There was also a more vigorous attack on many traditional institutions in the name of the market and efficiency. The civil service, health service and law profession were all targeted. Thatcher attacked important elements of the post-war consensus and was prepared to go beyond Parliament and the Cabinet by direct appeals to the electorate.

Hall has referred to local councillors and press officers simply as primary definers of the news agenda (*Policing the Crisis: Mugging, the State and Law and Order*; S. Hall, C. Critcher, J. Clarke, T. Jefferson, B. Roberts; Macmillan; London; 1978). As such, they attempt to control the flow of official information and define particular situations and issues. Local news journalism has become highly dependent on accredited local sources and the council's news managers. Thus, much local news reproduces the interpretations of these primary definers. For example, Chibnall has argued that institutions attempt to protect their images, control understandings and promote particular ideologies in such a way (*Law and Order News*; S. Chibnall; Tavistock; London; 1977).

According to Byrne local newspapers remain the chief means of communication about local issues and the link between council and community (*Local Government in Britain*; T. Byrne; Penguin; Harmondsworth; 1986). Most electors in Glasgow learn about issues through the local press, some eight in ten being regular readers. Cox and Morgan found that about a quarter of columns in local newspapers were devoted to news and about 10 per cent were devoted to news about local politics (*City Politics and the Press*; H. Cox and D. Morgan; Cambridge University Press; Cambridge; 1973).

However, there have been criticisms about the rather parochial content of local newspaper coverage:

- *Presentation*: they provide too little interpretation and analysis. Cox and Morgan found that issues are reported in relation to specific council meetings rather than being placed in a wider context (*City Politics and the Press*; H. Cox and D. Morgan; Cambridge University Press; Cambridge; 1973).

- *Sources*: journalists are too dependent on the local council for information, over-emphasising the views of senior officers, press officers and leading councillors. Newsroom handling of local government stories has become a matter of routine, with an over-use of a call system and press releases, council agendas, press conferences and "off-the-record" press officer briefings. This has restrained criticism or investigation and often led to a climate of co-operation, blurring the division between news and publicity (*The Silent Watchdog*; D. Murphy; Constable; London; 1976).

- *Editorials*: these have tended to portray the local community as a prosperous, harmonious community. Excessive criticism of the local council is seen as "not good for the town" (*The Provincial Press and the Community*; I. Jackson; Manchester University Press; Manchester; 1971).

- *Social and political values*: these are largely biased towards the conformist, conservative and traditional. Hence local papers tend to defend family values, discipline in schools and the Protestant ethic at work. However, Jackson found that the local press were less partisan than their national counterparts (*The Provincial Press and the Community*; I. Jackson; Manchester University Press; Manchester; 1971) and Curran's study of the loony left showed how the local political agenda became defined by the national tabloids (*Media Coverage of London Councils*; J. Curran; Goldsmiths' Media Research Group; Interim Report; Goldsmiths' College, London; 1987).

The shape of local government

IN 1996 the shape of local government again underwent major change following a review of local government structure in the non-metropolitan areas of England and throughout Scotland and Wales. In Scotland the old two-tier system of regions (or counties) and districts has been replaced with a system of unitary all-purpose authorities. In England change has been more limited with the two-tier system being mostly retained in 34 of the 39 existing counties. Avon, Cleveland, Humberside and Berkshire have disappeared from the local government map, with the Isle of Wight already a unitary council. Some 35 new unitary authorities have been established, like Milton Keynes, Nottingham, Southampton and Leicester (large cities outside metropolitan areas), which will now run all local government services.

These changes have come on top of a general process of change initiated by the Thatcher Government in the mid-1980s. In 1985 the GLC (Greater London Council) and the six metropolitan authorities in Tyne and Wear, South Yorkshire, West

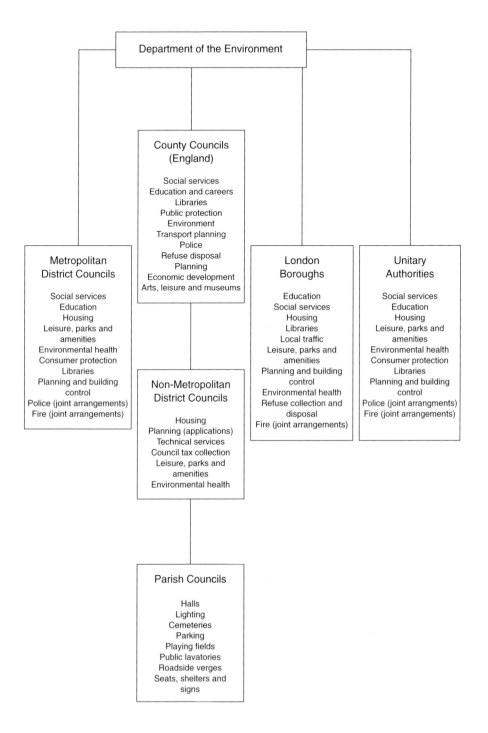

Figure 9.1 Local government in England and Wales

Yorkshire, Merseyside, Greater Manchester and the West Midlands were abolished. Various joint boards were established to co-ordinate services like fire and civil defence, passenger transport, waste disposal and the police (not in London). In London the Inner London Education Authority was abolished as well, with inter-borough arrangements being set up to manage London-wide services.

With the election of a Labour Government in 1997 further changes can be expected. A London-wide authority is proposed, to be headed by an elected mayor (more on the lines of how US cities are run). This will constitute a major departure in the history of local government. Also Labour are intent on establishing a Scottish Parliament whereby decisions affecting Scotland will be devolved from Westminster to Edinburgh. There has been some controversy as to whether a Scottish Parliament will have the power to raise higher levels of taxation. Also a Welsh Assembly is planned with more limited powers.

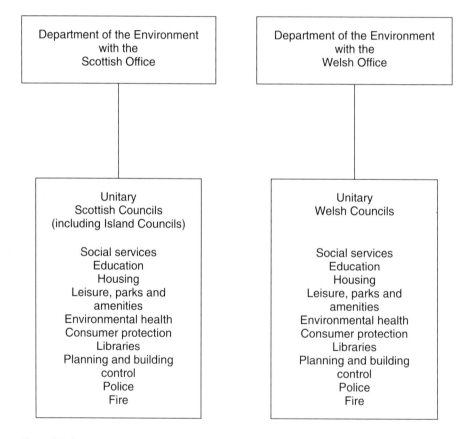

Figure 9.2 Scottish and Welsh local government

Councillors

A N article in the *Association of Metropolitan Authorities News* ("Town Hall Turnover"; A. Bloch; *Municipal Review & AMA News*; Vol. 63, No. 727, p. 40; London; 1992) reported that about a third of councillors drop out of politics at each election. Most do so because of personal reasons related to family and work pressures. Unlike MPs, the 24,000 local councillors in the main local councils are neither full-time nor paid for their services. Council work is often undertaken at the end of a councillor's normal day's work and, to be effective, they must master both policy detail and the work involved in looking after the interests of their constituents (*Local Government in Britain*; T. Byrne; Penguin; Harmondsworth; 1986). A chair of a social services or education committee may be responsible for a budget of many millions of pounds. They are given limited expenses and allowances for loss of earnings and, unlike MPs, there are strict controls over gains. Councillors must declare an interest if any meeting deals with an issue which might lead to a personal gain. Smith, Hender and Kett have pointed out that "one of the commonest of many misinformed criticisms of local government is that people only go into it for what they get out of it" (*Local Government for Journalists*; D. Hender, D. Kett and G. Smith; LGC Communications Information and Research; London; p. 31; 1992).

A district, borough or city councillor represents a ward and a county councillor a county district. A ward may have more than one councillor. Most council matters need to be grounded in terms of a human interest. A local journalist will be able to obtain reaction to a school closure or a new day centre from a local councillor who represents people who are directly affected. The councillor will have knowledge of what is happening on the ground and may even have views conflicting with those of their local party. Elections take place every four years, although in some more urban county districts there are elections in three years out of four, when a third of councillors are elected each time.

Surveys show that councillors are mainly white, older, middle-class men, either retired or in professional jobs. In the big urban areas there has been an increase in councillors under the age of 45, and in the Liberal Democrat and Conservative parties there are slightly more women councillors. Labour has a larger representation of manual workers among its councillors, some 35 per cent (*Report of the Committee of Inquiry into the Conduct of Local Authority Business*; D. Widdicombe; HMSO; London; 1986).

The council system

T HE following simplified diagram (Figure 9.3) shows the main parts of the local government system.

Party group meeting

Most councillors are motivated by their support for a particular party and the Widdicombe report showed that the party group was the most dominant factor in local government. In Labour-controlled councils 99 per cent of groups voted together, and 92 per cent in Conservative councils. Eighty-seven per cent of councillors in Labour councils and 61 per cent in Conservative councils said their main task was to implement the party manifesto (*Report of the Committee of Inquiry into the Conduct of Local Authority Business*; D. Widdicombe; HMSO; London; 1986).

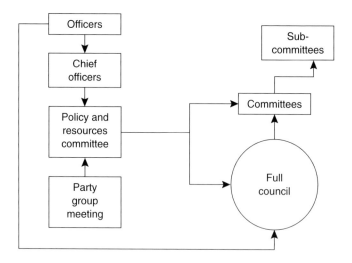

Figure 9.3 The structure of local government

The party group meeting is outside the formal local government system but is the most important meeting. The ruling group is made up of members with the majority in the council and meets between the meetings of the full council and committees. The ruling group decides policy, elects the leader and deputy leader of the council and selects the committee chairman. The group develops a collective view and this line is then reinforced by the whips. These party managers, like those in Parliament, use the carrot (political preferment) and the stick (discipline and possible de-selection) to ensure party support for the leadership.

Group meetings are often held away from the town hall and other council buildings. Groups sometimes meet at the local party's headquarters. The local reporter should attempt to build up contacts with key members of the groups. Although held behind closed doors, journalists can obtain information about the meetings, often through leaks perhaps motivated by political infighting within the group. Political parties are coalitions of contending interests. Consequently, group meetings can be heated affairs, highlighting policy divisions which are hidden from the open council and committee meetings.

Full council meeting

This is often the least interesting meeting to attend as a journalist. The parties have already agreed their positions on policy and the meeting is devoted to ratifying decisions and reports made by the committees.

The full council is chaired by the (Lord) mayor or chairperson (chair). They sit at the front of a semicircle of desks, with party leaders, deputy leaders and the committee chairs sitting in the front rows. The mayor is often joined by a chief officer while other officers usually sit in the back rows of the chamber. The council clerk is in administrative charge of procedure and an important person to cultivate if you are a reporter. Journalists may occupy a table outside this semicircle or be given a special place in the public gallery. Reporters should ensure they know the names of the principal speakers – the leaders, committee chairs and opposition speakers, though the clerk is normally available to help with names after the meeting.

Full council procedures

Councils have set procedures for dealing with points of order and votes. The council meeting will have an *agenda* which will outline matters to be discussed and indicate parts of the meeting open to the public and those parts when the public and press will be excluded. The full council meeting usually begins with the *approval of the minutes* of the last full council meeting. The mayor reports back on any matters arising and outlines any relevant correspondence, changes in the membership of the council or petitions from the public. Petitions from council-house residents or from parents of under-fives about the provision of services may be heard directly from the public in the council chamber itself.

The rest of the full council meeting is mainly taken up with the approval of committee minutes and reports arising from meetings which have been held since the last full council. Committee minutes are received, adopted and then approved by the full council. The committee chairman may present the report and explain any details. There are four courses of action which the full meeting may decide:

- It may automatically accept items in the minutes which are *resolved* items. This is when the full council has already given delegated powers to the committee to decide on issues on its behalf.

- The meeting can *approve recommendations* made by the committee. The opposition may move that a recommendation should not be accepted and, in this case, there may be a debate and vote. Each recommendation is dealt with in turn, some meetings choosing to take them in blocks. It is important for the journalist to follow the proceedings carefully, making a note of the item number or the page reference given by the mayor.

- A *recommendation* may be amended, in which case there may be a vote.

- The meeting can ask the committee to look at the item again. In this case the matter is referred back to the committee.

Councillors do have the opportunity to ask the committee chair questions, and may give *written notice* where they require detail and further explanation.

The newsroom will be given three days' notice of the meeting and will be sent copies of the relevant minutes. Reporters need to read through these papers for items which may form the basis of a news story.

Committees

Most of the council's work is done in committees and subcommittees. Each is a microcosm of the full council, with the majority party taking most of the seats in the committee. Some councils have a tradition of allowing the opposition to chair some committees although, in the main, the dominant party takes all the chairs. Journalists are allowed to attend committee meetings, although their access to subcommittees may be restricted.

Committee work is detailed and greatly informed by officers. Heads of the council's departments, such as the director of social services or the education director, tend to ensure councillors do not go beyond their powers, *ultra vires*, and will often stop councillors from making decisions which break the law (D. Hender, D. Kett and G. Smith; see Ch. 5; "Control of Local Government"; 1992).

There are four main types of committee:

- *Standing committees*: an authority must have these if they run particular services. Hence a county must have an education and social services committee and a district must have a housing committee (G. Smith, D. Hender and D. Kett; ibid.; see more detailed discussion of local government services in Chs 6–10; 1992).

● *Ad hoc committees*: these are set up at the discretion of the council and cover areas which are seen as important but not statutorily required. For example, these may include a women's committee, an employment committee or a race relations committee.

● *Subcommittee*: these are smaller groupings of a committee handling specific issues or covering specific areas. The housing committee of Haringey Borough Council, for instance, has a subcommittee covering the Broadwater Farm housing estate.

● *Policy and resources committee (P and R)*: the most important committee, it is the Cabinet of the council. Composed of the leader, deputy leader and committee chairs, it co-ordinates policy and allocates finance to other committees.

Procedures in committee

Each committee will start by approving the minutes of the previous meeting and go on to consider reports prepared by the council's departments. In a social services committee, the director of social services may present a paper on the implementation of the Children Act 1989. This may be about the issue of taking children into care when parental abuse is suspected. A recommendation may be passed which will be sent to the full council.

Journalists will be able to obtain such reports and may quote points made in the committee.

Officers

Officers are officially the servants of the council and try to resist attempts to politicise their role. However, as with civil servants in central government, politicians increasingly favour officers who are prepared to work with the policy of the ruling party group.

The work of officers is circumscribed by legal constraints and they are greatly influenced by their professional training. Many still think of themselves foremost as engineers, architects, planners, social administrators or accountants.

A journalist usually has to go through the public relations or press department of the council. They have their own agenda and the journalist must be careful to clarify the difference between publicity and news. Increasingly, press officers have found it difficult to be an intermediary between committed politicians and a more hostile national press and this has changed their role significantly. They are much more interested in negotiating a compromise between both sides.

The press office is likely to direct the reporter to the head of a department. The department will want to give a corporate view on an issue and will resent any attempt to contact and deal with a less senior officer who has only a partial view of the issue. Recent adverse reporting of issues related to social services and education have made officers much more sensitive as to what they say.

National politics

AT the national level the main local contact is the constituency MP and there may be three or four in the local area. It is even better if a local MP is also a government minister or an outspoken critic on the backbenches. Speeches, general interviews, votes in the Commons, local party contacts and other public duties can provide material for stories. Background on an MP's personal and business life provides background for the local reporter.

A local paper will obtain a report of their local MP's speeches in the House from a stringer or news agency. Many regional and local papers have correspondents based at Westminster, some of whom are members of the lobby. The local newsroom will use Hansard Parliamentary Reports and local MPs will be more than forthcoming in sending journalists copies of speeches. This may also include speeches at party conferences in October, when a local paper may wish to send a reporter or will again use a stringer.

Local political parties

THE local party holds regular meetings, selects the prospective MP or de-selects the sitting MP, chooses candidates for the local elections and, with other constituencies, for the European Parliament (*British Political Parties*; A.R. Ball; Macmillan, London; 1981). Again, the journalist should build up a relationship with local party activists because they can provide information about the content of local meetings.

The Labour Party

The Labour Party has a federal structure, controlled by a National Executive Committee which is elected by the party conference and meets at Walworth Road in South London. The NEC is made up of representatives from the trade unions, constituency parties, socialist groups, co-ops and a women's section. In recent years the NEC has strongly supported the process of reform in the party initiated by Kinnock, and carried through by Smith and Blair. The leadership has moved power in the party away from the constituency parties and activists and has given ordinary members voting rights in the election of the party leader so replacing the old electoral college system which gave votes to the trade unions, MPs and constituency parties. The Blair leadership has also distanced the party from the trade unions, although most of its income still derives from the trade union political levy.

There are 12 regional councils with their own executive committees which co-ordinate activities in relation to local, national and European elections. At the local level the party is organised on a constituency basis, with an elected general management committee which has representatives from ward organisations. The ward may have 20 to 30 activists, whereas the constituency organisation may have 100 representatives.

Blair has completed the process of policy reform moving the party further to the right and away from policies which were associated with the left. This has involved, for example, a rewriting of the party's constitution, especially Clause 4, which advocated public ownership as an ultimate objective. After 18 years in opposition New Labour won its largest majority in the 1997 general election.

The Conservative Party

The Conservative Party has a more top-down structure with considerable power residing with the leadership. The party leader chooses the party chairman who runs the party organisation at Smith Square, London. At the regional level there are the twice-a-year meetings of the Conservative Union which has delegates from the constituency associations and which elects an executive committee. At the local level there are the associations made up of ward organisations and which appoint a committee.

The party conference is always a stage-managed affair. Speeches by the leadership tend to be orchestrated and representatives are mainly out to display their loyalty. It is not a policy-making body, although it is a good barometer of party feeling. The Conservative Party leader is elected by Conservative MPs, under an electoral system which requires a candidate to win 50 per cent of the vote plus a clear lead over other candidates of 15. In 1990 it was the failure to secure this threshold which led to Thatcher's resignation. After the election defeat in 1997 and Major's resignation as leader the party continues to use this election method, although most candidates have pledged themselves to widening the electoral process by involving constituency chairmen and possibly allowing one member one vote in future leadership elections.

The Liberal Democrats

The Liberal Democrats also have a federal structure, with different organisations in England, Scotland and Wales. There are 12 regional parties who appoint representatives to the regional council. The conference is the most powerful body, electing a co-ordinating committee to oversee the day-to-day running of the party. At the constituency level there is the local party. The party leader is elected by the party membership on the basis of one person one vote.

The Scottish National Party (SNP)

The Scottish National Party was founded in the 1930s, although it only began to make inroads into the British political system with its victory at Hamilton in 1967. This gave the party a boost to membership and party organisation across Scotland, although the party suffered a setback with the rejection of a Scottish Assembly in 1979. The SNP is the main rival of Labour in Scotland, especially with the general decline in Conservative support. The SNP campaign for Scottish independence has led them to take a more pro-European line, and Labour has had to toughen its arguments for a devolved Scottish Assembly to ward off further Nationalist inroads.

The Welsh Nationalist Party (Plaid Cymru)

The Welsh Nationalist Party made a breakthrough at Carmarthen in 1966 and strongly contests seats against Labour in the valleys, West Rhondda and Caerphilly. Recently the party has moderated its illegal tactics, preferring constitutional means through self-government in the form of a Welsh senate. It has also dropped its linguistic nationalism, now accepting English as well as Welsh as national languages.

The Ulster Unionist Party

The Ulster Unionist Party dominated Ulster politics from 1922 when Northern Ireland was established. However, unionism was fractured in the 1970s when direct rule was imposed from Westminster in the wake of increasing violence. Unionism is now divided between the more traditional Official Unionist Party (OUP) and the more hardline Democratic Unionist Party (DUP). Both have remained opposed to attempts to develop an Anglo-Irish agreement on the future of Ulster and argue for a return of self-government.

The Social Democratic and Labour Party (SDLP)

The Social Democratic and Labour Party replaced the old Nationalist Party in 1971 and has been prepared to negotiate within the existing political framework despite its ultimate goal of a united Ireland.

Sinn Fein

Sinn Fein is often referred to as the political wing of the illegal Provisional Irish Republican Army (IRA) which has been engaged in an armed struggle against the British presence in Ireland since the 1960s. Sinn Fein received semi-illegal status when Thatcher imposed a ban on Sinn Fein politicians talking directly to radio and television. This ban has now been lifted as the Major Government sought to involve Sinn Fein in all-party talks on the future of Northern Ireland.

Elections

PEOPLE are most aware of politics and political parties at election times and national elections especially provide journalists with a good source of stories. By-elections can be used as a barometer of government popularity and will always attract the leading MPs from all parties, including ministers and frontbench opposition speakers. The local agent for the candidates is the most important contact for the reporter, pointing them towards the appropriate meetings and photo opportunities. An agent may distribute a copy of a proposed speech in advance, highlighting the key passages which the party wants reported.

Otherwise most reports will be centred around candidates' comments on each other's parties' programmes and the personal stance taken by specific politicians. Journalists should be prepared to challenge candidates about issues and party commitments. Local issues are important and questions should be asked especially of candidates who have been brought in from outside the area by their respective parties.

Parliament

THE House of Commons is the central focus for the reporting of national politics. Most political stories emanate from Parliamentary reporting and many local papers have their Parliamentary specialists, often located at Westminster. Otherwise, local papers will employ London-based stringers and the task of the local reporter will be to follow such stories up with a local angle and local interview.

Constitutionally, Parliament is the sovereign body having power to choose, maintain and reject governments. For the media in general the system of adversarial party politics provides a dominant agenda. This view over-emphasises the role and powers of ordinary MPs.

The power of government and especially that of the Prime Minister has increased in recent years. The government controls the business and procedures of the Commons, the Leader of the House outlining the timetable of business after Prime Minister's questions on Thursdays. The guillotine and closure motions are increasingly used to push legislation through, curtailing debate by putting a time limit on the discussion of amendments to bills. The Commons acts with the permission of government, most of its time devoted to the passage of public (government) bills through Commons procedures with the government's control of its majority ensuring legislation is passed. In three recent sessions of the committee stage of a bill, 906 out of 907 government amendments were accepted, whereas only 171 out of 3,510 backbench amendments were carried.

The work of government has grown in complexity. The state intervenes through economic and welfare politics and since 1945 this has led to a massive increase in public spending. Government requires more legislative time and the length of bills and Parliamentary sittings have grown in recent years. In one session there are about 150 government bills to be considered, most receiving the Royal Assent, and about 2,000 statutory orders and regulations. There were experiments with special standing committees to scrutinise policy during the passage of bills. Pressure groups were invited to play a part in the committee stage of the 1981 Education Act dealing with children with special educational needs. However, such experiments were quickly dropped ("Committees in the House of Commons"; P. Norton; *Politics Review*; Vol. 1, No. 1; Philip Alan Publishers Ltd; Deddington, Oxfordshire; 1991).

Backbenchers and the opposition parties can use the following limited devices for influencing government. Their interventions can provide copy for reporters:

Question Time: once a week for 30 minutes on Wednesday afternoons, Prime Minister's questions provide a set piece between government and opposition. There is little scrutiny here, with rhetoric crowding out information and the planted question from a government backbencher allowing the Prime Minister to attack the opposition.

Private Members' bills: a good source of news. MPs ballot for the opportunity to introduce them and are then inundated with suggestions from pressure groups on suitable topics. There is very limited parliamentary time for such bills and few get through, the more controversial being usually talked out by the use of the filibuster.

Ten-Minute Rule bill, Adjournment debate and Early Day Motions: ways for backbenchers to draw public attention to specific issues.

Supply Days and Emergency debates: used by the opposition parties to debate and vote on issues of importance. The government ensures it has a majority to ward off such attacks, the main intention of the opposition being to embarrass ministers and the government.

Select committees

I N recent years the most notable attempt to increase the Commons' influence over government has been the introduction of new select committees. With the televising of Parliament these now have a much higher profile. They are made up of about 12 MPs and can call ministers, civil servants, union leaders and business chiefs to give evidence on particular topics. Since 1980 select committees oversee the work of the main government departments, including Agriculture, Defence, Education, Employment, Environment, Foreign Affairs, Home Affairs, Social Services, Trade and Industry, Transport, the Military and the Civil Service.

They produce reports, sometimes critical of government policy, but are weakened by the evasiveness of ministers and civil servants, hiding behind collective Cabinet responsibility. Select committees hold sessions which journalists can attend. Usually, officials and ministers are questioned by MPs about aspects of a contemporary issue. Sometimes discussions can be a little heated, and notes from the meeting can be used in conjunction with follow-up interviews with interested parties. Civil servants have a set of instructions, the Osmotherly Rules drawn up in 1977, which govern their evidence before select committees. They are instructed to be helpful, but guarded to ensure good government and national security. As a result many important issues relating to government are kept from select committees, including advice to ministers, how decisions are made in departments, the level of consultation, the work of Cabinet committees and how policy is reviewed.

The relative impotence of select committees was dramatically shown in the case of Clive Ponting who leaked information to the Foreign Affairs Select Committee on the way Parliament had been deceived by the Ministry of Defence about the sinking of the General Belgrano during the Falklands War. The chairman of the committee, Sir Anthony Kershaw, instead of establishing an inquiry about government accountability, gave the documents to the Minister of Defence who immediately set up a leak inquiry to punish the person who had provided the information. Other members of the select committee tamely acquiesced to their chairman's actions.

Standing committees

STANDING committees of 20 to 50 MPs are appointed to examine the details of bills as they progress through Parliament. The committee can be of the whole House, as with the Maastricht Bill or the Finance Bill, and amendments to a bill can be tabled.

A local MP may be on a standing committee or may have a particular interest in the legislation. There is a *First Reading*, when a bill is formally introduced without a vote; a *Second Reading*, when the general principles of the bill are discussed; a *Committee Stage*; a *Report Stage*, when committee amendments are considered by the House; and a *Third Reading*, when the bill is reviewed and further amendments added. The bill then goes to the *Lords*, the Committee Stage usually being of the whole House, and the bill returns to the Commons with *Lords' amendments* and these then need to be resolved before the bill receives the *Royal Assent* and becomes an *Act*.

Government and the civil service

THE decline in the power of Parliament is matched by a growth in the power of the executive, and in particular the power of the Prime Minister's office. Much of this power emanates from party control and the growth of the Cabinet office since the First World War. The anonymity of civil service procedures reinforces this power at the centre (*Whitehall: Tragedy and Farce*; C. Ponting; Sphere Books; London; 1986). The Prime Minister appoints the government, dismisses ministers, chooses appropriate ministers for Cabinet committees, controls Cabinet agendas and chairs discussions with the Cabinet Secretary writing the minutes on behalf of the Prime Minister. The Prime Minister also controls the system of patronage, approving ministerial preferments to the chairmanship of quangos (Quasi autonomous non-government organisations) like the Independent Television Commission.

Cabinet government remains secretive and divisions between ministers are usually concealed by the notion of *collective Cabinet responsibility*. Under this convention decisions of the Cabinet are collective and ministers are not allowed to contest the view emanating from the Cabinet Office. This makes it difficult for journalists to record the true flavour of the political debates and discussions taking place at the heart of government. The work of the civil service is also kept secret by means of *ministerial responsibility*. This convention states that the buck stops with departmental ministers, ensuring that, when questioned in select committees, senior civil servants can dodge answering by referring to their minister.

Cabinet committees

THE issues concerning the resignation of Lawson and Howe from Thatcher's government raised questions about the relevance of the notion of collective Cabinet government. In the 1980s the Cabinet met less often, some 45 times a year compared with nearly 100 times in every year since 1945, and the number of Cabinet committees and papers also fell (*Cabinet*; P. Hennessy; Basil Blackwell; Oxford; 1986).

Under Thatcher a large proportion of Cabinet work was determined by Cabinet committees. Many major items of public policy were dealt with by committees, including the abolition of the GLC and six metropolitan authorities, the introduction of the poll tax, the banning of trade unions at GCHQ, the privatisation of British Telecom and reforms of the NHS.

The three principal committees deal with economics, overseas and defence and home affairs. With more decisions made in committee, the whole Cabinet system has become fragmented with policy being decided by relatively isolated groups of ministers and civil servants.

Prime Minister's Office

ANOTHER recent trend has involved the by-passing of the Cabinet system altogether. Increasingly, policy has been determined by informal groupings centred around the Prime Minister. Government information flows as much through the Prime Minister's Office as it does through the Cabinet secretariat. As a consequence, policy reaches the Cabinet and departments in a fairly developed form, providing ministers with a *fait accompli* and little time to organise opposition to it. The Broadcasting White Paper of 1989 was developed in a series of breakfast meetings between Thatcher and like-minded newspaper editors.

The lobby

THE lobby is made up of some 200 journalists with privileged access to the corridors of power. Tunstall has outlined four types of access – (a) off-the-record talks with MPs in the Commons' lobby; (b) receiving embargoed copies of official documents; (c) attending regular briefings by press staff; and (d) having permanent offices at Westminster (*The Media in Britain*; J. Tunstall; Constable; Ch. 2; London; 1983). The price that journalists pay is in their collusion with a system which reinforces the culture of confidentiality and deference. The lobby is particularly useful to government. For example, after the 1987 election Thatcher became displeased with one of her ministers, John Biffen. Through a press office briefing she let it be known that he had become "a semi-detached politician". He was then subsequently sacked.

Lobby journalists do not write reports about the proceedings in Parliament. Rather, they provide background on current political issues, culled from ministerial briefings and gossip from MPs and press officials. Journalists become insiders, keeping their sources anonymous. Public documents, like committee reports and White Papers are embargoed, with lobby journalists being given personal copies long before they are presented to Parliament.

A meeting of government information officers takes place every Monday afternoon at the Cabinet Office, with the lead taken by the Prime Minister's chief press officer. Techniques involve ensuring that unwelcome news is managed in a way to reduce its damaging effect. No two ministers are allowed to announce unpopular measures on the same day, whereas bad news may be released on a strong news day when there are other important stories. Failing this, news can be released late on a Friday afternoon.

Under Mrs Thatcher the press office became much more aggressive, mixing news management with public relations and advertising. Increasingly government has used lobby briefings to package policy and fly kites. For example, before the 1993 Budget, the Treasury let it be known that it was contemplating putting VAT on zero-rated goods, including food and books. This was then widely reported and there was much public concern. In the actual Budget no such measures were announced and the opposition were wrong footed, although the sting had been taken out of the issue. During the 1980s the government increasingly used advertising to sell policies. The budget for the sell-off of nationalised industries came at the same time as central government was restricting the right of local government to publicise its policies.

Every civil servant and journalist who has close links with Whitehall is subject to negative vetting. This involves an investigation by MI5 and Special Branch using the Criminal Record Computer of individuals' private lives, addresses, financial standing, politics and social views.

Profile | The journalist as contemporary chronicler:

● ● ● ● ● ● profile of

David Shaw, lobby correspondent

"I ENJOY the sense of chronicling contemporary history; the sense that you sometimes are able to shape decisions and events," says David Shaw.

Lobby correspondent of the London *Evening Standard*, Shaw cites as an example of press power the story he wrote in July 1986 about a boy beaten by his headmaster for getting low marks.

"It was just before the House of Commons was due to vote on an education bill. A clause would outlaw corporal punishment. I interviewed the mother and boy, and the editor took the courageous decision to publish a picture showing the little boy beaten black and blue. Lo and behold, that evening MPs calling for the ban were waving copies of the picture and story in the House and referring to it in their speeches.

"In the end the clause passed by a majority of just one. Had it not been for our picture and story the course of history might have been different."

He admits reporters in off-the-record briefings can be used as sounding boards by contacts. They might want to flag an idea or a possible policy change in a story to see the reaction it draws. But he dismisses criticisms of the lobby. Many other journalists operate within similar systems, he argues. Thus there is a health lobby, a crime lobby. They routinely meet prominent politicians and acquire information off the record. The Parliamentary lobby faces more flak because it's bigger and a lot more prominent. "We generate that much more copy by the day."

Shaw, one of a five-man Westminster team, certainly has a hectic schedule. Writing eight stories in a day is not unusual and at least a couple every week tend to make the front page. Maximum length, except for major stories, is 300 words.

He has regular contacts with ministers and keeps in close touch with MPs and civil servants – both prominent and not so prominent. "It's as well to know the people who sweep the floors as well as those who make policy," he says.

Most days Parliament begins at 2.30 pm, late for an evening newspaper's deadlines, so debates in the chamber are not of crucial significance. Instead, his journalism becomes a kind of crystal-ball-gazing. He has to wander around the House trying to find out the news about to break. He meets people informally in corridors or over tea in the canteen, attends lobby briefings at No. 10 Downing Street and at the Foreign Office. All the time he has to keep his eyes and ears open for news and gossip.

Government documents are placed during the day at certain positions in the House which have to be closely watched. "With our rolling programme of constantly shifting copy there are very few periods of quiet, few flat patches."

Not surprisingly, he finds the work "physically and mentally demanding . . . I know that my copy is read by the Queen, politicians, civil servants and opinion-formers in general. None of them would be averse to ringing up to complain if I made a mistake. But working in a friendly team helps coping with the stress."

Good shorthand is an absolute necessity. Shaw has a Teeline 120 wpm certificate. "Almost all Westminster correspondents have good shorthand. Those who don't, have traumatic experiences as a result. There are some safeguards available to them. They rely on PA or swapping notes around. You can't take tape recorders into the House though some people do. Why they take the risk I don't know."

Every work day, he wakes up at 4.10 am and immediately begins his news-gathering routine. He watches the television news, checks Teletext, and listens to the headlines in the car as he heads for London from his home near Milton Keynes.

Arriving at Westminster around 5.30 am (along with the cleaners and a few security men), he reads all the day's papers, possibly writes up a story left over from the previous evening, checks PA and other agency reports on the computer and monitors the radio and television for interviews with politicians. Particularly important for him is Radio 4's *Today* programme which he will tape when an important politician is being interviewed. "Over the last few years the government have increasingly used the media interview. It's like a press conference of the airwaves. They know that through programmes they can set the agenda."

In addition, some senior politicians have agreed with the *Evening Standard* to be rung at 6 am when appropriate and so he might contact them for reaction to a breaking story.

His first copy deadline is around 7 am and for this edition he will write two, maybe three, stories. "There is a lot of pressure to find something the morning papers haven't got. But when you do succeed, with the first deadline thrown so far forward, you do help set the agenda for the following day's papers. And that's rewarding."

Then at 8 am the Westminster team have their first planning meeting. There are six and sometimes seven editions through the day so work is intense until he finishes at around 2 pm. At home he routinely watches the news at 9 and 10 pm and can even continue pursuing story leads. It's a long day.

Shaw believes his grounding in the broad skills of provincial newspaper reporting was to prove invaluable in his later career. He started in 1968 when just 16½, reporting for the Lindsey Group of Newspapers in Lincolnshire (taking in the *Grimsby and Immingham News, Horncastle News* and *Market Rasen Mail*).

At one time or another he was news reporter, feature writer, sub-editor and news editor. "I learned a lot awfully quickly. I learned about sources of information, the importance of keeping confidences and how to write a story, not in a direct way but with a lot of grey areas to protect the contact and avoid any legal pitfalls."

While on the *Kent Evening Post* he was voted in 1973 Young Journalist of the Year by the Institute of Journalists. One of his major scoops was an interview with the widow of the first Securicor guard murdered while on duty. The whole of Fleet Street seemed to be doorstepping her home and she was refusing interviews. But then, just when the pack left for breakfast, she suddenly opened the door. "She decided she just wanted to talk. She poured out her heart to me and brought out all the family albums. I borrowed pretty well every picture she had. I didn't want our rivals to get them."

In 1976 he moved to the *Birmingham Post and Mail* and, after developing an education specialism, moved to the *Evening Standard* in 1981 as education correspondent. Just before the 1987 election was called, he took his current position. "It was an exciting baptism of fire going straight into the election campaign," he says.

Over recent years he has witnessed with concern the rise and rise of the party polit-ical spin doctors at Westminster. "They stalk the corridors of the press gallery, several times a day, every day. I've actually seen them try to browbeat a journalist into following their line. I guess it's the way elections are now fought. But it's going to get worse over the next few years: the parties are playing for such high stakes."

A week in the life of David Shaw

Monday
Westminster is on an alert with MPs on tenterhooks waiting for a possible announce-ment of Election Day. So he composes a "scene-setter" for first edition: "MPs braced for election being called". The Cabinet are due to meet during the day and he has learned through his contacts that they are likely to discuss their manifesto ideas, in particular the selling off of London Underground. "In fact they do decide on this policy and announce it the following day."

He also previews a health service debate in the House. But the actual debate produces little new and so is given only skimpy coverage in the paper.

Arriving home in the late afternoon, he is rung by a long-standing contact in the Health Department about a bogus doctor practising in south London and treating hundreds of patients for sexually transmitted diseases. The department is planning to launch a nation-wide alert, asking people who have been treated by the man to contact them. Test results they had been given could well be wrong.

"I immediately ring the news editor aware that I am on to a splash exclusive."

Tuesday
"I was enormously relieved to see the story as the front page lead in the first edition complete with the name and all the details, the in-house lawyer having gone through it carefully. Our man at Scotland Yard then rang to say the bogus doctor had been arrested and was being questioned. So we faced deep legal problems, committing a possible contempt if he were to be charged. Or should the 'public interest' defence over-ride these considerations? We decided to get a QC's opinion. Certainly in the second edition we decided to play safe and took out the name and addresses. But by the time of the third edition, the health authority had named the 'doctor' and supplied all the addresses. So after that the lawyer decided to let the story flow in all the remaining editions just as it had appeared at the start of the day.

"So I got an exclusive which was followed up by all the papers and had done a 'public good' into the bargain."

In between all the excitement generated by this story, he writes up the results from an opinion poll from Reuters which showed that while most people didn't trust the Labour Party on taxes, they were still prepared to vote for Blair. And he covers a row over nursery vouchers with the Liberal Democrats claiming they are a "bribe to voters".

"After all that I went home and simply slept," he says.

Wednesday
Previews a speech by Gordon Brown, the Shadow Chancellor, in which he was due to stamp his "iron man" image, claiming that Labour would "meet and beat" the Tory inflation target.

Mid-morning he attends press conference at which the Social Security Department announced proposals on pension provision for divorced women. And then covers a statement by the Shadow Home Secretary Jack Straw proposing improved treatment for witnesses in court cases. Over lunch, he meets a No. 10 Downing Street contact.

Thursday

Covers David Blunkett, Labour's education spokesman, outlining plans for a "revolution in reading" and follows up a press release from the office of Frank Dobson, vowing that Labour would improve water conservation without imposing compulsory meters. "I then preview the Wirral South by-election along the lines of 'Tories braced for a kicking'. It's a sort of pot-boiler: we have a reporter up there covering the actual event."

Then deals with a report from the Defence Select Committee suggesting that the military are so short of medics, troops could be sent into action without proper medical back-up.

"Then through trawling around I got from a Minister a letter sent to the chair of London Transport complaining that LT employees had been allowed to distribute anti-privatisation leaflets."

Friday

The result of the Wirral by-election is out. The political editor composes the predictable story: "Tories shell-shocked". Shaw early in the day handles Labour attempts to win government co-operation in rushing through a Building Societies Bill which aims to curb the carpet-baggers. The government refuses but the Bill goes through all the same.

Shaw then meets his local MP for breakfast. "My working routine makes it increasingly difficult to meet contacts for lunch so instead I try to meet them for breakfast," he says.

[Profile by Richard Keeble.]

10 *Law and disorders* Covering the courts

Henry Clother

....

Why court reporting?

THE first time you are sent to court as a reporter can be a daunting experience. The buildings, old or new, are grim and forbidding. The police, lawyers and court officials speak in legal jargon. If you are lucky you will find an experienced court reporter to show you the ropes, introduce you to people and warn you about the terrible acoustics. You will still have a lot to learn.

Court reporting matters not only because courts are a marvellous source of human interest and crime stories. It matters because the law is the basis of a civilised society and, in principle, should protect the weak and vulnerable (though, in practice, they often find themselves on the wrong side of the law). Every citizen has the right to a fair trial. Without this basic right all other rights are meaningless because they cannot be enforced. Thus a court reporter has to remember to do nothing to prejudice a fair trial. This is the basis of the strict rules of contempt of court (which will be explained later). It should not impede the journalist's basic duty to report the facts accurately and fairly.

Court reporters do not have any special status in the courts: they are essentially the eyes and ears of the public. However, court reporters have one big advantage in possessing by law what is called "qualified privilege" which gives exemption from swingeing libel laws. "Privilege" in this context does not refer to status, but means that reporters are free to report allegations and statements made in court without liability to actions for libel. This immunity does not apply to interviews outside the courtrooms.

The "qualification" is that court reports must be accurate, balanced and contemporaneous. That last word means reports should appear in the paper's next available edition, not held back for maximum effect. The other two criteria are more difficult to define and have led to bitter confrontations between journalists and judges. None the less, this limited protection is better than having a £1 million libel hanging over your head. The law may be the basis of civilised society. But it can still be used to oppress minorities and commit injustice, as was seen in the cases of the Birmingham Six, the Guildford Four and Broadwater Farm. The journalist should be more than a human tape recorder but represent the social conscience of the people, which exists outside the law and can act as a check when the law becomes corrupt. While journalists respect the law, they must never fail in their duty to criticise its faults and suggest improvements.

In recent years there has been a deluge of legislation on the operation of the courts, police procedure and civil rights. Much of this legislation has been populist in nature, aimed more at the denizens of the saloon bar than serious reformers, in a period of mass unemployment and growing social inequality.

The situation has been further complicated by the fact that some highly question-able changes have not in practice been implemented and others have been swiftly withdrawn. To take one example, the former Conservative Government's proposals under the Criminal Justice and Public Order Act 1994 to substitute for committal proceedings a transfer for trial procedure were vigorously opposed by journalists as restrictive and unjust. The Government caved in and abandoned the half-baked scheme and the present position is set out in an addendum to the 1995 edition of McNae's *Essential Law for Journalists.*

The new Defamation Act 1996 follows political realities by extending the principle of absolute privilege for fair and accurate court reports to the European Court of Justice, the European Court of Human Rights and war crimes tribunals. The Act provides a new fast-track procedure under which a judge can award damages up to £10,000. A new defence by an offer of amends for innocent libel is now available.

The Criminal Procedure and Investigations Act 1996 severely limits committal proceedings by excluding oral evidence by witnesses, so that magistrates have only written evidence and lawyers' statements to go on. The present strict reporting restric-tions continue.

In the run-up to the 1997 general election various ambitious schemes for law reforms were put forward by the politicians. These included everything from fixed penalties for repeat offenders to restriction of the right to trial by jury in a crown court and even a "Three strikes and you're out" law on the American model. On past form, many of these tough-talking notions will fall by the wayside. Journalists will have to be eternally vigilant if the law is not to become ever further removed from justice and humanity.

It is sometimes argued that court reporting, following in the tradition of public hang-ings, is part of the judicial process. The reporter, by publicising a crime and its punishment, holds up the crime to public view, warning others and adding public shame to the punishment of the convicted. Reporters are often approached by people found guilty asking them to "keep it out of the paper". Such requests are always referred to the news editor or editor and, although the individual circumstances have to be consid-ered, they sometimes mean an item which might not have appeared is included on principle.

There are two arguments against this traditional view of the report as part of the punishment. The first is that courts, like other civic events, are not reported as fully or regularly as they used to be. Newspapers and local radio stations do not have enough reporters to cover courts all the time, even with the help of freelances. The same applies to local councils and committees. Good reporters use their contacts to keep track of inter-esting cases but most court cases, even at the Old Bailey, are not covered today. Some quite large crown courts receive only the occasional visit from an agency reporter.

The second point is that reporters are not qualified to act as judges and juries; they do not have all the papers and facts available to the jury and they are just as biased as anyone else. It is not the function of the press to add to the burdens of those who have already been punished enough. There are few less edifying sights than the rat-pack of the popular press in hot pursuit of some poor man or woman who has drawn a few pounds extra unemployment pay.

The lack of effective coverage of courts and councils means that not only criminal courts but civil courts and coroners' courts have become less meticulous and even perfunctory in dealing with cases, with a profound effect on the lives of ordinary people. One of the most common complaints of those involved in court cases or inquests is that the full facts, say, of an industrial accident or police brutality, were never given. Witnesses may sometimes keep their oath to tell the truth and nothing but the truth, but the whole truth, never.

How is court reporting different?

FIRST of all, it isn't. The basics of reporting apply only more so. Accuracy is even more important because people's lives are being decided. A wrong name or address can cause untold harm to innocent people. A basic knowledge of media law and the various professional codes such as the NUJ Code of Conduct is essential.

Getting down to basics, a shorthand notebook with plenty of pages and two pens (always carry a spare) are the tools of the trade (since tape recorders and cameras are not allowed in courts). The other basic tools are your contacts book, with all those special numbers such as the Law Society, Justice and Liberty (formerly the National Council for Civil Liberties), and a local street map enabling you to check addresses and place-names.

Dress should be suitable for the job in hand. In the formal surrounding of the courts, neat and inconspicuous clothing is customary, which means a collar, tie and jacket for men and smart outfit for women. You won't be thrown out for wearing scruffy clothes, but you may find judges, counsel and court officials less helpful.

Shorthand

Shorthand is a tremendous help in court reporting and is a skill required by the National Council for the Training of Journalists (NCTJ). However, it is possible to get by without it if you can sub-edit as you write, concentrating on the basic facts and the key quotes. The approved shorthand systems such as Teeline, Pitmans and Gregg are much better than speed writing and although 100 words a minute is the required NCTJ and the Periodicals Training Council (PTC) proficiency speed, in practice you need about 120 wpm for a full note of evidence and judgements. But, as one editor said: "Shorthand should be a walking-stick, not a crutch."

The most important piece of equipment is a good knowledge of the law. This chapter is intended to ease your way into court reporting, but to understand the law as it applies to journalists (in particular libel and contempt) you need two books. The first is essential: *McNae's Essential Law for Journalists*; Walter Greenwood and Tom Welsh (eds); Butterworth; London; twelfth edition; 1992.

The second gives a deeper and more detailed account of the finer points: *Media Law*; Geoffrey Robertson QC and Andrew Nicol; Penguin Books; London; third edition; 1992.

Read all the law reports and columns you can find, especially in *The Times*, *Daily Telegraph*, *Guardian* and *The Independent*, and watch programmes such as ITV's *Rough Justice* and listen to radio features such as the BBC's *Law in Action*.

Reporting the courts

YOU first need to know the cases being heard and their starting times. Unfortunately, there is no standard system for lists to be displayed or copied although the Home Office has recommended in a circular that reporters should have the lists as soon as they are compiled. Lists are almost always displayed outside magistrates' and crown courts but only on the day of the hearings. In the case of crown courts and coroners' courts, preliminary lists are compiled days or weeks ahead but may be varied on the day, for instance when a key witness cannot be traced or when some legal issue arises.

Once the list is obtained or displayed it will give the name and age of the accused, with the charge, the Act and Section under which it falls and the rank and number of the presenting police officer. In some courts addresses are also given, but occupations are not given on the lists. In the coroners' court, lists of cases with the name, age and address of the dead can be collected or put on a side table. For addresses and occupations you usually have to check with the clerk of the court or the gaoler.

Contacts

Journalists have very little contact with magistrates or judges because of the need for judicial detachment. The most important contact in a magistrates' court is the clerk to the court who effectively controls its workings. In a small court with only one courtroom they may sit in front of the magistrates, keeping track of all the voluminous files and forms on all but the most trivial cases. In a large magistrates' court with two or more courts sitting there will be clerks sitting in each court. They are dignified and remote figures when the court is sitting but they have an interest in accurate reporting and, approached with courtesy, are usually informative. Barristers are particularly aware of the value of publicity to their careers and are loftily helpful.

The second most important group, an essential source of information in and out of court, is the police. Until quite recently magistrates' courts were termed police courts and the flow of prisoners and charges is in their hands. Today, the Crown Prosecution Service, staffed by lawyers, is responsible for prosecutions, not the police.

The police staffing criminal courts or working as coroners' officers are usually experienced and specially trained. Cultivate the police as much as you can without compromising your objectivity. Police and journalists have a symbiotic relationship, feeding off each other, and it pays to cultivate both uniformed officers and the detectives who (sometimes) catch the criminals. Police involved in crime prevention speak in underworld argot. They talk about "the manor", "shooters" and "blagging" to signify their local district, guns and robbery.

However much you cultivate your police contacts, if there is a big story like the discovery of a serial killer you will find your best contacts develop unsuspected Trappist tendencies and the stupidest PC in the force is posted outside the Incident Room (they are the hardest to talk your way round). Relations with court staff are necessarily formal but clerks and ushers can be helpful once you have won their confidence by behaving in a sensible manner.

This reliance on contacts means there is a big advantage for the specialist court reporter who attends court regularly, builds up contacts and watches for developing stories. The general reporter who is sent out by the news desk to cover a part-heard case without proper briefing on the background is at a considerable disadvantage and will often rely on the court reporter to help out.

In court

The most important parts of a court case normally come at the beginning and at the end. At the start the charges and the case for the prosecution are set out, often with an indication of the line the defence will take. At the end the judge sums up for the jury, the verdict is given and, if it is guilty, sentence is passed with any comments the judge cares to add. The case for the defence should provide another peak of news, and must be reported to balance the report. However, a good story can appear at any time, sometimes in the middle of the cross-examination of some minor witness when most of the press have adjourned for a cup of coffee. Old hands make sure someone is watching the court, just in case.

Enter and leave the court as quietly as you can, watching for a pause in the proceedings. Some reporters sit in public seats if they are moving from court to court. Keep as full a note as you can, as set out in the checklist below, with proper names printed or in clear longhand. Details which may seem unimportant when first mentioned may turn out to be key points. Watch out for the significant detail. The prosecution says a man in a blue suit attacked a young woman: the man in the dock was wearing a brown suit that day. Be careful of being so agog at a dramatic piece of evidence or cross-examination that you forget your note: your pen should be flying across the page, getting it all down.

Watch for courtroom drama, with a witness breaking down, an outburst from the dock or a disturbance in the public gallery. These are all reportable, but only if they are real events, not publicity stunts, which most reporters can detect.

Checklist

- Keep a full note, especially of the key facts, charges, pleas, names, ages, addresses, dates, sentences and fines. Put names and addresses in capitals or clear handwriting.

- Do not become so absorbed in the action that you forget to note significant detail.

- Note anything that could possibly make a good quote. Quotes add liveliness and corroboration to your report.

- Take a full note of the prosecution and defence cases and the judge's summing up and comments on sentence. They often make the story.

- Check any facts of which you are not sure with the clerk of the court or other contact.

- Avoid legal jargon. Technical terms such as "defendant", "plaintiff" and even "arraignment" and "indictment" puzzle the reader and slow down the story. The same applies to grisly medical evidence in coroners' inquests. And as for Latin – it's Greek to the reader!

- Write your story as soon as possible after the case, before memory fades. Phone, modem or fax it as soon as possible. Early copy gets in and gets the best show.

- Read through your story with special care for literals and errors. It is frightening how many even the most careful reporter will find.

- Watch for the follow-up. Ask: "What happens next?" Every story has a future: the man presented as a monster by the tabloid press found not guilty by the court; the woman who lives in fear when a rapist walks free. You should not retry the case or libel a specific person but you can describe the woman's sufferings with sensitivity.

- Unfinished business. If the case is not finished, say so: "The case continues" or "The case continues today". If the jury is considering its verdict or the judge is to pass sentence on a certain day, tell the reader.

- Keep your notes. Traditionally, reporters kept their notes for six months in case of libel writs, but generally three months is enough. There may be readers' complaints or other legal problems over the story.

● Keep your balance. The law requires court reports to be balanced but it does not specify whether that balance is to be observed in every story or, in a case running for several days, whether the balance is to be achieved over the sequence of stories on the case. The practical difficulties arising when different reporters may cover different days and pressure on space may vary are formidable. Lawyers and reporters tend to understand "balance" as giving equal prominence to both sides of the case, prosecution and defence.

This sounds eminently reasonable, but in practice the prosecution case is set out first in the trial, which gives prosecuting counsel a big advantage in public relations terms. Often the defence case will be given the following day, or days later, but it is the prosecution case in all its gory detail which stays in the reader's mind. The reporter may write a strong and full report of the defence case, demolishing the prosecution point by point, but the story does not have the same news value. It is essentially negative focusing on what the accused person did not do, rather than the positive assertions of the prosecution.

Example 1

MY local paper carried a prominent story on a disturbing event at a local public house with the headline across four columns. With names and places changed, it read:

Teenage thugs terrorise local pub

A gang of young skinheads armed with knuckledusters and hammers terrorised a local pub last month, Tanbury magistrates were told yesterday.

Twenty-year-old John Robinson and three friends from the Harley Cross area were "looking for trouble" when they entered the Crown and Anchor public house, Endwell Street, Tanbury, on a Saturday night.

Robinson, James Smith, 23, Robert Brown, 20, and Joseph Doe, 21, all denied charges of violent disorder and causing grievous bodily harm to a barman who ordered them out of the pub.

Prosecutor Mr Jonathan Jones said Robinson and his friends were members of a skinhead gang called the Barehead Boys and they had been angered by graffiti on a wall saying: "Barehead Boys is Bustards".

They entered the pub, but "the word had got around" and the Camwell Crew, the local gang, had armed themselves with knives and machetes.

Robinson asked: "Where are the Camwell poofters? I heard they done it."

A fight began in which Robinson was subjected to a "ferocious attack", suffering stab wounds and a broken nose.

After hearing the charges and legal argument the stipendiary magistrate dismissed the case.

This case sounded shocking at first glance and the gang-fight was indeed a nasty business, but the lurid headline broke the first rule of sub-editing by not faithfully representing the story beneath. It and the intro. did not give a fair account of the story which had two sides to it. The intro. led one to expect a major breach of public order had been committed, whereas the story, deplorable enough, was a gang-fight. I would have thought charges of carrying offensive weapons were justified but the case was dismissed.

Example 2

I LIKED this report in an evening paper:

Man jailed for highest B-test

A man who was seen crawling on all fours before getting into a car has been jailed for the "safety of the public".

Ludford magistrates jailed Vernon Duckson, 43, for three months, saying no other sentence was suitable for a man who was so heavily over the limit, and banned him for five years.

Prosecutor Donald Gaiter told the court that Duckson, of Lidsing Close, Ludford, had given the highest breathalyser reading he had ever known – 212mg of alcohol per 100 ml, when the limit was 35mg.

Duckson was seen by a witness on the morning of December 17 crawling around on all fours before getting into a Mercedes. There was a bottle of vodka in the glove compartment.

But Frank Forthright, defending, said Duckson was an epileptic whose fits became worse when he stopped drinking. He had been in custody and receiving hospital treatment after failing to turn up for a hearing because he was drunk in bed.

"Since then he has learned that his health is in a very serious state indeed. He has been told that if he drinks again that within two days he will be dead," said Mr Gaiter.

Medical evidence could show that the state of Duckson's liver was responsible for the incredible breath test reading, he added.

"Although the reading was so high he had not been drinking for 24 hours before the police saw him."

The court heard that Duckson had been found guilty of drink-driving five times before and had been disqualified for a total of 18 years.

A sad story, but I feel that defending counsel and the reporter did their best, and may even have saved a life. This kind of full and balanced reporting is rare in national newspapers nowadays, but fortunately is still to be found in the provincial press.

After the case

If the story calls for it, you may need to interview a person who has been acquitted, or friends or family of those found guilty. There is nothing against such interviews after the case, but during the case the strict rules of contempt make them inadvisable. It is forbidden to approach jury members about discussions or voting in the jury room. When interviewing non-jurors try to avoid the rat-pack in the corridor and steer your interviewee to the tea-room for a quiet chat.

In big cases involving prominent people there may often be features to be written giving the background to the story – the extravagant life-style of the disgraced tycoon or the deprived childhood of a murderer – and this has to be gathered during the trial for use after the verdict. This research has to be done outside the court and outside normal office hours. It involves burning the midnight oil and working with libraries and other reporters.

The court system

JOURNALISTS are not lawyers. But they are required to have a working knowledge of the law as it affects their work. Thus it is important for reporters to know, not only the heavy constraints which the law places on them, but also how far they can go in reporting the facts within the law. Many journalists, through ignorance, have an exaggerated awe of libel and contempt of court which creates imaginary fears and leads to unnecessary self-censorship. Restrictions apply not only when a person is arrested and charged but from the time an arrest is imminent. Thereafter, the case is *sub judice* (under consideration) and nothing may be written that could prejudice a fair trial. The following is a brief guide to the court system.

Criminal courts

There are two types: magistrates' courts and crown courts. Magistrates' are the courts of first recourse. All criminal cases start there, and the less serious ones are heard and decided. They are presided over by at least two lay magistrates, non-salaried local worthies, or, in cities, stipendiary magistrates, full-time professionals who sit alone.

At one time when people had time to read about bicycles without lights, magistrates' courts provided the staple news for all local papers. Nowadays the courts process cases like a sausage-machine and only a small number of cases are reported. This means special attention has shifted to the first hearing of cases which are to be transferred or "committed" to the crown court for trial by jury. Only the bare essentials of the case as outlined to the magistrates can be given from such a committal. These include name, age, address and occupation of the accused, the charges, names of counsel, bail arrangements and any lifting of reporting restrictions.

An Eastbourne local paper which mentioned in a report that a man committed for trial wore spectacles and a dark suit was heavily fined in 1973. Minor infringements of this kind are quite common 20 years later, but the principle of minimal reporting is maintained. However, if famous people are involved or the case has other news value, it is amazing what can be done with very few facts, a photo and tabloid layout skills.

Crown courts

These are held in large towns and cities and sit with a judge and jury to try serious criminal cases. Some cases, such as murder and rape, must be tried in the crown court. For some less serious charges, the accused person is given a choice (or "election") whether to be tried by the magistrate or by the crown court. In some drink-driving cases motorists have chosen to be tried by crown court in the hope that a jury mainly composed of fellow-motorists will acquit on the grounds of "there but for the grace of God go I". While it is possible juries might feel this way, crown court judges are no less severe on drink driving in their sentences than magistrates.

Always check the title of judges in the crown court who may be circuit judges, recorders or assistant recorders. Circuit judges are called Judge Joseph Oaks or Judge Joan Oaks, never Judge Oaks. High Court judges, who are very grand, are Mr Justice Oaks or Mrs Justice Oaks. When covering Appeal Court cases in the High Court in the Aldwych, check titles with the Press Association which has an office in that mausoleum.

Crown court juries of 12 are taken at random from the voters' list, minus peers, MPs, lawyers, felons and clergymen, all barred but for different reasons. Judges encourage juries to find a unanimous verdict, but if they cannot agree and a jury has been out of court for at least two hours ten minutes a majority verdict of at least ten votes to two is allowed. The jury room is sacrosanct and any attempt to report jury discussion and voting is regarded as a most serious contempt of court.

Counsel for the prosecution and the defence are normally barristers in crown court cases although solicitors have limited right to be heard. The Law Commission set up in 1992 to look into the reform of the legal system recommended an end to the ridiculous class division between barristers and solicitors.

The Old Bailey, as the Central Criminal Court is known, is a crown court dealing with serious cases and where high security is necessary. Its judges are all full-time. Cases may last for several days, weeks or, in the case of complicated fraud, months. Do not be overawed by the august surroundings or by the barristers giving spirited imitations of John Mortimer's *Rumpole of the Bailey*.

Reporting restrictions

Juveniles: You may not name or identify any child or young person under 18 in a juvenile court or other court proceedings except on the rare occasions when restrictions are raised. A young offender's school must not be named, and naming of friends, relations or places which might identify a juvenile is banned.

Sexual offences: Victims of sexual attacks are granted anonymity under the law and may not be identified in any way unless the restriction is lifted by the judge. There is no such general provision of anonymity for rape defendants except where naming the alleged rapist would identify the victim, as in the case of a husband charged with raping his wife.

Civil courts

Civil courts are concerned with disputes between individuals or groups seeking redress for claims and wrongs under civil law. A civil wrong which can be compensated by money is known in legal jargon as a tort. There is a mass of civil law on breach of contract, payment of debt, negligence, defamation, property, bankruptcy, wills and family law. Given half a chance lawyers can argue these cases for weeks, and in the High Court they do.

County courts

These were originally set up as cheap and cheerful people's courts to settle small claims. In recent years the 290 county courts across the country have become the main civil courts dealing with everything except the complicated and expensive cases heard in the High Court. They are presided over by circuit and district judges and the procedure encourages litigants to agree out-of-court settlements whenever possible.

County courts are limited to cases dealing with property up to a value of £330,000 and personal injury actions on claims up to £50,000. County court cases can be revealing and intriguing with neighbours behaving in unneighbourly ways and tradesmen overcharging old ladies by 1,000 per cent, but most of their work is on a small scale. A weekly check to skim the cream of interesting cases is usually enough.

The High Court

This is to county courts what the Old Bailey is to magistrates' courts – the biggest and most interesting cases end up there. The High Court of Justice normally sits in a cakey mausoleum off the Aldwych, although when it comes to issuing writs a High Court judge can call a session in his living-room if necessary. The person bringing the case, quaintly termed the plaintiff, takes out a writ against the defendant and cases are heard by a High Court judge sitting alone. The only civil cases heard by a jury are for libel and slander, wrongful arrest and malicious prosecution.

The Court of Appeal

This sits in the High Court and hears appeals, mainly criminal, usually with three High Court judges sitting together. Appeal may be against the verdict, or sentence or both. Each case is succinctly presented by counsel and after a brief recess the majority judgement is given by one of the judges, followed very occasionally by a dissenting judgement by the minority judge. Since appeals need a strong legal basis, the success rate is high and frequently prisoners walk free from the court, their sentence squashed or reduced. The highest court of appeal in this country is the House of Lords – not all of them, but five law lords who decide on a simple majority basis.

The European Court of Justice

This is the highest court of appeal on European Community law, and its rulings are binding on British courts. In recent years it has proved a useful recourse on civil rights issues where European law is notably more liberal than British statute and common law.

Coroners' courts

The coroner, whose job is to inquire into violent, unnatural and sudden death, holds the oldest office under the Crown, going back 1,000 years. The basic point about a coroner's court is that it is inquisitorial, not accusatorial. This means no-one is on trial and the court is forbidden to attribute blame to any named person, which is the job of the criminal courts. An inquest must be held in the case of death on the roads, railway premises or in custody of the police or prison.

The inquest is to find out three things: who was the dead person? How, when and where did they die? And what was the cause of death? There is normally no problem about the first two questions but the last is often difficult and sometimes impossible to answer. The court has a range of possible verdicts including natural causes, accidental death, misadventure, killing oneself (suicide to the press), unlawful killing, lack of care and an open verdict.

The coroner normally sits alone, but if there is any public concern or doubt he or she will sit with a jury of 7 to 11 members of the public. Sitting alone, the coroner records the verdict: the jury returns its verdict. Coroners' courts are a rich source of stories. Social ills such as the plight of the elderly living and dying alone, the homeless, drunkenness and drug abuse, appear there in all their human poignancy. Sometimes in a city court there may be four or five cases of old people who have died alone in flats with nobody to know or care.

As with all courts, there is a certain amount of jargon, notably in the post-mortem reports for which a medical dictionary comes in useful. Coroners and their officers (senior policemen chosen for tact and sympathy) are much more helpful than other court officials. Some coroners, like Dr Douglas Chambers of St Pancras and Sir Montague Levine of Southwark, were notably outspoken and used their power to make recommendations to government departments to campaign against hazards to life such as faulty traffic lights and railway carriage doors.

Changing the law

A REPORTER would have to be blind or insensitive not to see that most of those who end up in inner-city courts are black, and often unemployed. Their "crimes" are often motivated by poverty. If a middle-class youngster arrives in court he or she is well-dressed, with a good lawyer and respectable parents promising it will never happen again. The child of the ghetto, inarticulate and alone, expects nothing from the system and gets little except the proverbial "short sharp shock" prescribed by recent governments.

It is particularly depressing that court reporters and other observers on the courts are commenting on a vast increase in crimes of violence, and especially assaults on children, including sexual abuse in the family and in the very institutions which were set up to protect children and young people. At the same time, more and more judges and magistrates have attempted to apply reporting restrictions to investigative reporters trying to expose cases of abuse in public institutions. Fortunately, in a number of cases involving both national and regional newspapers and television programmes, journalists have put up a fight. And when they fight they almost always win.

There is more to court reporting than merely reporting the courts. The legal reporters of tomorrow will have to get out into the community and report the society which stands around the courts and which, if it was a healthy society, could make the courts unnecessary.

11 *Deeper, diverse and detailed* Feature writing

N EWS features tend to contain more comment, analysis, colour, background and a greater diversity of sources than news stories and explore a larger number of issues at greater depth. It is the extra length which accounts for many of the distinguishing elements of features. In particular, their intro. sections, where the overall tone of the piece is set, tend to be more colourful and varied in style than those of hard news. A feature may argue a case; the personal views of the writer may be prominent. But the emphasis is still on the news.

The intro.

T HERE are an enormous number of different styles for news feature intros. To identify a few:

The narrative with a twist at the end

A S an international horserider, Lena Ulrika Bidegärd was a creature of habit. Every morning the 26-year-old blonde sportswoman would drive to a stables in her black BMW, returning to her father's villa in a leafy Brussels suburb for lunch after a couple of hours of coaching. Last week the Swedish rider did something out of the ordinary: she disappeared.

Sunday Times (24 January 1993)

The teaser

ROSAMOND Chamberlin, 60, of Leeds, is one of a number of women her age who have received a curious letter from the DSS Benefits Agency.

Independent on Sunday (28 February 1993)

Eye-witness description

THE SLOGANS fall on fertile ground. "Thieves of Monza, your time is over," the posters warn. "The thief-hunting season is open. You have only one bullet, don't waste it."

"The Mafia is coming north with the parties," others warn. "We must stop the Mafia in the voting booth," cries the star speaker, and some 1,500 citizens who have skipped the Milan-Eindhoven football match to listen to him rise to their feet, to thunderous cheers and applause.

In this *Independent* feature (12 December 1992) the focus is on the small town of Monza and the way its political tensions reflect the broader complexities of Italian politics.

Historical background

IN 1972, Highbury Grove school in north London had the most famous headteacher of any comprehensive in the country. Rhodes Boyson possessed an accent which murdered vowels at 30 paces. He had Dickensian sideburns which he grew after a bet with his pupils, and an educational philosophy which seemed to hail from the same era as his facial hair.

He believed in treating boys from working-class backgrounds as if they were at public school, all houses and games and teachers in gowns. But, said his many supporters in the press (he had splendid public relations skills), he got results: he ran the most academically successful inner-city comprehensive in the country.

Twenty years later, Highbury Grove is again one of the most famous headmasterships of any comprehensive in Britain. Last Thursday, at midnight, Peter Searl was suspended from his post by his employers, Islington council, pending investigation of a complaint from the school governors.

This *Independent* report (27 November 1992) focuses on the Highbury Grove School of 20 years ago and on the celebrity headmaster Rhodes Boyson. After two succinct pars, it shifts to the present day highlighting the contrast with the head's suspension. Notice the brackets in par. 2. They are rarely seen in hard news stories since they disturb the urgent flow of copy.

News peg

As the fragile Middle East peace conference moves into important bilateral talks, **socialist** looks at grassroots opinion in the occupied territories and examines the international background

Israel settles for conflict

Arab left aligns with Islam as anger grows

ben cohen

PALESTINIANS in the West Bank and Gaza Strip are sceptical that the Madrid conference will deliver anything concrete. Mass rallies opposing it have been held all over the Israeli-occupied territories.

Five thousand people were at Bethlehem University on the Monday before the conference. The rally was organised by supporters of the radical Popular Front for the Liberation of Palestine, the Islamic fundamentalist Hamas, and the Naif Hawatmeh-led faction of the Democratic Front for the Liberation of Palestine (which has split over the conference).

These events demonstrate a growing anger with US plans for Palestine and a worrying alignment between the Palestinian left and the Islamic movement.

This *socialist* intro. (6–19 November 1991) has much of the feel of a hard news story. But from the famous five Ws and H of the traditional hard news intro. the "when" is missing. This gives the piece its feature-ish feel. It explores the background to the contemporary "fragile Middle East peace conference" rather than news of the conference itself.

Colourful description of an individual with a twist

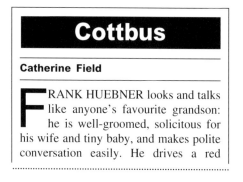

Cottbus

Catherine Field

FRANK HUEBNER looks and talks like anyone's favourite grandson: he is well-groomed, solicitous for his wife and tiny baby, and makes polite conversation easily. He drives a red

BMW and enjoys a night at the pub with his mates.

Yet Huebner, 26, leads a gang of about 500 militant fanatics grouped under the neo-Nazi banner of the Deutsche Alternative party, and during their regular Wednesday pub night they plot their path to power.

Catherine Field the *Observer* © 1992
Published by permission of the *Observer* © 1992

In this *Observer* feature (29 November 1992) Field describes in some detail her subject. But there is dramatic tension in the contrast between the first and second pars; between "well-groomed" and "polite" and "militant fanatics" plotting their "path to power". The writer begins with a close-up shot of an individual and pans out to take in the broader scene, in this case the rise of German neo-Nazis. This "filmic" strategy (from close-up to broad-view) is one of the most popular for opening features.

Ironic comment

by John Passmore and Tony Maguire

THE LATEST interest rate cut is, say estate agents, the starting gun. It will trigger the recovery. In the coming months, according to the 10,000-strong National Association of Estate Agents, the stagnant housing market will begin to move, those forests of rotting For Sale signs can come down at last, the bright new dawn is here – and pigs might fly.

Notice the colourful language of this intro. section from the London *Evening Standard* (28 January 1993), as in "those forests of rotting For Sale signs can come down at last, the bright new dawn is here". But the sting comes at the end with the ironic "and pigs might fly". That language and tone immediately identify the story as a feature.

Emphasising the idiosyncratic

Painful parting as Yanks go home at last

by Christy Campbell
Defence correspondent

THE United States Air Force sent out a priority signal last week. Would friends and neighbours at Bentwaters fighter base, Suffolk, please state their preference for hamburgers, ham or baked beans and franks. One step in the gradual withdrawal of American air power from Britain will be marked next month when the base closes with a "Mission Completed Hangar Dance", featuring the wartime music of Glenn Miller.

Christy Campbell begins his *Sunday Telegraph* feature (3 January 1993) on the US retreat from the UK with a surprising stress on hamburgers, ham or baked beans and franks.

Personal narrative

THE white bus driver's eyes widened in astonishment as I boarded behind an elderly passenger and produced R1 (25p) for a five-minute journey into the centre of Pretoria. "You can't ride on here," he blustered. I asked why not. "We don't carry your kind. You must get off," he replied.

"I don't understand. Is this bus not going to the city centre?" I said, feigning ignorance of Pretoria's strict apartheid bylaw which prevents black and white people using the same buses.

Hard news stories rarely emphasise the personal involvement of the reporter. But a news feature, in contrast, can have the witness of the reporter at its very centre, as in this Angella Johnson feature in the *Guardian* (9 May 1990).

Or here in the *Observer* (18 April 1993) where John Pilger compares his contrasting experiences of Cambodia:

> I HAD not been to Cambodia for two years and was not prepared for the astonishing transformation. Two years ago the sun beat down on a languid Phnom Penh decaying after 15 years of international isolation. There was no "peace process" then; there were no UN blue berets and white vehicles. This was a city of gentle anarchy, of bicycles and mopeds and silhouettes strolling at night down the centre of a road, backlit by a single headlight.
>
> Now the streets were a cataract of white vehicles, jeeps with flashing lights, Mercedes with brocade seat covers, Suzukis with whores on call, bicycles with filing cabinets on delivery, elephants announcing Cambodia's first takeaway pizza and, at the margin, legless or armless young men in military green, like crabs awaiting their chance.
>
> John Pilger the *Observer* © 1993
> Published by permission of the *Observer* © 1993

Stress on contrasts

> N OTHING much seems to happen at Comberton – but probe beneath the serene and tranquil surface and it is a hive of activity.
>
> The pace of change has slowed since the huge expansion that began in the Sixties, yet nearly 50 village organisations cover a multitude of interests for all age groups

This intro. by David Waterson from the *Cambridge Evening News* (26 January 1993) contrasts the tranquil appearance of the village with the reality.

A question

> REMEMBER that horrible feeling? A long day at school – double maths, boring biology and the rigours of French grammar – followed by yet more slog at home.
>
> You really wanted to tune in to Top of the Pops, but dared not risk the wrath of Miss Smith whose stern attitude to late French homework contributions was well-known.
>
> Today's pupils might not face the rigours of the "set today, hand in tomorrow" homework I remember, but their burden of out-of-school study is probably more arduous.

The *Eastern Daily Press* (16 February 1993) begins with a question, setting the scene back in time and then bringing the story up to date with the contrasting "Today's pupils . . ."

The sex angle

> AT WHEELOCK, a small mixed college in Boston, they have "safe sex" parties where a variety of games are played. One of the more bizarre, according to Sarah, an attractive 19-year-old student, is a relay race in which girls are divided into teams of six, each of whom is provided with a condom.
>
> At the other end of the room is a line of appropriate-sized wooden sticks which serve as penis-substitutes. Each of the girls has to run down the room, fit her condom onto the stick correctly, take it off again and run back. The first team to complete the course wins. "When we played," said Sarah ruefully, "one of our girls put the condom on the wrong way and it popped off – so we only came second!"

This *Daily Mail* intro. (8 February 1993) focuses on sex, an intro. angle the tabloids exploit endlessly to attract attention.

The necessary urgency

WHILE news feature intros use a wide range of stylistic devices their content has to be acutely relevant to the news peg which usually appears high in the story. Feature intros have to carry as much interest as hard news openings to attract attention. The writing is more flexible but it is still extremely concise.

MIRO had more reasons than most to wake up with a splitting headache on New Year's Day.

The creek which divides his ramshackle farmhouse from his hectare of land became part of the world's newest international border as the bells rang in 1993, leaving his property dissected by the disintegration of Czechoslovakia.

In future, every time the 54-year-old Slovak farmer crosses the small bridge from his home to his potato field, he will depart Slovakia and enter the Czech Republic – central Europe's two fledgling states.

This *Sunday Telegraph* feature (3 January 1993) focuses on the human interest surrounding Miro and his ramshackle farmhouse but the news peg is quickly stated in par. 2: namely the creation of the "newest international border".

CORPORAL Sonny and his mate Terry, having evaded their officers while on patrol, sat in the shade of an acacia bush and ripped open the heavy flak jackets which have reduced the fast-deploying US Marines to desiccated turtles under the intense Somali sun.

"All I want is a cold beer," sighed Sonny, who arrived in Mogadishu, the Somali capital, two weeks ago. On Christmas day in Baidera the most aggressive act that he encountered came from a goat which, impressed by his MI6 rifle and grenade launcher, munched the grass beside a wadi the young marine was patrolling.

© Times Newspapers Ltd 1993

The Times (26 December 1993) homes in on Corporals Sonny and Terry but quickly identifies the news peg surrounding the US marines in Somalia on Christmas day.

The body of the text

WHILE colour, description, opinion, analysis, narrative, quotes, dialogue, historical contextualising might all be important in a news feature they are all still built on the cement of factual detail and a sharp news sense.

Just as in news stories the most important information comes first with the details declining in importance thereafter, so the same is true of news features.

Greece taxed by refugee influx
Migrants are forced to resort to prostitution

**Helena Smith
writes in Athens**

CHRISTINA, a shy and pretty teenager, came to the brothel about three weeks ago. "She's yours for 2,000 drachmas [£6]," says her pimp.

"We will never tell our children how we started out, but there was nothing else to do," he whispers in halting Greek.

Christina and the young boy are Albanians. But in the seedy red-light district of Athens she could be a Bulgar or an Iraqi, a Russian or a Romanian – all immigrant groups who have in desperation taken to the trade.

From the Middle East and Africa, the Balkans and eastern Europe, refugees are pouring across Greece's borders at a rate described by officials as "terrifying".

Virginia Tsouderou, the deputy foreign minister, sighs: "There are now close to half a million, which means they comprise some 6 per cent of Greece's workforce and are an enormous strain on our already crippled economy. A lot are a security risk and have been caught with arms."

The influx of immigrants began in 1989 with the collapse of communism. Since then about 300,000 Albanians alone have trekked across the mountains and over the frontier.

Only a fraction, including about 40,000 ethnic Greeks from the Soviet republics and 50,000 political refugees – Turks, Kurds, Iraqis, Iranians, Ethiopians and Somalis – are legal. Many of the immigrants are brought to Greece by organised gangs of traffickers.

"The most serious threat comes from the east, where huge numbers are being ferried from Turkey to our islands," says Mrs Tsouderou.

In the past year more than 2,000 Iraqis have been dumped on Greece's outlying islands in the eastern Aegean after paying Turkish fishermen as much as £2,500 to transport them.

Last October, Athens and Ankara were at loggerheads when 68 Iraqis trying to enter Greece illegally from Turkey were stranded for 18 days at sea.

Now the conservative government is bracing itself for a mass influx of refugees from former Yugoslavia in the event of civil war spreading south.

Yasmina Chourfi, acting representative of the United Nations High Commissioner for Refugees in Athens, said: "We've heard that it [the government] is already creating reception centres along the northern frontier."

She added that Greece's 37,000 miles of coastline were impossible to control. "With the tightening of visa requirements across Europe, Greece will become the flank for an influx."

The majority are economic migrants. Although hundreds have been forced to resort to prostitution, the flow has meant cheap labour and bigger profit margins for employers. But to the Greeks at large, their arrival has been unwelcome.

Helena Smith © the *Guardian*

Take this feature from the *Guardian* (26 January 1993). Notice the build up of factual detail. Par. 3 identifies immigrants as Bulgars, Iraqis, Russians, Romanians. The next par. carries the newsy quote "terrifying". Next the authoritative source, the deputy foreign minister, is quoted. In the next par., there is the reference to "about 300,000" Albanians. Notice how specific that number is. The reporter did not say simply "thousands". More specific details, figures follow in the next par. A quote dwells on "the most serious threat".

Next, specific details about Iraqi numbers and the price they are prepared to pay Turkish fishermen are given. A sense of news values has determined the placing of all these details and quotes just as in hard news stories.

Thematic structure

SIMILARLY, news features are structured around logically interlocking thematic blocks arranged in order of news value. The same inverted pyramids concept applies as in news stories. Take the Christy Campbell feature (*Sunday Telegraph*, 3 January 1993):

Painful parting as Yanks go home at last

by Christy Campbell
Defence correspondent

THE United States Air Force sent out a priority signal last week. Would friends and neighbours at Bentwaters fighter base, Suffolk, please state their preference for hamburgers, ham or baked beans and franks. One step in the gradual withdrawal of American air power from Britain will be marked next month when the base closes with a "Missions Completed Hangar Dance", featuring the wartime music of Glenn Miller.

It will be an emotional occasion – half a century since the first US Flying Fortresses arrived in Britain to attack Hitler's Reich. Bentwaters was already earmarked for closure as part of the Bush administration's post Cold War pull-out of forces to leave just 150,000 in Europe.

President-elect Clinton says he could push that Europe-wide figure down, possibly as low as 75,000, a move opposed by General Colin Powell, the current chairman of the Joint Chiefs of Staff.

Last year more than 20,000 US servicemen were based in Britain, largely air force personnel, many with families. Under the Bush plans 9,000 of them are already on their way home. More than 15,000 British workers directly depend on the US presence.

The economic pain will be felt in a clutch of East Anglian communities where the scream of jets overhead is part of the way of life. "Each base closure takes around £15 million a year out of the local economy," says Michael Roberts of *The American* newspaper – "and towns like Woodbridge and Ipswich are going to take a beating".

"Hell, we don't know what Clinton's going to do – perhaps you can tell us," said a captain at Mildenhall, the USAF headquarters in Britain. But as the new administration reshapes US forces for global peace-keeping, Britain, the unsinkable aircraft carrier anchored off Europe, is still set to play a vital role.

The nuclear age is ending. Cruise missiles have gone from Greenham Common and the US Navy's Poseidon submarines have departed Holy Loch. Britain has sought and reportedly won assurances from the incoming administration that any run-down of the US Trident programme will not compromise the supply of missiles on which the future British independent nuclear deterrent depends.

But in a fitfully de-nuclearising world Pentagon planners still see Britain as a vital springboard for low intensity operations in Eastern Europe. And one major nuclear punch will be kept at Lakenheath in Suffolk, where brand new F-15E Strike Eagles have just been deployed.

Mildenhall, also in Suffolk, has become the base for USAF's European tanker task force, a giant filling station for aircraft which are already flying forces to Somalia and aiding the UN in the Balkans. It is also a staging point for US transatlantic troop movements.

The Upper Heyford F-111 bomber base in Oxfordshire will be mothballed in 1994 and Bentwaters and Woodbridge,

home to the A-10 tankbusters that operated in the Gulf War, are on the verge of closure. But a £100 million investment programme is under way at Lakenheath to make it a major nuclear strike base.

Defence analysts predict that the British based F-15E Strike Eagles, capable of carrying nuclear and conventional bombs, will remain a cornerstone of US defence policy as medium-range nuclear firepower is withdrawn from Germany.

Britain could be more important than ever as an intelligence listening post and springboard for secret missions. Alconbury in Cambridgeshire is now home to U-2R spy-planes and a Special Forces wing withdrawn from Germany. They fly black-painted Hercules for SAS-style missions anywhere across Europe.

The important electronic listening post at RAF Chicksands remains in service and any move to dismantle the network of information gathering and early warning bases intimately shared by the British and US intelligence communities will be strongly resisted.

Whatever President Clinton cuts from defence, America's "unsinkable aircraft carrier" looks set to stay afloat.

Block 1: pars 1 and 2 – the closure of Bentwaters fighter base.

Block 2: pars 3 and 4 – Clinton's plans for cutting down on troop numbers in Europe and the implications for Britain.

Block 3: par. 5 – focus on East Anglia; quote from journalist.

Block 4: par. 6 to end – but Britain still to play major role in US military strategy (with specific details relating to Lakenheath, Upper Heyford, Alconbury, RAF Chicksands).

The piece can be divided into two distinct blocks. The first (pars 1–6) looks at the withdrawal of US troops. The second (pars 6 to the end) looks at the paradoxical phenomenon of the continuing vital role of British bases for the US. That contrast between apparent withdrawal and continued presence gives the article its originality and "bite".

A hard news story would have introed: "Britain's role as the 'unsinkable aircraft carrier' for the US is set to become increasingly important as President-elect Clinton plans a major withdrawal of troops from Europe." That goes straight to the news. The feature carries that news element but tackles it more obliquely.

Notice the build-up of factual details. Par. 4 gives the figures of 20,000, 9,000 and 15,000. The roles of Lakenheath, Upper Heyford, Alconbury, and Chicksands are covered in detail. War/defence are fields notoriously clouded in the mists of jargon but Campbell's language is always accessible. The only esoteric reference comes with the mention of *The American* newspaper. It's a newspaper for US service men and women in Britain but the general reader is not likely to know that.

The feature is also significant for what it omits. For instance, there are no quotes from the peace movement to "balance" the coverage.

The final flourish

A HARD news story carries information in order of news value. The last par. is the least important and is cuttable without destroying the overall impact. A news feature can be different. News values still apply but the final section can often carry its own importance. A feature may explore a range of views on a subject and conclude by passing a comment on them; another may argue a case and come to a conclusion in the final section. A final par. may raise a pointed question; it may contain a striking direct quote or summon up an argument (*Writing Feature Articles*; Brendan Hennessy; Focal Press; Oxford; second edition; 1993).

Feature subs have to be particularly sensitive to this. Writers often include the words "Must par." in brackets before a final section to stress its importance to the sub.

The Campbell article is typical. It draws together the central argument and puts it in colourful, though direct language.

This *Independent on Sunday* feature (31 January 1993) ends with a direct quote; a cryptic answer to a pointed question.

Pete Millac, 24, a chef, agreed: "Grunge meant not worrying about your appearance and not spending any money on clothes. Now it's hip it's ridiculous. You read about it in magazines like *Elle*, and the clothes cost a fortune. Grunge is as low-grade as you can find. Or at least it was before the fashion people got their hands on it."	By the original definition, Mr Millac was out-and-out grunge, wearing a battered leather jacket which he said he had found, a check shirt that cost £1 in Brixton market, a £2 scarf from Camden market and jeans. What did he think of those who paid thousands to achieve a similar look? "If people want to spend their money on looking bad, that's fine by me."

In an *Evening Standard* feature (5 February 1993) Rory Ross's intro. argument is that polo is "a game played mainly by yobs in the hope that a little royal stardom will rub off". The piece ends with a newsy reference to Major Ronald Ferguson, at the time engaged in the scandal over an alleged affair, and these conclusive and cryptic words:

> Meanwhile, the man who first exploited the sponsorship potential of linking the royal family to polo is now perceived as the sport's biggest liability – Major Ronald Ferguson, who is in charge of sponsorship at the Royal Berkshire.
>
> Yet the idea that he is bringing the good name of polo into disrepute is laughable. It could be argued that polo has tarnished The Major.

John Pilger's *Guardian* feature about miners' families in the Durham pit village of Murton (30 January 1993) draws a general conclusion from their specific plight:

> On the bitter March morning in 1985 when the Murton miners went back to the pit, their prize brass band emerged from the mist with the women marching first. This had not happened before. What their long and heroic action meant, at the very least, was that ordinary men and women had once again stood and fought back. And that, for me, is Britain at its best. The shadow that has since lengthened over them – that of the centralised state progressively shorn of all countervailing power – is now the shadow over most of us.

Analysis of "Israel settles for conflict";
socialist (6–19 November 1991)

As the fragile Middle East peace conference moves into important bilateral talks, **socialist** looks at grassroots opinion in the occupied territories and examines the international background

Israel settles for conflict

Arab left aligns with Islam as anger grows

ben cohen

PALESTINIANS in the West Bank and Gaza Strip are sceptical that the Madrid conference will deliver anything concrete. Mass rallies opposing it have been held all over the Israeli-occupied territories.

Five thousand people were at Bethlehem University on the Monday before the conference. The rally was organised by supporters of the radical Popular Front for the Liberation of Palestine, the Islamic fundamentalist Hamas, and the Naif Nawatmeh-led faction of the Democratic Front for the Liberation of Palestine (which has split over the conference).

These events demonstrate a growing anger with US plans for Palestine and a worrying alignment between the Palestinian left and the Islamic movement.

Palestinian frustration was apparent at a meeting in east Jerusalem in September, just before the Palestine National Council (the PLO's policy-making body) convened in Algiers to debate the peace conference. Among the delegates were Sa'eb Ariqat and Ghassan al Khatib, both members of the

Palestinian negotiating team in Madrid.

All the speakers reaffirmed the PNC's 1988 declaration of the establishment of an independent Palestinian state and called for a halt to Israeli settlements in the occupied territories. Ariqat called for total Israeli withdrawal from the territories occupied after the 1967 war, the inclusion of Jerusalem on the conference agenda and the right of Palestinian refugees to return and exercise self-determination.

Only PFLP supporter Riad Malki opposed participation in the conference, saying "there are hundreds of questions ... the American conference will not answer even one of them ... the Palestinian decision must be a big No to Baker's conference, and we must say Yes to Palestinian and international legitimacy". Even so, Palestinian attendance at the conference was never really in doubt – it was Israel that dragged its feet.

Tikva Parnass, a journalist based at the left-wing Alternative Information Centre in Jerusalem, says: "Israel is going to the conference to save time in order to build more settlements. You can drive for hours in the West Bank now and not see one Arab village or one Arab car."

Israel has been building roads in the occupied territories which bypass Palestinian villages, in a frenzied construction programme aimed at making its presence permanent.

This leaves the Palestinian negotiators with a tough job. "The masses in the refugee camps are desperate," says Parnass. "If the negotiators return empty-handed, that will be the end of them."

The PLO hopes the conference will pressure Israel to withdraw from the West Bank and Gaza Strip, where 250,000 settlers live. Research by Jerusalem Media and Communications Centre shows that Israel plans to increase this figure to 500,000 by the end of 1994, using Soviet Jews.

London PLO representative Afif Safieh says: "The settlers will not forgive Shamir for misleading them into the occupied territories." Safieh is adamant that the settlements will have to be evacuated, pointing to the Camp David agreement between Israel and Egypt, which led to total Israeli withdrawal from the Sinai peninsula.

Increasing numbers of Israelis are expressing opposition to settlement. On the Saturday before the Madrid talks, 13,000 gathered in Tel Aviv for a rally organised by the Peace Now movement.

However, despite renewed self-confidence in the wake of the rally, Peace Now has decided not to send a delegation to Madrid. This reflects its long-held position that the government should be criticised inside Israel, but not embarrassed outside.

Those Israelis who go further by openly meeting the PLO, are turned into criminals. After meeting Yasser Arafat last month, peace activist Abie Nathan was sentenced to 18 months in prison under a law which forbids Israelis to contact the PLO.

Madrid does not mean that independent political activity will stop. Safieh says contacts between Israelis and Palestinians will continue. Senior Palestinian leader Hanan Ashrawi has said that the intifada, nearly four years old, will intensify as negotiations go on. And the radical left in Israel remains vocal. Up to 90 women now attend weekly Women in Black vigils in west Jerusalem.

Although Israel is set to accelerate its colonisation of Palestine, bricks and mortar may not prevent the Palestinians from winning their state. As Afif Safieh says: "We cannot make the mistake of being absent at a time when the destiny of the Palestinians will be decided."

HARD news stories carry implicit biases in their selection of sources, their exclusion of others, their highlighting of some details, their down-grading or exclusion of others. They might even contain some small amount of comment and analysis.

News features can make this "subjective" dimension a prominent element of their structure. They are still rooted in the conventions of news reporting (the strong sense of news values, the emphasis on specific details, the use of quotes, concise use of language). But many news features overtly argue a case.

Story structure

Thematic block 1: par. 1 – Palestinian opposition to the Madrid conference.

Block 2: pars 2 and 3 – supporting intro. with details of rally followed by general comment.

Block 3: pars 4–6 – more information to support intro. drawn from east Jerusalem meeting of Palestinians.

Block 4: pars 7–9 – quotes from left-wing journalist.

socialist 6-19 November 1991

middle east focus 5

As the fragile Middle East peace conference moves into important bilateral talks, **socialist** looks at grassroots opinion in the occupied territories and examines the international background

Israel settles for conflict

Arab left aligns with Islam as anger grows

ben cohen

■ Determined to learn: inside and outside the Women's Affairs literacy centre at Shati refugee camp, Gaza Strip. PICTURES: SALLY RAMSDEN

PALESTINIANS in the West Bank and Gaza Strip are sceptical that the Madrid conference will deliver anything concrete. Mass rallies opposing it have been held all over the Israeli-occupied territories.

Five thousand people were at Bethlehem University on the Monday before the conference. The rally was organised by supporters of the radical Popular Front for the Liberation of Palestine, the Islamic fundamentalist *Hamas*, and the Naif Hawatmehled faction of the Democratic Front for the Liberation of Palestine (which has split over the conference).

These events demonstrate a growing anger with US plans for Palestine and a worrying alignment between the Palestinian left and the Islamic movement.

Palestinian frustration was apparent at a meeting in east Jerusalem in September, just before the Palestine National Council (the PLO's policy-making body) convened in Algiers to debate the peace conference. Among the delegates were Sa'eb Ariqat and Ghassan al Khatib, both members of the Palestinian negotiating team in Madrid.

All the speakers reaffirmed the PNC's 1988 declaration of the establishment of an independent Palestinian state and called for a halt to Israeli settlements in the occupied territories. Ariqat called for total Israeli withdrawal from the territories occupied after the 1967 war, the inclusion of Jerusalem on the conference agenda and the right of Palestinian refugees to return and exercise self-determination.

Only PPLP supporter Riad

Malki opposed participation in the conference, saying "there are hundreds of questions ... the American conference will not answer even one of them ... the Palestinian decision must be a big No to Baker's conference, and we must say Yes to Palestinian and international legitimacy". Even so, Palestinian attendance at the conference was never really in doubt – it was Israel that dragged its feet.

Tikva Parnass, a journalist based at the left-wing Alternative Information Centre in Jerusalem, says: "Israel is going to the conference to save time in order to build more settlements. You can drive for hours in the West Bank now and not see one Arab village or one Arab car."

Israel has been building roads in the occupied territories which bypass Palestinian villages, in a frenzied construction programme aimed at making its presence permanent.

This leaves the Palestinian negotiators with a tough job. "The masses in the refugee camps are desperate," says Parnass. "If the negotiators return empty-handed, that will be the end of them."

The PLO hopes the conference will pressure Israel to withdraw from the West Bank and Gaza Strip, where 250,000 settlers live. Research by Jerusalem Media and Communications Centre shows that Israel plans to increase this figure to 500,000 by the end of 1994, using Soviet Jews.

London PLO representative Afif Safieh says: "The settlers will not forgive Shamir for misleading them into the occupied territories." Safieh is adamant

'You can drive for hours in the West Bank now and not see one Arab village or one Arab car.'

■ Palestinian women were briefly visible at the start of the Intifada but an incendiary mix of Israeli repression and a home-grown conservative backlash have swept away many gains, writes Graham Usher.

Co-operatives to nurture self reliance were crushed by the clampdown on all forms of Palestinian organisation. The few jobs women had have gone to Soviet Jewish immigrants or Palestinian men made redundant in Israel. A fundamentalist reaction, coaxed by Israel and fulled by despair, has sought to impose a rigid version of Islam on women.

Yet on the Gaza Strip, under Israel's harshest repression, resistance continues in the shape of Women's Affairs – set up by and for Palestinian women. "We want to provide women with the

intellectual and practical skills of independence so that they can think, speak and act in and through public life,' says Rita Giacaman of the WA steering committee.

The group's Gaza centre runs courses including sociology, computers, women's history, politics and health. It publishes a journal and offers library and translation facilities. It needs cash and contacts with kindred organisations – educational or otherwise – abroad.
● Sally Ramsden of the World University Service's Palestinian Education Programme is urging trade union, education and women's organisations to back Women's Affairs. Details from her at WUS, 20 Compton Terrace, London N1 2UN. Tel 071 226 6747.

that the settlements will have to be evacuated, pointing to the Camp David agreement between Israel and Egypt, which led to total Israeli withdrawal from the Sinai peninsula.

Increasing numbers of Israelis are expressing opposition to settlement. On the Saturday before the Madrid talks, 13,000 gathered in Tel Aviv for a rally organised by the Peace Now movement. However, despite renewed self-confidence in the wake of the rally, Peace Now has decided not to send a delegation to Madrid. This

reflects its long-held position that the government should be criticised inside Israel, but not embarrassed outside.

Those Israelis who go further by openly meeting the PLO, are turned into criminals. After meeting Yasser Arafat last month, peace activist Abie Nathan was sentenced to 18 months in prison under a law which forbids Israelis to contact the PLO.

Madrid does not mean that independent political activity will stop. Safieh says contacts between Israelis and Palestinians will continue. Senior Palestinian

leader Hanan Ashrawi has said that the intifada, nearly four years old, will intensify as negotiations go on. And the radical left in Israel remains vocal. Up to 90 women now attend weekly Women in Black vigils in west Jerusalem.

Although Israel is set to accelerate its colonisation of Palestine, bricks and mortar may not prevent the Palestinians from winning their state. As Afif Safieh says: "We cannot make the mistake of being absent at a time when the destiny of the Palestinians will be decided."

Courtesy *socialist*

Block 5: par. 10 – PLO views on Madrid conference and *par. 11* – quotes from London PLO representative.

Block 6: pars 12 and 13 – pro-Palestinian views among Israelis.

Block 7: pars 14 and 15 – return to Safieh.

The sources contrast with those normally seen in the mainstream press: a mass rally at Bethlehem University, a meeting of Palestinians in east Jerusalem, a left-wing journalist, Jerusalem Media and Communications Centre, London PLO representative, Women in Black. And those sources are used, in general, to develop the angle outlined in the intro.

The argument is also sustained by the reporter's interventions. He describes the alignment between the Palestinian left, generally ignored or seen only in a negative light by the mainstream press, and Islamic movement as "worrying" in par. 3. The final par. sums up the argument that Israeli "bricks and mortar may not prevent the Palestinians from winning their state" with a quote from a major source supporting it.

Negotiating the subjective: *the eye-witness sporting event*

JOURNALISTS often attend sporting events, not to record the happenings and results from a specialist perspective but to describe simply the experience of being there. The journalist becomes the outsider looking in.

Such an assignment presents a varied challenge. You will need to extract a range of factual details relating to the event and highlight any news elements. It will provide you with opportunities for descriptive colour, eye-witness reporting, the development of sources and the use of quotes and for the exploration of your subjective response.

The experience of attending an event as "an ordinary member of the public" is very different from being a reporter there. As a journalist you are likely to have a note-book and tape recorder to record any interesting sights, interview, facts. You are on the look-out for the unusual, perhaps even the slightly bizarre, the newsworthy. You need to keep all your senses alive to collect a mass of details, quotes, impressions which will go towards the creation of your article.

You are unlikely to provide a simple chronology of your experience: arrival, watching spectators, the highlights of the event, the results, and departure. Instead, special jour-nalistic values should come into play. You may want to intro. on a lively quote or a striking incident which happens towards the end. It may be good to start with a colourful description of a participant and then pan out to take in the overall event.

Eye-witness writing is always overtly subjective. It should never be self-indulgent. If you are describing an underwater hockey match, the reader does not need to know at length your fears of underwater swimming originating in some early childhood trauma in Lake Ontario. This constraint does not apply to celebrity writers. Their own subjectivity is often, in news value terms, as interesting as the event they are describing and so their own self-indulgence is legitimate. But, in general, subjectivity works best when handled delicately. It is not easy striking the right balance between egotism and sensitive, effective "subjectivity".

Eye-witness features within this genre are usually aimed at non-specialist readers. Thus, you might need to explain the rules of the game if it is an unusual one, and the level of its support in the country.

Evidence of class, race and gender bias run through whole segments of British life and is prominent in sporting activities. Certain sports are more distinctly working class (football, ten-pin bowling, rugby league, darts) than others (polo, hunting). There may be opportunities in your feature to explore these aspects.

Unusual sports are played all over the country. It's a challenge to search them out in your own area. Don't worry if you have never seen it played before. The newness of the experience will make it all the more intense for you.

All the same, it is advisable to prepare as far as possible before covering the event. Consult local libraries for contacts and information; ring the Sports Council.

You may find the event boring and unintelligible. That merely poses you with the challenge of conveying that dullness in an interesting way. Always try to stay true to your feelings. Given the many pressures and constraints on journalists that is not easily achieved. Try never to transform what you experience as dull into something lively simply to "beef up" your copy. It will, almost inevitably, appear unauthentic.

The tone will be an important ingredient of your piece. Humour, irony, wry self-criticism, mock chauvinism: any of these may be appropriate. But the tone has to emerge from your own experience. The eye-witness piece will only work if that tone is genuine.

To explore the subjective element in eye-witness reporting, I'll examine critically a piece I wrote while on the staff of the *Cambridge Evening News*.

Analysis of "Bingo: Eyes down for that elusive jackpot"; *Cambridge Evening News (15 January 1977)*

Bingo: Eyes down for that elusive jackpot

By Richard Keeble

I AM with more than 450 people packed in a hall in the centre of Cambridge. And I'm staring – in the silent thrall of my bingo fling – at a small piece of paper full of figures.

A man stands on a balcony and reads out nothing but numbers. He commands total attention as we sit poised with pens and pencils praying for the elusive jackpot.

"All the eights, 88," says the man on the balcony.

A cry of "Yes" is heard. A whistle is blown. Great chattering breaks out. A young man dashes (so quick it is as if his life depended on it) towards the crier, takes a card from him and reads out again nothing but numbers. The crier is £80 richer: another game is over, another drama has been enacted.

Indeed it is the theatrical, almost surreal, aspects of the surroundings that I find so fascinating in the Central EMI Bingo and Social Club in Hobson Street.

This converted cinema could quite comfortably have found a place in the zaniest of science fiction movies – with its brash, psychedelic mish-mash of colours (silver, yellow, red, green, rust, cream to name a few) and its huge, electrically operated board that rises high behind the caller, a confusing conglomeration of figures blazing out like the strange invention of a mad mathematician.

And then there's the peculiar bingo lingo – housey housey, full house, last'un, flyer, ling double, quickie – that flows so naturally off the lips of the cognoscenti.

Since the game first burst upon the British public 15 years ago the number of participants has been growing dramatically. It's an even bet that at some time or other you've had a bingo fling.

The four-year-old Cambridge Central club alone has 10,000 members. And Britain's big four bingo businesses – Mecca, Rank, EMI and Ladbrokes – have between them 422 clubs dotted about the country.

Britain is, in fact, going through a bingo boom. But bingo players remain the great unnameables. It's an almost dead cert that if you play bingo you don't want your neighbour to know it.

Last Saturday I could find no-one prepared to give me his or her name, so strong is the social stigma attached to the game.

EMI's Press officer, Mr Eric Sullings, blamed this on the "class consciousness of the town."

"If you go to Lancashire and Yorkshire, the real bingo playing country," he said, "people are happy to talk freely about playing bingo but the further south you go the more careful people become."

This wall of silence was not my only problem. Bingo, be warned, is almost submerged beneath rules and regulations.

Before you can play you have to be a member of a club. On my first approach to the Central I was membershipless and told I just could not play.

I had to sign like everyone else a free application card and wait a week for my membership. My second visit revealed still more hazards. I arrived at 8.15 p.m. expecting to launch into a game but was told it was impossible – no cards are sold after 7.45 p.m. and members are not allowed guests.

So last Saturday it was a case of third time lucky. Even then the manager Mr John Jones, aged 41, first said I could not talk to any of the players or any of his staff. Then, after ringing his regional chief, he allowed me to talk to the players. His staff were to remain mute.

The bingo men are clearly still smarting from recent "bingomania revelations" in the national popular Press. Bashing bingo, they feel, has become a national newspaper sport and reports of women spending their rent money on the game have given it a bad image.

Certainly the Central is an addict's paradise – open every afternoon and evening except Sunday afternoon and with hundreds of pounds at stake at each session.

On Saturday the club linked up by phone to the EMI club in Oxford for a game which boasted a £400 jackpot

Moreover the players I spoke to were quick to comment on the addictive aspects of the game. "That fruit machine is a disease," said one.

Indeed I looked on somewhat amazed at people dashing for the fruit machine (which spills out its £30 jackpot in 50p pieces) in the few seconds between games and then at the long queues forming in front of them during the interval.

But Mr Jones was eager to stress the social aspects of the game. "We have people from all walks of life – police officers off duty, traffic wardens and doctors as well as housewives. It's a happy place. We get lots of pensioners in the afternoons who come for the warmth and companionship."

Clearly lots of people get lots of fun from bingo. I felt I had a good £1.80 worth playing in all the games – even though I did not come within a mile of winning any prize let alone the £400 jackpot.

But the final word goes to manager Mr. Jones: "I can't stand the game. It's too boring."

Par. 1: the "I" presence stated clearly at the start. Notice the use of the dramatic present tense. The tone is slightly ironic ("in the silent thrall of my bingo thrill"); perhaps over-consciously literary with the use of alliteration "full of figures". And the local angle is stressed.

Par. 2: more colour, eye-witness reporting and contrived alliteration.

Par. 3: short, direct quote to maintain the narrative flow.

Par. 4: a sense of drama is conveyed through contrasting sentence lengths: three short ones followed by a much longer one. Then comes a clear conclusion to the opening section's narrative "another drama has been enacted".

Par. 5: a general comment about the subjective "I" experience and the "where" of the piece is detailed: the Central EMI Bingo and Social Club in Hobson Street.

Par. 6: an enormously long sentence whose home could only be a feature. There is an emphasis on the building up of descriptive details about what is seen. Again, the rather self-consciously literary and alliterative "confusing conglomeration" and the simile "like the strange invention of a mad mathematician".

Par. 7: an emphasis now on what is heard. And I am conveying some delight in the sounds of unusual, jargon words.

Par. 8: general British historical background details and I take up the gambling jargon with "an even bet".

Bingo: Eyes down for that elusive jackpot

I AM with more than 450 people packed in a hall in the centre of Cambridge. And I'm staring — in the silent thrall of my bingo fling — at a small piece of paper full of figures.

A man stands on a balcony and reads out nothing but numbers. He commands total attention as we sit poised with pens and pencils praying for the elusive jackpot.

"All the eights, 88," says the man on the balcony.

A cry of "Yes" is heard. A whistle is blown. Great chattering breaks out. A young man dashes (so quick it is as if his life depended on it) towards the crier, takes a card from him and reads out again nothing but numbers. The crier is £80 richer; another game is over, another drama has been enacted.

Indeed it is the theatrical, almost surreal, aspects of the surroundings that I find so fascinating in the Central

Membership card in hand, Richard Keeble enters the bingo hall.   827716

By Richard Keeble

EMI Bingo and Social Club in Hobson Street.

This converted cinema could quite comfortably have found a place in the zaniest of science fiction movies—with its brash, psychedelic mish-mash of colours (silver, yellow, red, green, rust, cream to name a few) and its huge, electrically operated board that rises high behind the caller, a confusing conglomeration of figures blazing out like the strange invention of a mad mathematician.

And then there's the peculiar bingo lingo—housey housey, full house, last'un, flyer, ling double, quickie—that flows so naturally off the lips of the cognoscenti.

Since the game first burst upon the British public 15 years ago the number of participants has been growing dramatically. It's an even bet that at some time or other you've had a bingo fling.

The four-year-old Cambridge Central club alone has 10,000 members. And Britain's big four bingo businesses—Mecca, Rank, EMI and Ladbrokes — have between them 422 clubs dotted about the country.

Britain is, in fact, going through a bingo boom. But bingo players remain the great unnameables. It's an almost dead cert that if you play bingo you don't want your neighbour to know it. Last Saturday I could find no-one prepared to give me his or her name, so strong is the social stigma attached to the game.

EMI's Press officer, Mr Eric Sullings, blamed this

on the "class consciousness of the town."

"If you go to Lancashire and Yorkshire, the real bingo playing country," he said, "people are happy to talk freely about playing bingo but the further south you go the more careful people become."

This wall of silence was not my only problem. Bingo, be warned, is almost submerged beneath rules and regulations.

Before you can play you have to be a member of a club. On my first approach to the Central I was membershipless and told I just could not play.

I had to sign like everyone else a free application card and wait a week for my membership. My second visit revealed still more hazards. I arrived at 8.15p.m. expecting to launch into a game but was told it was impossible—no cards are sold after 7.45 p.m. and members are not allowed guests.

So last Saturday it was a case of third time lucky. Even then the manager Mr. John Jones, aged 41, first said I could not talk to any of the players or any of his staff. Then, after ringing his regional chief, he allowed me to talk to the players. His staff were to remain mute.

The bingo men are clearly still smarting from recent "bingomania revelations" in the national popular Press. Bashing bingo, they feel, has become a national newspaper sport and reports of women spending their rent money on the game have given it a bad image.

Certainly the Central is an addict's paradise — open every afternoon and evening except Sunday afternoon and

with hundreds of pounds at stake at each session.

On Saturday the club linked up by phone to the EMI club in Oxford for a game which boasted a £400 jackpot.

Moreover the players I spoke to were quick to comment on the addictive aspects of the game. "That fruit machine is a disease," said one.

Indeed I looked on somewhat amazed at people dashing for the fruit machine (which spills out its £30 jackpot in 50p pieces) in the few seconds between games and then at the long queues forming in front of them during the interval.

But Mr Jones was eager

to stress the social aspects of the game. "We have people from all walks of life —police officers off duty, traffic wardens and doctors as well as housewives. It's a happy place. We get lots of pensioners in the afternoons who come for the warmth and companionship."

Clearly lots of people get lots of funs from bingo. I felt I had a good £1.80 worth playing in all the games — even though I did not come within a mile of winning any prize let alone the £400 jackpot.

But the final word goes to manager Mr. Jones: "I can't stand the game. It's too boring."

Courtesy *Cambridge Evening News*

Par. 9: more background about bingo in Cambridge and in Britain generally.

Par. 10: more general background with "an almost dead cert" continuing the gambling theme. Social stigma theme emerges.

Par. 11: social stigma theme developed and related to my own experience.

Pars 12 and 13: strong quote to back up social stigma theme from good source.

Pars 14–16: details, rules and regulations of game drawn from my own experience.

Par. 17: "third time lucky" continues gambling theme as I continue the narrative of my visits. Return to social stigma theme with indirect quote from manager.

Par. 18: new "bashing bingo/addiction" theme.

Pars 19 and 20: extra detail about Cambridge club continuing addiction theme.

Par. 21: short quote to support the continuing addiction theme.

Par. 22: eye-witness reporting supporting the addiction theme.

Par. 23: quote to present positive view of the game in the interests of "balance".

Par. 24: balancing comment from myself plus extra details about costs and prize money.

Par. 25: short, snappy concluding remark which is somewhat surprising: a "sting in the tail" ending. In retrospect, I regret using this quote. Mr Jones did say it (a photographer was there to confirm) and it did provide me with a quirky finishing flourish. But it reflected badly on Mr Jones and caused him unnecessary problems afterwards. I should have exerted some self-censorship in that instance.

Looking back at the feature, written after I'd been a journalist for around seven years, the detached, ironic tone is most striking. I think it probably emerged from my class orientation. Here I was, a middle-class man intruding into the world of the working class who felt themselves ostracised in academically-dominated Cambridge. From this tension emerges the self-conscious, over-literary style of my writing. The tone of dry irony (common in the media), in fact, was my attempt to negotiate this feeling of being an "outsider".

To what extent can and should journalists remain outsiders? How much do journalistic notions of neutrality, objectivity, balance conflict with inevitable feelings of sympathy, compassion, alienation, confusion?

George Orwell grappled with such dilemmas by going to "live" the experience he wanted to write about. He became a plongeur (a dish-washer in a hotel kitchen) and tramp before writing *Down and Out in Paris and London*; he fought alongside the Republicans in the Spanish civil war. But even the "Orwell solution" is not without its problems and limitations.

The best the journalist can do is to seek to understand their own histories, their own subjectivities as well as the broader political dynamics of their society. It's perhaps a tall order – but worth striving for.

Painting pictures in words: *profile writing*

OPEN a newspaper and you are likely to find a profile somewhere. People, according to Harold Evans, former editor of *The Times* and *Sunday Times*, are news. And the profile, the drawing of a portrait with words, is the archetypal manifestation of this "people/human interest bias" in the media.

The portrait need not be only of a person. Organisations, buildings, cemeteries, roads, parks, schools, Father Christmas, even weapons can all be profiled. But people profiles are the most common.

Profiles succeed in satisfying a wide range of interests:

- *Readers*: profiles are immensely popular. They feed people's curiosity about other people. What makes them tick, what hurdles have they overcome, what is the person really like behind the public face, what accounted for their downfall? This kind of questioning has great appeal. We become voyeurs into other people's private/professional lives.

- *Reporters*: writing profiles is fun, challenging and can often help a journalist to build up contact with a useful source. Reputations can be made on the strength of profile writing.

- *Editors* like profiles because they often appear in series which guarantee a certain space being filled each week. Readers like the series format also, perhaps because they provide a feeling of continuity, stability and order. They occupy the same spot at regular intervals and so simplify the reading process.

- *Proprietors*: there is another important commercial aspect to profiles. In terms of cost-effectiveness they are particularly attractive to newspaper proprietors. An interview with accompanying picture can easily provide half a page (broadsheet) or a page and more (tabloid or magazine). Compare this with the cost effectiveness of investigative reporting. A journalist may spend hours, months even investigating a story and get nowhere.

- *People like being profiled.* It can pander to their vanity.

- *And profiles can help promote business.* A writer, for instance, hopes the publicity will help sell more of their books. The PR industry is forever pressurising the press to profile their clients.

Types of people profiles

There are many kinds of profiles and no standard format. There are no profile rules. To highlight a few styles within the genre:

- A short profile may highlight some newsworthy feature of the subject. A variation on this theme are the tiny portraits of people drawn in diary/gossip columns.

- There is the profile focusing on the person's views about a contemporary issue or experience or highlighting a recent achievement/failure.

- A longer profile will aim to provide an overview of a life. The person will be chosen probably because of a newsworthy element (a new job, a new book/film/television series/political campaign, a visit to this country) which will be highlighted.

- A person may be profiled because of some unusual feature of their lives. They may have the largest collection of football programmes in the country; or an unusual job, such as travelling the country advising gypsies on educational matters. The news element here is not significant.

- There is the "authoritative profile" in which the newspaper tries to present its definitive view on the subject. These will not carry a by-line since it is the publication speaking.

- An obituary is a form of profile.

- There is the profile, common in the tabloids, which focuses on some aspect of the subject's private, rather than public life. Thus the *Guardian* might run a profile of Michael Grade, head of Channel 4, and concentrate on his professional activities. The *Daily Mail*, in contrast, will carry a profile concentrating on his relations with his mother and wife. The *News of the World* might profile some film star and paint a broader picture based on his or her recent love affairs and what he or she has supposedly learnt from them.

- There are a whole range of "special focus" profiles which build a picture of a person around a specific angle. The *Independent on Sunday*'s colour supplement has a "How we met" feature each week, while the *Sunday Times* has its "Life in the Day" series and "Relative Values", in which two members of the same family give their own impressions of growing up with the other person. Brian MacArthur reveals that the most letters ever received on any one subject at the *Sunday Times* followed a "Life in the Day" of May Philpott, a totally unknown woman of 57 who had spent her life looking after her parents (*Deadline Sunday: A Life in the Week of the Sunday Times*; Hodder & Stoughton; London; 1991).

- The *Guardian* Saturday supplement and many other local and national papers have people responding briefly to a range of questions (What do you most regret? How would you like to die? Did you pay the poll tax? Which person do you most despise? etc). The *Sunday Express* colour supplement built profiles around the idea of taking celebrities out shopping. Another series, popular in many papers, has personalities talking informally at their homes. And so on.

- A profile becoming increasingly popular focuses on a particular possession of the subject and builds a more detailed picture around that idea. There is the *Observer*'s "A Room of my Own" which shows the subject sitting in a favourite room with their most-dearly-loved possessions laid out around them (here a Ming jug, there a Picasso to convey culture, there a pile of books to convey intelligence, the family photographs on the table top to convey a sense of human affection, warmth and security).

- Occasionally a couple are profiled in the same article; they may be married, living together or in a business partnership. Some newspapers profile families.

Preparing the profile paint

Focus

The journalist has to be aware of the particular kind of profile sought by their publication. Is it to be an overview of the life, or a focus on the latest achievements or affairs, or on their home improvement work, or a "life in their day" (very different from a "day in their life")? In every case the focus will influence the questioning.

Very often the journalist identifies to the subject during the initial contact the kind (and possibly length) of profile envisaged.

Background research

Absolutely crucial. Quite simply, the more knowledge of the subject and their special area you bring to the interview the more respect they will have for you and the more they are likely to "open up".

Thus, if you are interviewing a writer/film director/television or sports personality/local council leader/political campaigner you should be aware of their previous achievements. People featured in *Who's Who* will not expect questions about the fundamental details of their life. The challenge is very different when the subject is unknown. Then, the journalist needs to convey an interest in their subject and their specialist area.

Before (and if possible after) the interview ask other people about your subject. You may want to include some of these views in your profile. Consult the cuttings but don't presume they are accurate without checking. Immerse yourself in your subject.

Place of interview/s

Most profiles are built on the basis of one-off interviews. Describing the time and place of the interview might provide colour to the piece. The good journalist uses all their senses. Sometimes the profile is the result of a series of interviews. On one occasion they may be relaxed; at another completely different. They may be extremely busy people; describing snatches of conversation in various places can convey a sense of their hectic life-style. Occasionally a person is so famous they are extremely difficult to get hold of. Describing the hunt can provide colour to the profile. If the hunt ends in failure, the non-story can become the story. Again some people are very shy of interviewers. When they finally agree, this "rareness" is worth highlighting.

Sometimes personalities are unwilling to be interviewed. Profiles of them are still written, often containing comments about the person from other people. The person might have revealed something about themselves in a rare television interview and quotes and details from that may be used.

Occasionally a profile might be built around a press conference but then the copy loses the feeling of intimacy that a face-to-face interview provides. Increasingly profiles are amounting to nothing more than re-writes of cuttings with some newsy element in the intro.

Those important brush-strokes: *constructing a profile*

The influence of the news agenda

Profiles need not begin with the newsworthy aspect. They might seek to highlight a particularly significant or unusual event in the past. They might open with a particularly revealing quote. They might be descriptive, focusing on the appearance of the person or the environment where the interview took place.

But many profiles are influenced by the news agenda and in these cases their news aspect will never be buried in copy. It will be near the start.

Interview

Gillian Slovo

COINCIDENCE is a word which Gillian Slovo uses often, so it must please her that a whole set of coincidences surrounds the publication on Thursday of her fifth novel, *The Betrayal*, the theme of which is the price paid for political commitment.

Her father, Joe Slovo, one of only two white members of the executive council of the ANC, and former head of MK, its military wing, is in London for the first time in nine months. (So is his former enemy, President F. W. de Klerk, with whom he is now negotiating.) And *A World Apart*, the film written by her sister Shawn, based on the relationship between herself, at 13, and their mother, the ANC activist Ruth First, who was detained in solitary confinement for 117 days in South Africa in the early 1960s, is screened on Channel 4 tonight.

Gillian Slovo the *Observer* © 1991
Published by permission of the *Observer* © 1991

Here the focus in the *Observer* interview by Yvonne Roberts (21 April 1991) is on the publication of Ms Slovo's fifth novel in the coming week.

ASK anyone who knows Gennadi Rozhdestvenksy – or Noddy, as he is called affectionately – for their impressions of this garrulous Russian conductor and you get some unequivocal replies: clown, conjuror, modern Medici, a prince and protector of new Soviet music, a ghastly yet masterly, daring, wild conductor – and one of the strangest men you will ever hope to meet.

With that reputation to precede him, the grizzly bear of a fellow who turns up for his interview, apologetically late, black beret pulled down over straggly grey curls, a single tooth protruding through thick, smiling lips, already holds a certain mystery – endorsed by his insistence on speaking through an interpreter, though his English is said to be very good.

Rozhdestvensky, no stranger to London, is here to conduct Mussorgsky's Boris Godunov, the revival of which opens at Covent Garden tonight – a work he has performed, he says, waving a hand, "one hundred and one times, at least". He will also participate in the South Bank's extensive Russian Spring series, conducting a concert of contemporary Soviet music by Schnittke, Firsova and Smirnov later this month.

Here *The Independent* intro. section (6 April 1991) culminates with the reference to the visit to London to conduct *Boris Godunov*.

O N his 30th birthday he was unemployed. A bearded, balding figure who walked on Wandsworth Common, on the dole, wondering what life was all about. At 44, he is one of the most powerful men in television, chauffeur-driven in a Mercedes, linked to his job by golden handcuffs and wearing a smile that won't rub off. Has success changed Greg Dyke? Not much.

Some profiles are "timeless", without a specific news angle. The person themselves may simply be newsworthy or there may be something particularly interesting about them. This *Sunday Times* profile of Greg Dyke (20 October 1991) highlights the startling contrast between his life at 30 and now at 44.

The importance of quotations

Most profiles will carry the views of the person through the use of direct quotes. The importance of these to the profile cannot be overstated. Given that the profile is attempting to paint the most vivid portrait possible, the language of the interviewee is a vital ingredient of their personality. A profile in which all the views are in reported speech will be deadly dull.

The profile writer, then, needs to be a confident note-taker. Interviews are often taped, helping eye contact and conversation flow. But this always should be backed up with written notes. Lynn Barber, in her profile of Gore Vidal in the *Independent on Sunday* (27 October 1991), managed to use her subject's comments on tape recording since they revealed an aspect of his personality she was keen to stress: his vanity (rather than his political ideas):

H E leads me to the study, and urges me to check that my tape-recorder is working properly: no point in having an unreliable Boswell.

She also compared his formal conversation, when the tape was functioning, to his talk later on:

E VENTUALLY my tape ran out, but Gore urged me to stay anyway and chat. I wondered if he would talk about Howard Austen, or reveal more about his mother, but in fact what he chose to talk about was books. For all his frequent protestations that literature is dead, twentieth-century fiction "a chartered flight to nowhere", he still cares passionately about the dying art. He raved about Jeanette Winterson and, without the tape recorder, was even prepared to rave a bit about Martin Amis. This Gore, the Gore talking about books, was far more modest and likeable than the Gore who gives interviews. I noticed as we went on talking, and the light faded over the Tyrrhenian sea, that the bravura fell away – but so did the wit. Perhaps, like Barry Humphries with Dame Edna, he needs to turn on a false persona to get the humour juices flowing.

Notice the use of "Gore" there. It's more intimate than the formal "Mr Vidal" or "Gore Vidal" which is appropriate for news.

Some profiles will carry snatches of conversation (sometimes remembered rather than noted) verbatim. As here, from a Hunter Davies profile of Alan Yentob, programme controller at the BBC (*The Independent*, 9 March 1993):

> JACOB'S mother, Philippa Walker, has lived with Alan for 12 years. She is tall, thin, blonde. Why aren't you married? "If it's not broken, why fix it?" she says, getting Jacob's tea. She is a TV director but has taken two years off to have Jacob. Her parents don't mind her not being married, or that Alan is Jewish. Alan's mother, however, was a bit upset when they set up house together, because Philippa is Catholic.
>
> "I was there when Jacob was being born," says Alan. "When I saw him coming with those blond curls I thought, is this mine?"
>
> "He had no curls when he was born," says Philippa.
>
> "Well, you know what I mean," says Alan. "It reminded me of *South Pacific* – the colours were so lurid, especially the reds and greens. It was a Caesarian, so it was top-lit."

Hard news stories rarely begin with direct quotes but profiles quite often do. A striking phrase can encapsulate so much of the person's personality. As here, from *The Voice* (2 February 1993):

> "ANY fool can father a child but it takes a *man* to be a father," says Larry Fishburne's character Furious Styles in *Boyz N The Hood*.
>
> And anyone who has seen *Boyz* will confirm that Fishburne's performance is central to the success of the film.

Some profiles will be based totally on a verbatim (or edited) account of the interview. This is more common in magazines than British national or local newspapers.

Other profiles will merge quotes from a conversation into one long direct quote such as the "Life in the Day" profile in the *Sunday Times* colour supplement each week. The interviewee will often be consulted to see if they approve of the editing. A particularly common profile genre is the TOTS (Triumph over Tragedies) in which someone (movingly) narrates their success against tremendous odds. This example from the *Sun* (31 March 1993) combines the genre with the long direct quote:

I wanted to die but my tot sobbed: Please don't go Mummy

TURNING POINT

Sam's husband left when cancer nearly killed her . . . now she is a business owner, car racer and model

by Robin Corry

SAMANTHA Raeisi was happily married with two young sons when her world fell apart. She developed cancer of the womb, which made her Muslim husband declare her "unclean".

He told her he didn't love her and she thought there was no point going on – until her elder son, who was two, restored her faith in life and gave her a reason to live.

Now Samantha, 27, who lives in Swindon with her boys Kurosh, ten and Arash, nearly nine, tells how she battled and won.

"I was 19 and blissfully happy. I had the perfect marriage and the family life I'd always dreamed of.

I'd met my Iranian husband on a graphics design course at college.

It was love at first sight. Any worries I had about our cultural and religious differences quickly disappeared.

He was caring and a great dad to our sons Kurosh, who was two, and Arash, one. But my world began to fall apart one day in 1985 when I began to haemorrhage. There was no warning.

One minute I was playing with the boys, the next I was in terrible pain. It was like really bad labour.

Tumour

I rang a neighbour who called an ambulance. In the hospital the doctor told me there was a massive tumour in my womb. If it wasn't removed I'd be dead within six weeks.

The tumour was removed and after eight days I was allowed to go home.

I was desperate for the support of my husband. But once I came home he rejected me.

He said I was unclean because I'd had cancer, adding 'I don't want you – nobody else will.' I was in tears. We had been so close. Even when he visited me in hospital he had given no hint anything was wrong. Now he was saying it was all over.

He refused to do anything in the house.

I should have been resting to conserve what little strength I had.

Instead I was dragging myself around on my hands and knees to cope with the children.

Six days after I got home, I started to bleed again.

A further scan showed they hadn't removed all the tumour. I had to return to hospital and go through it all again.

I couldn't stop crying. I just lay there sobbing: 'Why me?' By the next day I'd given up caring. My life was in the balance but it didn't seem to matter.

What had I got to live for? I even thought of suicide.

But then my mother brought Kurosh in to see me. He clambered up on my hospital bed and put his arms around me.

He knew I was very sick and with tears rolling down his cheeks, he said: 'Don't go, Mummy, don't go.'

Sessions

That was the turning point. I made up my mind to fight back and win. I would beat the cancer and make a new life for myself and my sons.

They gave me a sense of purpose, the will to go on.

After ten days I went home, but my battle wasn't over. Six weeks later, tests showed it had spread.

Doctors tried chemotherapy, but I reacted to it so badly that I had a series of ten operations over five months.

Finally it looked like the cancer was beaten.

My husband came back saying he realised he still loved me. I soon realised it was a sham.

His parents were coming over from Iran and the only reason he came back was so they could stay at our house and see their grandsons.

Even his parents told me I wasn't a good wife because I'd had cancer and couldn't have more children.

But I've since learned I can.

As soon as they went back to Iran I took my sons and moved into a council house.

A few weeks later my husband turned up, saying he wanted to make a new start for the children's sake.

As they were pining for him I agreed, but refused to let him share my bedroom.

I decided it was time for a career.

It was the booming Eighties and I got a job as a financial consultant.

I took to it like a duck to water and was soon earning more than my husband. He hated that, making the strain of living together worse.

Finally he left for good. Our marriage had long been dead. We divorced and I felt free to rebuild my life.

My career thrived and I won awards as one of my firm's top consultants.

I bought myself the Alfa Romeo car I'd always dreamed of.

Life just got better – I tried a motor-racing talent-spotting event and came sixth out of 350 men and six women.

Then a week later I took part in my first race at Brands Hatch in Kent – always an ambition – and came 21st out of 50.

It's like the novice Formula, where the maximum engine size is 1.6-litre. This season I'm competing in 15 such events, called Formula First.

My aim is to be the British Formula First champion, and later the first woman to drive in a Grand Prix. The great thing about racing is that I'm totally in charge.

It's thanks to racing that I met my manager Mike Theobald. He's the boss of AWS, who make fireproof overalls for motor-racing, the emergency services and armed forces.

We met when I went to his factory to get some racing gear. He'd just spent seven months in hospital having spinal surgery.

Because of my own experiences I had some idea of what he was going through. That was one of the things that brought us together.

Career-wise, I'd gone as far as I could working for someone else, and last year I left to set up on my own.

I'm modelling as well. It began with brochure shots for some of the clothing Mike makes, and since then I've done sportswear and Lancome beauty products.

Disastrous

I'm proud of what I've achieved. My dad was an electrician and I was one of five children brought up in a council house. I don't regret anything – not even my cancer or my disastrous marriage. The pain and grief I've suffered have made me the strong person I am today.

None of us knows how long we've got to live. I believe in doing the things you want to do today. You only have one life.

On the health front the news isn't all good. I was told I was clear of cancer in 1989, four years after having the tumour.

But 18 months ago a smear test showed abnormal cells. It doesn't mean I have cancer, but it was a shock.

I'd been doing everything by the book, eating the right foods, getting lots of exercise and avoiding stress.

Now I'm being tested every six months and no one can tell what the future holds. It's a constant battle. But I'm living proof that cancer doesn't mean you're finished.

You can change a trauma into something positive.

It's your attitude that's most important. I'm still as determined to win my fight as I was when my little boy begged me not to die."

Some profiles carry quotes from people about the interviewee, their personality and/or their work. This is particularly the case in "authoritative" profiles which attempt to provide an overview of the person and their achievements.

For instance, a profile of Harold Pinter in *The Times* (19 October 1991) focused on his new play *Party Time*. But it included comments on Pinter and his work from a variety of sources: playwrights Simon Gray and Tom Stoppard; "the distinguished drama critic", Martin Esslin; professor of English at Ohio State University, Catherine Burkman; a member of the *Party Time* cast, Dorothy Tutin; Warren Mitchell; Donald Pleasance; drama professor and friend, Henry Woolf.

Descriptive colour

Many profiles carry descriptions of the person, their appearance, their mannerisms perhaps, their asides, the environment where they live, work or are interviewed. All this adds colour and variety to the copy, as here, from Neroli Lawson's profile of Christopher Heath (the country's former highest paid employee who that week joined the ranks of the jobless) in the London *Evening Standard* (18 March 1993):

HE is wistful but not dented. He likes Sloaney blondes but doesn't seem to allow them under his skin. Business, it seems, comes first.

Occasionally he draws on a small cigar. Briefly a rim of perspiration appears above his lip. Otherwise he is still and circumspect.

I wanted to die but my tot sobbed: Please don't go Mummy

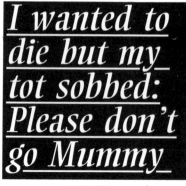

By ROBIN CORRY

SAMANTHA Raeisi was happily married with two young sons when her world fell apart. She developed cancer of the womb, which made her Muslim husband declare her "unclean".

He told her he didn't love her and she thought there was no point going on—until her elder son, who was two, restored her faith in life and gave her a reason to live.

Now Samantha, 27, who lives in Swindon with her boys Korush, ten and Arash, nearly nine, tells how she battled and won.

MOTHER'S PRIDE . . . Samantha with her sons Kurosh and Arash

● I WAS 19 and blissfully happy. I had the perfect marriage and the family life I'd always dreamed of.

I'd met my Iranian husband on a graphics design course at college.

It was love at first sight. Any worries I had about our cultural and religious differences quickly disappeared.

He was caring and a great dad to our sons Kurosh, who was two, and Arash, one. But my world began to fall apart one day in 1985 when I began to haemorrhage. There was no warning.

One minute I was playing with the boys, the next I was in terrible pain. It was like really bad labour.

Tumour

I rang a neighbour who called an ambulance. In the hospital the doctor told me there was a massive tumour in my womb. If it wasn't removed I'd be dead within six weeks.

The tumour was removed and after eight days I was allowed to go home.

I was desperate for the support of my husband. But once I came home he rejected me.

He said I was unclean because I'd had cancer, adding: "I don't want you—nobody else will." I was in tears. Even when he visited me in

TURNING POINT

SAM'S HUSBAND LEFT WHEN CANCER NEARLY KILLED HER ....NOW SHE IS A BUSINESS OWNER, CAR RACER AND MODEL

hospital he had given no hint anything was wrong. Now he was saying it was all over.

He refused to do anything in the house.

I should have been resting to conserve what little strength I had.

Instead I was dragging myself around on my hands and knees to cope with the children.

Six days after I got home, I started to bleed again.

A further scan showed they hadn't removed all the tumour. I had to return to hospital and go through it all again.

I couldn't stop crying. I just lay there sobbing: "Why me?" By the next day I'd

given up caring. My life was in the balance but it didn't seem to matter.

What had I got to live for? I even thought of suicide.

But then my mother brought Kurosh in to see me.

He clambered up on my hospital bed and put his arms around me.

He knew I was very sick and with tears rolling down his cheeks, he said: "Don't go, Mummy, don't go."

Sessions

That was the turning point. I made up my mind to fight back and win. I would beat the cancer and make a new life for myself and my sons.

They gave me a sense of purpose, the will to go on. After ten days I went home, but my battle wasn't

ON THE RIGHT TRACK . . . Samantha aims to be be the first woman to drive in Grand Prix

over. Six weeks later, tests showed it had spread.

Doctors tried chemotherapy, but I reacted to it so badly that I had a series of ten operations over five months.

Finally it looked like the cancer was beaten.

My husband came back saying he realised he still loved me. I soon realised it was a sham.

His parents were coming over from Iran and the only reason he came back was so they could stay at our house and see their grandsons.

Even his parents told me I wasn't a good wife because I'd had cancer and couldn't have more children.

But I've since learned I can.

As soon as they went back to Iran I took my sons and moved into a council house.

A few weeks later my husband turned up, saying he wanted to make a new start for the children's sake.

As they were pining for him I agreed, but refused to let him share my bedroom.

I decided it was time for a career.

It was the booming Eighties and I got a job as a financial consultant.

I took to it like a duck to water and was soon earning more than my husband. He hated that, making the strain of living together worse.

Finally he left for good. Our marriage had long been dead. We divorced and I felt free to rebuild my life.

My career thrived and I won awards as one of my firm's top consultants.

I bought myself the Alfa Romeo car I'd always dreamed of.

Life just got better—I tried a motor-racing talent-spotting event and came sixth out of 350 men and six women.

Then a week later I took part in my first race at Brands Hatch in Kent—always an ambition—and came 21st out of 50.

It's like the novice Formula, where the maximum engine size is 1.6-litre. This season I'm competing in 15 such events, called Formula First.

My aim is to be the British Formula First champion, and later the first woman to

drive in a Grand Prix. The great thing about racing is that I'm totally in charge.

It's thanks to racing that I met my manager Mike Theobald. He's the boss of AWS, who make fireproof overalls for motor-racing, the emergency services and armed forces.

We met when I went to his factory to get some racing gear. He'd just spent seven months in hospital having spinal surgery.

Because of my own experiences I had some idea of what he was going through. That was one of the things that brought us together.

Career-wise, I'd gone as far as I could working for someone else, and last year I left to set up on my own.

I'm modelling as well. It began with brochure shots for some of the clothing Mike makes, and since then I've done sportswear and Lancome beauty products.

Disastrous

I'm proud of what I've achieved. My dad was an electrician and I was one of five children brought up in a council house. I don't regret anything—not even my cancer or my disastrous marriage. The pain and grief I've suffered have made me the strong person I am today.

None of us knows how long we've got to live. I believe in doing the things you want to do today. You only have one life.

On the health front the news isn't all good. I was told I was clear of cancer in 1989, four years after having the tumour.

But 18 months ago a smear test showed abnormal cells. It doesn't mean I have cancer, but it was a shock.

I'd been doing everything by the book, eating the right foods, getting lots of exercise and avoiding stress.

Now I'm being tested every six months and no one can tell what the future holds. It's a constant battle. But I'm living proof that cancer doesn't mean you're finished.

You can change a trauma into something positive.

It's your attitude that's most important. I'm still as determined to win my fight as I was when my little boy begged me not to die.

Courtesy the *Sun*

> The photos of Samantha remain on display. The ones of himself are mainly as country gent – he raises Gloucester Old Spot pigs in his Hampshire retreat, together with other rare breeds. There are paintings of terrier dogs. His unusually long motor yacht is pictured off Portofino – all 141 feet of it. Periodically he wags an index finger and frowns – then it's off with the tape recorder. It's not himself he's worried about revealing. But merchant banks are cautious creatures and Heath will remain a consultant to the group.
>
> © *Evening Standard*/Solo

But be careful. Appearances can be deceptive. Don't presume that the persona your subject presents at your short meeting is necessarily their real personality. Someone shy today might be relaxed and talkative tomorrow.

Chronology

Only rarely do profiles begin at the beginning of a life and end with a focus on the present. That chronology will appear extremely dull since it reflects no concept of news values.

Instead, profiles can highlight a newsworthy aspect of the person and then, in the body of the article, take up the chronological theme. It is important to keep this section clear, as in this par. from Leone Ross's profile of the writer Chinua Achebe in *The Voice* (2 February 1993):

> ACHEBE was born Albert Chinualumogu, in Ogidi, in eastern Nigeria, on November 15, 1930. One of six siblings, his grandfather was one of the first people in Nigeria to embrace Christianity, and his father was a dedicated evangelist. He was always bright, throughout his education at the local mission school and his university career at the University of Ibadan – where he switched from studying medicine to literature.

Illogical disturbances to the chronological flow (first talking about 1975, then 1965, then 1968, then 1952) can be confusing. But this personal, historical section can be important in establishing the class origins of the subject and the political/cultural influences on their lives. Often having covered the biographical background the profile will return to more up-to-date aspects of the life.

Occasionally newspapers carry biographical details briefly in a box accompanying the article leaving the profile the space to concentrate on more up-to-date matters.

The presence of the reporter

In any representation of an individual there is bound to be a subjective element. But some profiles tend to exploit the journalist/interviewee relationship and make the journalist intentionally visible and intrusive. Reporters may present their own views on the subject or on some of the issues raised in the interview. They may describe the dynamic in the relationship and how the interviewee responded to some of the questions (abruptly, hesitantly). Part of the interview might be reproduced verbatim. Lynn Barber, formerly of the *Independent on Sunday* and more recently of the *Observer*, has a particular style which is intrusive, confident, witty and often critical.

For instance, here, at the end of her profile of the writer J. G. Ballard (*Independent on Sunday*, 15 September 1991):

He finds my persistence with the subject at first funny and then irritating: "You're saying, why haven't I moved my life into a much more glamorous phase? Would it satisfy you if I moved to a typical piece of Twenties stock-broker Tudor in Chertsey and furnished it all from Harrods? You'd like that, would you?" No, but . . . "Living in this house is a political statement. I'm identifying myself with a social class that stands outside the self-strangulating, taboo-ridden world of the English middle classes. Put that in your article: build it up a bit." And then, as I laugh merrily at what I take to be a joke, "I *mean* it."

The truth is, he doesn't particularly care where he lives, because he lives inside his head. He would quite like to live in Roquebrune, in the South of France, where he goes every summer for his holidays, and will do so one day when his girlfriend retires. But meanwhile Shepperton is as good as anywhere. He likes the fact that many of its inhabitants work at the film studios or Heathrow; he likes the used-car lots, the Thirties Modernist buildings that remind him of air traffic control towers, and the proximity of the motorways – not for convenience, because he rarely travels anywhere, but because he admires their architecture. He finds Shepperton "American" and there is no higher compliment in his book. And because he brought his children up in Shepperton, the house, the streets, the park, the river bank, are filled with happy memories.

When I was leaving, he asked me, "How many of the people you interview do you envy?"

"Not many. You more than most."

"What?" he laughed. "Living in a house like this!"

No . . . there is nothing enviable about his material circumstances. But there is something extremely enviable about his indifference to them. "There *are* people," he says cheerfully, "who are constantly rediscovering the world on a second-by-second basis, for whom every minute is a new excitement. Whether it's a sort of naïveté or not I don't know, but I've always been one of those. I wake up in the morning and look out at Shepperton and I'm always always amazed and think, What *is* this?"

In the opening paragraph of the extract, she conveys the intensity of the conversation. She laughs and he responds forcefully. Then she presumes to comment on his life-style, almost psychoanalysing him. Barber says at the start she has known Ballard "since the Sixties" and her profile conveys a sense of intimacy and depth (which would not have been feasible on the basis of a single interview) as well as a sense of detachment.

Notice the use of verbatim dialogue and direct quotes at the end of the extract.

Often the journalist makes no attempt to intervene. As here from the *Mirror* – bar the last par. (24 April 1993):

Solo Ernie brings back the sunshine

By Alec Lom

IT'S TAKEN almost ten years, but at last Ernie Wise believes he is more than just the surviving half of British comedy's most famous double act.

With Eric Morecambe he commanded viewing figures of more than 26 million – a feat never equalled.

Now *Forty Minutes* has filmed *The Importance Of Being Ernie*, in which he looks to the future once more.

Says Ernie: "If one of a true double act dies then the other one usually cannot perform.

"It doesn't work. They are so integrated.

"Well, I'm still performing. I'm going on. I'm not giving up. I know I've been Ernie Wise all my life but now, at last, I feel I'm a whole person." He runs a boat on the Thames, keeps a home in Florida and enjoys the trimmings of success.

But although he can't put his finger on the reason, he needs to carry on working.

"People must look at me and think 'He must be mad. He's got all the goodies, a car, a house.'

"But I still want to perform. I have this compulsion. I have to have some purpose.

"The work could be just connected with showbusiness. I'm quite capable of producing or directing.

"But I've been working since the age of six and I can't stop."

Forty-six of those years were spent with Eric Morecambe. "We were ordained for one another," Ernie tells the programme.

"I think it happened because somebody up there liked us. We created this double act which wasn't perfect by any means.

"But I don't think I would have teamed up with anybody else. There was only Eric.

"I would have done a single act otherwise. We always went everywhere together and shared everything."

If he were here, Eric would no doubt give his old friend a slap on the cheek to celebrate Ernie's new-found completeness.

The tone

This is the most vital ingredient of the piece. Is it to be an affectionate piece? Is it to be respectful, gently mocking, a damning exposé, intellectually discursive, witty, "neutral" (hopefully you will never write a sycophantic one)? In each of these the language used will be very different.

You may spend a couple of hours, even days with your subject. They may offer you a meal. Some form of human contact is established. It is then very tricky to write a damning (though obviously non-libellous) profile of that person. Equally there is a danger of solving this dilemma by lavishing praise on your subject.

SINGLE-MINDED: Ernie has finally laid the ghost of Eric Morecambe to rest

Courtesy *Daily Mirror*

There can be no standard response. At all times passing judgement should always be handled delicately. A crook, a racist, a sexist needs to be exposed. But the interview is an extremely artificial environment and the impression the subject provides should always be viewed as partial and superficial.

Analysis of Benazir Bhutto profile: "Rise of a dutiful daughter"; *Observer (9 July 1989)*

PROFILE

Benazir Bhutto

Rise of a dutiful daughter

IN DECEMBER 1971, Benazir Bhutto was in New York to hear her father address the UN Security Council. The war with what would soon be Bangladesh was nearing its end; Pakistan was on the verge of defeat. But the theme chosen by Zulfikar Ali Bhutto was, characteristically, both brave and aggressive. Realities change, he said.

"It had the most profound effect on me," she admitted to an *Observer* interviewer years later. "That speech substantially influenced me. It kept me going." For Benazir, realities have certainly changed, more than once; from pampered daughter of a wealthy family, to years of detention, isolation and exile, and now the modern world's first woman leader of an Islamic nation.

Last week, she came to London, where she seemed to be happiest when denouncing the sins of Pakistan's multifarious opposition parties. At breakfast on Friday with 100 or so of the great and good, she appeared to slip almost with relief once more into the ways of the Western world.

For at home, the problems are huge, and in the nearly eight months since her election as Prime Minister, she has made little headway in tackling them. It would be unjust after so short a time to deliver a verdict, yet there is no shortage of opponents prepared to judge her inadequate for the task she faces.

Her critics say she has done no more than react to crises as they erupt; there is no government-set agenda for reforms aimed at winning public support and offering solutions. Yet her power is far from absolute, and her dependence on American support all too obvious. What, after all, can a Prime Minister realistically achieve if, to win office, she has had to accept a deal with the military (brokered by the US) under which she undertook not to "interfere" in her country's nuclear policy, not to vary its support for the mujahideen in Afghanistan, and not to change the Constitution?

But she has had her successes too. She has released all the political prisoners, liberalised the media, freed the trades unions and student organisations. In the past six months, not a single politician has been arrested, an all-time record. And in foreign policy, relations with India's Rajiv Gandhi – like Benazir, inheritor of a myth-laden family mantle – are unexpectedly warm, leading to a dramatic defusing of tensions between their two countries. Yet, even here, the seeds of future difficulties are being sown, for both the opposition and the Army are wary of Pakistan's giant neighbour.

Benazir's biggest problem, however, lies in the relationship between central government and the provinces. Both Punjab and Baluchistan are headed by administrations implacably hostile to her, and even in the family's home province of Sind, the government of her Pakistan People's Party is hanging on only by a thread following the break-up of its alliance with smaller parties. The control exercised by the centre is at its most marginal in the country's history.

Part of the reason for all these difficulties is the widespread belief that, at heart, like her father before her, she remains unconvinced by the need for a genuine multi-party system. Asked last week how the balance of power will lie over the coming decade, she replied: "There is no one who can challenge us in that time, but the opposition is constantly trying to arouse the army to trouble." She accuses the opposition of trying to undermine her economic initiatives at state level, but her critics counter that it is she and her party who cannot tolerate regional dissent and insist on putting through rural and local aid schemes only through the party structure.

Benazir Bhutto was born, the first of four children, grand-daughter of Sir Shahnawaz Khan Gutum Murtaza Khan Bhutto, founder of the political dynasty which has dominated the southern province of Sind for more than a century. Her mother, Nusrat, is a Shia, daughter of an Iranian trading family who had settled in Bombay. For her father, Zulfikar, it was a second marriage; the first, to a cousin 10 years his senior, had been celebrated when he was only 13, and didn't last. Benazir was named after his sister, who had died in adolescence (the name means "unique").

By her own account, she was a shy but well-adjusted child; when her father used to return from New York where he led his country's delegations to the UN, he always returned with huge boxes of chocolates and clothes from Saks Fifth Avenue. It was a comfortable and privileged life, so comfortable that when she was sent to school in the United States at the age of 16, she cried because she had never had to walk to school before. "It was tough," she recalled later, "but it forced me to grow up."

She adored, even worshipped, her father, and to this day will not hear a word against him. She refers to him sometimes as "Papa", sometimes as "Mr Bhutto", sometimes as *shahid*, the martyr. "You see," she says, "my father was brilliant, he was the shining star." Salman Rushdie, reviewing her autobiography in *The Observer*, called her "still Zulfikar Ali Bhutto's little girl, still unwilling to admit that the martyred parent ever committed the tiniest of sins".

Terrible years

But when she returned to Pakistan in 1977, after eight years away (Radcliffe had been followed by Lady Margaret Hall, Oxford, where she was elected President of the Union), her father's government was crumbling. Two days after her return, he was arrested by the Army. "Look," he said when she visited him in jail, "how realities change."

The new military ruler, General Zia ul-Haq, charged him with conspiring to murder a political opponent. He was convicted and sentenced to hang; 18 months later, he was executed. For Benazir it was to be the start of the terrible years – six of them spent either in prison or under house arrest, sometimes in solitary confinement.

She insists that she does not believe in revenge: "I think there are too many better things to do in the world than to fill up your heart with hate." But despite her relentless determination (Rushdie, in his novel "Shame", created an all-too-identifiable character dubbed The Virgin Ironpants), she came close to giving it all up in 1985, after the mysterious death in Paris of her brother Shahnawaz. "I asked myself: Why am I going round in circles? Why am I leading a life that is physically exhausting, financially exhausting, emotionally barren, socially barren – for what?"

Her spirits were rekindled when she returned to Larkana, the Bhutto family capital, for Shahnawaz's funeral. A vast crowd had gathered: "I realised that these were the people for whom we have made the sacrifice. It's for them that we have put up with our pain and grief. One gets strength from one's own country. One literally feels renewed."

In December 1987, Benazir was married to Asif Zardari, a fellow-Sindi, in a wedding arranged in the most traditional of ways. She had met him, by arrangement between the two families the previous June, and seven days after the first meeting, agreed to the marriage. "Though I certainly did not – and do not – want to be seen as an advocate of arranged marriages," she wrote in her autobiography, "I realised there was something to a relationship based on acceptance. We were coming into our marriage with no preconceptions, no expectations of each other other than goodwill and respect."

Less than a year later, while Benazir was in the throes of an election campaign following General Zia's death in an air crash, a son, Bilawal, was born. From being a single woman leading an opposition party, she had become a married Prime Minister with a baby. Once again, the realities had changed.

"I admire Mrs Thatcher for winning an election three times," she said last week. "But what any leader will be remembered for in our part of the world is presiding over the transition to democracy." It is a fair enough point, but there remains a gap between her image abroad – the valiant democrat who won power from a military dictatorship in a free election – and the perception at home, where she is regarded in a less positive light.

Her job now is to move ahead on several fronts simultaneously: to set a long-term domestic agenda which will win public support; to crack down on corruption inside her own party; to act against the drugs barons, some of them senior military figures; to obtain US agreement for a move towards a dialogue with Kabul; and to wrest control of Pakistan's nuclear programme from the Army.

Her popularity has already slumped dramatically since she came to power; scarcely surprising, confronted as she is by a massive economic crisis, a continuing war in Afghanistan, and an over-active opposition waiting to pounce at every opportunity.

And, perhaps just as important, she should spend more time actually in Pakistan: since becoming Prime Minister she has already been to Turkey, Iraq, Japan and the United States, and she plans to visit another 10 countries in the next two months. Overseas support is, of course, crucial to success, but being feted in the banqueting halls is no substitute for genuine popular support back home.

THIS is a typical "authoritative", no-by-line profile, though untypical in that it does not feature a white, western male. The *Observer* (which by 1997 had switched to by-lining its major profile, carried on the back page of its Review section) is delivering its definitive assessment of the subject. It is not built from a one-off interview but is more of a critical overview looking at Ms Bhutto's career in general and using a variety of sources to support a general argument. The tone treads a delicate path between the critical and respectful. She is head of a state, after all, which has close political ties with the West – the tone and language used would have been very different had she been head of a state opposed to the West.

The alliteration in the headline is intended to provide a certain lilt and colour. The head and shoulders cartoon has a caption supporting the overall critical argument. Significantly, most profiles are accompanied by a photograph or illustration; it is as if words are felt insufficient to paint the full picture. Often a reporter will be accompanied by a photographer on a profile assignment and the interactions there can provide copy.

Pars 1 and 2: soft, feature style. Historical background focusing on the famous father. Contrasts highlighted: he is "brave and aggressive", both attributes being viewed positively in the British media; she is described as "pampered daughter".

The "realities change" theme is established strongly early on, first in par. 1 and echoed in the next par. This motif is to be developed throughout the piece acting as a sort of thematic stem around which the rest of the copy can flower. But it is rather contrived. The statement "realities change" seems hardly profound and inadequate to inspire a woman to daring political deeds.

By the end of the second par. we have moved rapidly from 1971 to the present: "from pampered daughter of a wealthy family, to years of detention, isolation and exile, and now the modern world's first woman leader of an Islamic nation". How the three stages contrast so dramatically with each other. In those last words the news peg for the profile is established.

There is no further development of the Islamic theme. Perhaps this is not surprising given the remoteness of Islam to the dominant culture in Britain. But by excluding it, the picture of both Ms Bhutto and Pakistan is seriously distorted, lacking a crucial religious/cultural ingredient.

Par. 3: the news element is heightened with reference to the visit to London "last week". The *Observer* is a Sunday and routinely deals with the previous week's news.

PROFILE

BENAZIR BHUTTO

Rise of a dutiful daughter

IN DECEMBER 1971, Benazir Bhutto was in New York to hear her father address the UN Security Council. The war with what would soon be Bangladesh was nearing its end; Pakistan was on the verge of defeat. But the theme chosen by Zulfikar Ali Bhutto was, characteristically, both brave and aggressive. Realities change, he said.

'It had the most profound effect on me,' she admitted to an *Observer* interviewer years later. 'That speech substantially influenced me. It kept me going.' For Benazir, realities have certainly changed, more than once; from pampered daughter of a wealthy family, to years of detention, isolation and exile, and now the modern world's first woman leader of an Islamic nation.

Last week, she came to London, where she seemed to be happiest when denouncing the sins of Pakistan's multifarious opposition parties. At breakfast on Friday with 100 or so of the great and good, she appeared to slip almost with relief once more into the ways of the Western world.

For at home, the problems are huge, and in the nearly eight months since her election as Prime Minister, she has made little headway in tackling them. It would be unjust after so short a time to deliver a verdict, yet there is no shortage of opponents prepared to judge her inadequate for the task she faces.

Her critics say she has done no more than react to crises as they erupt; there is no Government-set agenda for reforms aimed at winning public support and offering solutions. Yet her power is far from absolute, and her dependence on American support all too obvious. What, after all, can a Prime Minister realistically achieve if, to win office, she has had to accept a deal with the military (brokered by the US) under which she undertook not to 'interfere' in her country's nuclear policy, not to vary its support for the mujahideen in Afghanistan, and not to change the Constitution?

But she has had her successes too. She has released all the political prisoners, liberalised the media, freed the trades unions and student organisations. In the past six months, not a single politician has been arrested, an all-time record. And in foreign policy, relations with India's Rajiv Gandhi — like Benazir, inheritor of a myth-laden family mantle — are unexpectedly warm, leading to a dramatic defusing of tensions between their two countries. Yet, even here, the seeds of future difficulties are being sown, for both the opposition and the Army are wary of Pakistan's giant neighbour.

Benazir's biggest problem, however, lies in the relationship between central government and the provinces. Both Punjab and Baluchistan are headed by administrations implacably hostile to her, and even in the family's home province of Sind, the government of her Pakistan People's Party is hanging on only by a thread following the break-up of its alliance with smaller parties. The control exercised by the centre is at its most marginal in the country's history.

Part of the reason for all these difficulties is the widespread belief that, at heart, like her father before her, she remains unconvinced by the need for a genuine multiparty system. Asked last week how the balance of power will lie over the coming decade, she replied: 'There is no one who can challenge us in that time, but the opposition is constantly trying to arouse the army to trouble.' She accuses the opposition of trying to undermine her economic initiatives at state level, but her critics counter that it is she and her party who cannot tolerate regional dissent and insist on putting through rural and local aid schemes only through the party structure.

Benazir Bhutto was born, the first of four children, grand-daughter of Sir Shahnawaz Khan Gutum Murtaza Khan Bhutto, founder of the political dynasty which has dominated the southern province of Sind for more than a century. Her mother, Nusrat, is a Shia, daughter of an Iranian trading family who had settled in Bombay. For her father, Zulfikar, it was a second marriage; the first, to a cousin 10 years his senior, had been celebrated when he was only 13, and didn't last. Benazir was named after his sister, who had died in adolescence (the name means 'unique').

By her own account, she

There is no shortage of opponents who judge her inadequate for the task she faces.

was a shy but well-adjusted child; when her father used to return from New York where he led his country's delegations to the UN, he always returned with huge boxes of chocolates and clothes from Saks Fifth Avenue. It was a comfortable and privileged life, so comfortable that when she was sent to school in the United States at the age of 16, she cried because she had never had to walk to school before. 'It was tough,' she recalled later, 'but it forced me to grow up.'

She adored, even worshipped, her father, and to this day will not hear a word against him. She refers to him sometimes as 'Papa', sometimes as 'Mr Bhutto', sometimes as *shahid*, the martyr. 'You see,' she says, 'my father was brilliant, he was the shining star.' Salman Rushdie, reviewing her autobiography in *The Observer*, called her 'still Zulfikar Ali Bhutto's little girl, still unwilling to admit that the martyred parent ever committed the tiniest of sins'.

Terrible years

But when she returned to Pakistan in 1977, after eight years away (Radcliffe had been followed by Lady Margaret Hall, Oxford, where she was elected President of the Union), her father's government was crumbling. Two days after her return, he was arrested by the Army. 'Look,' he said when she visited him in jail, 'how realities change.'

The new military ruler, General Zia ul-Haq, charged him with conspiring to murder a political opponent. He was convicted and sentenced to hang; 18 months later, he was executed. For Benazir it was to be the start of the terrible years — six of them spent either in prison or under house arrest, sometimes in solitary confinement.

She insists that she does not believe in revenge: 'I think there are too many better things to do in the world than to fill up your heart with hate.' But despite her relentless determination (Rushdie, in his novel 'Shame', created an all-too-identifiable character dubbed The Virgin Ironpants), she came close to giving it all up in 1985, after the mysterious death in Paris of her brother Shahnawaz. 'I asked myself: Why am I going round in circles? Why am I leading a life that is physically exhausting, financially exhausting, emotionally barren, socially barren — for what?'

Her spirits were rekindled when she returned to Larkana, the Bhutto family capital, for Shahnawaz's funeral. A vast crowd had gathered: 'I realised that these were the people for whom we have made the sacrifice. It's for them that we have put up with our pain and grief. One gets strength from one's own country. One literally feels renewed.'

In December 1987, Benazir was married to Asif Zardari, a fellow-Sindi, in a wedding arranged in the most traditional of ways. She had met him, by arrangement between the two families, the previous June, and seven days after the first meeting, agreed to the marriage. 'Though I certainly did not — and do not — want to be seen as an advocate of arranged marriages,' she wrote in her autobiography, 'I realised there was something to a relationship based on acceptance. We were coming into our marriage with no preconceptions, no expectations of each other other than goodwill and respect.'

Less than a year later, while Benazir was in the throes of an election campaign following General Zia's death in an air crash, a son,

Bilawal, was born. From being a single woman leading an opposition party, she had become a married Prime Minister with a baby. Once again, the realities had changed.

'I admire Mrs Thatcher for winning an election three times,' she said last week. 'But what any leader will be remembered for in our part of the world is presiding over the transition to democracy.' It is a fair enough point, but there remains a gap between her image abroad — the valiant democrat who won power from a military dictatorship in a free election — and the perception at home, where she is regarded in a less positive light.

Her job now is to move ahead on several fronts simultaneously: to set a long-term domestic agenda which will win public support; to crack down on corruption inside her own party; to act against the drugs barons, some of them senior military figures; to obtain US agreement for a move towards a dialogue with Kabul; and to wrest control of Pakistan's nuclear programme from the Army.

Her popularity has already slumped dramatically since she came to power; scarcely surprising, confronted as she is by a massive economic crisis, a continuing war in Afghanistan, and an over-active opposition waiting to pounce at every opportunity.

And, perhaps just as important, she should spend more time actually in Pakistan: since becoming Prime Minister she has already been to Turkey, Iraq, Japan, and the United States, and she plans to visit another 10 countries in the next two months. Overseas support is, of course, crucial to success, but being feted in the banqueting halls is no substitute for genuine popular support back home.

Published by permission of the *Observer* © 1989

The reference to the breakfast "with 100 or so of the great and good" conveys colour (for how extraordinary to eat breakfast with over 100 people, we are bound to think). Perhaps it satisfies the voyeuristic side of the reader for how often are we given a peep into the breakfast habits of the world's most famous and powerful women?

The reference to slipping "almost with relief once more into the ways of the Western world" contrasts with the Islamic nation reference at the end of the previous par. And as good Westerners we readers can perhaps be expected to identify with her feeling of relief. Is there not a subtle form of cultural bias slipping into the copy?

Pars 4 and 5: the play of contrasts is a prominent feature of this profile. Here, in contrast to the "happiness" and "relief" of London in the previous par. we are thrown back again to the "huge problems" and criticisms of her opponents in Pakistan.

In the first three pars Ms Bhutto has been presented in a sympathetic light. Pars 4 and 5 attempt to balance that view. The emphasis switches to her critics' comments. Even here the paper comes out in her support: "What, after all, can a Prime Minister achieve if, to win office, she has had to accept a deal with the military?"

Par. 6: contrasts again. After the "difficulties" of the previous par. we move on to "successes" qualified by new "difficulties" at the end of the par.

Par. 7: more problems but the urgency of the copy is maintained by describing these as the "biggest". Useful details about the central government's conflicts with the provinces.

Par. 8: a delicate balancing act: accusation (she remains unconvinced by the need for a genuine multi-party system) followed by answer (in direct quote with the newsy reference "last week"). Then comes a Ms Bhutto allegation (opposition trying to undermine her initiatives) followed by critics' counter argument (that she cannot stand regional dissent).

Par. 9: having opened with a critical, up-to-date overview, the profile launches into a brief chronology. Notice how strictly the chronology is followed: birth/parentage/childhood/schooling/relationship to father (again). Here the private and intimate contrast with the emphasis on the public at the opening.

Par. 10: it is a picture which appears influenced to a certain degree by Hollywood, with daddy returning with chocolates and clothes to the adoring little girl. (Just missing are the violins in the background.)

The father theme culminates with superlatives. He is worshipped, he is brilliant.

The reference to Salman Rushdie was strikingly newsworthy at the time since it was soon after he had been condemned to death over his novel, *The Satanic Verses*, by the Iranian leader, the Ayatollah Khomeini. The reference to her being "still Zulfikar Ali Bhutto's little girl" is profoundly patronising but supports the general theme and tone of the par. Again the newspaper is keen to stamp its identity on the profile, this being the second reference to its title. The *Observer* is trying to stress its exclusive knowledge of Ms Bhutto.

Par. 11: back to the chronological run-through. Placing the reference to Oxford in parenthesis suggests her achievements there, substantial though they may have been, were relatively insignificant in her life. And back again to the "realities change" theme. Here the reference also appears trite but its purpose is journalistic, providing a structure to the piece.

Par. 12: execution and the start of the "terrible years". The profile is built around emotional extremes (normally associated with the tabloids): the adoring child in domestic innocence is thrown a few pars later into the horror of prison confinement.

Par. 13: but she has heroic qualities: she suffers yet does not believe in revenge, this sentiment developed with the use of a succinct direct quote. And she is a woman of all-too-human contradictions/contrasts. While she has a "relentless determination" she also has her doubts about the ultimate value of political commitment. "Why am I leading a life that is physically exhausting, financially exhausting, emotionally barren?" she asks.

It's a significant section because it highlights one of the appeals of this kind of profile. We are given little insights into the vulnerabilities and tragedies of those who rule over us. They become more human, more sympathetic. We are perhaps encouraged, if not to like them, to tolerate them.

But this is a very selective, politically influenced process. People such as Col Gaddafi, of Libya, or Saddam Hussein, of Iraq, whom the West vociferously opposes, are not permitted to possess such human frailties. In contrast, they (and their supporters) are often depicted in the media as one-dimensional and non-human – beasts, mad dogs, missile targets.

Par. 14: dwells on the impact the vast crowd at her brother's funeral had on her. Indeed, while she had described her life as a politician as "emotionally barren" she is defined here almost exclusively with reference to her feelings. Nowhere is she given space to articulate her thoughts, her political ideas, her policies. Reason, according to the sexist stereotype, gives way in women to emotion. So here in this par. her spirits are being rekindled, she is feeling renewed.

Par. 15: the chronological flow arrives at her wedding. Again the contrasts/contradictions motif emerges. She is not an advocate of arranged marriages but accepts one. The reference to her autobiography says something useful about Ms Bhutto (she writes in addition to doing all the other things – what a wonderwoman!) and as a source for quotes provides some useful colour.

Par. 16: birth of son. Reiteration of "realities change" theme again appearing rather contrived.

Par. 17: again Ms Bhutto as the feeling woman. She "admires" Mrs Thatcher. Has she any criticism of her policies? We aren't told. There is a superficial reference to her wanting to preside "over the transition to democracy" but this is immediately countered by the newspaper seemingly rigidly committed to its notion of balance.

Pars 18–20: the newspaper advises her on the policies she should adopt. She should set a long-term domestic agenda (though the paper has given her little space to articulate any ideas on this theme), crack down on corruption and so on.

The profile concludes saying she should spend less time abroad. Paradoxically, without her visit to London it is unlikely this profile would have ever seen the light of day. The activity which provided the newspaper with its news peg and some of its quotes becomes a source of criticism.

12 *Some specialist areas*
Personal columns, reviewing, freelancing

The "I" witness: *personal columns*

ALL news is subjective, the result of a complex process of selection. Personal columns make this subjectivity overt. There is no attempt to hide the "I" of the reporter behind claims of objectivity, balance, truth, neutrality. The "I" speaks loud and clear.

Personal columns "work" when the voice speaks in particularly original tones. They may be witty, controversial, no-nonsense, hard-hitting, culturally eclectic, conversational, quirky, bitchy, whimsical, ironic, confessional, authoritative, subversive, irritating. At their worst they combine crude ranting with personal abuse. But the writer's personality should always shine through the copy.

The reader enters into a kind of relationship with the writer. Often accompanying the column is a head-and-shoulders picture or drawing of the writer to help "personalise" this relationship further. Readers can come to love them and look forward to their regular slots or hate them. The worst fate for a columnist is to be ignored.

Personal column styles, language and tones are also appropriate to their newspapers. They make up and are influenced by the overall "personality" of the newspaper. Quotations from novels by contemporary East European novelists might appear in a column in the *Observer* but not in the *Star*. A slow-moving narrative about a strange appointment at the hairdresser's might be appropriate for a local weekly but not for the *Guardian*. A Marxist or a Muslim is unlikely to be offered a regular platform in a national or local newspaper. Their views are marginal and press treatment reinforces this marginalisation. But in a small circulation newspaper they are more likely to find a home.

The value of good columnists is acknowledged by all newspapers. The nationals pay enormous salaries (more than £100,000) to writers they want to promote. Similarly many local papers, in particular smallish, weekly freesheets hit by the slump in advertising revenues, will use personal columns strategically. Rather than attempt to be "journals of record" like their daily rivals, they will carry an opinionated column on a major event of the preceding week. In this way, the paper is striving to make its mark on the local community, intervening with a column aimed at getting people talking and hopefully provoking letters (either for or against).

There are many forms of personal column. They may be straight opinion or involve a small amount of journalistic research. They might be a selection of short features or news stories reflecting the interests of the writer. Most personal columns respond to the dominant news agenda but this is not always so. Perhaps too many columns by journalists end up talking about other journalists, other media.

Keith Waterhouse, the eminent Fleet Street columnist, has provided a 25-step plan to writing the perfect column ("Talking of which . . ." the *Guardian*; London; 25 September 1995). His advice includes:

- Every columnist needs a good half-dozen hobby horses. But do not ride them to death.

- On cuttings, he suggests: "The more cuttings you accumulate, the more you will be tempted to offload them on to your readers . . . Packing the column with other people's quotes is the columnar equivalent of watering the milk. Assimilate the material and then discard it."

- Never try to fake it. "Nothing is so transparent as insincerity – pile on the adjectives though you may, false indignation has the ring of a counterfeit coin."

- A column should not be used to pursue a personal grudge unless it is going to ring bells with most of your readers.

- Allow your readers only a few restricted glimpses into your private life.

- "Columnar feuds are amusing to other columnists and may even yield them copy, provided they don't mind living vicariously. The readers, or what Craig Brown describes as 'that diminishing minority of people who do not write newspaper columns', find them bemusing."

To all papers, personal columns provide an invaluable ingredient to the overall mix. Hard news (perhaps broken up where relevant with "fact files"), soft news, features, profiles, analysis, humour, reviews, investigative pieces, vox pops, specialist pages, sport, editorials, cartoons should all feature in a well-balanced, colourful publication. Students planning college-based publications should think in terms of creating this kind of mix. Ideally among all that should appear the personal column.

Thus, the *Evening Telegraph*, Peterborough (20 February 1993) carried columns by Rosie Sandall ("Rosie Sandall writes") and Mike Colton ("Colton on Saturday"). In addition, a pop column "Sounds New" with a mug shot of Paul Stainton, and a soap series review column, with accompanying drawing of a smiling Suzanne Ostler, were given the "personality" treatment.

Let's look at "Colton on Saturday":

The politicians who are definitely for turning
Colton on Saturday

U-TURNS may be disappearing from the A1 in the interests of road safety, but they seem to be spreading like maggots in bad meat in the world of politics.

John Major and his team have made enough U-turns to complete several circles and finish up travelling in the original direction, each a marvel of audacity.

The latest saw him shopping around for legal advice over Maastricht like somebody searching for a speak-your-weight machine making the right noises.

And within weeks of being elected, the President of the United States has made remarkable progress in the art of U-turning by telling people they would be taxed after telling them they wouldn't.

That is a laboratory demonstration of bending a promise round the lavatory pipe, which is where it should have been in the first place.

The curious thing is that politicians and other people in high places keep telling us to mend our ways and behave morally.

Only the other day I heard the Bishop of Liverpool say crime was all my fault (and his, and yours), even though I've only ever been done for parking without lights.

Is there anybody who can just keep going in a straight line?

This is a cleverly crafted short piece using a variety of grammatical skills, even though sentence lengths remain short in keeping with the rest of the paper. An idiosyncratic voice is maintained throughout. The focus is on the news of Major and Clinton U-turns but the style is literary with much built around metaphors and similes associated with U-turns.

Par. 1: the opening sentence, with the A1 reference, immediately highlights the local angle. The imagery associated with the simile "like maggots in bad meat in the world of politics" is strong and conveys a feeling of contempt which is to run through the piece. But there is a slight grammatical awkwardness with the use of "in" three times.

Par. 2: this continues the U-turn metaphor wittily, the tone and rhythm culminating with the phrase "each a marvel of audacity".

Par. 3: the tone of contempt is maintained with the reference to "shopping around" and the use of another simile "like somebody searching for a speak-your-weight machine making the right noises".

Par. 4: a sudden shift to America with the "And" link word. Irony is one of the most difficult tones to convey. Only through clear contextualising will the reader understand the opposite of what is written. Here "remarkable progress" is said ironically and the tone is clear.

Par. 5: somewhat obscure. Perhaps Colton is tripping up over his wordiness. The reference to "laboratory" is strange; the "bending a promise round the lavatory pipe" is intriguing, but the meaning of the final subordinate clause remains a mystery.

Par. 6: those opening five pars constitute a section presenting the main problem. Now, in the second section, emerges the moral of the tale: the hypocrisy of "people in high places". "The curious thing" has a conversational tone as do "only the other day" and "been done for" in the next par.

Against the moralising of the bishop to the impersonal masses ("us"), he presents the down-to-earth evidence of his own experience: "I've only ever been done for parking without lights."

Final par.: he returns to the U-turn theme using the "straight line" metaphor to ask the pointed question.

The politicians who are definitely for turning

U-TURNS may be disappearing from the A1 in the interests of road safety, but they seem to be spreading like maggots in bad meat in the world of politics.

John Major and his team have made enough U-turns to complete several circles and finish up travelling in the original direction, each a marvel of audacity.

The latest saw him shopping around for legal advice over Maastricht like somebody searching for a speak-your-weight machine making the right noises.

And within weeks of being elected, the President of the United States has made re-

Colton on Saturday

• •

markable progress in the art of U-turning by telling people

they would be taxed after telling them they wouldn't.

That is a laboratory demonstration of bending a promise round the lavatory pipe, which is where it should have been in the first place.

The curious thing is that politicians and other people in high places keep telling us to mend our ways and behave morally.

Only the other day I heard the Bishop of Liverpool say crime was all my fault (and his, and yours), even though I've only ever been done for parking without lights.

Is there anybody who can just keep going in a straight line?

Courtesy the *Evening Telegraph*

In many people, contempt for authority mixes with respect. A democratic if not anarchic streak competes with fascination for power and fear of radical change. Newspapers tap those ambivalent feelings. On the one hand they build up personalities into stars, heroes, demi-gods almost. The next minute they are casting them to the ground. Here "Colton" speaks directly to the reader's contempt for "people in high places". It's very effective.

Analysis of Julie Burchill "Comment"; *Mail on Sunday* *(26 January 1992)*

ONE of the most famous and highly-paid executors of the barbed comment and pugnacious put-downer is Julie Burchill. Her *Mail on Sunday* column usually comprised a series of short, punchy and deliberatively provocative comments on largely trivial news points of the moment. There are lots of word plays. This extract captures some of the basic elements of her style:

Par. 1: the put-down. Mick Hucknall is described as a "crooner" but not until the final par. is it said he *is* Simply Red. To readers unacquainted with pop chart personalities the piece might appear a bit of a mystery. Why all the fuss?

Anyway, Ms Julie is determined to insult the poor chap. His achievements, she says, have nothing to do with singing but all to do with looking like the "Duchess of York in drag". Royalty, pop stars, and drag – a potent brew.

Par. 2: an important discovery: he has a tattoo. (But how was this discovery made? Did she read it in a paper? Did a friend tell her? Did she see it in the flesh? I think we should have been told.) We are not allowed to forget that he has a tattoo. Over 16 words she mentions it three times.

It's all just tattoo much

UNTIL now the flame-haired crooner Mick Hucknall has been most remarkable for his striking resemblance to the Duchess of York in drag.

But now I discover he has a tattoo. And not just any tattoo.

It's "a tattoo of a cross surrounded by yellow stars; it's the federal symbol of Europe, each star representing a different European nation."

Can you credit that? Only a Euro-bore could call up the po-faced pomposity it takes to have "Federation" tattooed on one's arm! In the old days, pop stars had themselves slathered in slogans like "Born To Be Wild", "Death before Dishonour" or "Blood And Glory".

Even "Mother" showed a certain, insouciant watcha-gonna-do-about-it daring.

Absence

But *having the logo of a business cartel emblazoned on yourself?* – what comes next? McDonald's?

"I feel more European than English," Hucknall explains. So let us leave him to the inspiring glories of the food mountain, red tape run riot and two-thousand-word directives on the export of marzipan.

One thing remains unexplained; if Hucknall feels so "European", why are balalaika and bouzouki and accordion and zither so absent from his music?

Which is, like 75 per cent of Anglo-American pop being churned out today, a bare-faced, watered-down rip-off of black American soul.

One minute – I concede my case. In one way, Simply Red music is the sound of the new Europe. Bland, smug and very, very boring.

© *Mail on Sunday*/Solo

Par. 3: the man is now dubbed a Euro-bore but "po-faced pomposity" is straining the possibilities of alliteration for largely meaningless effect. Much media comment is built on the nostalgic fantasy of a "better" past – when men were braver, or less violent, or ate more wholesome food and drank less polluted water etc. Here Burchill dabbles in her own nostalgia summoning up the words of earlier, less po-faced tattoos. The reader has heard the word "tattoo" too often but indulging in the contrived "slathered in slogans" to avoid repeating it again is over-the-top.

Notice the use of the threesome "Born To Be Wild", "Death Before Dishonour" or "Blood And Glory". Max Atkinson, in *Our Master's Voices: Language and Body Language of Politics* (Methuen; London; 1984) has identified how lists of three consti-tute an important ingredient of rhetoric as well as other forms of communication. "One of the main attractions of three-part lists is that they have an air of unity or complete-ness. Lists comprising only two items tend to appear inadequate or incomplete." Here Burchill parades her list of three and she ends on one, too: "Bland, smug and very, very boring." Intriguing.

It's all just tattoo much

BLAND: Hucknall

UNTIL now the flame-haired crooner Mick Hucknall has been most remarkable for his striking resemblance to the Duchess of York in drag.

But now I discover he has a tattoo. And not just any tattoo. It's 'a tattoo of a cross surrounded by yellow stars; it's the federal symbol of Europe, each star representing a different European nation.' Can you credit that? Only a Euro-bore could call up the po-faced pomposity it takes to have 'Federation' tattooed on one's arm! In the old days, pop stars had themselves slathered in slogans like 'Born To Be Wild', 'Death Before Dishonour' or 'Blood And Glory'.

Even 'Mother' showed a certain, insouciant watcha-gonna-do-about-it daring.

Absence

But *having the logo of a business cartel emblazoned on yourself?* — what comes next? McDonald's?

'I feel more European than English,' Hucknall explains. So let us leave him to the inspiring glories of the food mountain, red tape run riot and two-thousand-word directives on the export of marzipan.

One thing remains unexplained; if Hucknall feels so 'European', why are balalaika and bouzouki and accordion and zither so absent from his music?

Which is, like 75 per cent of Anglo-American pop being churned out today, a bare-faced, watered-down rip-off of black American soul.

One minute — I concede my case. In one way, Simply Red music *is* the sound of the new Europe. Bland, smug and very, very boring.

© *Mail on Sunday*/Solo

Par. 4: this comes as a surprise. After the macho bravado of "Blood And Glory" and the like comes the reference to "Mother". It's an idiosyncratic shift of focus which works well. The use of "insouciant" continues this mood. It's a surprising word, not on the lips of the average *Mail* reader. And "watcha-gonna-do-about-it daring" is a great, invented phrase which, following the mandarin, esoteric "insouciant" has all the gusto of street language and slang.

Par. 5: a joint put-down for Hucknall and the EC described, with brutal brevity, as a "business cartel".

Par. 6: the ironic tone emerges with the reference to "inspiring glories". "Red tape run riot" allows her to indulge her affection for alliteration; the reference to the marzipan report is mocking in tone.

Par. 7: a strange point here. Does it mean that any musician who supports the EC has to include balalaika, bouzouki, accordion and zither in their scores? Surely not?

Par. 8: from Hucknall she moves to slag off the bulk of Anglo-American pop. "Churned out" conveys her contempt which continues with the trio of hyphenated words (full of clashing hard consonants).

Par. 9: back to the Hucknall theme. Again her trio of adjectives conveys the strength of her feeling: "Bland, smug and very, very boring." The implication is that her views and writing are the very, very opposite of that.

Analysis of "Rat for a sinking ship?" by Lucy Orgill;
Derby Evening Telegraph (25 February 1993)

Rat for a sinking ship?

HANDS up those out there who allow themselves the luxury of a good wallow in breakfast telly. Not many, I wouldn't wonder.

So who cares if Fiona Armstrong has failed the F-factor, or if the sexual chemistry between her and Michael Wilson has gone down the tubes? We're usually too busy scraping the burnt bits off the toast and wondering if we've still got a job to go to to worry about the state of Ms Armstrong's legs or which bleary-eyed potato-on-the-couch the "team"

will be pandering to today.

GMTV, however, are so concerned about the drop in viewing ratings that they're bringing in Greg Dyke, the man who "rescued" TV-am 10 years ago when he introduced Roland Rat and Kevin the Gerbil – which only serves to show the mentality of the early-doors viewing public.

Perhaps he could poach Wogan?

After all, the ratings have only gone down since he returned to the breakfast spot on the wireless.

THIS was the bottom piece in her column suitably titled "Sounding Off". Other pieces included a suggestion to vegetarians to "swallow their diets and their ideology" and dip into "a little drop of home-made chicken soup"; a jibe at Prince Charles; and a swipe at John Major who was told to "put his own house in order before swanning off to America".

Par. 1: the style is conversational. But she maintains a certain distance. Instead of saying: "Hands up those of you who allow yourselves ...", which would have been more intimate, she calls her readers "those out there" and "themselves". All the same, there is an attempt to identify with those who don't, she says ironically, "allow themselves the luxury of a good wallow in breakfast telly".

Par. 2: she adopts a dismissive attitude to the media hype surrounding the launch of the GMTV independent television station. Prominent in this coverage was Fiona Armstrong's supposed "F (for fanciability) Factor". The reduction of the television host to a sexual object, in particular by the popular press, was both predictable and appalling. The response of the public is complex, ambivalent.

Here Orgill is articulating those feelings of contempt for media hype which must resonate with many of her readers: "Who cares if Fiona Armstrong has failed the F-Factor." Notice there is no need to explain who Fiona Armstrong or Michael Wilson are; nor what the F-Factor is. Orgill presumes, probably correctly, the story's background is sufficiently well known to her media-consuming readers.

In contrast to the pretentious media talk of "sexual chemistry" and Ms A.'s legs, Orgill presents the down-to-earth reality of "scraping burnt bits off the toast and wondering if we've still got a job". And the phrase "bleary-eyed potato-on-the-couch" captures with its length and inventiveness her struggle to convey the depths of her contempt.

Par. 3: contempt for the media hype surrounding Ms A. translates into contempt for the "not many" of par. 1 (though they are, in fact, millions) who watch breakfast telly.

Rat for a sinking ship?

HANDS up those out there who allow themselves the luxury of a good wallow in breakfast telly. Not many, I wouldn't wonder.

So who cares if Fiona Armstrong has failed the F-factor, or if the sexual chemistry between her and Michael Wilson has gone down the tubes? We're usually too busy scraping the burnt bits off the toast and wondering if we've still got a job to go to to worry about the state of Ms Armstrong's legs or which bleary-eyed potato-on-the-couch the "team" will be pandering to today.

GMTV, however, are so concerned about the drop in viewing ratings that they're bringing in Greg Dyke, the man who "rescued" TV-am 10 years ago when he introduced Roland Rat and Kevin the Gerbil — which only serves to show the mentality of the early-doors viewing public.

Perhaps he could poach Wogan?

After all, the ratings have only gone down since he returned to the breakfast spot on the wireless.

Courtesy *Derby Evening Telegraph*

They are the kind of people who took to Roland Rat and Kevin the Gerbil – which shows their "mentality".

Pars 4 and 5: a dig at Wogan. A columnist like Orgill can summon up the name of a media "personality" and we immediately understand. "Wogan" is like someone living down the road. We see him regularly, we have our own feelings about him. We can like him, hate him or we can give him a little dig – as here. Is this anything more than gossip in the global media village we all inhabit?

The art of reviewing

REVIEWS serve many functions. They provide basic information: for example, that a film has just been released and can be seen at the cinemas indicated.

For people who intend to see, read or hear a work (or, in the case of a broadcast show, have already seen or heard it) the review gives an opinion carrying some authority to compare with their own.

Yet often the vast majority of readers will never experience directly the work under review. A concert may have been attended by no more than a few hundred people. The review must then exist as a piece of writing in its own right. It must entice in the reader through the quality and colour of its prose. It must entertain, though different newspapers have different conceptions of what entertainment means.

For the producers of the work the review (good, bad, or indifferent) offers some vital publicity. Many journalists like reviewing. They often come from a humanities academic background where arts reviewing is common. Science is still on the margins of the journalists' culture.

And for the newspaper, reviews can attract advertisements. A newspaper carrying substantial book reviews, for instance, is more likely to attract advertising from book publishers than one which largely ignores books.

On many local weeklies, the review might serve a different purpose. The newspaper is acting as a journal of record for the local community, carrying all the names of the performers, say, in a school play.

Accompanied by a photograph of a scene, the report will serve as a souvenir for many.

At the heart of reviewing lie some basic journalistic challenges. A great writer does not necessarily make a great reviewer.

- Names of performers, producers, writers and of any fictional characters and places must be carried accurately. Where relevant their titles must be given.

- Direct quotes from the works, similarly, must be given correctly.

- Plots (or, say, the contents of an exhibition) should be summed up clearly and in accessible language.

- Any esoteric elements should be conveyed in language likely to be understood by the majority of the readers.

- In some cases special sensitivity is required. A reporter, for instance, approaches a work by a group of committed amateurs or by children with different aesthetic standards from when reviewing a work by professionals. The reviewer may do the reader a service by not spoiling the suspense of a thriller; they may choose not to reveal a sudden twist in the plot at the end.

- In criticising a work, the journalist must not stray into libel.

- The journalist has to be true to their own experience and find the words to convey that accurately and concisely without falling into cliché.

- The reviewer must be able to write, handling variations of tone and sentence structure confidently in accordance with the overall style of the newspaper. The thematic structure (as in all features) must be clear and not contain any contradictions or repetitions.

- As in all journalistic writing, the intro. must carry sufficient weight to attract the reader. It might encapsulate the main theme of the piece, it may contain a striking quote or description, a joke or a narrative. If it's dull, pretentious, long-winded, off-target it has failed.

- Reviewers usually write to a specified word count. As Irving Wardle, veteran theatre critic of *The Times* and *Independent on Sunday* comments: "Reviewers soon learn to write to length knowing that if they overwrite it is their opinion that will be cut while all the plottery will be kept intact" (*Independent on Sunday*, 12 July 1992).

- Reviewers have to be sensitive to the particular bias of the newspaper and its readers. For instance, a review in *Tribune* or the *Catholic Herald* will be very different from one in the *Sun* or *The Independent*.

The style, content, length, and tone of an arts review are influenced by many factors. For instance, the personal bias of the reviews editor can influence the choice of reviewer and the work reviewed.

Reviews in the popular press tend to be short, focusing on the entertainment level of the work. The language, as in the rest of the paper, is usually brisk and straight-to-the-point. Any sexual, sensational, human interest elements are highlighted.

The tone can be varied: mocking, ironic, damning, praising. But it is rarely analytical. In films and theatre/showbiz reviews, the focus is often on the performances of any leading "star", particularly if they are British. Because of the shortness of the piece there is rarely any chance for the reviewer to express any distinct style.

Many local papers tend to mix elements of the popular with those of the middle brow. The language and sentence length follow the style in the rest of the paper. But an extra overall length gives the chance for a more idiosyncratic approach. Plots can be explored in greater depth; themes can be explored further. Often in local and middle-brow papers the emphasis tends to be more on the personalities involved – with news and profile features dominating the arts sections.

Heavies tend to put greater emphasis on reviewing, though there is a distinct London bias in their coverage. They draw important advertising from the arts and many of their readers, educated past 18, have either an active or passive interest in "culture". Reviewers in the heavies aim to impress with the depth of their knowledge and appreciation. As Edward Greenfield, for 40 years *Guardian* music critic, commented (30 July 1993): "My own belief is that the music critic must aim at appreciation above all, trying never to let the obvious need to analyse in nit-picking detail get in the way of enjoyment."

Heavies carry short and snappy (and probably much read) reviews as well as much longer ones. The language, particularly in art, classical music and book reviews, might be esoteric since the writer is presuming a certain level of knowledge among their readers. For instance, Andrew Graham-Dixon wrote in his *Independent* review of a National Gallery exhibition (30 March 1993):

Chardin's great gift was his ability to make the mundane seem consequential, to aggrandise (but inconspicuously, subtly without banging a drum) everyday activities like eating, cleaning, unpacking the groceries. The painting may even covertly refer to its own transformative potency, its transubstantiation of ordinary stuff into an image fit for moralised contemplation.

The extra length of the reviews in the "heavies" allows the writer greater scope for expressing their personality and idiosyncrasies. As a result, reviewers of theatre, books, films and television in the heavies often acquire celebrity status – Kenneth Tynan, John Carey, Cyril Connolly, Graham Greene, Dilys Powell, Nancy Banks-Smith, to name but a few.

A lengthier review in a heavy might be expected to contain some of the following ingredients, in addition to those outlined above:

● The analytical element tends to be more prominent.

● Comparisons are more likely to be made with previous works by the artists involved or by others in the same field thus conveying a greater sense of knowledge and authority in the review; if a film, or television programme, say, is based on a book, then comparisons between the two works are likely.

● Nuances of tone (through wit, mockery, the subtle use of parentheses, through contrasting sentence rhythms and lengths, through the use of slang perhaps juxtaposed with rarefied, intellectual "highbrow" writing) can be explored.

The distinctions made here between popular, middle-brow/local and heavy are over-simplifications. There are countless different styles overlapping these areas. But, for the purposes of further analysis, let us look at the following reviews:

What's on at the movies

William Hall

ONE look at those alligator eyes and a girl knows she's in B-I-G trouble. The eyes belong to Jack Nicholson and in **MAN TROUBLE** (Cert 15, on release next week) he proves again that he is to lechery what other leading men are to charm.

He plays a shady dealer in the newest growth industry amid the neurotic world of Hollywood: breeding guard dogs to protect the multi-million-dollar properties.

Hired by a famous concert singer (Ellen Barkin), Jack is bitten by the love bug the moment he sets eyes on his new client.

Blonde and spirited, she is being harassed by her jealous ex-husband (Harry Dean Stanton) as well as by a sinister neighbourhood burglar.

Jack arrives at the gates with an alsatian named Duke, an appealing creature which prefers to gnaw a rubber bone than an ankle. The fur starts to fly when the four-legged friend is let off the leash to patrol the grounds, while Jack sets out to prove himself a master detective.

Nicholson can normally win over any script. But he has an uphill task with this one. He treads an uneasy line between lust and laughter as he pursues the reluctant singer through the rose bushes.

There's an awful lot of shrieking and running about, and the pair get into some amusing shouting matches. But what should have been a biting suspense comedy from director Bob Rafelson veers too closely on the border of farce.

Down, boy! Only a small rosette for this one.

© William Hall 1993

The review from the *People* (17 January 1993) bears the headline "What's on at the movies" stressing the informational function of the copy. It is basically telling the readers this is the major new film (since it features a Hollywood "superstar", Jack Nicholson) and that it will be on release next week.

All the focus is on Nicholson. The caption, the intro., the body of the text revolve around him, not the character he plays. Nowhere is his fictional name identified. He is always referred to as "Jack", reality merging with fantasy. Most of the rest of the piece is devoted to a lively description of the plot with adjectives used to provide extra impact (as in "shady dealer"; neurotic world", "blonde and spirited", "sinister, neighbourhood burglar", "appealing creature").

Comment is restricted to two pars with an over-indulgence in alliteration in one ("an uneasy line between lust and laughter" and "the reluctant singer through the rose bushes"). The last sentence has a jokey feel to it, the critic mixing his judgement with the jargon of dog shows. This also seems rather contrived, Duke the alsatian having been mentioned only briefly in the text.

WHAT'S ON AT THE MOVIES

JACK THE LAD: Nicholson and Barkin

ONE look at those alligator eyes and a girl knows she's in B-I-G trouble. The eyes belong to Jack Nicholson and in **MAN TROUBLE** (Cert 15, on release next week) he proves again that he is to lechery what other leading men are to charm.

He plays a shady dealer in the newest growth industry amid the neurotic world of Hollywood: breeding guard dogs to protect the multi-million-dollar properties.

Hired by a famous concert singer (Ellen Barkin), Jack is bitten by the love bug the moment he sets eyes on his new client.

Blonde and spirited, she is being harassed by her jealous ex-husband (Harry Dean Stanton) as well as by a sinister neighbourhood burglar.

Jack arrives at the gates with an alsatian named Duke, an appealing creature which prefers to gnaw a rubber bone than an ankle. The fur starts to fly when the four-legged friend is let off the leash to patrol the grounds, while Jack sets out to prove himself a master detective.

Nicholson can normally win over any script. But he has an uphill task with this one. He treads an uneasy line between lust and laughter as he pursues the reluctant singer through the rose bushes.

There's an awful lot of shrieking and running about, and the pair get into some amusing shouting matches. But what should have been a biting suspense comedy from director Bob Rafelson veers too closely on the border of farce.

Down, boy! Only a small rosette for this one.

WILLIAM HALL

Courtesy William Hall/*the People*

Nilsen's victory for truth

David Thomas
TV Review

TELEVISION reporters like to look down on the ink-stained hacks of Fleet Street. They adopt an air of superiority when covering the tabloid Press and its struggles against government restrictions.

But they should beware. For they may be next in the firing line.

As if to prove the point, last week saw a determined effort by the Home Office to prevent the broadcasting of an interview with the mass killer Dennis Nilsen. It appeared in **A MURDER IN MIND (ITV, Tues)**, a serious, responsible documentary about the psychology of serial killers.

Unlike The Silence of the Lambs (**SKY MOVIES, Weds**), it did not glamorise these evil men. Instead it did what good journalism should. It searched for the truth and it increased understanding.

Attempts to black out the interview were justified by claims that the families of his victims might be offended. Yet none of the dead were mentioned and Carl Stotter, who survived a Nilsen attack, supported it. In truth, Whitehall was, as always, doing everything it could to limit the public's knowledge and restrict information.

We are governed by an Establishment obsessed by secrecy to an extent unknown in any other Western democracy. A Murder In Mind represented one small victory and I applaud its producer Mike Morley and Mr Justice Aldous for allowing it.

Frightening

All week long, those programmes not about murderers were about vampires. On Wednesday, Holmes and Watson investigated **THE LAST VAMPYRE (ITV)** in a lavish production whose most frightening aspect was the enormous amount of weight which had settled about Jeremy Brett's once-emaciated frame. Meanwhile, **THE SOUTH BANK SHOW (ITV, Sun)** turned its gaze on Dracula. The programme illustrated the difficulty this venerable flagship is having in finding a new identity.

On the one hand, it was a serious investigation of the Dracula myth, from Bram Stoker's book, through all the subsequent films and dramatisations. But alongside this ran an unashamed promotional puff for Francis Ford Coppola's new Dracula film. It is one thing to celebrate the arts, but quite another to act as an unofficial PR team.

Still, it could have been worse. It could have been **BLOOD LINES: MAKING COPPOLA'S DRACULA (BBC, Sat)**. This programme was bought from Columbia Pictures. By a quite remarkable coincidence, Columbia happens to be the studio which made . . . yes, you guessed it . . . Coppola's Dracula. It was, in other words, a 30-minute advertisement. I wonder what John Birt has to say about that?

Better news for Mr Birt was that by far the best programme of the week appeared on BBC2, **EUROPE ON THE BRINK (Tues)** was a dramatisation of a conflict between Europe and America in the year 2013.

Devastation

Produced by Glynn Jones and directed by Marsh Marshall, the film set out the path that led from Maastricht to Armageddon. It used superb computer graphics, designed by Chris Fynes, but even more chilling were the genuine newsreels of riots, nuclear bombs and environmental devastation, and all horrifyingly real.

By the time it was all over, I was ready to book my passage to New Zealand. In 20 years time, it might be the only peaceful spot left.

This *Sunday Express* column (31 January 1993) captures some of the elements of a middle-brow review. The logo stresses the celebrity status of the reviewer, David Thomas. You may not have watched any of the programmes but the colour of the writing should provide its own entertainment.

Compare this to the *People* piece where the critic's name was buried at the end and where comment occupied only a small amount of space.

The Thomas piece is also typical of a popular review format which links a number of works under the same headline.

It is fascinating to see how the dominant news agenda seeps into the various sections of any newspaper such as features and arts. Here Thomas opens with an oblique reference to the controversy current at the time over the Calcutt committee recommendations for constraints on the press.

He links that with a comment on the Home Office's attempt to ban the showing of an interview with the mass killer Dennis Nilsen, which had also been given massive media coverage over the previous week. A sense of news values has clearly influenced the choice of opening subject.

The reference to "ink-stained hacks of Fleet Street" is metaphoric. With the introduction of new technology, reporters no longer end up "ink-stained" (though sometimes RSI-afflicted, see Chapter 13). And while he has a point over television reporters' attitudes to the popular press, it was strange to single out the tabloids in this context. All the press were facing government restrictions.

All the same, Thomas's opening comments flow easily into his discussion of the programme *A Murder in Mind* (channel and day shown clearly given). "As if to prove the point" is the crucial linking phrase.

The comments are concise. He manages to compare it to the most famous, recent film about a serial killer and make a pointed comment about the purpose of good journalism: it should search for the truth (a highly problematic concept, though) and increase understanding.

In the next par. he answers arguments of those who sought the ban and concludes with a comment about Whitehall's propensity to restrict information. He continues with a criticism of a "secrecy-obsessed" Establishment. In part this rings true. But the paradox lies in the fact that the view appears in the *Sunday Express* which, it could be argued, is itself part of the Establishment.

From murder Thomas moves on to his next subject with the link phrase "All week long, those programmes not about murderers were about vampires" (a bit of journalistic licence/exaggeration there, though). He tackles three programmes on this theme in a clearly presented thematic block running through pars 7 to 9.

A bit of wit emerges from the former editor of the now relaunched *Punch* when he subverts expectations saying the most frightening aspect of the film comes not from the plot but from the enormous amount of weight put on by Jeremy Brett. He presumes his media-consuming readers know to whom he is referring here. With the link word "meanwhile" Thomas shifts to his new programme. He states his case – the *South Bank Show* is finding it difficult establishing its new identity – and then elaborates on that point.

Nilsen's victory for truth

DAVID
THOMAS
TV REVIEW

TELEVISION reporters like to look down on the ink-stained hacks of Fleet Street. They adopt an air of superiority when covering the tabloid Press and its struggles against government restrictions.

But they should beware. For they may be next in the firing line.

As if to prove the point, last week saw a determined effort by the Home Office to prevent the broadcasting of an interview with the mass killer Dennis Nilsen. It appeared in **A MURDER IN MIND (ITV, Tues)**, a serious, responsible documentary about the psychology of serial killers.

Unlike The Silence of the Lambs **(SKY MOVIES, Weds)**, it did not glamorise these evil men. Instead it did what good journalism should. It searched for the truth and it increased understanding.

Attempts to black out the interview were justified by claims that the families of his victims might be offended. Yet none of the dead were mentioned and Carl Stotter, who survived a Nilsen attack, sup-

ported it. In truth, Whitehall was, as always, doing everything it could to limit the public's knowledge and restrict information.

We are governed by an Establishment obsessed by secrecy to an extent unknown in any other Western democracy. A Murder In Mind represented one small victory and I applaud its producer Mike Morley and Mr Justice Aldous for allowing it.

Frightening

All week long, those programmes not about murderers were about vampires. On Wednesday, Holmes and Watson investigated **THE LAST VAMPYRE (ITV)** in a lavish production whose most frightening aspect was the enormous amount of weight which

had settled about Jeremy Brett's once-emaciated frame. Meanwhile, **THE SOUTH BANK SHOW (ITV, Sun)** turned its gaze on Dracula. The programme illustrated the difficulty this venerable flagship is having in finding a new identity.

On the one hand, it was as serious investigation of the Dracula myth, from Bram Stoker's book, through all the subsequent films and dramatisations. But alongside this ran an unashamed promotional puff for Francis Ford Coppola's new Dracula film. It is one thing to celebrate the arts, but quite another to act as an unofficial PR team.

Still, it could have been worse. It could have been **BLOOD LINES: MAKING COPPOLA'S DRA-**

CULA (BBC1, Sat). This programme was bought from Columbia Pictures. By a quite remarkable coincidence, Columbia happens to be the studio which made ... yes, you guessed it ... Coppola's Dracula. It was, in other words, a 30-minute advertisement. I wonder what John Birt has to say about that?

Better news for Mr Birt was that by far the best programme of the week appeared on BBC2. **EUROPE ON THE BRINK (Tues)** was a dramatisation of a conflict between Europe and America in the year 2013.

Devastation

Produced by Glynn Jones and directed by Marsh Marshall, the film set out the path that led from Maastricht to Armageddon. It used superb computer graphics, designed by Chris Fynes, but even more chilling were the genuine newsreels of riots, nuclear bombs and environmental devastation, and will horrifyingly real.

By the time it was all over, I was ready to book my passage to New Zealand. In 20 years time, it might be the only peaceful spot left.

Courtesy Sunday Express

From there, with the link phrase, "Still, it could have been worse. It could have been ..." he tackles *Blood Lines*. He makes another important, though debatable, point, highlighting the way both these programmes show how distinctions between journalism and PR are constantly being broken down.

The John Birt theme is used to link his Coppola section with his final programme. But how many people knew John Birt was the director-general of the BBC? Certainly many more became aware after a scandal blew up over his tax affairs some months following this review. At the time, journalists like Thomas knew. He was perhaps expecting too much of his general reader. A simple reference to Birt's title would have solved that problem.

Television

Allison Pearson

SUMMERTIME, AND the living is queasy. What with the heat and the bodies piling up under the floorboards, Dennis Nilsen started worrying about the "smell problem". Then he had an idea: "I thought what would cause the smell was the innards, the soft parts. So on a weekend I'd pull up the floorboards and begin dissection." It was horrible work: Nilsen explained that he would get blind drunk and occasionally run into the garden to throw up. If it made a serial killer sick, what did the makers of **Viewpoint 93's Murder**

in Mind (ITV) think it would do to viewers? Make them watch it, stupid.

The Home Office was most co-operative in this endeavour. Its attempt to ban the interview with Nilsen guaranteed a ratings boom, and the warning before the programme will have pulled in any stragglers: "This contains pictures and language that many viewers may find disturbing." "We hope" is traditionally left off the start of that sentence. As it turned out, *Murder in Mind*, ostensibly about new ways to catch serial killers, *was* shocking: shockingly thought out, shockingly edited, shockingly gullible.

TELEVISION

ALLISON PEARSON

SUMMERTIME, AND the living is queasy. What with the heat and the bodies piling up under the floorboards, Dennis Nilsen started worrying about the "smell problem". Then he had an idea: "I thought what would cause the smell was the innards, the soft parts. So on a weekend I'd pull up the floorboards and begin dissection." It was horrible work: Nilsen explained that he would get blind drunk and occasionally run into the garden to throw up. If it made a serial killer sick, what did the makers of **Viewpoint 93**'s **Murder in Mind** (ITV) think it would do to viewers? Make them watch it, stupid.

The Home Office was most co-operative in this endeavour. Its attempt to ban the interview with Nilsen guaranteed a ratings boom, and the warning before the programme will have pulled in any stragglers: "This contains pictures and language that many viewers may find disturbing." "We hope" is traditionally left off the start of that sentence. As it turned out, *Murder in Mind*, ostensibly about new ways to catch serial killers, *was* shocking: shockingly thought out, shockingly edited, shockingly gullible.

Courtesy *Independent on Sunday*

The opening of Allison Pearson's review in the *Independent on Sunday* (31 January 1993) usefully reveals some of the possibilities of the genre in the heavies.

Again a logo carrying a photograph of the reviewer accompanies the piece, stressing the personal flavour of the writing.

Immediately, she uses a wide range of tones and styles, the opening par. here containing more stylistic interest than the previous two combined. "Summertime and the living is queasy" plays on the opening words of the George and Ira Gershwin song "Summertime", the changing of easy to queasy creating a sense of dislocation and unease while the sense of awkwardness is maintained in the grammar and grotesque content of the next sentence: "What with the heat and the bodies piling up under the floorboards . . ." Concern over the "smell problem" appears almost banal given the enormity of the horrors (the real problem) committed.

The dead-pan way in which Nilsen is quoted mixing the normal (the weekend break) with the macabre ("I'd pull up the floorboards and begin dissection") adds to the dramatic effect of the writing. Pearson asks a question and provides the answer in the blunt tones of the vernacular ("Make them watch it, stupid"). In this way she subtly raises the issue of the ratings war as the background for the making of the programme.

The ironic voice continues with her suggestions that the Home Office's intervention along with the pre-programme warning merely pulled in the audience. She goes on to play with the word "shocking". For her, the programme was shocking, not so much in being alarming but in being so poor. Through repetition ("shockingly thought out, shockingly edited, shockingly gullible") she emphasises her point.

Film

Derek Malcolm

LOUIS MALLE directs **Damage**, the script is by David Hare, and Josephine Hart wrote the book upon which this study of British *amour fou* is based. And the problem with the film is that you are not really sure who has had the most influence on it. Someone, however, has failed to have a decisive one.

On the whole, though, this looks much more like a David Hare film than one by Louis Malle. It seems to be trying to tell us something. But in the end all it vouchsafes is that, if you let your genitals rule your life, you might as well kiss goodbye to everything else.

So much for Lloyd George and JFK, since this is about a rising politician. The politician (Jeremy Irons, looking more and more wracked as the film progresses) is a high-flying Tory junior minister with an orthodox family life (Miranda Richardson and kids) who falls obsessively for his journalist son's girlfriend (Rupert Graves is the son and Juliette Binoche his fiancée). She, despite a fear of possessiveness engendered by her brother's suicide – owing to his apparently incestuous love for her – plays both ends against the middle by deciding to marry the boy and still screw the man. This leads inevitably to tragedy and, perhaps fortuitously, the nation loses a Minister of Health who might not have had his mind totally on the job of closing wards in hospitals.

If this sounds a slightly flip way of summing up Damage, I can only say that unfortunately the film's pretensions do not quite square up to its stylish but less than resonant presence on the screen.

Malle and Hare's examination of the British class system is accurate without being illuminating, and you get the feeling that the inevitability of tragedy is being signalled too hard too early, without the saving grace of making us care about the characters.

This does not preclude some very decent performances taking hold, though the frequent Irons/Binoche sex scenes are an oddly unsatisfactory mixture of the stylised and the realist which get a bit dull. Besides, we never glimpse the emptiness of the politician's emotional life which in the book explains what happens when he is at last suffused with desire.

Malle bathes London in suitably wintry light, secures a number of subsidiary performances that do not murder probability (Ian Bannen, Gemma Clarke and Leslie Caron are particularly good) and allows his principals enough space to do what they can to persuade us to watch them. The fact that something is seriously missing is not their fault but the inevitable consequence of gaping holes in the screenplay, and possibly the direction, which never manages to show us, like certain of Malle's other films, the sheer ferocity of sexual obsession. That is rarely accomplished by cinematic grapplings, as 9½ Weeks found to its cost. It is much more a matter of getting emotion on to the screen, like Kieslowski or Pialat do, without necessarily dropping a stitch of clothing.

Derek Malcolm's *Guardian* review (4 February 1993) has a very clear structure:

Pars 1 and 2: statement of main "problem" and of what the film is "about".

Par. 3: brief outline of plot and listing of who plays whom.

Pars 4 to end: more comments – on film's pretensions, on the sex scenes, on minor roles and its general failures.

The underlying motif of the piece lies in a play on contrasts and paradoxes. All the time Malcolm seems to be saying: "On the one hand this . . . but on the other hand this . . ."

So in par. 1, on the one hand he is saying a lot of talent went into the film. But on the other hand it fails because no one stamped their authority on it. In par. 2, on the one hand it's trying to tell us something, on the other hand it doesn't amount to very much. In par. 4, the film is said to have pretensions and be "stylish" but the reality is something different. In the next par., the tragedy is represented as inevitable – but on the other hand the characters are not worth caring about. And so on. Indeed, this play on contrasts and paradox becomes too predictable after a while.

Reference is made in the intro. to the film being based on a book. We next hear about the book deep in par. 6. This is good journalism. Malcolm is indicating he has done his homework but is not bragging about it. The point he draws from the comparison is pointed and concisely put.

At the beginning of the second par. he says the film looks more like a David Hare work than one by Louis Malle. This is an esoteric point needing more explanation for it to mean anything to the general reader.

The use of the word "vouchsafes" is strange too. It's an archaic word, appearing awkward here – as do the references to Lloyd George and JFK in par. 3.

In par. 3 brackets are used to good effect to make the telling of the tale (and the major roles) as concise as possible. With the self-critical link phrase "If this sounds a slightly flip way of summing up . . ." he moves on to more general comments. The reference to "the British class system" seems tokenistic and surprising since there is no hint in the earlier plot description of the possibility of any such theme emerging while the phrase "accurate without being illuminating" is obscure. Perhaps the reference to the class system is an attempt to extract some deeper "social meaning" from the film – "balancing" the largely critical review with some positive comment.

The readers are then told they are not likely to "care about the characters" which seems to contradict the next statement that the film contains some "very decent performances" (itself a cliché).

In the final par., brackets are again used to good effect – doing the crucial journalistic job of conveying details concisely. But again some elements of confusion emerge. Earlier Malcolm has said viewers are not encouraged to "care for the characters". Now he seems to be saying they are eminently watchable. Is there not some contradiction there? The final flourish involves references to the popular *9½ Weeks* and the more esoteric Kieslowski or Pialat together with the telling point that nudity does not necessarily help convey the "sheer ferocity of sexual obsession".

Freelancing: *a survival guide*

JUST as there are many kinds of staff reporters, so there are many kinds of freelances. Some are the country's best paid and busiest writers. Many are finding life extremely difficult with the widespread cuts in journalists' jobs intensifying competition among freelances. Increasingly freelancing is becoming a euphemism for "being unemployed".

All the same, if you are determined, organised and talented, good chances are still available to break into the freelance world.

There are good and bad sides to the freelance life. To a certain extent they enjoy some "freedoms" not permitted staff writers. They can work from home, they are not forced to abide by a strict daily routine, they can avoid all the hassles of office politics.

They may even be given the opportunity to pursue a specialism which no other journalistic route has allowed. They may be fascinated by food and wine. A full-time food specialist is a rare commodity on daily and weekly newspapers. Freelancing for a number of publications in this area is more of a possibility.

But freelances can rarely free themselves from the constraints of the market. You may be contemptuous of the capitalist rat-race of the newspaper world but freelancing hardly provides a refuge from this. Freelances have to go where the money is. You can have lofty ideas about ideologically sound journalism but it usually pays badly if at all.

If your interest is in progressive journalism then secure a steady job (with a charity, a pressure group or a progressive think-tank, for instance) and build up your freelance experience on that foundation.

A freelance's working day is in many respects more demanding and stressful than that of a staffer. Not only do they have the pressures of finding work, promoting new ideas and meeting deadlines. They have, in addition, a range of other issues to worry about. They have to sort out taxation problems. They may have to chase finance departments to pay up on time. They have to negotiate rates and make sure all their equipment is maintained properly. Without the regular inflow of money enjoyed by staff journalists, freelances have, in short, to be far more financially organised.

On top of all this, the freelance has no job security. When jobs are on the line, they are invariably the first to suffer. Without the companionship that goes with a full-time job, the freelance's life can be lonely.

But with the job cuts in the industry, more and more journalists are becoming freelances. Unable to secure full-time appointments they mix a variety of roles – they may work two days on a publication, send features on a regular basis to another two and write booklets on commission. They may do some media consultancy work and be writing a commissioned book while sending off the occasional feature. Some will be supplementing freelance work with sessions of teaching at their local journalism training centre. Basically, in the post-Thatcherite world of individual enterprise, they are getting what work they can.

If you are thinking of becoming a freelance, bear in mind that you need to be resilient, imaginative and self-motivated. Are you sure you've got the temperament to go freelance? Without it you will have an awful time. With it you will survive.

Starting up

Launching into a freelance career is not easy. Many freelances are former full-time staffers who have developed a specialism, sent out linage (freelance copy paid by the line) to nationals and then, through either choice or redundancy, taken the plunge and gone solo or started a small agency.

Sometimes a non-journalist professional may build up contacts and a specialist knowledge. They may have enjoyed close links with the media and even contributed the occasional article to the press. On this basis they may decide to switch to journalism as a career.

The feature linking all these examples is a specialism which can be exploited jour-nalistically. Very few freelances are generalists.

Many aspiring freelances imagine themselves sitting at home in front of a computer, bashing out their words of wisdom on the major issues of the day for ever-grateful newspapers. Nothing could be further from the freelance reality. Local newspapers either take little such work or have former staffers submitting on a freelance basis. Freelances succeed on the strength of their contacts and their specialist knowledge which together convert into news or feature stories. And freelances need to be imag-inative, always able to come up with colourful, original ideas for features.

Basic requirements

- *A personal computer and printer*: this will save you endless retyping and aids orderly storage of your stories. All hard copy should be laid out according to the standard guidelines of the publication. Otherwise, many newspapers are now geared up to receiving copy via modems. If you become a regular freelance for a news-paper they may well supply you with a modem to transfer copy directly over a telephone line to their computer system or they may supply you with an appro-priate computer and/or disk to save retyping. Some freelances by arrangement with a newspaper's systems editor will also use their PCs to access databases.

- *Telephone and answering machine*: many freelances also have portable telephones. Some have a built-in facility for taping telephone conversations. For tax purposes it is necessary to keep separate records of business and personal calls.

- *Ideally a fax machine*: given the speed of newspaper operations, the normal mail is often too slow; many freelances are now linked up to the Internet and correspond through email.

- *A small tape recorder* for interviews.

- *A television*: many freelances follow the Ceefax and Oracle services to keep up with breaking news. And a radio.

- *An accountant to advise on tax*: if you become particularly successful you will have to pay VAT. Most freelances keep in regular touch with their local tax inspector.

- *An office with a working desk*: but there are problems relating to capital gains tax if you sell your home and have used a room exclusively as an office. Consult your accountant on this. Your office will normally contain a library of reference books, dictionaries, collections of quotations, newspapers and magazines (often small cir-culation and specialist). In addition, the *Writer's Handbook* and *Writer's and Artist's Yearbook* are essential tools, providing tips and valuable lists of newspaper contacts. Access to public and specialist libraries is essential. Established freelances will also take the opportunity to use the library facilities at newspapers to which they file copy.

- *A filing cabinet*: this should be used to store cuttings, photocopies of crucial arti-cles and chapters, and notes from interviews and written sources. Organising a tidy filing system is a special art providing enormous rewards. So much time can be lost looking for information when the filing system is chaotic. Your files will also need constant attention. Some files become redundant and can be thrown out, or new files need to be set up to take in new issues.

- *Headed notepaper and business cards.*

- *Notebooks and pens.*

- *An invoice book* for sending off demands to accounts departments.

- *Transport*: most reporters drive (and set some of the costs against their taxable income) but it is not absolutely essential. Some freelances rely on bikes, others on public transport.

- *Camera*: not essential but handing in a story with a good pic helps attract the eye of an editor.

- *The ability to discipline your work schedule*: and a sound pension plan.

All this makes it clear you need some capital before starting out on the daunting freelance road.

Finding an outlet

Get to know the market for your specialist area of interest. Study the different writing styles, the lengths of sentences and articles in the different publications. Try to establish through examining by-line patterns the amount of freelance work accepted and in which specific areas: it may be in celebrity profiles, in authoritative, fact-based comment, or in timeless features. Read carefully recent issues to make sure you do not duplicate anything already done.

It is not a good idea to ring a publication to gather this kind of information or even their general views about freelancing. You are expected to do all the basic groundwork and then approach the publication with a potential article.

With a hot news story you will obviously contact the paper by phone. But with other kinds of stories there are no rules. Some prefer contact by phone, others by letter. Always direct your approach to the most appropriate person on the editorial staff. If you have a news story for your local paper, ring the news editor. Expect to go through a range of "protective" secretaries before speaking to them in person. Best time to ring a national daily is before 12 noon; a local daily is best contacted in the afternoons.

Explain the main point of the story and the likely word length you envisage. In covering news, there is always the danger the paper will take down the details and then send out their staffer to handle it. Try to convey the story's importance and the fact that you have the story ready to send over by fax or phone. You may even be able to drop it in by hand. Don't give too much away on the phone. Even if they use your phone call as a simple "tip off" for a story they cover themselves you are still owed a payment for that.

If you are not known to the paper they are unlikely to commit themselves to carrying a story on the basis of a rushed phone call. The news editor is most likely to say: "That sounds interesting. Send in the copy but I can't promise anything."

Don't expect to have your copy returned. Even a stamped addressed envelope offers no guarantee. But always make sure you have a copy of all your submitted work. If it is rejected, you may want to direct it to another newspaper or rearrange it with some new angles for a different outlet. There may be queries over the story which can only be cleared up with reference to your original hard copy; you may need it to protect yourself against libel where the publication has subbed in a comment or error.

Feature ideas

Fast-breaking news tends to be covered by staffers so freelances usually specialise in features (for which magazines are often more suitable than newspapers). Once you have a few published you are in a position to adopt a different approach. You may ask to meet the commissioning editor you have dealt with to discuss some further ideas for features. Or you may send in a couple of short synopses of planned features.

There are always dangers here. The publication may steal your ideas and give them to someone else to follow up. And the freelance has absolutely no protection in law against this kind of theft. While written work can be copyrighted, ideas can occur to two people at the same time and can also be stolen.

There is no easy solution to this problem that constantly faces freelances. One approach is to provide only the bare minimum of background information before the idea is accepted. Personal contact with the commissioning editor helps in creating mutual trust and confidence. The best solution is to prove your abilities to the newspaper in a series of stories sent on spec or to commission so they will be concerned not to lose your work to other competitors. It's also worth emphasising you are the only person with the unique knowledge, contacts, idiosyncratic viewpoint or desire to compile the article. Clearly freelances have to develop special negotiation skills.

Once the idea is accepted

If the commissioning editor has said: "OK, I'll be pleased to look at your story but I can't promise we'll use it," they are free to reject your story without incurring any financial liability. But if they have commissioned your piece and then do not publish it they should (though not all do) pay you a "kill" fee comprising part or all of the original amount agreed.

How much should you be expected to be paid for your hard work? Well, the NUJ draws up a list of minimum freelance rates which are regularly updated and which will give you some idea of what to expect. But many freelances are finding payments are either standing still or going down.

Make sure you also negotiate expenses when your piece is commissioned since without that agreement you may end up using the payment simply to fund your research. And send an invoice soon after the appearance of your story.

Remember that if you are a self-employed freelance you own the copyright in your work: it's your "intellectual property" whether submitted speculatively or commissioned. Thus you are strongly advised to hold on to your copyright. This does not mean refusing further use of the material: you can license it, giving permission for a specific use for an agreed fee.

In fact, you should accept commissions for one use only – usually called first British serial rights. As the NUJ advises: "Despite all the techno-guff, there is no difference between licensing the use of an item to another conventional publisher and licensing it to a database operator or CD-Rom producer. Payment for a licence to reuse material in any medium, old or new, can be made either as a one-off fee, upfront, or a percentage of the client's income from the licensed item." ("Copy takers"; the *Journalist*; April/May 1996).

Further reading

The Freelance Journalist: How To Survive and Succeed; Christopher Dobson; Butterworth-Heinemann; Oxford; 1992.

Magazine Journalism Today; Anthony Davis; Heinemann Professional; Oxford; 1988.

Freelance Writing for Newspapers; Jill Dick; A. & C. Black; London; 1991.

The Complete Guide to Working from Home; Sue Read; Headline; London; 1992.

National Union of Journalists Freelance Fees Guide and *Freelance Directory*; both annually updated; Acorn House, 314–320 Gray's Inn Road, London WCIX 8DP.

Life at the End of a Wire; Chris Stephen; *UK Press Gazette*; 16 April 1991. Useful article on freelancing abroad.

Interviewing for Journalists: How to Research and Conduct Interviews You Can Sell; Joan Clayton; Piatkus; London; 1994.

The Universal Journalist; David Randall; Pluto Press; London; 1996.

Journalists and Copyright; Clive Howard; National Union of Journalists; London; 1994.

13 *New technology*
How journalism can damage your health

· ·

J OURNALISM can damage your health. Many in the industry find it extremely stressful. A recent survey of media workers by the London College of Printing School of Media (entitled *The News Breed: British Journalism in the 1990s*; Anthony Delano and Professor John Henningham; London; 1995) found that 51 per cent considered they experienced high levels of stress in their job while 24 per cent felt the levels were very high.

Another survey, commissioned by Guardian Financial Services and published in July 1996, found that more than 75 per cent of media employees had seen stress play a significant part in causing physical ill health. Migraines, headaches, ulcers, irritable bowel syndrome, digestive problems and heart disease were among the stress-related conditions suffered. Almost half those surveyed felt their bosses were doing nothing to reduce stress levels.

Occupational psychologist Dr Stephen Williams has studied hundreds of workplaces but says journalism beats all for stress (see "A job to die for?"; the *Journalist*; June/July 1996).

And according to government figures, published in 1996, journalists are out-performing other professions at booze and tobacco consumption, and dying young as a result.

Deadlines can be short, competition can be fierce, criticisms from colleagues can be sharp. Get some information wrong and not only is your mistake very public but a costly libel action may result. Pressures from all sides (news desk, editors, sources, advertisers, politicians) are faced by journalists every day. As cutbacks in the industry deepen, job security dwindles and the pressures to conform and work harder to justify the job grow.

The introduction of new technology has, for many, brought new stresses. Over recent years the newspaper industry has gone through a revolution. The old stereotype of the journalist hunched over a noisy typewriter with a cigarette drooping from his lips (the image always was masculine) no longer applies. Except in a few outposts of old technology, journalists today sit at computer screens in open-plan offices. Gone is all the bashing on typewriters. Now the sounds of the news room are of the gentle tap-tap of computer keyboards. Smoking is likely to have been banned there too.

In the late 1960s, photocomposition (by which page images are composed photo-graphically) began to replace hot metal setting in the provincial press. The compositor would retype journalists' copy on a keyboard attached to a visual display unit (VDU). Text would be automatically hyphenated and justified while strips of bromide from the photosetter would be pasted down to form the page.

But on Fleet Street, the introduction of photocomposition was delayed until the mid-1970s, the result of management incompetence and trade union conservatism. Even as late as 1985 three Fleet Street newspapers were still hot-metal-set while five others used a mix of hot and cold systems. Then came Eddie Shah's launch of the new-tech, all-colour *Today* in 1985 and the sudden shift of Rupert Murdoch's News International titles from Gray's Inn Road to Wapping. Since then, all the nationals have quit Fleet Street and taken on new technology.

Today was launched with an editorial staff of just 130, less than a quarter of the staff levels then at the *Express* or *Mail*. So began a wave of editorial staff cuts, by Murdoch at News International, by Maxwell at Mirror Group Newspapers and by others, which have decimated the industry and which are continuing today. One of the consequences of these job cuts is inevitable extra stresses for those remaining.

Printers' numbers have been reduced even more drastically. With journalists typing and subbing stories and then inputting directly to the central computer typesetter, the printers' job of retyping copy to the correct size and measure has been eliminated. Now, newspapers are increasingly moving to the full-page, on-screen make-up system which virtually eliminates the printers' role.

The silent sufferers

The journalist's VDU screen is an extremely flexible tool which has transformed the job. For instance, it can be split so that the reporter accesses on one side agency copy, the results of a database search or a previous edition story, while dealing with their own copy on the other side.

New technology has also brought many new hazards. Particularly notorious is repetitive strain injury (RSI). This swept the industry from the mid-1980s so that a decade later the NUJ was claiming it knew of more than 1,000 sufferers. Nationally, with 7m keyboard users, it became the biggest cause of time lost through illness in office work. A 1997 survey at the giant IPC Magazines group in London found that a third of journalists had some symptoms of RSI.

In the States, computer manufacturers were facing multi-billion dollar compensation bills as lawyers representing thousands of RSI sufferers claimed they had known of the risks for years – but failed to warn users adequately.

Research in the USA and UK has found that the use of the mouse (and in particular the dragging of the mouse with the button depressed) can prove particularly dangerous (see "Of mice and balls"; the *Journalist*; August/September 1995).

Among those to have been seriously affected were journalists at the *Financial Times* and the *Guardian* in the UK and at the *Los Angeles Times* and *Newsday* in the USA. Hardly a newsroom in Britain was unaffected. At one time in the mid-1990s, the NUJ was preparing around 100 compensation cases against employers but most of these looked likely to be settled out of court, thus saving the journalists the ordeal of the trial.

By the late 1990s most of the larger newspaper companies had come to terms with RSI and were dealing with affected journalists compassionately. At the *Guardian*, for instance, a technology committee was set up, combining management and the NUJ. The emphasis was on supporting people in continuing to work, not getting rid of them.

As Tim Gopsill, NUJ health and safety officer, commented: "The bigger the company the better. After all, they've got the money to spend. The *Financial Times*, for instance, has spent a fortune getting their newsroom up to acceptable ergonomic standards."

He said that, apart from "some judges and bent doctors", most people now acknowledged RSI as a serious injury. But in smaller newsrooms journalists could still be "badly treated" and throughout the industry there remained many silent sufferers afraid that if they revealed their symptoms they could be unemployable or sacked.

What is RSI?

Research into RSI is already considerable but explaining its causes (why it strikes one person and not another) remains difficult. The Health and Safety Executive prefers to call it an upper limb disorder since it argues that repetition is not the only cause. Others have dubbed it the Occupational Over-use Syndrome.

RSI and the symptoms associated with it have been around for more than 150 years. Piano players, factory workers, farmers, anyone involved in repetitive activities with their limbs, is prone to suffer. But it is only recently, since journalists have been seriously affected, that concerns about it have been widely expressed in the media.

Symptoms can develop slowly over a period of time or appear suddenly as a devastating shock. One journalist recorded: "I simply woke up one morning unable to move my neck or use my hands properly. I dropped newspapers, couldn't grasp a cup and, panic-stricken, didn't know what could be wrong." While using a computer is often the main problem, first symptoms might appear while turning a screwdriver, mowing the lawn, writing, washing your hair, driving, carrying shopping, turning taps, knitting or playing the piano.

How to avoid RSI

- If you are a staffer, try to insist that your employer follows European Community regulations which came into force on 1 January 1993. These insist that chairs must have height adjustable seats and backs that are height and tilt adjustable. Employers are obliged to provide stands to raise screens and footrests when these are required.

- Concentrate on getting your posture right at the keyboard. Your forearms should be parallel to the floor when you type and both feet should be firmly on the floor. If you have short legs, you may need a footstool, a specially adjustable chair or both. In front of the keyboard there should be sufficient space to place wrists during rest periods or while reading the screen. You should be able to sit straight, using the back-rest of the chair, with relaxed shoulders and chin up, looking down at the screen at an angle of 15 degrees. There should be no pressure on the thighs from the chair since this can limit circulation and put pressure on the sciatic nerve.

- You need to take regular breaks from the screen. The NUJ recommends breaks of 15 minutes in every 75 minutes of continuous VDU work or formal breaks of 15 minutes after each hour. A leaflet produced by News International, following a survey of workers at the Wapping plant, suggested 30-second breaks from screen every five minutes were better than longer breaks every hour (*Posture and VDUs for Journalists*; Occupational health and safety department; News International, 1 Virginia Street, London E1 9XS). It added that where possible journalists should take longer breaks and their lunches away from their desks. Even so, lunch-at-the-desk is an increasing trend among hard-pressed, under-staffed news rooms across the country.

- Journalism lecturer Robert Jones has suggested a number of two-minute exercises drawn from a variety of sources to help keep any RSI symptoms at bay (*The Journalist's Locoscript 2: Word Processing on the Amstrad PCW*; City University, London; second edition; 1992).

If symptoms emerge

- If you suffer pain during or after working at the keyboard but not at other times when using your hands, take regular breaks, reduce your typing speed and adjust the height of your chair so that you can type more efficiently. And talk to your union representative if there is one where you work. They should be able to advise on what to do.

- If the pains persist during other uses of the hands, seek medical advice immediately. Fear, anxiety and guilt don't help. Robert Jones stresses the importance of being treated by an experienced doctor. He says: "Physiotherapy can help but it can also make the condition worse, unless there has been a diagnosis first and unless the physio is really experienced in dealing with RSI."

- For some people RSI can have a devastating effect on their careers. The inflammation and pains remain and they have to quit regular employment. Subs are generally worse affected than reporters and where employers are sensitive, sufferers are moved to work a reporter's post requiring much less screen work.

But not all RSI sufferers remain permanent sufferers. Some respond to treatment, others find a period of rest from the screen and careful attention to all possible precautions thereafter clears the pains. Often a change of job, and a shift away from a stressful situation, can remove the symptoms.

Concerns remain

According to the 1991 European directive which came into force on 1 January 1993, all employers are obliged to assess any foreseeable risks to employees using workstations and premises and should inform workers of the results of these assessments. They have to provide health and safety training, plan work to allow for regular breaks from screens and pay for employees' eye tests and special glasses if required.

Tim Gopsill, NUJ health and safety officer, says enforcement of the regulation depends entirely on employee pressure. But job cuts make it increasingly difficult for workers to pressure managements on new technology. "They are frightened of losing their jobs so there is an unfortunate tendency for people to keep on working when they shouldn't. Employers are starting to ask people when they apply for jobs whether they have RSI." Research from the Health and Safety Executive, published in February 1997 revealed that only one in five VDU users – about 1m workers – had exercised their right to a free eye-test.

Gopsill stresses: "The main cause of RSI is not the furniture but the amount of work people have to do and the pressure they are under to do it."

Other ailments

- In addition to RSI, people have suffered eye complaints from sitting at VDU screens. Headaches, blurred vision, fuzzy images, stress and irritability can result. The NUJ recommends that keyboard, desk, walls and other major surrounding areas should be non-reflective and avoid excessively bright or dark colour schemes. No VDU or operator should face a window.

- Dust is attracted to a switched-on screen and this, together with positive ions and static, can lead to blocked pores, dry eyes and irritated skin. Author Peggy Bentham suggests every operator should have a dust cover to put over the screen when not in use, an antistatic floor mat and an antistatic desk mat. In addition, she advises people to wear natural fibres at the VDU to reduce static.

- Because of the radiation risks in sitting in front of VDUs, the NUJ recommends pregnant women should have the right to switch to non-VDU work without loss of pay, status and career prospects.

- The London Hazards Centre also points out that photocopiers and laser printers, which produce ozone, can pose health risks if they are poorly positioned or maintained, or used for long runs. Areas in which they are sited should be well ventilated and no one should have to work within 3 metres of the machine.

- Health concerns have also been raised over the use of mobile phones. Research by US experts Dr Henry Lai and Dr Narenda Singh warns that exposure can damage the body's genetic building-block DNA, leading to Alzheimer's and cancer. If you have to use a mobile phone, keep calls short; if you have to make a lengthy call, switch the phone from ear to ear.

- There is an Internet site for discussion on RSI. Subscribe, free, to Listserv@tictac.demon.co.uk

Further reading

VDUs, Health and Jobs; Labour Research Department; 78 Blackfriars Road, London SE1 8HF.

The VDU Hazards Factpack; City Centre; 32–35 Featherstone Street, London.

TUC Guidelines on VDUs; TUC publications department; Congress House, Great Russell Street, London WC1.

Muscle Over-use Syndrome (RSI); Dr R.M. Pearson; MRCP; The Musicians' and Keyboard Clinic, 7 Park Crescent, London WIN 3HE.

VDU Terminal Sickness: Computer Health Risks and How to Protect Yourself; Peggy Bentham; Green Print; 1991.

14 *On and off the job – or both?* Training and careers

⋯⋯⋯⋯⋯⋯⋯⋯⋯⋯⋯⋯⋯⋯⋯⋯⋯⋯⋯⋯⋯⋯⋯⋯⋯⋯⋯⋯⋯⋯⋯⋯⋯⋯⋯⋯⋯⋯

THE best way to learn about journalism is "on the job". You may have great ideas about the nature of reporting, you may know all about ideology and the history of the press in 18th century Britain. But if you can't bash out a quick story on a local murder you're useless.

That was the dominant view in the industry at the beginning of the century. It remains largely the same today. There have been slight changes. Training courses have developed with the support of newspaper managements and trade unions. They have even spread into the learned corridors of universities. But mutual suspicion still persists between the press and academia.

On the one hand there is a prevalent belief that journalists are born, not made. You've either got the nose for the news, or, sadly, you haven't. As Sir David English, former editor of the *Daily Mail*, says: "Journalism is a skill that can only be acquired on the job and at the end of the day it depends on whether someone has a burning individual talent."

On the other hand there is the belief that journalism is a profession with its own ethical and work-related standards which can be both taught and assessed. Thus, certain educational qualifications are laid down for entrants while the development of training courses becomes an essential part of the formation of the journalist's professional identity.

Caught between these two views are students and trainers. A further twist emerges when attempts are made by trainers to promote reflective, critical approaches to dominant professional attitudes. Scepticism about the value of theoretical studies for aspiring reporters remains widespread.

The contrasting US/UK traditions of training

THE training of journalists in Britain is a relatively new phenomenon. In the United States, university training started at the beginning of the century with the first journalism school founded in 1908 at the University of Missouri. Ten years later there were 86 US schools offering at least some journalism coursework while by 1940 this figure had jumped to 542 (*Training and Hiring of Journalists*; Lee B. Becker, Susan L. Cavdill and Jeffrey W. Fruit; Ablex Publishing Corporation; Norwood, NJ; 1987).

Currently around 325 colleges and universities offer programmes in which the student can major in journalism.

In Britain, in contrast, it was not until the mid-1960s that any major programme of journalism training was launched. A diploma course had run at King's College, University of London, between 1922 and 1939 but this was not restarted after the war.

After the 1949 Royal Commission on the Press drew attention to the need for better training, the National Advisory Council for the Training and Education of Junior Journalists was set up in 1952 (*Journalism Training in Europe*; Hugh Stephenson and Pierre Mory; European Community; Brussels; 1990). Three years later this body changed its title to the National Council for the Training of Journalists (NCTJ) and brought together representatives from the NUJ and the Institute of Journalists (the two trade unions), the Newspaper Society (owners of provincial newspapers in England and Wales and suburban London weeklies) and the Guild of British Newspaper Editors.

Later they were joined by the Newspaper Publishers Association (linking owners of national newspapers) and by the two bodies formed by the owners and managers of newspapers in Scotland.

Since the 1960s a range of colleges and universities have developed courses in journalism. Initially, the media were considered largely within their sociological or broader theoretical contexts in courses usually titled Mass Communications. But over recent decades the focus has shifted, largely in response to student demands, to the development of practical skills. Many mass communication courses have integrated a practical element while both postgraduate and (in the early 1990s) undergraduate journalism degrees have emerged.

Yet despite all this, many newspaper journalists still learn the ropes on local papers.

Educational qualifications

In 1965 the trade unions and Newspaper Society agreed the minimum qualification for entry to the profession was three GCEs, one being in English. Since 1970 the required minimum has been five passes at O level (or GCSE) at grades A, B or C with English language still being among them.

Some other examinations have been approved by the NCTJ as being educationally equivalent and in exceptional cases (when the editor has their eye on an individual) the qualifications are waived.

For those who seek to enter via a college course, the requirements are two A levels and two GCSE or O levels, including English at either GCSE O or A level.

The trend over recent decades has been towards the formation of an increasingly graduate profession. In 1965 only 6 per cent entering local newspapers had a university degree while a further 33 per cent had one or more A levels. Some 25 years later, 53 per cent of entrants to provincial papers boasted degrees while most of the others had two or more passes at A level.

Even so, academic qualifications in themselves have never been sufficient to guarantee a chance to become a trainee journalist. Colleges and newspapers are inundated all the time with applications. In addition to showing academic abilities, the successful applicant must be able to demonstrate a special commitment to working in the field. Many school pupils go to newspapers on work attachment schemes, others manage to persuade editors to let them observe the newspaper operations during their holidays. Some pupils help with hospital radios; others send in letters and articles to their local newspapers. All this counts well for any applicant whether to a newspaper or college.

Pre-entry training: post-A level

One-year pre-entry courses are provided at centres dotted about the country such as Darlington College; Gwent Tertiary College; Harlow College; Highbury College; the Centre for Journalism, University of Central Lancashire, Preston; Stradbroke College, Sheffield; Cornwall College, Centre for Arts Media and Social Sciences, Redruth.

You may win sponsorship from a local paper. Or you may be able to secure a grant from your local authority to cover the fees and possibly living expenses. The grants are discretionary, dependent on the authority's willingness to support you. They have no legal obligation to fund you. With the local authority spending cuts, discretionary grants have been severely cut. All the same, you should approach your authority to establish their position when you make your application.

As an alternative route, Brighton College of Technology offers a 36-week part-time course operating only three days each week which enables unemployed students to continue claiming state benefit.

Pre-entry training: the post-graduate diploma route

In 1970, the first university journalism course was launched at the University College, Cardiff. Largely the inspiration of Tom Hopkinson, former editor of *Picture Post*, and modelled on a programme at Columbia University, New York, it initially attracted 15 to 20 postgraduate students. A similar one-year postgraduate diploma course was begun at City University, London, in 1976, initially with 13 students.

By the late 1980s these had both grown enormously, spanning a range of diploma and MA courses: newspaper, periodicals, broadcast, European (linking Cardiff with colleges in Utrecht, the Netherlands, and Aarhus, Denmark) and international. And in the late 1990s, City University launched an electronic publishing MA.

Also during the 1990s, one-year postgraduate diplomas were started at centres such as City of Liverpool Community College; De Montfort University, Leicester; Strathclyde University; Trinity and All Saints College, Leeds; and the University of Central Lancashire, Preston. Trent University, Nottingham, launched a diploma in investigative journalism.

But suspicions persisted between the press and the universities. As Professor Hugh Stephenson, of City University, comments: "The academic community in this country has always been distrustful of courses in journalism and media employers have been distrustful of people with education."

Brian Hitchen, former *Daily Star* editor, put an industry view bluntly:

"I've only met one graduate from journalism who was any good. Most of them are appalling. There's only one way to learn journalism and that's by starting at the bottom. There is a sieve in our profession that is the cruellest and the finest and only the best get to the top."

The degree route

Then in the early 1990s, just as the recession-hit industry was showing evidence of serious decline, for the first time the US-style undergraduate route to journalism emerged with the launch of degrees at five centres: Bournemouth University; University College, Cardiff; the University of Central Lancashire, Centre for Journalism; and the London College of Printing; while City University, London, offered a Journalism with a Social Science degree course (with an optional third year "out", studying abroad or on work attachments).

These were to be later joined by Teesside University, the University of Sheffield and Liverpool John Moores University, Surrey Institute of Art and Design and Harlow College/Middlesex University (offering journalism with another optional subject).

For some of the postgraduate courses local authority discretionary grants are available. Some national newspapers offer awards (watch the newspapers themselves for details). There are also special awards for applicants from ethnic minorities.

The international MA or diploma course at City University (largely aimed at foreign, more mature students) is open to a few home students hoping to work abroad.

On-the-job training

Roughly 40 per cent of entrants to newspaper journalism start by training on a local. Take a look at the media directories (such as *Benn's* and *Willing's Press Guide*) which your local library should hold and which list all newspapers and periodicals in the country. It is advisable before writing to ring any chosen newspaper just to make sure it is worth your while and to get the editor's name correct on the letter. Editors tend to come and go.

Once accepted, a direct entrant for their first six months takes a course of home study in addition to receiving on-the-job training and experience. Most will then attend a 12-week block release course though some will attend day-release courses.

Each trainee will have to pass seven qualifying examinations: newspaper journalism, handling handouts, law (two parts), local and central government (two parts) and short-hand to 100 words per minute. For direct entrants the qualifying period is two years, for pre-entry and postgraduate diploma students it is 18 months. Once through all these hoops, the journalist can then take the National Council for the Training of Journalists' National Certificate Examination to be fully qualified.

A number of regional and national newspaper groups have set up their own training schemes including: Emap, Midland News Association, Trinity and United Provincial Newspapers, Liverpool Daily Post and Echo Ltd, and News International (*The Times* and *Sunday Times*).

National Vocational Qualifications

In the early 1990s, the National Vocational Qualifications (and Scottish Vocational Qualifications) in newspapers emerged. Organised by the Newspaper Society, the NVQs were almost entirely focused on work-based assessments.

Following the setting-up of the National Council for Vocational Qualifications in 1986, the Newspaper Society's steering group drew up a set of standards under three headings – writing, production journalism and press photography (a graphics jour-nalism option followed).

A reporter covering a diary event, for instance, is required to display accurate fact-gathering skills, an appreciation of any legal and ethical issues arising and the ability to file copy to a deadline.

All assessment is carried out by work-based assessors, appointed either internally (e.g. news editors) or externally. No specific timetable is attached to the award of an NVQ but a trainee could be set a period for completion in their contract of employment. The Newspaper Qualifications Council supervises the awards (in Scotland the Scottish Vocational Education Council) together with the Royal Society for the Encouragement of Arts, Manufactures and Commerce (RSA) Examinations Board.

Other routes

In addition to these entry routes there are many others. For instance, there are two-year HNDs; BTECs; and many evening class centres now run courses in freelancing, feature writing or press photography. There are privately run journalism training centres (most of them claiming extraordinary success for their graduates in gaining jobs in the industry) and you can even learn journalism via a correspondence course or the Internet. Many universities and colleges (in response to massive student demand) provide media studies courses. In fact, during the 1990s, media-related courses became the most fashionable to study and inevitably attracted the kind of suspicions from Fleet Street once reserved for sociology and peace studies ("A degree in futility"; Lucy Hodges; *Evening Standard*; London; 14 May 1997).

Many editors argue that they require applicants with broad interests and knowledge rather than bookish experts in the narrow academic discipline of communications studies. As Sarah Niblock (*Inside Journalism*; Blueprint; London; 1996) comments: "Some editors may feel journalists who are well read in media criticism may lead them to question editorial policy, so do not think having such a qualification will automatically give you a head start."

Yet, increasingly, theoretical media courses are incorporating practical, vocational elements (with students also undertaking placements in the industry). And hopefully journalists' traditional reluctance to encourage the reflective approach will dwindle as more graduates enter the industry.

Moreover, research by the Standing Conference in Cultural, Communication and Media Studies in Higher Education found that media studies graduates had a slightly better chance of finding work than other graduates: 57 per cent of them finding work after six months compared with the average of 56. But these findings were challenged in research conducted by Professor Alan Smithers and his colleague Pamela Robinson, of Brunel University, west London. And so the Great Debate continued.

Further reading and contact addresses

Careers in Journalism: National Union of Journalists; Acorn House; 314–20 Gray's Inn Road, London WC1X 8DP. Tel: 0171-278 7916; fax: 0171-837 8143.
(The NUJ also provides a list of useful books on journalism, drawn up by Humphrey Evans.)

Making the Decision; Newspaper Society; 4 Great Russell Street, London WC1B 3DA. Tel: 0171-636 7014; fax: 0171-631 5119

A World of Challenge; National Council for the Training of Journalists, Latton Bush Centre, Southern Way, Harlow, Essex CM18 7BL. Tel: 01279-430009; fax: 01279-438008; Net: http://www.itecharlow.co.uk/nctj/[;] email: NCTJ@itecharlow.co.uk

The Media Guide (annually updated); edited by Steve Peak and Paul Fisher; Fourth Estate; London; 1997 etc.

The foot in the door: *getting your first job*

JOURNALISM has always been a notoriously difficult world to enter. With staff cutbacks in virtually all the media since the late 1980s, the job hunt has become still more difficult. Not only are colleges producing more trained young aspirants but the jobs market is becoming jammed full with experienced journalists made redundant and on the hunt for employment.

Contacts are crucial. Students on journalism courses at colleges should exploit every opportunity to build up useful contacts in the industry. A reporter comes from a local paper to give a talk. Ask her intelligent questions at the seminar, if possible chat informally afterwards, later ring her for an interview over a media-related story or project you are working on.

If you are hoping to move into a specialist area, for instance, the ethnic, religious, trade union or political press, there is all the more reason for you to concentrate on building up contacts. These are relatively small worlds on the look-out for people with specialist knowledge and commitment.

While on the courses try to get freelance work published. The number of students leaving colleges with formal journalistic qualifications is growing all the time; being able to produce some published work will help you to stand out slightly from the rest.

The application

Because newspapers are inundated with job applications there is little need to advertise many of the jobs that fall vacant. But a number are still advertised in the *Press Gazette* and the *Guardian* Media Section every Monday and all aspiring journalists are advised to scour those columns for any possible openings.

The letter of application should be brief and to the point. More important is the CV (curriculum vitae) which, in a formalised way, should summarise your achievements to date. It should list your name, address, date of birth, education (school, college, university, evening classes etc.) with dates and qualifications, professional qualifications, any job/s you have held, desktop publishing skills, publications, special interests, references (with addresses and telephone numbers) (see *Preparing Your Own CV*; Rebecca Corfield; Kogan Page; London; third edition; 1992).

Some newspapers may be on the look-out for a CV with a particularly imaginative format and content.

Even if you are applying while still at school you can still list your periods of work attachment on a newspaper, say, or your contributions to your school magazine or local hospital radio.

It is also advisable to have your CV printed out in an attractive font. It is a very important document and you are more likely to impress if it looks good.

The interview

It is vital to prepare for any job or college interview. Find out about the paper, get some copies and look at them critically. The interviewer will also expect you to be able to speak confidently about the national press. When you are asked about your favourite newspapers it is disastrous to say: "I like the *Mail* and the *Observer* because my mum and dad get them every week." You must show more initiative, being able to comment on a range of national papers.

It also impresses if you can use some journalistic jargon. If words like "follow-up", "page lead", "splash" and "stringer" flow off your lips (at the appropriate moments, of course) this shows your newspaper ambition is more than a Hollywood-induced fantasy and that you are beginning to absorb the jargon of newspapers.

You may be asked if you have any favourite journalists. It is not good enough simply to say either John Pilger or Kate Adie. These names are often mentioned and interviewers will be expecting something more original. Certainly, be prepared to talk about television reporting. All the mainstream media feed off each other and follow broadly similar news values while a newspaper specialist is likely to keep their eye on the television and ear to the radio. Ignorance of television reporting would demonstrate a hyper-specialism at too young an age.

Make sure you arrive on time for the interview and dress tidily. Take any cuttings of your work in a folder. If you have written stories from handouts while on an attachment and they do not carry your by-line make sure you have asked the editor or news editor to sign a note indicating your authorship. Without that there is no proof you were the reporter. And many are the games played at interviews . . .

Always go prepared to ask some questions. An interviewer will often be aware that in the short time of the formal discussion some major issues have been passed over. If no question about any of them is forthcoming then the interview will fall flat. The technology used by the company may not have been mentioned. A question about that would show good initiative. Good luck.

Appendices

....

Appendix 1   The NUJ Code of Conduct

1   A journalist has a duty to maintain the highest professional and ethical standards.
2   A journalist shall at all times defend the principle of the freedom of the press and other media in relation to the collection of information and the expression of comment and criticism. He/she shall strive to eliminate distortion, news suppression and censorship.
3   A journalist shall strive to ensure that the information he/she disseminates is fair and accurate, avoid the expression of comment and conjecture as established fact and falsification by distortion, selection or misrepresentation.
4   A journalist shall rectify promptly any harmful inaccuracies, ensure that correction and apologies receive due prominence and afford the right of reply to persons criticised when the issue is of sufficient importance.
5   A journalist shall obtain information, photographs and illustrations only by straightforward means. The use of other means can be justified only by overriding considerations of the public interest. The journalist is entitled to exercise a personal conscientious objection to the use of such means.
6   Subject to justification by overriding considerations of the public interest, a journalist shall do nothing which entails intrusion into private grief and distress.
7   A journalist shall protect confidential sources of information.
8   A journalist shall not accept bribes nor shall he/she allow other inducements to influence the performance of his/her professional duties.
9   A journalist shall not lend himself/herself to the distortion or suppression of the truth because of advertising or other considerations.
10   A journalist shall only mention a person's race, colour, creed, illegitimacy, marital status (or lack of it), gender or sexual orientation if this information is strictly relevant. A journalist shall neither originate nor process material which encourages discrimination on any of the above-mentioned grounds.
11   A journalist shall not take private advantage of information gained in the course of his/her duties before the information is public knowledge.
12   A journalist shall not by way of statement, voice or appearance endorse by advertisement any commercial product or service save for the promotion of his/her own work or of the medium by which he/she is employed.

Appendix 2   The PCC Code of Practice

The PCC is charged with enforcing the Code of Practice, ratified by itself, which was framed by the newspaper and periodical industry. All members of the press have a duty to maintain the highest professional and ethical standards. In doing so, they should have regard to the provisions of this Code of Practice and to safeguarding the public's right to know. Editors are responsible for the actions of journalists employed by their publications. They should also satisfy themselves as far as possible that material accepted from non-staff members was obtained in accordance with this code. While it is recognised that this involves a substantial element of self-restraint by editors and journalists, the code is designed to be acceptable in the context of the system of self-regulation. The code applies in the spirit as well as in the letter. It is the responsibility of editors to co-operate as swiftly as possible in PCC enquiries. Any publication which is criticised by the PCC under one of the following clauses is duty bound to print the adjudication which follows in full and with due prominence.

1 Accuracy

(i) Newspapers and periodicals should take care not to publish inaccurate, misleading or distorted material
(ii) Whenever it is recognised that a significant inaccuracy, misleading statement or distorted report has been published, it should be corrected promptly and with due prominence.
(iii) An apology should be published whenever appropriate.
(iv) A newspaper or periodical should always report fairly and accurately the outcome of an action for defamation to which it has been a party.

2 Opportunity to reply

A fair opportunity for reply to inaccuracies should be given to individuals or organisations when reasonably called for.

3 Comment, conjecture and fact

Newspapers, while free to be partisan, should distinguish clearly between comment, conjecture and fact.

4 Privacy

(i) Intrusions and enquiries into an individual's private life without his or her consent, including the use of long-lens photography to take pictures of people on private property without their consent, are only acceptable when it can be shown that these are, or are reasonably believed to be, in the public interest.
(ii) Publication of material obtained under (i) above is only justified when the facts show the public interest is served.

Note: private property is defined as (i) any private residence, together with its garden and outbuildings but excluding any adjacent fields or parkland and the surrounding parts of the property within the unaided view of passers-by, (ii) hotel bedrooms (but not other areas in a hotel) and (iii) those parts of a hospital or nursing home where patients are treated or accommodated.

5 Listening devices

Unless justified by the public interest, journalists should not obtain or publish material obtained by using clandestine listening devices or by intercepting private telephone conversations.

6 Hospitals

(i) Journalists or photographers making enquiries at hospitals or similar institutions should identify themselves to a responsible executive and obtain permission before entering non-public areas.
(ii) The restrictions on intruding into privacy are particularly relevant to enquiries about individuals in hospitals or similar institutions.

7 Misrepresentation

(i) Journalists should not generally obtain or seek to obtain information or pictures through misrepresentation or subterfuge.
(ii) Unless in the public interest, documents or photographs should be removed only with the express consent of the owner.
(iii) Subterfuge can be justified only in the public interest and only when material cannot be obtained by any other means.

8 Harassment

(i) Journalists should neither obtain nor seek to obtain information or pictures through intimidation or harassment.
(ii) Unless their enquiries are in the public interest, journalists should not photograph individuals on private property (as defined in the note to Clause 4) without their consent; should not persist in telephoning or questioning individuals after having been asked to desist; should not remain on the property after having been asked to leave and should not follow them.
(iii) It is the responsibility of editors to ensure that these requirements are carried out.

9 Payment for articles

(i) Payments or offers of payment for stories or information should not be made directly or through agents to witnesses or potential witnesses in current criminal proceedings except where the material concerned ought to be published in the public interest and there is an overriding need to make or promise to make a payment for this to be done. Journalists must take every possible step to ensure that no financial dealings have influence on the evidence that those witnesses may give. (An editor authorising such a payment must be prepared to demonstrate that there is a legitimate public interest at stake involving matters that the public has a right to know. The payment or, where accepted, the offer of payment to any witness who is actually cited to give evidence should be disclosed to the prosecution and defence and the witness should be advised of this.)
(ii) Payment or offers of payment for stories, pictures or information, should not be made directly or through agents to convicted or confessed criminals or their associates – who may include family, friends and colleagues – except where the material concerned ought to be published in the public interest and payment is necessary for this to be done.

10 Intrusion into grief or shock

In cases involving personal grief or shock, enquiries should be carried out and approaches made with sympathy and discretion.

11 Innocent relatives and friends

Unless it is contrary to the public's right to know, the press should avoid identifying relatives or friends of persons convicted or accused of crime.

12 Interviewing or photographing children

(i) Journalists should not normally interview or photograph children under the age of 16 on subjects involving the welfare of the child or of any other child, in the absence of or without the consent of a parent or other adult who is responsible for the children.
(ii) Children should not be approached or photographed while at school without the permission of the school authorities.

13 Children in sex cases

(1) The press should not, even where the law does not prohibit it, identify children under the age of 16 who are involved in cases concerning sexual offences, whether as victims or as witnesses or defendants.
(2) In any press report of a case involving sexual offence against a child:
(i) The adult should be identified.
(ii) The word "incest" should be avoided where a child victim might be identified.
(iii) The offence should be described as "serious offences against young children" or similar appropriate wording.
(iv) The child should not be identified.
(v) Care should be taken that nothing in the report implies the relationship between the accused and the child.

14 Victims of sexual assault

The press should not identify victims of sexual assault or publish material likely to contribute to such identification unless there is adequate justification and, by law, they are free to do so.

15 Discrimination

(i) The press should avoid prejudicial or pejorative reference to a person's race, colour, religion, sex or sexual orientation or to any physical or mental illness or disability.
(ii) It should avoid publishing details of a person's race, colour, religion, sex or sexual orientation unless these are directly relevant to the story.

16 Financial journalism

(i) Even where the law does not prohibit it, journalists should not use for their own profit financial information they receive in advance of its general publication, nor should they pass such information to others.

(ii) They should not write about shares or securities in whose performance they know that they or their close families have a significant financial interest without disclosing the interest to the editor or financial editor.

(iii) They should not buy or sell, either directly or through nominees or agents, shares or securities about which they have written recently or about which they intend to write in the near future.

17 Confidential sources

Journalists have a moral obligation to protect confidential sources of information.

18 The public interest

Clauses 4, 5, 7, 8, and 9 create exceptions which may be covered by invoking the public interest. For the purpose of this code that is most easily defined as:

(i) Detecting or exposing crime or serious misdemeanour.
(ii) Protecting public health and safety.
(iii) Preventing the public from being misled by some statement or action of an individual or organisation.

In any cases raising issues beyond these three definitions the PCC will require a full explanation by the editor of the publication involved, seeking to demonstrate how the public interest was served.

- Comments or suggestions regarding the content of the code may be sent to the Secretary, Code of Practice Committee, Merchants House Buildings, 30 George Square, Glasgow G2 1EG.
- The PCC has published the code and its *How to Complain* leaflet in Urdu, Bengali and Welsh.

PCC: 1 Salisbury Square, London EC4 8AE. Tel: 0171-353 1248 (text phone for the hard of hearing: 0171-583 2264); fax: 0171-353 8355; Web site: www.pcc.org.uk

In March 1997, the commission members were: Lord Wakeham (chairman); Arzina Bhanji, director, Royal Hospitals NHS Trust; Jenny Brown, literature director of the Scottish Arts Council; Lady Browne Wilkinson, solicitor, Allen & Overy; Iris Burton, editor in chief of *Woman's Realm* and *Woman's Weekly*, *CHAT* and *Eva*; Jim Cassidy, editor, *Sunday Mail*; Tom Clarke, editor, the *Sporting Life*; Graham Collyer, editor, *Surrey Advertiser*; Sir Brian Cubbon, Permanent Secretary, Home Office 1979–88; Baroness Dean of Thornton-le-Fylde, chair, Independent Committee for the Supervision of Standards of Telephone Information Services; Sir David English, chairman and editor in chief, Associated Newspapers; Professor Robert Pinker (privacy commissioner), Professor of Social Administration, London School of Economics; Baroness Smith of Gilmorehill, chair, Edinburgh Festival Fringe; Lord Tordoff, principal deputy chairman of committees, House of Lords; John Witherow, editor, the *Sunday Times*.

Glossary

ABC – Audit Bureau of Circulation: organisation providing official figures for newspaper circulation

access provider – a company that sells Internet connections (also known as an Internet Access Provider or Internet Service Provider)

ad – abbreviation for advertisement

add – additional copy as when Press Association (PA – see below) follows lead of major story with new paragraphs

advertorial – where distinction between editorial and advertising becomes blurred

agencies – main news agencies (supplying both stories and pictures) are PA, Reuters, Agence France Presse, Itar-Tass, Associated Press. Also a large number of smaller agencies serving specialist and general fields. Copy (known as wire copy) arrives in newspaper offices from them on computer screens or occasionally on teleprinters

agony aunt – women who offer advice to people who write in to newspapers with personal/emotional problems. One of the most famous was *Daily Mirror*'s Marje Proops. Agony uncle: male equivalent. Not many of these around but likely to grow in number

alignment – ranging of copy text (and headlines) over column. Copy ranged/aligned left begins on extreme left of column; all lines of copy ranged right are flush to the extreme right of the column and ragged on the left

alternative press – loose term incorporating wide variety of non-mainstream newspapers. Can include left press (*Tribune*, *Socialist Worker* etc.), religious press (*Catholic Herald*, *Church Times*, *Q News*), ethnic press (*Asian Times*, *The Voice*), municipal press, trade union publications

ambush interview – when an interviewee is surprised by suddenly different line of questioning or by the sudden appearance of journalist (or group of journalists). Has theatrical flavour when done on television. Generally only done when reporters are convinced they are dealing with crook or hypocrite whose "crimes" it is important to expose

angle – main point stressed in story usually in intro. US: peg

AP – Associated Press news agency

apology – a newspaper may admit to error and publish correction in apology. Complainant can still claim libel in court and publication of apology provides no defence for newspaper. But if newspaper loses case, fact that it took prompt and adequate steps to correct error and to express regret provides plea in mitigation of damages tending to reduce the size of damages awarded

artwork – all illustrations, maps, charts, cartoons that accompany copy

asterisk – * occasionally used in text to link footnote or to indicate letters of words considered obscene

attachment/internship (US) – time spent by student journalists training (or occasionally just observing) at media organisation

attribution – linking information or quote to original source

backbench – group of top level journalists who meet to decide the overall shape and emphases in that day's newspaper. Positioning of important pictures, choice of page leads, subject and angle of editorial comments will be among their decisions

background – section of news or feature story carrying information which serves to contextualise main elements. Varies in length and positioning though most news stories will contain only small amount of background detail while length of features often allows them to carry longer background sections. Also, in computer jargon, indicates hyphenation and justification system is operating while copy is being input

backgrounder – feature exploring the background to main story in news

back issue – previous issue of paper

back-up – fallback supply of equipment, data or copy

banner – front page headline extending across full page

baron – newspaper proprietor (e.g. Murdoch, Black, Maxwell, Rothermere). Other words – mogul, magnate, boss

beat – when story is gained before rival. US: refers to specialist area covered by reporter, e.g. education, politics, transport

bill/billboard – poster giving headline of main story of day

black – in days of typewriters this was carbon, back-up copy of top, hard copy typed by reporter. Many contemporary computer systems still call copies of top story blax

blob par/s – follows small black marking (usually a square, outline of a square, a circle or sometimes in the tabloids a star) at start of paragraph. Bullet in computer jargon

body – copy following intro.

boil down – shorten copy

bold face – heavy-face type (in contrast to lighter type of most stories' body text) used for emphasising in copy, headlines, subheadings

box – copy with rules around all four sides

break – moment when news story emerges. But bad break refers to ugly-looking hyphenation at end of line of text

breaker – any device (such as crosshead or panel) which breaks up text on page

brief – (1) short item of news often of just one par. but occasionally with up to four or five pars. Other names: snip/nib/bright/filler; (2) short advice given to journalist before they cover a story

broadsheet – large-size newspaper such as *Daily Telegraph*, *The Times*, *Financial Times*, *Guardian*, as opposed to tabloid (see below)

browser – software program for navigating the Internet, in particular the World Wide Web

bureau – newspaper office in foreign country

bury – when important information or quote (see below) is carried within the body of text so its impact is lost

bust – when copy text or headlines run over allotted space

buy-up – see chequebook journalism

by-line – gives name of journalist/s who has/have written article. Otherwise called credit line. (Subs often call this the blame-line.) When it appears at end of story known as sign-off

calls (sometimes known as check calls) – routine telephone calls (or sometimes face-to-face visits) by reporters to such bodies as police, ambulance, hospitals, fire brigade (usually supplying information on tapes) to check if any news is breaking

campaigning journalism – overtly partisan journalism promoting particular cause: e.g. greener Britain; save Bart's hospital; restore David Gower to England cricket side. US: advocacy journalism

caption – words accompanying any picture or artwork. Basic details are supplied by photographer. Final content of the caption is compiled by sub-editor (see below). A caption amounting to a small story is a caption story

casting off – estimating length of copy

casual – journalist employed by a newspaper only on temporary basis. Since it's cheaper for employers, numbers growing

catchline – usually single word identifying story which is typed in right hand corner of every page. Sub-editor will tend to use this word to identify story on layout. US: slug

CD-Rom – abbreviation of Compact Disk-Read Only Memory. CD holding computer-accessible data. For instance, dictionaries and back issues of some newspapers are available in this form

centre spread – copy and pictures running over two pages in centre of newspaper

chapel – newspaper branch of National Union of Journalists (30,000 members). Chair, if male, is known as Father of Chapel; if female, Mother of Chapel

chequebook journalism – activity in which newspapers compete to purchase rights to buy up someone's story, e.g. mistress of minister. Figure can reach phenomenal levels when person's story considered of high news value. Some newspapers routinely offer much smaller amounts of money to people in exchange for information

city desk – section of newspaper running the financial page/s

classified – small ads classified according to subject area and carrying no illustrations

clips/clippings/cuttings – stories cut from newspapers and usually filed. Most newspapers have cuttings libraries to assist journalists' research activities. Individual journalists usually have their own cuttings files

colour – section of newspaper copy focusing on descriptions, impressions. Thus a colour feature is one which puts emphasis on description and the subjective response of the journalist though the news element might still be prominent

column – vertical section of article appearing on page. Also known as leg

columnist – journalist who provides comment in regular series of articles. Usually adopts individual writing style

column rule – usually light line between columns of type

conference – meeting of editorial staff to discuss previous issue/s and plan future ones

contact – journalist's source

contacts book – pocket-sized booklet carried by reporter listing phone numbers (occasionally addresses, faxes and email details) of contacts

copy – editorial material. Hard copy refers to editorial material typed on paper

correspondent – usually refers to journalist working in specialist areas, e.g. transport, education, defence. Particularly used with reference to foreign assignments, e.g. Moscow correspondent, Cairo correspondent

crop – to cut picture

crosshead – small heading usually of one or two words within body text of larger typesize than body text, sometimes underlined (see below). Used for design purposes in tabloid papers to break up grey of body text. Word is usually drawn from text following but carries no great news value. Written by sub-editor and not reporter

cross ref – indication that story continues or begins on another page

cub reporter – trainee

cursor – usually dash or arrow on the computer screen indicating position of the next input

curtain raiser – story which provides background to forthcoming event. Otherwise known as scene-setter

cut – remove copy from script, screen or page proof

cut-out – illustration with background cut, masked or painted out so that the image appears on the white of the page background

database – storage of electronically-accessible data

dateline – place from which story was filed (see below). Usually applied to stories from abroad

day in the life of – profile feature focusing on particular day of subject. Not to be confused with "Life in the day of" profile which covers the subject's life but in context of talking about currently typical day

deadline – time by which copy is expected to be submitted

deck – a unit of headline

Deep Throat – secret whistle-blower (see below) on major scandal. First given to secret source for Woodward and Bernstein in Watergate scandal. Derived from title of in/famous pornographic film starring Linda Lovelace

delete – to cut/remove

desks – departments of newspapers are often known in terms of desks; thus picture desk; news desk; features desk etc.

diary column – (1) a gossip column; (2) a day-to-day personal account

diary piece – article derived from routine sources (press conferences, press releases, council meetings, Parliament) listed in diary (originally in written form, increasingly on screen) which helps news desk organise their news gathering activities. Off-diary stories are those which come from reporter's initiative (not prompted by desk) and from non-routine sources

dig – to do deep research

direct input – process by which text goes straight from editorial screen into computer for typesetting thus cutting out process in which printers typed out copy

discussion list – individuals communicating via email subscribe to the list and then receive all messages other subscribers send to the list

disk – hard or floppy disk containing computer information

display ads – large advertisements usually containing illustrations (cf. classified ads) and appearing on editorial pages. Advertising department will organise the distribution of ads throughout the newspaper which is usually indicated on a dummy (see below) handed to the sub-editors before layout of paper begins

district office – any office away from newspaper's main one

domain name – system of names to describe precise position of a computer on the Internet (e.g. city.ac.uk is the domain for City University, London)

doorstepping – journalists pursuing sources by standing outside their front doors. Now journalists increasingly wait in cars

double column – text/heading/graphics over two columns. Double page spread is a feature occupying two facing pages

downpage – name given to story appearing in bottom half of newspaper page

downtable – subs other than chief and deputy subs (who often used to sit at the top table of the subs room) are known as downtable subs

drop cap – capital letter at start of par. occupying more than one line of text

dummy – small version of editorial pages used for planning overall contents of newspaper and usually containing details of display advertising. Dummy will often be considered at early news conference where decisions on newspaper size and advertisement distribution are made

editor – person (mostly male) in overall charge of the editorial content of the newspaper

editorial – (1) all non-advertising copy; (2) column in which newspaper expresses its own views on issues (sometimes known as leader)

email – electronic mail carried on the Internet

embargo – time (often found on press releases) before which information should not be published. System based on trust between source and media outlet. Some newspapers, however, have habit of breaking embargoes – and attracting considerable publicity (good and bad) in process

exclusive – story supposedly uniquely carried by newspaper. Vast number of stories in every newspaper would qualify for this description so should really be limited to few major stories. Description becomes devalued when attached to stories too frequently or when the same story is carried in other newspapers on the same day (as often happens) (see below – scoop)

eye-witness reporting – presence of reporter at news event can provide unique opportunities for writing descriptive, colourful copy

e-zine – electronic magazine

fact file – listing of facts (often boxed) relating to story. Useful way of creating visual and copy variety on page

feature – as distinct from news story tends to be longer, carry more background information, colour, wider range of sources and journalist's opinion can be prominent

feedback – response (from colleagues/public) to journalist copy

file – (verb) to send story from foreign country; (noun) anything stored on a computer such as a document, program or image

filler – a short story, usually of one or two pars, filling in space when a longer story runs short (also known as brief)

fireman – person sent out from newspaper's headquarters to cover major story (either at home or abroad). Notice gender bias in word

fit – when text or picture does not overrun (bust) its allotted space

Fleet Street – though most newspapers have dispersed from this street in East London between the Strand and St Paul's Cathedral, national newspapers as a collective group are still known by this name. Often known as Street of Shame

floppy disk – flexible disk used for storage of information on computers

follow-up – when newspaper uses report in another media outlet as basis for its own news story

font – this spelling is now more common than fount (see below)

fount – typeface of one particular size and style

Fourth Estate – press supposedly occupying the position of fourth most powerful institution after Lords Spiritual, Lords Temporal and Commons. (Lord Macaulay: "The gallery in which the reporters sit has become a fourth estate of the realm.")

free – free newspaper

freebie – range of services and entertainments (e.g. drinks, meals, trips abroad funded by governments/tourist organisations, transport companies, tickets to concerts, theatres) provided free to journalists. Some journalists believe acceptance of freebies compromises "objectivity" and refuse to accept them

freelance – journalist contributing to several media outlets and not on permanent staff of any one organisation (increasingly a euphemism for unemployed). Freelancer in US

FTP – File Transfer Protocol, used to transfer files across the Internet

gopher – a menu system allowing you to navigate the Internet, now being displaced by the World Wide Web

gutter – space between pages in centre spread (see p. 300). Sometimes used on computer layout screen to describe space between columns

gutter press – sometimes applied to tabloid press

hack – insult word for journalist which journalists are happy to use to describe themselves

hamper – story displayed horizontally usually at top of page

handouts – story sent to media outlets by press relations office of organisation or PR company

hard copy – copy typed on sheets of paper (usually A4 size). Each page is known as a folio

hard news – news focusing on who, what, where, when, why based on factual detail and quotes and containing little description, journalist comment or analysis. Cf. soft news (see p. 309)

heavies – broadsheet "serious" papers such as the *Guardian*, *The Times*, *Financial Times*

hold – instruction (usually known as set and hold) ensuring copy is prepared for publication but not printed as for instance an obituary of some eminent figure

home page – either the first page loaded at start-up by your browser, or the main Web document for a person, group or organisation

house – a media organisation. Thus in-house (meaning within a particular media organisation). House organ is company's own newspaper or magazine. See also style (p. 310)

HTML – HyperText Markup Language comprising the codes for writing Web pages

human interest story – story focusing on success, failures, tragedies, emotional/ sexual histories of people, eliminating or marginaling more abstract and deeper cultural, economic, political, class-based factors

hypertext – divides a document into clickable links that connect Web pages to each other

imprint – name and address of printer and publisher required by law; often at the foot of the back page

indent – abbreviation for indentation: providing white space at start or end of line

in-depth reporting – coverage of issues/events in considerable detail

index – front page (or sometimes elsewhere) listing of stories in rest of paper. To ease reading and "sell"/"flag" the contents in prominent place

input – to type copy into computer

insert – copy injected into story which is already written or set

inside story – reporter bases investigation on their experiences and research within organisation/s at the centre of controversy and/or on quotes from insiders within organisation/s

intro. – opening of news/feature story usually containing main angle (see p. 297). Not necessarily just single par. (see p. 307). Also known as lead. US: nose

inverted pyramid – traditional representation of news stories (with main point at start and information declining in news value thereafter and ending with short background). Tends to oversimplify structure of news story. Better to imagine series of inverted pyramids within an overall, large pyramid

investigative reporting – in one respect all journalism involves investigation. But investigative reporting tends to reveal something of social/political significance which someone powerful or famous wants hidden. US: investigative reporters are known as muckrakers

issue – all copies of day's paper and its editions

italic – typeface sloping to right. Not commonly used in body text. Sometimes in headlines. Some French newspapers put all direct quotes in italics but this style not adopted in Britain or US

journo – jocular term for journalist

justify – line of text set to fit given measure

kill – to decide not to use (or drop) story/feature. Newspapers are supposed to pay "kill fee" when they break an agreement to use freelance copy

knock down – to disprove story usually in rival newspaper

label – headline merely categorising the news: e.g. "Interview with PM"; "Woman addresses meeting". Or intro.: "A report on drugs was published yesterday."

layout – design of page, originally by sub-editor using pencil and sent to compositor for guidance but increasingly done totally on screen

lead (pronounced leed) – main story on page. On front page otherwise known as splash

lead (pronounced led) – space between lines of type (derived from former "hot metal" printing system when strips of metal, or leads, were used for this purpose). Leaded out copy has its lines spaced out to fit allotted space

leader – see editorial

legal (vb) – to send copy to lawyer to be checked for libel, contempt etc. Some nationals (e.g. *Daily Telegraph*) have night lawyers to advise on legal matters

lift – (1) to use whole or section of story from one edition to the next; (2) to pinch story from other media outlet changing and adding only a little. When only barest minimum is changed known as "straight lift"

linage – payment to freelances based on number of lines of copy used

line drawing – drawing made up of black lines as in cartoon

listings – lists usually of entertainment events giving basic information: data, times, venue, phone numbers etc.

Listserv – software for organising an email discussion list

literal – typing error either misspelling or transliteration

lobby – specialist group of correspondents reporting House of Commons

lower case – small letters in fount of type (as opposed to capitals)

masthead – newspaper's title on page one

middle-market – newspapers such as *Mail* and *Express* which lie (in terms of overall style and appearance) between heavies and pops

modem – telephone link-up for computers, most commonly used for sending email and accessing the Internet

mole – a secret source for investigative journalist buried deep in heart of organisation whose activities they are prepared to reveal

moonlighter – journalist who works during the evening for media organisation while holding another full-time post during day. Nice to be but it means moonlighter is depriving colleague of job

more – written at foot of each page of hard copy (see p. 304) except last when "end" is written. "More follows" (mf) or "more follows later" (mfl) used when reporter ends sequence of pages (or "take") temporarily (in order to give the news desk copy at earliest opportunity) but later returns to story

mug shot – photo showing just face (and sometimes shoulders). Otherwise known as head and shoulders

must – editorial copy which must appear e.g. apology, correction

new journalism – literary, subjective form of reportage pioneered in US in 1960s and 1970s by Norman Mailer, Tom Wolfe, Joan Didion, Truman Capote. (See: *The New Journalism*; edited by Tom Wolfe and E.W. Johnson; Pan Books, London; 1977)

newsgroups – discussion groups of the Internet

New World Information and Communication Order – a concept promoted by UNESCO in 1970s and 1980s to counter the dominance of international news flows by five major news agencies. Western countries, particularly US and UK, saw it as threatening "free flow of information"

obit – abbreviation of obituary, an account and appreciation of life. For famous people usually prepared in anticipation of their death

off-beat – unusual story often with a humorous twist. Can be used on front page to provide light relief from all other major hard news stories

off the record – when statements are made not for publication but for background only. Information derived from comments should in no way be traceable back to source

on spec – uncommissioned article submitted voluntarily to media

on the record – when there are no restrictions on reporting what is said

op ed – abbreviation of opposite editorial, being page opposite one on which newspaper's editorial/leader comment falls. Usually contains important features and commentary by prestigious columnists

opinion piece – article in which journalist expresses overt opinion

PA – abbreviation for Press Association which supplies national news and features service (as well as an international service from its link-up with Reuters) to most national and local papers

pack – collection of journalists (sometimes known as "rat pack")

panel – text larger than body text with lines top and bottom. Serves to break up grey block of copy. Written by subs

paparazzi – horde of photographers

par. – abbreviation for paragraph. Also para

pay-off – last par. with twist or flourish

PC – personal computer, normally either an Apple Macintosh or IBM-compatible

pic – abbreviation of picture meaning photograph. Plural: pix

pick-up – (a) journalist attending function might pick up or take away photograph supplied by the organisers. This is known as a pick-up job; (b) journalist following up an event after it has happened (speaking to participants and establishing views and outcome) is "picking up" meeting

picture-grabber – facility for taking pictures off television

podding – scheme originally promoted by Westminster Press in which multi-skilled subs, reporters and photographers worked in small teams

pool – privileged, small group of journalists with special access to event or source. Their reports and findings are then distributed to those news organisations outside group

pops/populars – mass-selling national tabloids

PR or PRO – abbreviation for press relations officer

press release – announcement made by organisation specially for use by media (not necessarily just press)

probe – investigation

profile – picture in words. Usually focuses on individual but organisations, cars, horses, weapons, buildings etc. can also be profiled

proof – print-out of part or whole of page. This proof is read, corrected where necessary and amended page (the revise) is then ready for final printing. Galley proof contains just columns of type

punchline – main point of story. Thus "punchy" means story has strong news angle

quote – (1) abbreviation for quotation; (2) when a reporter files copy over phone "quote" then means first inverted commas. End quote marks are often known as "unquote"

qwerty – standard keyboard for typewriter or VDU based on first five letters on top bank of letter keys

readership – number of people who read paper as opposed to number of copies sold

re-jig/re-hash – rearrangement of copy provided by reporter usually by sub-editor to produce better-structured piece

retrospective – feature looking back on an event

re-vamp – change story or page in light of new material

re-write – to use information provided in story but compose it in completely new language. Known as re-write job

ring-round – story based on series of telephone calls

roman – standard typeface

round-up – gathering together of various strands of story either under the same heading (otherwise known as umbrella story) or under a variety of headings

roving reporter – reporter who travels around a lot

RSI – abbreviation for repetitive strain injury which journalists can suffer through their use of computer keyboards and mice

run – period of printing edition

running story – story which runs/develops over number of editions or days

run on – continue from one line, column or page to the next

scoop – exclusive

screamer – exclamation mark (usually in headline)

search engine – provides for subject searching on the Internet through feeding terms into a database and returning a list of "hits" or correspondences

section – separately-folded part of the paper

server – computer that makes services and data available on a network

sexy story – story with popular appeal. But many "sexy stories" unfortunately give sex a bad name

sign-off – by-line at foot of story

silly season – supposedly a time (usually in summer holiday period) when little hard news is around and the press is reduced to covering trivia. For some newspapers silly season can last a long time. Wars and invasions often happen in silly season too

sister paper – when company owns more than one newspaper each is described as sister. Thus *The Times* is the *Sun*'s sister paper since both are owned by Rupert Murdoch

sketch – light, often witty article describing event. Most commonly used with reference to reporting House of Commons

slip – special edition for particular area or event. Can involve change of one or more pages or whole new paper (as in football slip carrying football results, news and features on Saturdays)

snap – brief information given by news agency before main story is sent

soft news – light news story that can be more colourful, witty, commenty than the hard news story (see p. 304)

spike – to reject copy or other information (e.g. press release). Derived from old metal spike which stood on wooden base on which subs would stick unwanted material. Had advantage over "binning" since material was accessible so long as it remained on spike

spin doctors – people who attempt to influence the political agenda (the "spin" in US jargon) such as press officers, communications specialists and other propagandists; trendy 1990s word for political PROs (see above)

splash – lead news story on front page

standfirst – text intended to be read between headline and story which can elaborate on point made in main headline, add new one, raise question which will be answered in story (a teaser). Sometimes contains by-line. Helps provide reader with a "guiding hand" into reading large slice of copy – thus mainly used for features and occasionally for long news stories

stet – ignore deletion (Latin for "let it stand")

stone sub – sub-editor who checks final proof of pages

stop press – column on back page of newspaper left blank and allowing for slotting in of news which had broken just before publication

strap/strapline – headline in smaller type appearing over main deck. Otherwise known as overline

stringer – freelance, either in provinces, in London or overseas, who has come to arrangement with news organisation to supply copy on agreed basis. Super-stringer will contract to devote most of time working for one organisation but still be free to freelance for other media outlets for rest of time

style – special rules adopted by newspaper relating to spellings, punctuation, abbreviations. Often contained within a style-book though increasingly carried on screens. Many newspapers somehow survive without them

sub-editor/sub – responsible for editing reporters' copy, writing headlines, captions, laying out pages etc. Stone sub makes final corrections and cuts on page proofs

tabloid – newspaper whose pages are roughly half size of broadsheet. All popular papers are tabloids as are sections of some of the heavies (e.g. *Guardian 2*; *The Independent*'s *Eye* section). Despite their popularity, tabloid often used as a term of abuse when press collectively are criticised. Serious tabloids exist on Continent (*Liberation* and *Le Monde*, in France, for instance) and in US (*Los Angeles Times*, for instance) and only matter of time before heavy in this country takes plunge and goes tabloid (*Guardian* seems most likely bet)

tabloidese – shoddy, over-sensational, cliché-ridden copy most commonly associated with the tabloids

take – page or number of pages comprising a section of longer piece

taster – journalist who checks copy, selecting good and removing unwanted. Process is known as tasting

think piece – analytical article

tip-off – information supplied to newspaper by member of public

top – story at the top of a page

tots – abbreviation for "Triumph over Tragedy Story", particularly popular human interest genre

underline – to carry line/rule under headline

upper case – capital letters when used alongside small (lower case) letters. When just capital letters are used (as in headline) they are known as caps

URL – Uniform Resource Location: a string of characters identifying the Internet resource and its location; the most common one is http://

vox pop – series of quotes on particular theme. From Latin *vox populi* ("voice of the people")

wall newspaper – journalism training schools often produce wall newspapers when final pages are produced but not sent away to be published. Simply stuck on walls. In some countries (e.g. China) newspapers gained most of readership through being pinned to walls in public places

war – word beloved of reporters and subs, used often in relation to press: hence tabloid wars, circulation wars

Web – the World Wide Web (www): text and graphic documents on the Internet which are interconnected through using clickable "hypertext" links

whistle-blower – person revealing newsworthy and previously secret information to press

widow – short line left at top of column

Index